# Agricultural and Agribu

This introductory textbook provides an overview of the concepts necessary for an understanding of agricultural and agribusiness law. The text will help students of land-based industries with little or no legal background to appreciate and identify issues that may require referral or consultation with legal counsel. This new edition is fully revised and updated, particularly addressing developments in taxation and trade, and includes a new chapter on criminal law, an area of increasing relevance to agriculture.

Each concise chapter addresses a different legal issue that those employed in agriculture and agribusiness may face, and both federal law and representative examples of state law are included. In addition to traditional topics such as contracts, property law, and estate planning, the book also covers more contemporary issues such as organic certification, animal law, genetically engineered crops, and food safety.

Agricultural law extends beyond those directly engaged in farming to those in agribusiness who provide services and inputs to farmers, buy farmers' products, store or transport products, manufacture food products and serve as intermediaries between farmers and consumers. The book will, therefore, also serve as a reference and a guide for those employed in agribusiness and agriculture.

**Theodore A. Feitshans** is Professor of Agribusiness in the Agribusiness Program at the University of Mount Olive and Extension Professor Emeritus in the Department of Agricultural and Resource Economics at North Carolina State University, Raleigh, USA. He is a past president of the American Agricultural Law Association.

"This is the best textbook available in agricultural law specifically geared towards non-lawyers. It is clear, easy to read and covers the major topics of relevance for agribusinesses."

*Marne Coit, MSEL, JD, LLM, North Carolina*
*State University, USA*

**Praise for the first edition**

"Excellent in terms of coverage, in terms of substantive content in each chapter, in organization, and in writing style. Professor Feitshans conveys a great amount of information crisply and clearly. He also uses examples to explain and to clarify the text, which greatly enhances the reader's understanding of the legal concepts and issues."

*Drew L. Kershen, Earl Sneed Centennial Professor of Law*
*(Emeritus), University of Oklahoma, USA*

"There has been a great need for an agricultural law textbook and *Agricultural and Agribusiness Law* fills that need. Theodore Feitshans is one of the preeminent agricultural law professors in the United States and does an excellent job of outlining complex legal issues in a practical way for law students."

*Tiffany Dowell, Assistant Professor and Extension Specialist,*
*AgriLife Extension Service, Texas A&M University, USA*

"This textbook is perfect for undergraduates or others trying to gain a basic understanding of legal issues impacting agriculture. From contracts to environmental law, topics are covered in a quick and easy to understand fashion. I highly encourage faculty and students alike to take a look at Professor Feitshans' book."

*Paul Goeringer, Research Associate and Extension Legal Specialist,*
*Agricultural & Resource Economics, University of Maryland, USA*

# Agricultural and Agribusiness Law

## An Introduction for Non-Lawyers

Second Edition

# Theodore A. Feitshans

Routledge
Taylor & Francis Group
LONDON AND NEW YORK

from Routledge

Second edition published 2019
by Routledge
2 Park Square, Milton Park, Abingdon, Oxon, OX14 4RN

and by Routledge
52 Vanderbilt Avenue, New York, NY 10017

*Routledge is an imprint of the Taylor & Francis Group, an informa
business*

© 2019 Theodore A. Feitshans

First edition published by Routledge 2016

*British Library Cataloguing-in-Publication Data*
A catalogue record for this book is available from the British
Library

*Library of Congress Cataloging-in-Publication Data*
Names: Feitshans, T. A., author.
Title: Agricultural and agribusiness law : an introduction for non-lawyers /
    Theodore A. Feitshans.
Description: Second edition. | Abingdon, Oxon ; New York, NY : Routledge,
    2019. | Includes bibliographical references and index.
Identifiers: LCCN 2018051770 (print) | LCCN 2018053793
    (ebook) | ISBN 9780429467837 (eBook) | ISBN 9781138606036
    (hardback) | ISBN 9781138606104 (pbk.) | ISBN 9780429467837
    (ebk)
Subjects: LCSH: Agricultural laws and legislation–United States.
    | Agricultural credit–Law and legislation–United States. |
    Agricultural industries–Law and legislation–United States. |
    Agriculture–Economic aspects–United States. | Agriculture and state–
    United States.
Classification: LCC KF1682 (ebook) | LCC KF1682 .F45 2019 (print) |
    DDC 343.7307/6–dc23
LC record available at https://lccn.loc.gov/2018051770

ISBN: 978-1-138-60603-6 (hbk)
ISBN: 978-1-138-60610-4 (pbk)
ISBN: 978-0-429-46783-7 (ebk)

Typeset in Goudy
by Apex CoVantage, LLC

Visit the eResources: www.routledge.com/9781138606104

This book is dedicated to the memory of Richard Benson Feitshans, who taught me the business of farming, and to my mother, Jean Heim Feitshans, who continues to be an avid gardener. She taught me the joy that can be found in plants.

# Contents

# Preface

This book is addressed to three audiences. The first two are closely related: students in two-year associated degree programs and students in four-year bachelor degree programs. The third group that this book is intended for are farmers, prospective farmers, and those in closely allied businesses. It is hoped that this book may serve as a reference that those in agriculture may use to help to identify the questions that they need to ask of their attorneys. Legal problems, like guests that have overstayed their welcome, do not improve with age. The sooner a legal problem is addressed, the more likely is a positive outcome.

Unlike fields of law such as intellectual property and bankruptcy law, agricultural law is not a unified area of law. That means that it draws from areas of law as diverse as intellectual property and bankruptcy law, often with a twist unique to agriculture. Any author coming to the topic of agricultural law will be much more versed in some topics than others. Many of these topics are very esoteric. The great challenge in writing this book has been to write in a manner that can be understood by the audiences intended for this book, while preserving accuracy. This is further complicated by the dramatic variation in laws, such as those governing the right to use water, from one state to another. If this book helps agricultural students and those already in agriculture to decide when legal assistance is needed and formulate appropriate questions, this author will consider this book a success.

The second edition provides needed updates, especially for taxation and trade. It also provides a new chapter on criminal law, an area of increasing relevance to agriculture. Chapter 19 on criminal law is entirely new. While criminal law is not a new issue in agricultural law, the Justice Department has shown increased enthusiasm for prosecuting food safety cases. Chapter 23 has been substantially revised to reflect changes made by the 2017 Tax Cuts and Jobs Act. The 2017 Tax Cuts and Jobs Act is the first major revision of the Internal Revenue Code since 1986. Significant changes to Chapter 22 have been made reflecting changes made to the Affordable Care Act by the 2017 Tax Cuts and Jobs Act. The early chapters have also been reordered to move contracts up to the position of Chapter 5, reflecting the preferences of those who have been using the first edition for their classes.

Theodore A. Feitshans
Raleigh

# Disclaimer

No book about the law is complete without a disclaimer. The information provided in this book is for educational purposes only; nothing herein constitutes the provision of legal advice or services or tax advice or services, and no attorney-client relationship is formed. Though every effort has been made to avoid errors, individual situations may vary. There is no substitute for the advice of a private attorney, licensed in the jurisdiction where the matter arose.

Examples are not based upon any actual individuals, either living or dead, except for those that cite a judicial decision in the public record. No implication beyond the facts stated in the public record should be taken.

# Acknowledgments

Janis Epton, my partner in my life, has once again supported the effort to bring forth this second edition. The department of agricultural and resource economics, North Carolina State University, of which I am now emeritus faculty, has continued to support this effort. My colleagues at NC State, Marne Coit, Andrew Branan, and Guido van der Hoeven, have provided invaluable peer review and suggestions for selected chapters. Guido van der Hoeven provided me assistance incorporating recent tax changes. Paul Goeringer, extension legal specialist, in the department of agricultural and resource economics at the University of Maryland, and David Saxowsky, associate professor, in the department of agribusiness and applied economics, North Dakota State University, provided invaluable peer review and suggestions for revisions to selected chapters. As with the first edition, I bear sole responsibility for any errors that remain in this book.

## Acknowledgments to the first edition

There are people and organizations that I thank for their support as I endeavored to complete this book. First, I should thank Janis Epton, my partner in my life, without whose support and patience this book would not have been possible. She also read every draft for readability and grammar. I should also thank my department head, Charles Safley, and our IT and administrative staff, Scott Cravens, Kendell Del Rio, Jenny St. Jean, and Jean Weatherford, all of whom have directly or indirectly made it possible for me to find the time to write this book. The department of agricultural and resource economics, North Carolina State University, has been and is a truly outstanding place to work. I would be remiss if I did not thank our work study student, Brooke Stoll, who gave me a student's perspective on the text.

The peer reviews of this book were very useful and made the book much stronger. Those that provided peer reviews of all or selected chapters are Bryan Endres, associate professor, department of agriculture and consumer economics, University of Illinois; Shannon Ferrell, associate professor, department of agricultural economics, Oklahoma State University; Paul Goeringer, field faculty, department of agricultural and resource economics, University of Maryland; Drew Kershen, Earl Sneed Centennial professor of law (emeritus), University of Oklahoma, college of law; Tiffany Dowell Lashmet, assistant professor and extension specialist, Texas A&M AgriLife Extension Service; Frederick Parker, assistant professor, department of agricultural and resource economics, North Carolina State University; and Guido van der Hoeven, extension specialist, department of agricultural and resource economics, North Carolina State University. I should also add an additional note of appreciation to Professor Kershen, whose friendship and mentoring over almost three decades has been invaluable. I also thank my friends and colleagues in two organizations: the American Agricultural Law Association and the Environment, Energy, and Natural Resources Section of the North Carolina Bar Association. Many delightful conversations about the law have contributed in no small way to this book. Finally, I bear sole responsibility for any errors that remain in this book.

# Glossary

**abatement**   reduction or elimination of a nuisance.

**actuarially sound**   in reference to an insurance policy, a policy that is priced to cover the expected risk without a shortfall.

**addendum**   an additional document attached to the main document to modify or supplement the terms of the main document.

**adjudication**   the process of deciding conflicts between persons.

**adulterated**   in the context of food and feed, any such food or feed that contains a substance or pathogen at a level that exceeds the tolerance level established by the FDA, EPA, USDA, or other federal agency. An adulterated food or feed product may not be sold.

**affidavit**   a document, signed under oath or affirmation, in which the affiant (signatory) has attested to the accuracy of the information in the document.

**agronomic rate**   a rate of application of animal and poultry waste that is not in excess of the capacity of the crop or pasture to use the nutrients in the waste.

**alluvion**   the creation of new land through the gradual deposition of sediment by a natural body of water such as a sea, a river, or a lake.

**ambiguous term**   a term in a contract that is capable of more than one interpretation.

**anachronism**   something from an earlier time that continues into the present.

**arbitration**   a form of alternative dispute resolution in which a neutral third party decides a dispute much as a judge would.

**articles of incorporation**   basic document that creates a corporation when it is filed with the secretary of state in the state of incorporation. Articles of incorporation are also called the certificate of incorporation or corporate charter.

**back cruise**   a method of valuing timber at some date in the past. It usually is done to establish the value of standing timber at the date upon which the current owner acquired the property, either by purchase or inheritance.

**bailee**   the person who receives personal property in a bailment.

**bailment**   a transfer of personal property from one person to another without out a transfer of title. Giving the keys to your car to a valet at a restaurant is an example of a bailment. The relationship is not generally a fiduciary relationship; however, the bailee has a duty to care for the property in a non-negligent fashion.

**bailor**   the person who transfers the property to the bailee.

**basis**   the amount paid for property plus adjustments. When property is sold, the basis in the property is generally not subject to income tax.

**bench trial**   a trial without a jury. This usually happens when all parties have waived their right to a jury trial.

**beneficiary**   owners of the equitable interest in a trust that are entitled to the benefit of income and possibly principal of trust. Also refers to third parties named to receive contractual benefits of a contract such as the death benefit under a life insurance policy.

**bequeath**   transfer at death by will.

**bilateral**   having two sides. In the context of contract, a contract supported by an exchange of promises rather than an exchange of a promise for an act as in a unilateral contract.

**bioaccumulation**   the process by which toxins accumulate and are concentrated in living organisms.

**case in chief**   the initial direct examination of a party's own witnesses by that party's attorney. It excludes cross-examination and any redirect examination that follows the other side's cross-examination.

**civil code systems**   legal systems based upon detailed codes of laws. Unlike judges in a common law system, a judge in a civil code system has only the power to decide the case before her or him, not to make law for future cases.

**civil contempt**   used by a court to obtain compliance with its order. A party in civil contempt will usually be jailed until that party complies with the court's order.

**clandestine**   secret.

**codicil**   a document that makes changes to an existing will. The codicil must be signed by the testator and witnesses.

**common law system**   a legal system under which cases decided by judges make law. Common law legal systems are found only in Great Britain and those countries that were formerly British colonies or dependencies.

**community property**   a system in Louisiana, Arizona, California, Texas, Washington, Idaho, Nevada, New Mexico, and Wisconsin by which most property and most debts acquired during the marriage are 50 percent owned by each spouse. This is contrast to common law property states where ownership follows title.

**concerted activity**   an activity that is undertaken by two or more employees to address working conditions or pay.

**contempt**   violation of a court order or disruptive or disrespectful conduct to the court. Civil contempt is used to enforce court orders through incarceration until compliance with the court order is achieved.

**contribution action** a separate action against a co-defendant to recover an equitable share of damages paid the plaintiff where one defendant paid the entire award under the principle of joint and several liability. Under the principle of joint and several liability, a plaintiff may recover the entire award from one defendant even though all of the defendants shared in the fault for the wrongful act. Where the plaintiff failed to join a potentially liable party, the defendant may avoid the need for a contribution action by filing a third-party complaint against that potentially liable party. Filing a third-party complaint often faces procedural barriers and requires permission of the court. Where a third-party complaint cannot be filed, a separate contribution action is the only means for the defendant in the original action to recover an equitable share of the damages.

**corporeal hereditament** something that can be touched or felt (i.e., real property or tangible personal property that may be inherited).

**corrosivity** the characteristic of a waste or other substance to eat away flesh.

**covered facility** any facility regulated under EPCRA.

**coverture** under common law, the state of legal disability of a married woman.

**crop year** the 12 month period required for production of a particular crop, e.g., for wheat, July 1 to June 30 of the following year.

**cutting** a method of reproducing a genetically identical clone of a plant. Reproduction from cuttings is used extensively in the horticultural industry.

**de novo** a Latin term that means anew. In the context of an appeal, it means that the appellate court will hold a new trial and decide issues of both fact and law without any obligation to follow the decision of the lower court.

**derivative** a form of intangible personal property, created by contract, which is based upon some other type of property.

**derivative action** an action brought by a stockholder of a corporation or an owner of an LLC to recover funds owed the corporation or LLC by its managers.

**dicta** opinions of the judge that are not the decision in a particular case. Dicta have no legal effect.

**dilution** a trademark concept that involves acts that make it less likely that a trademark will be associated by members of the public with a particular company's product. If the trademark owner does not defend the trademark to stop dilution, the trademark may eventually be canceled.

**disregarded entity** a business entity with one owner that is disregarded for federal income tax purposes. All profits and losses are reported on the owner's individual income tax return.

**dominant tenement** the property that is benefited by an easement appurtenant.

**duress** force. No agreement made under threat of force is valid.

**easement appurtenant** a right of the owner of one tract of property to make some use of a neighboring property. The first property is call the dominant tenement, and the second property is called the servient tenement. A typical easement appurtenant is one that gives one tract an access road over a neighboring property.

**encumbrance**   an interest in land such as a lien that is security for a debt.

**enumerates**   lists, as in a power enumerated in the Constitution.

**equine**   any of the genus *equus* that includes domestic horses and donkeys.

**erroneously**   in error.

**escheat**   the process by which ownership of unclaimed property is lost to its owner and transferred to the state.

**estovers**   the right of a tenant to wood, food, and clothing produced from the land.

**eutrophication**   the process by which bodies of water age. The process is accelerated by nutrient pollution caused by excessive nitrogen and phosphorus compounds in the water, usually the result of pollution.

**feral**   animals or birds that were once domestic but have returned to a wild, self-sustaining state. Feral livestock and birds are generally considered to be the property of the landowner and are not subject to regulation as wildlife. Some, such as feral hogs and pigeons, are serious pests.

**fiduciary relationship**   a term generally applied to a relationship where one person, called a fiduciary, manages money for a beneficiary, in the beneficiary's best interest.

**freehold estate**   ownership of land, the ownership of which is potentially infinite in duration.

**futures contract**   a contract for the sale of some personal property at some point in the future for a fixed price.

**general jurisdiction**   refers to the power of a court to hear those matters not otherwise assigned to a specialized court.

**gestation crate**   a cage designed to limit the movement of a sow that is expecting piglets. Gestation crates prevent a sow from rolling on its piglets and crushing or suffocating them.

**grantor**   the one who creates the trust, future interest, or other right in property.

**guardian *ad litem***   a person appointed by the court to represent the interests of a person that is not competent to do so, either a child due to minority or other person that lacks of mental capacity.

**holding**   the portion of a judicial decision that makes law. It is the portion of the decision that serves as a precedent for future cases.

**hydric soil**   a soil that is saturated with water for part or all of the year and exhibits certain characteristics typical of such soils.

**hydrological connection**   a connection between two bodies of water. Typically used to describe the connection between percolating groundwater and natural surface bodies of water.

**ignitability**   the characteristic of a waste or other substance to catch on fire at room temperature.

**indemnification clauses**   a clause in a contract that requires one party to pay another party for defined losses should those losses occur. An insurance contract is a classic example of an indemnity agreement.

**information**   an alternative to indictment by a grand jury, used in some states, and by consent in federal courts, to begin a criminal prosecution.

**infringement**   violating a property right in intellectual property such as a patent or a copyright.

**injunctive relief**   a court order directing a person to either perform an act or refrain from certain behavior. It is granted under the equity power of a court and is enforceable through civil contempt.

*inter vivos*   during one's life.

**intestate succession**   a transfer of property at death under state law that governs the disposition of property of a decedent who died without a valid will. If there was a valid will that failed to transfer all of the probate estate, there will be a partial intestacy as to that property for which the will made no provision.

**irrevocable transfer**   a transfer of money or property to another person or a trust that cannot be taken back.

**jilted**   wronged.

**jointly and severally liable**   a plaintiff may recover the full sum due from one or more of several defendants and it is up to the defendants to sort out proportionate shares among themselves. If proportionate defendant shares are not resolved as part of the plaintiff's case then defendants that paid more than a proportionate share may bring contribution actions against underpaying parties with liability.

**karst**   a type of rock formation such as limestone, dolomite, and gypsum that is highly permeable to water and characterized by the presence of caves and sink holes.

**lien**   an encumbrance upon property reflecting a debt secured by the property.

**litigation**   the process of carrying on a lawsuit.

**livestock**   animals used in agriculture for meat, hides, fiber, milk, or other products.

**loss of consortium**   the loss of companionship and sexual relations with a spouse. The law of tort recognizes this as a compensable injury.

**mediation**   one type of alternative dispute resolution mechanisms. In mediation a neutral third party assists adverse parties with finding a solution to their dispute. Many court rules and state statutes require that parties attempt to resolve their dispute through mediation prior to filing a lawsuit.

*mens rea*   guilty mind. A required element for most criminal charges.

**microfiche**   an obsolete information media once used for storing a wide variety of information, including information relevant to the legal system. It is a film medium that requires a reader to view. A great deal of legal information, not currently available in electronic form, continues to reside on microfiche.

**minor use**   use of a pesticide for which the sales volume can be expected to be low.

**misbranded**   incorrectly labeled as to the content of the product.

**mitigate**   to make less, reduce, by making less harmful or onerous.

**monetary relief**   the usual remedy for claims at law consists of a judgment awarding some sum of money to the plaintiff as compensation for injury or damages. Damages is a synonym for monetary relief.

**natural objects of his/her bounty**   children, grandchildren, or other relatives that a testator would be expected to bequeath his/her property to.

**negotiable instrument**   a document that represents ownership in some underlying personal property that may be sold to another person.

**nexus**   a relationship such as that between a body of water that is navigable in fact and an associated body of water sufficient to bring that associated body of water under the jurisdiction of the Clean Water Act.

**notarized affidavit**   an affidavit (see affidavit) to which a notary public has affixed his/her signature and seal to attest to the genuine character of the affiant's signature.

**nuisance ordinance**   a law enacted by a local government to prohibit certain public nuisances such as noxious odors or rowdy bars.

**nuncupative will**   an oral will made under apprehension of impending death that is heard by at least two uninterested witnesses.

**offeree**   in contract law, the person to whom an offer is made.

**offeror**   in contract law, the person who makes an offer.

**omnibus**   in reference to Congressional legislation, a bill that addresses many topics.

**optionor**   the landowner who makes property available under an option contract.

**quasi-property**   something that has some but not all the characteristics of property.

**par value**   the arbitrary face value of a stock or bond. For stock, the price is usually set low and has no relationship to market values. Setting par value for stock in the corporate charter is required under some state corporations laws. The trend is away from setting any par value.

**percolating groundwater**   groundwater held in soil or rock that is diffused through the soil or rock in aquifers.

**perennial forages**   crops, such as grasses, used for grazing that do not require replanting each year.

**perfect**   to take the necessary steps that usually include filing the necessary paperwork with the proper government office to have an enforceable security interest in property.

**person**   any entity capable of bringing a lawsuit in its own name. Persons include flesh-and-blood persons, governments, churches and other religious institutions, associations, cooperatives, and business organizations such as partnerships, corporations, and limited liability companies.

**phytosanitary**   free from plant pests and diseases.

**pocket veto**   occurs when the President fails to sign a bill and Congress adjourns within ten days of presentation of the bill to the President. Such a bill does not become law and is not subject to being overridden.

**point source**   the Clean Water Act defines two types of surface water pollution: point sources that are discrete and concentrated as distinguished from nonpoint sources that are diffuse and dilute. There is no bright line that distinguishes these two types of surface water pollution.

**police power**   the inherent common law power of states to protect the health, welfare, and property of its citizens. Since the federal government has only those powers delegated to it by the states through the Constitution, it has no inherent police power. The police power of the states is protected from federal encroachment by the Tenth Amendment.

**possessory**   as applied to real property, the term means that the interest is a present interest, entitling one to use and enjoy the property.

**poultry**   birds used in agriculture for meat and related products, eggs, feathers, and other items.

**power of appointment**   the right granted by one person to a second person to confer property on a third person. It is a device often used to confer property on a minor or a person not yet born at the time the power was created.

**precedent**   a written judicial decision that is law for similar future cases in that court or a court below it in the same system.

**precipitously**   suddenly; rapidly.

**preemption**   federal preemption occurs when a federal law trumps a state law, meaning that only the federal law is enforceable. A second type of preemption occurs when a state law trumps a local government ordinance or rule.

**present use valuation program**   a program designed to tax real property on its value in an agricultural or forestry use rather than at its higher fair market value. Such programs vary from state to state but share a goal of making it possible for landowners to afford to keep property in agricultural or forestry uses.

**presumption**   something that the law considers established once a precondition is met. A rebuttable presumption shifts the burden of going forward with evidence to rebut the presumption to the party against whom the presumption operates. An irrebuttable presumption is one that is conclusive once certain evidence is produced.

**prevented planting**   a term from the federal farm commodity programs and the Federal Crop Insurance Program. Prevented planting usually occurs as the result of natural disasters such as drought. Typically, it triggers the payment of benefits under the federal farm commodity programs or triggers a claim under the Federal Crop Insurance Program.

***prima facie* case**   a case in which the plaintiff will prevail if uncontradicted by the defendant's evidence.

**private litigant**   a nongovernmental party to a lawsuit.

***pro se***   a litigant who represents himself or herself without an attorney.

**punitive**   in tort law, describes a type of damages designed to punish the defendant rather than compensate the plaintiff for economic losses. Punitive damages are paid to the plaintiff.

**purchase-money security interest**   a security interest held by the seller of property as security for the seller-financed portion of the purchase price.

**quasi-judicial**   like a court. Many agencies have administrative proceedings that are designed to resolve disputes between the agency and other persons. These proceedings are quasi-judicial.

**quiet title action**   method for extinguishing claims in real property.

**reactivity**   the tendency of a waste or other substance to explode or violently combine with other substances with which it may come in contact.

**recharacterize**   to change the character of something from what it is purported to be to something else. The IRS often does this to collect tax actually due where the taxpayer has avoided tax by mischaracterizing a transaction to one that is not taxed as heavily.

**reliction**   the permanent drop in water level of a natural surface water. The effect, where the water line served as a boundary between properties, is to change the boundary.

**remainderman**   a person, different from the grantor or his heirs, who holds a future interest in property. Such an interest is vested if the remainderman will come into possession at some point in the future. Such an interest is contingent if some uncertain event, that may never occur, must come to pass before the remainderman comes into possession.

**remand**   the act of an appellate court in sending a case back to a trial court for further proceedings.

**reporter**   A serial publication in which the decisions of a court or a group of courts are reported.

**rescission**   in contract law, a remedy of canceling the contract and treating the contract as if it had never existed.

**research**   the process of gathering disparate facts, testing hypotheses, conducting analyses, and drawing conclusions as to the validity of one's hypotheses.

**restitution**   in contract law, a remedy of restoring the aggrieved party to their position prior to entering the contract. Rescission and restitution are almost always granted together.

**reversioner**   the grantor or his heirs that holds a future interest in property. Such an interest is vested if the land will come into possession at some point certain in the future. Such an interest is contingent if some uncertain event, that may never occur, must come to pass before the land can come into possession.

**revocable transfer**   a transfer of money or property to another person or a trust that can be taken back.

**right of disposition**   right to dispose of property by sale, gift, or other means such as its destruction.

**right of first refusal**   a contractual right to buy real or personal property that is triggered when it be offered for sale by its owner. Nothing in the right requires the owner of the property to offer it for sale.

**right of survivorship**   the right of a surviving co-owner of property to the interest of the deceased co-tenant.

**riparian rights**   common law rights of landowners to use natural surface waters and underground streams where the water touches their property. The system of riparian rights was not adopted in most western states.

**scienter**   a guilty mind. Also *mens rea* or the knowledge of wrongdoing.

**security interest**   an interest of a creditor in real or personal property that allows the creditor to recover the amount of the debt by retaking or forcing the sale of the property.

**sentient**   having the ability to feel and perceive one's environment.

**servient tenement**   the property that provides the benefit to the dominant tenement through an easement appurtenant, such as an access road.

**share lease**   an agricultural lease of real property that involves the landlord and tenant sharing both providing inputs and sharing in the crops resulting therefrom.

**sharia law system**   legal system of some Muslim countries that is based upon the Koran and Haddith.

**silviculture**   forestry.

**solemnize**   to hold a ceremony in which a couple confirms the obligations of marriage. Marriages must be solemnized before a member of the clergy, justice of the peace, or other person of authority whom the state has authorized to solemnize marriages.

**sorghum**   a plant in the grass family that is grown as a crop for grain, forage, or sugar and syrup, depending upon the variety.

***stare decisis***   the common law doctrine that requires a court to follow its own precedents and those of courts above it in the same system.

**statistician**   a person trained in the science of statistics.

**statute**   a law enacted by a legislative body such as the U.S. Congress.

**statute of limitation**   a statute that limits the right to bring an action after the passage of a period of years following the date upon which the injury was discovered.

**statute of repose**   a statute that limits the right to bring an action after the passage of a period of years following the date upon which the action arose. A statute of repose bars an action even though the injury was not discovered until after the action was barred.

**stringent**   very strict.

**subordination clause**   a clause in a security agreement or other document that subordinates one interest to another.

**subordinate**   to make less or lower than. In the context of a security interest in property, to make junior to a senior security interest. If there is not enough money to pay both security interests in full, the senior interest gets paid first.

**subsequent lien holders**   holders of security interest in property that are junior to the senior lien holder. The senior lien holder is entitled to be paid first if the sale of the asset that serves as security does not provide sufficient funds to pay all of the lien holder claims.

**sub-therapeutic**    refers to a dosage level of an antibiotic or other medication that is below the level used to treat an illness. Low dosage levels of antibiotics are used as growth promoters in livestock and poultry.

**support**    the right of one landowner that requires neighboring landowners to avoid activities that result in subsidence or other destruction of that landowner's land. Support from underneath is called subjacent support. Support along the sides of the property is called lateral support.

**tenancy by the entirety**    a form of co-ownership of real property available only to a married couple.

**testate succession**    transfer of the property of a decedent according to the terms of the decedent's valid will.

**testator**    the person who made a will.

**third-party insured**    a beneficiary of an insurance contract that is not a party to the contract.

**tort**    a civil wrong for which a court will provide monetary or injunctive relief.

**tort-feasor**    a person who commits a tort.

**toxicity**    characteristic of being poisonous to humans or animals.

**trustee**    the person who holds legal title to property owned by a trust and who manages it for the benefit of beneficiaries.

**ubiquity**    widespread presence.

***ultra vires***    beyond the scope of statutory authority.

**upland**    for purposes of section 404 of the Clean Water Act, any land area that is not a wetland.

**vicarious liability**    responsibility imposed on one person for injuries to a second person that were caused by a third party. An example is the imposition of liability upon a parent for the torts of his child.

**void**    a contract that is unenforceable by all parties because the subject matter violates the law.

**voidable**    a contract that may be voided by one party to the contract but not the other. The party that may void the contract is the one protected by the law due to minority or mental incompetence.

**winding up**    the orderly termination of a business outside of bankruptcy or an insolvency proceeding.

**writ of certiorari**    a court order used by a superior court to require an inferior court to produce a certified copy of its records in a case for inspection. It is today used primarily by the U.S. Supreme Court to grant discretionary appeals.

**zoning ordinance**    a pervasive type of local law that is designed to reduce the occurrence of nuisances by grouping like land uses together.

# Acronyms

| | |
|---|---|
| ACA | Affordable Care Act |
| ACEP | Agricultural Conservation Easement Program |
| ADA | Americans with Disabilities Act |
| AFO | Animal Feeding Operation |
| AGI | Adjusted Gross Income |
| AMS | Agricultural Marketing Service |
| AO | Administrative Office |
| APA | Administrative Procedure Act |
| APHIS | Animal and Plant Health Inspection Service |
| ARC | Agriculture Risk Coverage |
| BSCC | Biotechnology Science Coordinating Committee |
| BT | Bacillus thuringiensis |
| CAFO | Confined Animal Feeding Operation |
| CCC | Commodity Credit Corporation |
| CDC | Centers for Disease Control and Prevention |
| CEO | Chief Executive Office |
| CERCLA | Comprehensive Environmental Response, Compensation and Liability Act |
| CFTC | Commodity Futures Trading Commission |
| CIGs | Conservation Innovation Grants |
| Corps | United States Army Corps of Engineers |
| CPM | Commission on Phytosanitary Measures |
| CPR | Cardiopulmonary Resuscitation |
| CRP | Conservation Reserve Program |
| CSA | Community Supported Agriculture |
| CSP | Conservation Stewardship Program |
| CWA | Clean Water Act |
| DHS | Department of Homeland Security |
| EA | Environmental Assessment |
| EEOC | Equal Employment Opportunity Commission |
| EIS | Environmental Impact Statement |
| EPA | Environmental Protection Agency |

| | |
|---|---|
| EPCRA | Emergency Planning and Community Right-to-Know Act |
| EQIP | Environmental Quality Incentives Program |
| EU | European Union |
| EUP | Experimental Use Permit |
| FAS | Foreign Agricultural Service |
| FAO | Food and Agriculture Organization of the United States |
| FDA | Food and Drug Administration |
| FFDCA | Federal Food, Drug, and Cosmetic Act |
| FERC | Federal Energy Regulatory Commission |
| FICA | Federal Insurance Contributions Act |
| FIFRA | Federal Insecticide, Fungicide and Rodenticide Act |
| FLSA | Fair Labor Standards Act |
| FMIA | Federal Meat Inspection Act |
| FMLA | Family and Medical Leave Act |
| FOIA | Freedom of Information Act |
| FONSI | Finding of No Significant Impact |
| FSA | Farm Service Administration |
| FSIS | Food Safety Inspection Service |
| FSMA | Food Safety Modernization Act |
| FUTA | Federal Unemployment Tax Act |
| FWS | Fish and Wildlife Service |
| GAPs | good agricultural practices |
| GATT | General Agreement on Tariffs and Trade |
| GDP | Gross Domestic Product |
| GE | Genetically Engineered |
| GINA | Genetic Information Nondiscrimination Act |
| GMO | Genetically Modified Organism |
| GRAS | Generally Recognized as Safe |
| HACCP | Hazard Analysis and Critical Control Points |
| HHS | Health and Human Services |
| HSWA | Hazardous and Solid Waste Amendments |
| IPM | Integrated Pest Management |
| IRB | Internal Revenue Bulletin |
| IRC | Internal Revenue Code |
| IRS | Internal Revenue Service |
| ITA | International Trade Administration |
| ITC | International Trade Commission |
| LGBT | lesbian, gay, bisexual, and transgender |
| LLC | Limited Liability Company |
| LPA | Limited Partnership Act |
| MSPA | Migrant and Seasonal Agricultural Worker Protection |
| NAD | National Appeals Division |
| NAFTA | North American Free Trade Agreement |
| NEPA | National Environmental Policy Act |

| | |
|---|---|
| NIH | National Institutes of Health |
| NIIT | net investment income tax |
| NLRB | National Labor Relations Board |
| NOAA | National Oceanic and Atmospheric Administration |
| NOP | National Organic Program |
| NPDES | National Pollutant Discharge Elimination System |
| NPPO | National Plant Protection Organization |
| NPRM | Notice of Proposed Rulemaking |
| NRCS | Natural Resources Conservation Service |
| NSF | National Science Foundation |
| OECD | Organization for Economic Cooperation and Development |
| OFPA | Organic Foods Production Act of 1990 |
| OMB | Office of Management and Budget |
| OSHA | Occupational Safety and Health Administration |
| PACA | Perishable Agricultural Commodities Act |
| PCN | Preconstruction Notice |
| PCT | Patent Cooperation Treaty |
| PDA | Pregnancy Discrimination Act |
| PDR | Purchase of Development Rights |
| PHS | Public Health Service |
| PIP | Plant Incorporated Protectants |
| PLR | Private Letter Ruling |
| PNS | Pre-Sale Notification System |
| POD | pay on death |
| POLST | Physician Orders for Life Sustaining Treatment |
| POTW | publicly owned treatment work |
| PPA | Plant Protection Act |
| PPIA | Poultry Products Inspection Act |
| PVPA | Plant Variety Protection Act |
| RCRA | Resource Conservation Recovery Act |
| RRA | Roundup Ready Alfalfa |
| SCO | Supplemental Coverage Option |
| SDS | Safety Data Sheet |
| STAX | Stacked Income Protection Plan |
| SWDA | Solid Waste Disposal Act |
| TAM | Technical Advice Memoranda |
| TD | Treasury Decision |
| TDR | Transfer of Development Rights |
| TMDL | Total Maximum Daily Load |
| TRIPS | Trade-Related Aspects of Intellectual Property Rights |
| TVA | Tennessee Valley Authority |
| UCC | Uniform Commercial Code |
| UCEA | Uniform Conservation Easement Act |
| UPA | Uniform Partnership Act |

| | |
|---|---|
| USCIS | United States Citizenship and Immigration Services |
| USDA | United States Department of Agriculture |
| USDOL | United States Department of Labor |
| USMCA | United States-Mexico-Canada Agreement |
| USPTO | United States Patent and Trademark Office |
| USTR | United States Trade Representative |
| WTO | World Trade Organization |
| WPS | Worker Protection Standard |

# Chapter 1

# Understanding the U.S. legal system

## Introduction

The key to understanding the U.S. legal system is that it is not one system but many. The U.S. legal system is a federal system composed of separate systems that include the states, other associated territorial entities, and the Indian tribes.[1] Over all of these entities sits the federal government. The relationship between the federal government and the states is governed by the Constitution. The relationship between the federal government and associated territorial entities and the Indian tribes is governed by the Constitution and a complex of treaties, statutes, and court orders. Most of these entities, but not all, use some version of English common law. This chapter provides an overview of these systems and how they are linked.

English common law is a system of judge-made law that is used in Great Britain and its former colonies and dependencies. Each published judicial decision creates law not only for the case but for all subsequent decisions by that court or any court below it. This is in contrast to civil law systems that are used in most other countries, except for some Muslim countries that use a sharia law system. Civil law systems use comprehensive codes that attempt to capture all possible situations that may arise. As one may imagine, such codes are very comprehensive. The Napoleonic code was the basis of the first modern civil law systems. Statutes in common law systems tend to be rather sparse by comparison. In common law systems, the gaps in statutes are filled by regulations promulgated by regulatory agencies and by judicial decisions. Common law will be discussed in more detail later in this chapter.

The rise of the modern regulatory agency has led to a convergence between common law and civil law systems. Regulatory agencies such as those of the U.S. Department of Agriculture, the U.S. Environmental Protection Agency, the U.S. Food and Drug Administration, and a host of others provide much of the detail missing from legislation through regulations and "guidance." State agencies, and even local agencies, function in much the same way, although often with less public input and transparency. The rise of the modern regulatory agency was one of the major developments in the law in the United States during the twentieth century. Agency law is usually referred to as administrative law. Much of the law applicable to agriculture in the United States is administrative law. An introduction to administrative law will be provided later in this chapter.

## Constitutions and key provisions of the U.S. Constitution

Most modern nations have written constitutions. A constitution is a written document that sets forth the powers and limitations of government. The U.S. Constitution represents an agreement between states to limit their own sovereignty in favor of a central government with the power to handle certain enumerated functions. The constitutions of the respective states provide the consent of the peoples of those respective states to a form of government and the exercise of certain sovereign powers. The powers of any government under its constitution are never absolute; some powers are always reserved to the people. Sovereignty is defined as the characteristics of an independent government. The federal government and state governments are all sovereign, but usually municipal and county governments are not. In many states, local governments have no power except that given to them by the state legislature. In some states, local governments have sovereignty delegated to them through the state constitution. This can be an important distinction because it determines whether a local government may act independently of the state legislature. Indian tribes are sovereign preexisting extra-constitutional entities whose relationship to the United States is governed by treaty or other law. U.S. territories are federal entities, like counties and cities of states that have no independent sovereignty. There are, in addition, a few associated entities that have sovereignty of their own.

The federal Constitution is the highest source of U.S. laws. No other law can override it. The federal Constitution divides sovereign powers between the federal and state governments. It grants some powers to the federal government only (called "exclusive" powers), grants some powers to the federal and state governments ("concurrent" powers), and refuses other powers to both the federal and state governments ("denied" powers). Any power not mentioned by the federal Constitution in one of these three categories is implicitly a power of the states. When a power is given to the states it is said that it is a power for the people. The federal government is, therefore, a government of limited powers. State governments are considered, conversely, as having plenary power, limited only by restrictions placed on them by their respective constitutions and by the explicit and implicit limits established by the U.S. Constitution.

Where federal law supersedes state law, state law is said to be preempted, meaning that it is not enforceable. There are three types of preemption: express, field, and conflict. Express preemption is found where either the Constitution or a statute expressly preempt state law. Field preemption is one of the two types of implied preemption. Field preemption occurs when the law enacted by Congress is so comprehensive that it leaves no room for states to regulate in the field. Example 1.1

provides an example of field preemption. This type of implied preemption is rare in agricultural law. Example 1.2 discusses a Supreme Court decision where field preemption was rejected. The second type of implied preemption is conflict preemption. Where federal law and a state law are in conflict, the federal law will preempt the state law. Example 1.3 discusses a Supreme Court decision where conflict preemption was rejected by a 5 to 4 majority. The dissent provided an excellent argument for why conflict preemption should be applied in an agricultural context.

---

**Example 1.1** The state of X decided to promote innovation by issuing certificates of innovation to inventors. No person in the state of X was allowed to make, use, or sell any product or service embodying an invention protected by a certificate of innovation without the written permission of the certificate holder. Federal courts have long held that protection of inventions through the patent system under Article I, Section 8, Clause 8 (the Patent and Copyright Clause) occupies the field, leaving no room for state protection of inventions. It would be an adequate defense for any person sued for violation of such a state certificate to assert field preemption.

---

**Example 1.2** Dow Agrosciences' label and its marketing campaign represented that its pesticide, Strongarm, was suitable for all peanut crops. The Supreme Court took as fact the finding of the trial court that Dow Agrosciences knew or should have known that its pesticide would severely stunt peanuts in soils with a pH level of 7.0 or higher. Dow Agrosciences eventually reregistered its label with the Environmental Protection Agency (EPA) to recommend that Strongarm not be used on peanuts planted in soils with pH levels of 7.2 or higher. EPA approved a supplemental label for New Mexico, Oklahoma, and Texas, the primary states where those soils are found. The plaintiffs, Texas peanut farmers who experienced severe crop damage prior to the label change, brought state tort claims based on strict liability and negligence. They also raised state law claims based upon fraud, breach of warranty, and violation of the Texas Deceptive Trade Practices-Consumer Protection Act. Dow Agrosciences countered that the Federal Insecticide, Fungicide and Rodenticide Act (FIFRA) preempts state law that imposes additional or different packaging or labeling requirements from those approved by EPA.[2] In *Bates v. Dow Agrosciences*,[3] the Supreme Court held that FIFRA's express preemption of different or additional labeling or packaging requirements for pesticides was limited. State laws are not preempted if they are sufficiently similar to the federal law or if the state did not require a change to federally mandated packaging or labeling.

The Supreme Court analyzed the boundaries of federal preemption and remanded the case to the lower courts for a determination of which state law claims survived and which were preempted. That the Bates decision was not unanimous underscores the difficulty determining the outer boundary of express preemption in a particular case.

**Example 1.3** In the Supreme Court decision in *Florida Lime & Avocado Growers v. Paul*,[4] the Court declined to invalidate a California standard for avocados based upon conflict preemption by the federal standard for avocados. The Court found no actual conflict and no actual intent by Congress to preempt the field. In this decision, only five of the nine justices on the court agreed that there was not conflict preemption, again illustrating the difficulties in drawing the boundaries of preemption. The four dissenting justices noted that the California standard for avocado maturity resulted in Florida avocados certified as mature under the federal standard being rejected and destroyed by California.

### Articles of the U.S. Constitution

The original text of the Constitution as ratified included seven articles that defined the original powers of the federal government. Article I of the U.S. Constitution defines the functions and powers of Congress, the legislative branch of federal government. Congress as established by the Constitution consists of two houses: the Senate and the House of Representatives. Each state has two Senators. Representation in the House is apportioned by population, with each state having at least one member. Congress has the exclusive authority to legislate through the enactment of statutes or laws. Every federal statute begins in a bill introduced in either house of Congress. For Congress to enact a bill, both houses must pass an identical version of the bill to be sent to the president. The president may either sign the bill, veto the bill and return it to Congress with an explanation of his or her objections, allow the bill to become law without his or her signature or, in rare cases, exercise a pocket veto. A regular presidential veto may be overridden by a two-thirds vote of each house of Congress.

Section 7 of Article I requires that all appropriations bills (spending bills) originate in the House of Representatives. The Senate must agree. All spending bills enacted by Congress must be submitted to the president. The process of authorizing funds for any federal activity is complex. Substantive legislation typically authorizes the spending of up to a certain amount of money. So for example, a bill that establishes a program to encourage farmers to use conservation practices may authorize spending of $200 million per year. That authorization is only the first step. Congress must pass a budget each year that funds the authorized program. It is not unusual for the actual funding provided to be much less than the authorization. Actual funds provided for some programs may even be zero. This two-step process is a source of both confusion and disappointment to the members of the public who attempt to plan their activities based upon expected federal funding.

Section 8 of Article I enumerates the legislative powers of Congress. These powers include those typical powers of government that include powers to tax and spend, borrow money, coin money, and establish post offices and roads. Powers important to agriculture include the power to establish rules for immigration (naturalization), exclusive authority over bankruptcies, authority to establish patent and copyright systems to protect the intellectual property of inventors and authors, and the power to regulate interstate and international commerce and commerce with Indian tribes. Two of these powers are the authority for most federal agricultural programs. The first of these is the power to spend money. This power is found in the first clause of Section 8. It is called the Spending Clause, or sometimes, the Taxing and Spending Clause. Many of the federal programs designed to help farmers protect soil and water are based upon the Spending Clause. Farmers are voluntarily enticed to participate to obtain the federal funds provided to participants. The second power, often called the Commerce Clause, is found in the third clause of Section 8. The Commerce Clause provides the express power to the federal government to regulate foreign and interstate commerce and commerce with the Indian tribes.

The Commerce Clause has been expanded to cover many situations and is the basis for much federal law. It is often called the elastic clause as Congress has stretched it to provide authority for federal laws covering many subjects including agriculture and protection of the environment. The test used by the Supreme Court to determine whether Congress is acting within the scope of its authority under the Commerce Cause is whether an activity has a substantial impact on interstate commerce. Example 1.4 illustrates the application of this test.

---

**Example 1.4** The Supreme Court decision in *Wickard v. Filburn*[5] affirmed that Congress may regulate an activity that is entirely intrastate based upon a substantial impact on interstate commerce. Indeed, the activity was not only intrastate but was confined to one farm. Mr. Filburn grew wheat that was entirely consumed on his farm. While his individual use was trivial, the Supreme Court found that the collective effect of farmers raising and consuming their own crop had a substantial impact on interstate commerce by reducing market demand, thereby undermining federal efforts to support the price of wheat.

The Commerce Clause may prohibit state action even when Congress has not acted. This doctrine is referred to as the dormant Commerce Clause. An action by a state that tends to burden interstate commerce may be prohibited by the Commerce Clause directly, without congressional action. Any state regulation that substantially burdens either interstate or international commerce risks being preempted by the dormant Commerce Clause.[6]

An explicit limitation on state power is found in the Contract Clause of Section 19 of Article I. The Contract Clause prohibits states from unreasonably impairing private contracts. This is an example of a denied power. Example 1.5 provides an example of how the Contract Clause limits state legislative options.

---

**Example 1.5** North Carolina enacted legislation to limit the exploration phase of oil and gas leases to ten years. The legislation applied only to those leases signed after the date upon which the legislation became law. Thus, the legislation did not apply to contracts already signed before the effective date of the legislation. To apply the law to such preexisting leases with terms greater than ten years would have substantially impaired existing contracts in violation of the Contract Clause.

---

Article II of the Constitution vests the executive power in the president. Article II defines the functions and powers of the executive branch. Section 2 of Article II defines the powers of the president, one of which is to make treaties with foreign countries with the consent of two-thirds of the senators present. Article I, Section 10 prohibits states from making treaties with foreign nations and from taxing exports and imports. There is an exception that allows for fees associated with inspections. This exception allows states to operate and charge for agricultural inspections to prevent transmission of disease and the introduction of unwanted species that may endanger valuable crops and livestock. States are prohibited from making agreements with other states unless Congress consents. Such agreements, formally approved by Congress, are called interstate compacts.

Under Article II, the president is the elected official who is responsible for enforcing the federal law. He or she is commander-in-chief of the armed forces. The president shares war-making powers with Congress. While the president has the authority to respond to crises and minor incidents, the president must notify Congress of extensive engagements and seek funding to support those efforts from Congress. Article II is the source of the president's power to appoint a cabinet and its officers. Political appointees to cabinet-level departments are subject to Senate confirmation. The president can grant reprieves and pardons to federal criminals. He or she makes diplomatic and judicial appointments, subject to Senate confirmation. As it is the responsibility of the president to execute the laws, the president may issue executive orders. Executive orders interpret or implement provisions of the Constitution, a statute, or a treaty. In recent years, the use of executive orders has been criticized for exceeding this limited function. The federal courts have not been reluctant to strike down executive orders that exceed executive powers under Article II. Although executive orders are law, they can both be rescinded by future presidents and overridden by Congress.

Article III vests the judicial power in the Supreme Court and other lower courts. The Supreme Court is the only court mentioned by name in the Constitution. It and the lower federal courts are empowered by Article III to hear and decide cases. Lower federal courts, including the U.S. Courts of Appeal and the U.S. District Courts, are established by Congress. Judges on these courts and the Supreme Court have life tenure. Judges on these courts are appointed by the president subject to confirmation by the Senate. These courts are sometimes called Article III courts. The Supreme Court has original jurisdiction in only a limited number of cases, including cases involving disputes between states. Original jurisdiction means that the Supreme Court is the only court that can hear such a dispute. These cases are relatively common in disputes involving water. Decisions in these cases can have drastic consequences for affected farmers.

Article I, Section 8, Clause 9, and Article III empower Congress to establish courts inferior to the Supreme Court. Article I courts are generally inferior to and under the appellate jurisdiction of Article III courts. Article I courts include bankruptcy courts and the U.S. Court of Federal Claims. The U.S. Court of Federal Claims is the only court with the power (jurisdiction) to hear a claim for money against the United States. Federal bankruptcy courts are the only courts in which a bankruptcy can be adjudicated. Judges who serve on Article I courts serve for fixed terms. When an Article I judge's term ends, that judge must be reappointed by the president, subject to confirmation by the Senate.[7]

### Amendments to the U.S. Constitution

There have been only twenty-seven amendments to the Constitution. The first ten amendments are called the Bill of Rights. The Fourth Amendment protects the privacy of citizens by prohibiting unreasonable searches and seizures (essentially those without judicially issued warrants). Originally, the Fourth Amendment applied only to the federal government; however, the Supreme Court applied it to the states through the Fourteenth Amendment. The Supreme Court has held that the use of warrantless high-technology surveillance (such as infrared scanning) of a home violates the Fourth Amendment.[8]

The Fifth Amendment prohibits the federal government from denying any person "life, liberty or property without due process of law." The concept of due process means that any person can expect to be treated fairly by the government. The Fourteenth Amendment places these same restrictions on state government. The Fifth Amendment also contains a Takings Clause that prohibits the federal government from taking private property for public use unless the owner is fairly compensated for it. The Fifth Amendment, as with most of the first ten amendments, has been applied to the states through the Fourteenth Amendment.

The Fourteenth Amendment contains the Equal Protection Clause that says that states must treat similarly situated people in the same manner. It is the Equal Protection Clause that prohibits racial and other forms of discrimination. It is the constitutional basis for equal access to federal agricultural program benefits.

## Administrative agencies

Most of the work of the federal government is done by entities that are not mentioned in the Constitution. These are administrative agencies. Administrative agencies are essential to the function of government, yet fit uncomfortably into the U.S. constitutional system. An administrative agency is a unit of the government (but not a court or legislative body) that is created by Congress to make rules, render decisions, and run programs. Administrative agencies are usually formed by an act of Congress. Such a statute is called an enabling statute in that it enables the creation of the agency. An enabling statute sets up the agency and the guidelines to be followed by the agency in performing its duties. Administrative agencies can also be created by an executive order of the president, but this is uncommon as there must be existing law passed by Congress that allows the president to do this. Most agencies, although created by Congress, are in the executive branch. There are a few agencies, such as the Library of Congress, that are agencies of Congress, and a few, such as the Federal Judicial Center, that are agencies of the judicial branch. There are also independent agencies, such as the Federal Reserve, that have a great deal of independence from any of the three branches of government.

The U.S. Department of Agriculture was established by an act of Congress in 1862.[9] Prior to that, its functions were part of the agricultural division of the Patent Office where it was established by an act of Congress in 1839.[10]

The duties of an administrative agency include rulemaking, adjudication of individual cases, and administrative activities. The rulemaking activity is a legislative activity of the agencies. It corresponds to the legislative branch of government. Agency adjudication is a quasi-judicial activity that corresponds to the judicial branch of government. Agency adjudication can look much like a court proceeding, or it can be much more informal. Administrative activities correspond to the activities of the executive branch of government. Administrative activities include research, property management, issuing permits, and enforcement of regulations (rules) and laws. While agencies generally have the power to withhold benefits for violations of rules, the ability of agencies to force a person to do something or to collect a fine is limited. To do this, agencies must generally go to court to seek either an injunction or court order requiring payment of a fine or penalty. It has often been noted that agency functions mimic the functions of all three branches of government.

Agency procedures for rulemaking and adjudication are governed by the Administrative Procedure Act (APA). The definition of an agency under the APA does not include Congress, courts of the United States, governments of territories, possessions of the United States, or the government of the District of Columbia. There are also exemptions for some military activities. Agencies are required to publish notice of their activities in the Federal Register. Both information associated with rulemaking and information associated with the adjudication of individual cases must be published in the Federal Register. Most agency records are open to the public, and copies are available either without charge or at cost. National security documents may be withheld and are protected. Most meetings conducted by agencies are required to be open to the public unless there are national security or other reasons for it to be closed.

## Types of agencies

Most administrative agencies are executive branch agencies. Heads of such agencies are appointed by the president subject to confirmation by the Senate. The head of such an agency serves at the pleasure of the president. All political appointees, including the agency head, are "at will" employees who may be dismissed at any time without cause. Political appointees are appointed by the president, vice president, or the agency head and are usually subject to Senate confirmation. Career or merit employees serve for longer terms. This latter group of employees does the technical and administrative work of the agency.

All policy decisions are made by political appointees. Political appointees generally do not serve beyond the term of the president that appointed them. Of course, a political appointee can be reappointed by a new president; however, there is a limited total number of politically appointed positions. These positions reward people who helped the president get elected and promote the policy of the president by ensuring that merit and career employees adhere to that policy. Prior experience with the subject matter responsibilities of an agency are not always required. Most likely to be appointed to these positions are individuals with previous experience working in the industry regulated by the agency, because the companies in those industries will generally promote such an individual for the position. It is felt that having such a person as a political appointee, particularly as an agency head, will ensure that industry viewpoints are considered in the agency's decisions.

In addition to executive agencies, there are three other types of agencies. The first of these is the independent agency. The head of an independent agency is appointed by the president subject to confirmation by the Senate; however, the head of an independent agency serves for a fixed term that may not be terminated except for cause. Candidates proposed by the president to serve as agency heads typically have extensive experience in the agency subject matter. As noted above, the Federal Reserve is an example of an independent agency. The Commodity Futures Trading Commission (CFTC) is an example of an independent agency that is important for agriculture. The CFTC regulates futures contracts including those for agricultural commodities such as corn and wheat. There are also agencies of the judicial system and of Congress. Examples of judicial agencies include the Administrative Office of the United States Courts and the Federal Judicial Center, mentioned above. The Federal Judicial Center has done important research on agricultural bankruptcy. As mentioned above, an example of a Congressional agency is the Library of Congress. The primary function of the Library of Congress is to provide information to the members of Congress. It also serves the very important secondary function of supporting research by the public through its functions of storing documents, many of which are much older than the United States itself. It conducts some research of its own in its efforts to answer requests from members of Congress. The Copyright Office, an agency located organizationally within the Library of Congress, is a historical anomaly in that it is a congressional agency whose primary mission is the executive function of serving the public by registering copyrights.

## Agency rulemaking

The rules (also known as regulations) promulgated by an administrative agency have the same effect as a law made by Congress and, to ensure that the rules are appropriate, the APA provides procedures for making such regulations. The types of rulemaking are informal, formal, hybrid, and exempt. Informal rulemaking involves five mandatory steps and one optional step. The mandatory steps are: (1) a review of the agency's proposed rule is made by the Office of Management and Budget (OMB); (2) after at least thirty days, notice of the proposed rule is published in the Federal Register; (3) written comments are received and evaluated; (4) a review of the draft final rule is made by the OMB; and (5) the final rule is published in the Federal Register. The optional step precedes development of the agency's proposed rule. It is called a request for information. Requests for information are published in the Federal Register. The second type of agency rulemaking, formal rulemaking, is less favored because it is expensive and time-consuming. It varies from informal rulemaking only at the third step. Rather than written public comments, the agency holds public hearings with all witnesses sworn and subject to cross-examinations. Formal rulemaking is used only where mandated by law. The most common type of rulemaking is called "hybrid" because it combines the formal and informal types. It also varies from formal and informal rulemaking only in the third mandatory step. Public comments are taken through written comments and unsworn oral testimony at informal public hearings. To emphasize the point, these three forms of rulemaking differ only in how public comments are taken.

The fourth type of rulemaking, exempt rulemaking, is characterized by the absence of opportunity for public comment prior to the regulation's becoming law. Exempt rulemaking is not favored by the courts. Exempt rulemaking is used only in special circumstances, such as where rules are made by a military service or national security agency (where speed and secrecy are needed),[11] in cases of emergency, or for interpretive rules or general policy statements. For those rules made in secret by military or national security agencies, the regulations themselves are secret, and no public comments are ever taken. For emergency rules, public comment is taken after the rule becomes law. This permits rapid agency response to an emergency. The agency may later revise the emergency rule based upon public comment and experience and issue a final rule.

Interpretive rules and general policy statements are not rules at all. They do not have the force of law. The purpose of interpretive rules is to provide the agency's interpretation of laws and its own regulations. A general policy statement is of a similar nature. Agencies sometimes seek to avoid the rigor of the APA-required process for making rules by using interpretive rules or policy statements. If the agency attempts to enforce interpretive rule or policy statement as law, courts will strike that attempted enforcement down. The agency will then be forced to go through APA rulemaking.

### Judicial review of agency rulemaking

A person with standing may challenge an agency's final rule in court. A person with standing is anyone who will be affected by the rule. Article III, Section 2, Clause 1 requires that there be an actual case or controversy for the plaintiff to have standing to bring a suit. Many federal statutes designate a specific court as the reviewing court for regulations made under the authority of those particular statutes. If no court is designated, standard rules of jurisdiction and venue apply. Courts with jurisdiction are those courts that have the power to review a rule. A court with venue is the one most convenient to the parties and witnesses. Some courts will have jurisdiction but not venue. The reverse is not possible. The purpose of judicial review is to ensure that agencies operate within their authority and with proper procedure. There are four grounds upon which a court may set aside an agency's final regulation. Those reasons are that the delegation of authority was unconstitutionally vague, a constitutional standard was violated, the action was beyond the scope of the agency's statutory authority, or the proper procedure was not followed.

Failure to follow proper procedure as set forth in the APA and other statutes is the most common reason that federal courts cite when setting aside regulations. If the court finds that the agency failed to follow proper procedure, it will not reach the merits of the regulation. While an agency may always reissue a regulation that is valid by following proper procedure, the delay itself, as illustrated in Example 1.6, may be beneficial to the regulated industry.

---

**Example 1.6** In 1982, the U.S. Secretary of Agriculture published a determination in the Federal Register setting a fifty-cent-per-hundredweight assessment on fluid milk. Plaintiffs were various milk producers and their respective associations who alleged that the regulation was invalid because it was substantive rulemaking subject to the notice and comment provisions of the APA. The District Court for the District of South Carolina agreed and issued an injunction against collecting the assessment. The secretary did not appeal but instead reissued the rule using notice and comment rule-making. The plaintiff sued again alleging the same violations of the APA. The District Court again found violations of the APA and violations of substantive law and issued a preliminary injunction. The United States Court of Appeals for the Fourth Circuit reversed.[12] That the Fourth Circuit reversed does not mean that the plaintiffs failed to accomplish their goal. In the more than six months that it took for the Fourth Circuit to set aside the preliminary injunction, the milk producer plaintiffs were saving about $6 million per day!

Federal courts look first to whether proper procedure was followed and then to whether an agency had proper statutory authority. A regulation or agency action that is beyond the scope of statutory authority is said to be *ultra vires*. As Example 1.7 illustrates, the power not granted to an agency by Congress may be a power that Congress had the constitutional authority to grant but did not.

**Example 1.7** The U.S. Army Corps of Engineers defined the Clean Water Act term, a "water of the United States," in part, upon whether migratory birds use or do not use a body of water. For the Corps to have jurisdiction under the Clean Water Act, a body of water must be a water of the United States. The U.S. Supreme Court in *Solid Waste Agency of Northern Cook County v. U.S. Army Corps of Engineers*[13] held that the Clean Water Act did not include the use of a body of water by migratory birds within its definition of a water of the United States. For that reason, the Supreme Court held that the regulation of the Corps was without statutory authority and, therefore, invalid. The Supreme Court noted that the power to regulate a body of water on the basis of its use by migratory birds was clearly within the commerce power conferred by the Commerce Clause; however, Congress, in enacting the Clean Water Act, chose to grant less power to the Corps than was available under the Constitution.

The nondelegation doctrine and constitutional violations are also possible grounds that a court may use to declare a regulation invalid. Federal courts try to avoid these last two grounds. The nondelegation doctrine prohibits Congress from delegating its legislative authority to an agency. The nondelegation doctrine is rarely violated as Congress rarely passes legislation that lacks sufficient guidelines for constitutionally sound agency rulemaking. Violation of a constitutional standard is even more infrequent. A statute, and a regulation based upon that statute, cannot authorize an action that violates the Constitution. Such a statute may violate the Constitution either by authorizing an act that violates the Constitution or by failing to provide a constitutionally required protection. Courts look at how the statute or regulation was applied to determine whether, as applied, the Constitution was actually violated. Although constitutional violations are relatively rare, they do occur, particularly in the area of Commerce Clause jurisdiction. As Example 1.8 illustrates, a Commerce Clause violation may depend upon whether the burden of the regulation is borne proportionally or primarily by out-of-state interests.

---

**Example 1.8** Massachusetts issued a pricing order that assessed a fee upon all fluid milk sold in Massachusetts. The proceeds of the fee were distributed to in-state milk producers. The vast bulk of fluid milk sold in Massachusetts comes from out of state. The Massachusetts Supreme Court upheld the assessment as not being discriminatory against out-of-state milk producers, reasoning that the fee applied to all milk producers evenly. The U.S. Supreme Court reversed, holding that the assessment was a tariff-like trade barrier that discriminated against out-of-state milk producers because they bore the vast share of the burden, in violation of the Commerce Clause.[14]

---

### Agency adjudication

Agency adjudication takes place when a person wishes to dispute an agency order that directly affects him or her. This does not include rulemaking. Final rules are directly appealable to federal court. Agency adjudication involves disputes between the agency and regulated persons.[15] Agency adjudication may be very formal and closely resemble a judicial proceeding, or it may be quite informal. The proceeding is usually conducted by an administrative law judge. Jury trials are not available in agency adjudication. One criticism of agency adjudication is that the administrative law judges are usually employees of the agency. This gives the appearance of bias towards the agency. Some departments such as the U.S. Department of Agriculture (USDA) have attempted to address this issue by taking the adjudicatory function out of individual agencies. The USDA created the National Appeals Division (NAD) in 1994 by taking the adjudicatory function out of individual USDA agencies.

---

**Example 1.9** Farmer John grows cotton for which economic adjustment assistance is available through the USDA Farm Service Agency (FSA). Farmer John believed that he was eligible for payment. The FSA county office denied him payment based upon a determination that he had farmed a wetland in violation of federal law. Farmer John appealed this decision first to the FSA county committee, then to the FSA state committee in an NAD, an entity separate from FSA. The NAD determined that he had not farmed ineligible wetland and restored his right to payment of economic adjustment assistance. Had Farmer John's appeal failed, he would have exhausted his administrative remedies. His next step would have been to petition a U.S. district court for review of the final NAD decision.

### Administrative duties

Administrative duties are many. These duties include managing and implementing federal programs, managing property, making grants, issuing permits, conducting inspections, and enforcement. The range of duties are too numerous to list.

### Limitations upon agency power

An agency's power is limited by the statute or executive order by which it is created. Each branch of government shares control over executive agencies. Executive branch controls are extensive. The president appoints the agency head and other political appointees. The president retains authority to remove political appointees without cause. The OMB recommends the budget each year. The OMB reviews both proposed and final rules and may send those rules back for revision. Agencies are subject to executive orders.

Congress has oversight over agency actions. Each house has oversight committees that may ask agency employees to explain the actions of the agency. Congress has the power to terminate or amend the enabling statute of any executive agency. Termination of an agency's enabling statute is an agency death sentence. Congress has ultimate authority to determine an agency's annual budget. As noted above, the Senate must consent to agency nominations.

The process of judicial review has been discussed earlier in this chapter.

## Local governments

County and municipal governments are the primary units of local governments. These governments have only the power that is granted to them by state legislatures or state constitutions. They are generally authorized to issue ordinances. Zoning and nuisance ordinances that attempt to reduce incompatible land uses are among the most important. There may also be other local agencies such as drainage authorities and health departments whose jurisdictions may include one or more counties. They are authorized to issue rules. Ordinances and rules are both forms of local law.

## Common Law

The federal and state courts base their opinions on written laws, such as the Constitution, statutes, regulations, and the common law. Common law is based upon case law or precedents. It is judge-made law. The making of law by judges is the characteristic of common law legal systems that distinguish them from civil code systems.

Common law systems apply the principle of *stare decisis*. Under the principle of *stare decisis*, a court is required to follow its own prior decision when the facts in the current and prior cases are the same. The principle of *stare decisis* requires a court to follow decisions of courts above it in addition to its own. However, the principle of *stare decisis* is limited to a single court system. Courts may consider, but do not have to follow, the precedents of different sovereign's court systems. Example 1.10 illustrates this principle. Under the doctrine of reception, the United States and each state, except Louisiana and Hawaii,[16] received the English common law so that English precedents prior to independence are generally part of the common law of the states and the federal government.

---

**Example 1.10** The XYZ Corporation brought a contract action for $100 million against the ABC Corporation in the Onondaga County Supreme Court. The Onondaga County Supreme Court is the trial court of general jurisdiction for Onondaga County, New York. The decision in the case turned on the legal interpretation of the contract between XYZ Corp. and ABC Corp. The trial judge found no applicable precedent in New York. He decided the case in favor of ABC Corp., using a decision by the Supreme Court of California, the highest court in the California system, as guidance. XYZ Corp. appealed to the Appellate Division of the Supreme Court, Fourth Department. The Fourth Department reversed, holding that a California precedent cannot be used by a New York trial court. ABC Corp. immediately appealed to the New York Court of Appeals, the highest court in the New York State Court system. The New York Court of Appeals reversed the decision of the Fourth Department. It held that nothing in the principle of *stare decisis* prohibited a trial court from using a precedent of another state as non-binding guidance where there is no applicable New York precedent.

---

A trial court decision may be used as a precedent only if the decision is published. With the widespread availability of unpublished decisions through the Internet, care must be taken to distinguish between published and unpublished decisions. It is common practice in many states that trial court opinions are unpublished and, therefore, without precedential value. Note from Example 1.10 that the names of state courts do not always reveal the rank of the courts in a particular state system. In New York, the Supreme Court is the trial court of general jurisdiction, not the highest court in the system.

Courts of different states are courts of different judicial systems. More difficult to understand is that state and federal judicial systems are separate judicial systems. Case law or precedents do not apply across systems. State courts are not bound under the principle of *stare decisis* by precedents of lower federal courts. States are bound only by constitutional decisions of the U.S. Supreme Court. States are bound not because of the principle of *stare decisis* but through application of the Supremacy Clause discussed above.

### Basic court rules and procedure

As Article III, Section 2, Clause 1 of the Constitution requires that there be an actual case or controversy for federal courts to have jurisdiction, federal courts cannot issue advisory opinions where there is no actual case or controversy. An advisory opinion is an opinion issued on the request of someone who wants clarification as to what the law is. Some state supreme courts issue advisory opinions. Obviously these opinions are limited to the state law of the state supreme court that issued the opinion. Jurisdiction is the power of a court to act. Article III, Section 2, Clause 1 defines the jurisdiction of federal courts to include all cases or controversies involving federal law, treaties, all cases involving admiralty (water traffic), and other listed matters. Under Clause 2 of Section 2, the Supreme Court is given original jurisdiction over all disputes between states. In these cases, the Supreme Court serves as a trial court rather than appellate court.

---

**Example 1.11** North Carolina levies a tax on illegal drugs such as marijuana and cocaine. Although state law prohibits possessing the substances, should one possess them, one has an obligation to pay the required tax. In the NC Court of Appeals decision in *State v. Adams*,[17] the NC Court of Appeals reversed the decision of the trial court that applied a precedent of the U.S. Court of Appeals for the Fourth Circuit. The Fourth Circuit held that the NC tax on illegal drugs was not a civil penalty but a criminal penalty. The Fourth Circuit held that applying the tax and its penalties for nonpayment along with the usual criminal penalties for possession and sale constituted double jeopardy under the Double Jeopardy Clause of the Fifth Amendment. The NC Court of Appeals held that the trial court improperly applied this Fourth Circuit precedent. The trial court had no duty under the principle of *stare decisis* to apply a precedent of another sovereign's court system. That the other sovereign was the United States did not matter.

---

Congress has further defined the jurisdiction of various federal courts by statute. Examples include federal courts such as the U.S. Court of Federal Claims and bankruptcy courts that have jurisdiction limited to monetary claims against the government, and bankruptcy, respectively. However, before discussing these technical matters the reader will probably find it useful to have a general description of how courts work. Courts are generally divided between trial courts and appellate courts. As seen in the previous paragraph, some courts may serve both functions under different circumstances, as is the case with the U.S. Supreme Court. A trial court is typically where resolution of the dispute begins. In the federal court system, this is usually a federal district court. However, disputes with agencies must generally begin in an administrative court within the agency. Administrative adjudication of disputes with agencies involving denial of benefits, denial of permits, fines and other sanctions, and other matters must begin with an administrative appeal in an administrative court for an administrative law judge. Administrative courts can be extremely informal, without formal meetings, or the court can look very much like a regular federal or state court. Some administrative appeals involve the submission of written documents with no meeting. Only after all administrative appeals to the federal agency that made the decision are exhausted may the dispute move to the federal court system. Some federal statutes allow certain agency actions to be immediately appealed to federal courts. States follow their own rules.

For a federal district court to have jurisdiction to hear a case, it must have both personal jurisdiction and subject matter jurisdiction. Jurisdiction is the power of the court to hear a matter. If the court lacks jurisdiction, any judgment or order that is issued in the case is void. Personal jurisdiction is acquired by service of process. Service of process requires delivery of the summons and complaint to the defendant. There are various means by which this may be accomplished that are somewhat different from one state to another. For federal district courts, proper service is defined in rules of civil or criminal procedure depending upon whether the case is civil or criminal. Process usually includes the summons and complaint. The summons tells the defendant when and where to appear at the initiation of the case. Failure to appear in a civil case may be punished by civil contempt or by a finding of default followed by a default judgment in favor of the plaintiff. The complaint tells the defendant the wrongs that she or he is alleged to have committed. Federal (and state) jurisdiction may also be obtained over property through *in rem* jurisdiction. *In rem* jurisdiction is used to resolve disputes about property where personal jurisdiction cannot be obtained because the owner is either unknown or cannot be found. Piracy cases are a rich source of federal precedents because pirates often left their loot ships behind. Their flight was incentivized by the prospect of hanging if apprehended.

Criminal cases in the federal system begin with an indictment. Indictments in the federal system are issued by grand juries that are groups of sixteen to twenty-three citizens who sit for eighteen months. Grand juries meet in secrecy. There is no judge present at their meetings. Their meetings are presided over by the U.S. district attorney (the federal prosecutor); however, the grand jury is independent of the district attorney. In addition to reviewing criminal charges proposed by the prosecutor and issuing indictments, federal grand juries have broad powers to investigate criminal activity. Grand juries may subpoena individuals to testify before them. No individual is allowed to be represented by an attorney when testifying before a grand jury. Some states no longer use grand juries as the Supreme Court has never applied the grand jury clause of the Fifth Amendment to the states. Most states use some sort of preliminary hearing to begin criminal matters. The basic outline of the case includes preliminary matters, pretrial motions, the trial, and post-trial motions. Preliminary matters include the defendant's answer to the plaintiff's complaint. The complaint and answer, together with amendments to either the complaint or answer, and other related documents constitute the pleadings in the case. From the pleadings, the court may determine whether the defendant has pled all the required elements in his or her cause of action. If not, the judge will dismiss the case upon a motion to dismiss the case. It may be that the pleadings reveal that the parties agree upon the facts and disagree only upon the applicable law. In such a circumstance the judge may decide the case without a trial. Trials are needed only where the parties disagree about the facts. Discovery exists to help the parties find all of the facts and follows the completion of preliminary matters. While discovery happens throughout the dispute's course through the trial court, most discovery occurs pretrial. The purpose of discovery is to allow each side to discover the evidence that the other side has. Discovery may occur by exchange of interrogatories (questions), depositions, document requests, and other requests such as those to examine physical evidence in the control of the other party. Each side is required to submit to the court lists of the witnesses and evidence that they intend to present. Electronic discovery has become a contentious issue in many cases. Electronic information is a form of documentary evidence. Often these disputes turn on the question of whether a party destroyed evidence through the failure to prevent routine deletion of e-mail and other documents. Discovery is often expensive and highly disruptive to business operations. Punishments for discovery violations can be draconian. Sanctions for discovery violations range from a warning to striking the offending party's pleadings, with the resultant loss of the case by that party. Some discovery violations such as the destruction of evidence are crimes and may result in criminal prosecution.

Pretrial motions cover a great deal of ground. Motions to amend either the complaint or the answer are common. Amendments to either the complaint or the answer require court approval once the case has begun. There may be motions questioning jurisdiction. For example, if service of process was inadequate, there is no personal jurisdiction. Subject matter or geographic jurisdiction may be questioned. If jurisdiction is lacking, the case must be dismissed because the court has no power to decide the matter. Venue may be questioned. Venue is the location of the trial. If venue is improper, the case may be moved to another court. In high-profile criminal cases, it is not uncommon for the defense attorney to request a change of venue due to the likely prejudice of the local jury pool. Motions may also be made as to applicable statutes of limitation. Motions also may be made questioning whether the case was brought either too soon or too late, ripeness, and mootness, respectively.

Discovery motions such as motions to limit discovery or motions to allow certain methods of discovery are quite common. Disputes over whether to allow the testimony of certain experts to be admitted are also usually resolved before trial. A common pretrial motion is a motion for summary judgment. Such a motion states that there are no factual issues in the case and that it can be decided on the legal issues without holding a trial. Cases may end at the pretrial stage for a variety of reasons.

A trial is somewhat like a game of ping-pong. It begins with opening statements by the attorneys for each party. The plaintiff's attorney or the prosecutor then presents her or his case "in chief" or main case. The plaintiff's attorney or the prosecutor's case in chief will include witnesses and physical and documentary evidence. It may also include the testimony of experts. Each witness is subject to cross-examination by the attorney for the defendant. Admission of physical evidence, documentary evidence, and the statements of any witness are subject to the objection of the defense attorney. The failure to object when evidence is offered bars an appeal. After the plaintiff's attorney or the prosecutor closes his or her case in chief, the trial moves to the case in chief of the defendant. Again, witnesses and evidence will be presented. The defense witnesses are subject to cross-examination by the attorney for the plaintiff. The plaintiff's attorney or the prosecutor has the opportunity to object to witness statements and to evidence produced by the defense. After the close of the defense's case in chief, attorneys for each side will present a closing statement. If either or both parties have invoked the right to a jury trial, the case will go to the jury. This type of jury is called a "petit jury" to distinguish it from a grand jury, discussed previously. Prior to the judge's sending the case to the jury, each party has the right to make a motion for directed verdict. In the federal system, this motion is called a motion for judgment as a matter of law. For such a motion to be granted, there must be no issues of material fact for the jury to decide. Typically, such motions are not granted. All jury deliberations are conducted outside the presence of other persons. After deliberation, the jury will deliver their verdict which is their determination of the facts in the case. The standard of evidence in criminal cases is beyond a reasonable doubt. In civil cases, the much lower standard of a preponderance of the evidence is used. Juries decide issues of fact. Judges decide all legal and equitable issues. If the parties elect not to have a jury trial, the judge will also decide the issues of fact in what is called a bench trial. Bench trials are usually less costly than jury trials.

Post-trial motions are made after the trial has concluded. Post-trial motions are typically made as an objection to the jury's verdict or the judge's order. A very common motion that is infrequently granted is a motion for a new trial. These motions may be based on a wide variety of errors that may occur in trials. There also may be motions to set aside the jury verdict. Such a motion would be granted if the jury verdict were irrational.

> **Example 1.12** The plaintiff presented evidence of damages in a breach of contract action involving a contract for the sale of Christmas trees. The defendant failed to honor a purchase contract with the result that the entire shipment of Christmas trees was rendered unsalable to another purchaser. The plaintiff presented evidence that the contract price was $100,000, growing expenses were $25,000, and the cost of disposal was $5,000. The jury awarded the plaintiff contractual damages of $250,000. The defendant made a motion for a new trial based upon the lack of evidence at trial to support this verdict.

Those issues to which proper objection was made during the trial may be appealed to an appellate court. There are two types of appeals: "as of right" and "discretionary." An appeal as of right must be heard by the appellate court, whereas discretionary appeals may or may not be heard by the appellate court. If the appellate court rejects a discretionary appeal, the decision of the court below is the final decision in the case. Appeals as of right typically involve important issues such as those involving constitutional rights. Appeals as of right are rare in the federal system. In many state systems such appeals are quite common. Appellate courts hear only legal issues and take no evidence. Their deliberations are confined to the trial record. There is one other type of appeal, called an "interlocutory" appeal. It is an appeal taken during the pendency of the trial. These appeals are disfavored and are allowed only at the discretion of the trial court. Trial courts allow interlocutory appeals where necessary to promote judicial efficiency and avoid injustice.

> **Example 1.13** John Doe got sick from eating kale contaminated with a pathogenic strain of *E. coli*. He sued the grocery store where he bought the kale, the broker who supplied the kale to the store, and Farmer Stan who grew the kale. John Doe handled the case *pro se* and served the farmer with a handwritten note that contained little information about the case. Both the grocery store and the broker voluntarily accepted personal jurisdiction, so that was not an issue for them. Through a limited appearance solely for the purposes of contesting jurisdiction, Farmer Stan demanded that the action against him be dismissed for lack of proper service. The court denied his motion to dismiss but granted his motion to file an interlocutory appeal. The court granted the motion, as the question of whether service was proper goes to the essence of whether he can be held liable for the plaintiff's damages. It would be unfair and a waste of resources to keep him in the case if he cannot be held liable.

Most appeals to the U.S. Supreme Court are discretionary. A party that wishes to ask the Supreme Court to review a decision of a lower federal court or a state supreme court must do so by filing a writ of certiorari with the Supreme Court. Of 3,000 to 4,000 such applications per year, the Supreme Court usually accepts 85 to 95 appeals to hear and decide.

## Notes

1 Though there is controversy about the term to apply to the indigenous peoples of North America, I will use the term used in the Constitution, Indian tribes. Native American and American Indian are also names commonly used. None of these terms are entirely satisfactory as no group of indigenous people historically used those names. Each has their own name. According to the U.S. Bureau of Indian Affairs there are 573 American Indian and Alaska Native groups in the United States that are accorded federal recognition. Retrieved May 18, 2018, http://www.bia.gov/WhatWeDo/index.htm. Some states accord state recognition to additional groups of indigenous people.
2 7 U.S.C. § 136v(b).
3 544 U.S. 431 (2005).
4 373 U.S. 132 (1963).
5 317 U.S. 111 (1942).
6 *South-Central Timber Development, Inc. v. Wunnicke*, 467 U.S. 82 (1984).
7 State-level judicial systems are separate systems established under state constitutions. For that reason, the U.S. Constitution is silent about state-level judicial systems.
8 *Kyllo v. United States*, 533 U.S. 27 (2001).
9 U.S. Department of Agriculture. *USDA Celebrates 150 Years*. Retrieved May 18, 2018, www.usda.gov/our-agency/about-usda/history.
10 National Archives. *Records of the Office of the Secretary of Agriculture*. Retrieved May 18, 2018, www.archives.gov/research/guide-fed-records/groups/016.html#16.2.
11 Classification authority is found in 28 C.F.R. §§ 17.1–17.47 (2015).
12 *South Carolina v. Block*, 717 F.2d 874 (4th Cir. 1983).
13 531 U.S. 159 (2001).
14 *West Lynn Creamery, Inc. v. Jonathan Healy*, Commissioner of Massachusetts Department of Food and Agriculture, 512 U.S. 186 (1994).
15 A person is defined under the APA to include not only natural persons but partnerships, corporations and associations, or probe book or private organizations other than a federal agency. Persons may include state agencies.
16 Louisiana is a civil law jurisdiction because it was a former French colony while Hawaii received the law of the Kingdom of Hawaii, which adopted the common law prior to becoming part of the United States.
17 132 N.C. App. 819 (N.C. Ct. App. 1999).

# Chapter 2

# Finding legal materials

## Introduction

With all the separate sovereign entities described in Chapter 1, an enormous quantity of legal verbiage is generated every year. To the uninitiated, sorting through these various sources can be intimidating and uninformative. If one is facing a serious legal issue, such an effort can be dangerous to one's legal cause. It is difficult for a layperson to separate the useful from the unuseful and the accurate from the inaccurate or even fraudulent materials. In general, search tools such as those available from Google, Yahoo, Bing, and other major free Internet-based search tools may provide a reasonable starting point; however, these search tools suffer from two major downsides for legal research. First, the number of hits returned may be overwhelming. Second, the search tools provide no indication of the reliability or accuracy of the sources. Online encyclopedias such as Wikipedia may also provide a good starting point. Such tools tend to provide fairly general descriptions and are secondary sources created through managed open source means. Some entries are quite good whereas others are quite limited.

Legal materials can be divided into primary and secondary sources. Primary sources are legally operative sources such as statutes enacted by legislatures and case law. Primary sources are law. For the U.S. government and state governments, these include constitutions, statutes, regulations, treaties (U.S. government only), judicial decisions, and executive orders. For counties, cities, and other local government entities such as drainage districts and water authorities, these sources include charters, ordinances, and rules. Though one must look to primary sources if one is to determine what the law is on any particular topic, these sources can be difficult to understand and often require the services of an attorney to interpret properly.

Secondary sources are commentary on the law. Law reviews published by most law schools are one of the largest categories of secondary sources. Many law firms provide information about legal topics related to the areas of practice on their websites. For a layperson, secondary sources are usually the best place to start one's research. Court websites and specifically those of clerks of courts may also be useful secondary sources. These sources are generally easier to understand,

and some provide a broad view of the issue. Some secondary sources are written specifically to aid laypeople in understanding the law. There are many treatises on various areas of law. Though these treatises, such as *Prosser on Torts*,[1] are written for attorneys, they can be useful references for non-lawyers.

At one time, not so very long ago, all legal resources resided in paper, microfiche, or some other physical form. Today, most legal resources exist in electronic form. There are some important exceptions. Many rural counties in the United States continue to keep important legal records in paper form. These include land and tax records. Smaller cities and rural counties often keep their ordinances and rules only on paper. Even where their ordinances and rules are available on their websites, those sites must be used with caution because they are often infrequently updated. The most recent and legally operative documents may reside only on paper.

The records of state trial courts, including opinions of the courts, are often not published and are available recorded only on paper or media such as cassette tapes. Accessing these records may be done only during business hours in the applicable clerk of court office or some other such location. Substantial fees may be charged to obtain copies or transcripts.

Citations to legal records often reference a particular paper series or publication that now resides only in electronic form. This can make searching somewhat confusing as the legal record may be found in multiple electronic services. A useful distinction to make is between the various available electronic databases and the specific legal serials available within those databases. Often a particular series is available in more than one database. We will begin our discussion with various electronic databases and then proceed to particular legal sources. The chapter will conclude with a discussion of how to read a judicial decision.

## Databases and websites

### Proprietary databases

There are two comprehensive legal databases used by attorneys: Westlaw and Lexis. Westlaw is a product of Thomson Reuters. Lexis is a product of RELX Group. These two competing products are the products most often used by practicing attorneys. To use them requires an account. Using these products can be quite expensive; however, these sources contain copies of official documents that are essential to legal practice. There is a third comprehensive legal database, Bloomberg Law. A fourth comprehensive legal database is Fastcase (formerly Loislaw) that is a product of Wolters Kluwer. Additionally, Findlaw Lawcrawler, another product of Thomson Reuters, is a database with free information for the general public.

### Government databases

The Library of Congress is an agency of the U.S. Congress, provides free access to the official records of the business of Congress. In it can be found bills, resolutions, committee reports, the Congressional Record, and treaties. The Law Library of Congress[2] provides a variety of free legal resources. The U.S. Government Publishing Office[3] provides free access to federal documents including public laws, statutes, and regulations. USA.gov is an excellent free source for links to the courts and agency websites. The Administrative Office of the United States Courts (AO) is a judicial agency that provides services and research to federal judges. The website of the AO provides links to the websites of each federal court. The U.S. Department of Agriculture Office of Administrative Law Judges[4] publishes its decisions on its website. Most other cabinet-level departments provide similar information. Of particular relevance to agriculture are the Environmental Protection Agency (EPA), the Food and Drug Administration (FDA), and the U.S. Army Corps of Engineers (Corps). The National Agricultural Library, part of the USDA, is a source of agriculture-specific information.

Each state government operates websites similar to those operated by the federal government. At the very least, there are websites for the executive, judicial, and legislative branches. Many state agencies operate their own websites that contain information about agency determinations. Many local governments such as cities and counties have websites on which their ordinances and rules can be found. Some of these sites are excellent, whereas others have limited information or are out of date.

### University and other databases

The National Agricultural Law Center[5] (NALC) provides links to both primary and secondary sources of information about agricultural law. It also provides its own publications on various topics in agricultural law. The Legal Information Institute[6] at Cornell University also publishes both primary and secondary sources. It differs from NALC in that it provides information about all legal topics, not just about agricultural law. It is also available without charge.

## How to find laws

### Legislative materials

The legislative process is initiated by the introduction of a bill in either the House or the Senate. Typically, similar bills are introduced in both the House and Senate at about the same time; however, that is not always the case. The House and Senate usually pass related bills that are somewhat different. After a bill has passed each house, it goes to a conference committee where a reconciled bill is produced. The reconciled bill must be passed by each house for the bill to become law. These enacted bills are known as public laws. Congress also passes private laws that are designed to address a problem of a particular individual. Private laws apply only to the individual that they were intended to benefit. Public laws apply broadly to everyone. The Congressional Record, discussed later, contains the text of bills as introduced along with all amendments to those bills as they were made in each house.

Public laws are published in the U.S. Statutes at Large. Public laws are listed by Congress in chronological order. Public laws may contain a variety of subject matter. As part of the process of passing a law, Congress may include many different subject matters in a single public law to obtain enough support to pass it. These laws may also be found listed by Congress in chronological order on the Congressional website, congress.gov.[7]

Compilations of public laws are not very useful for researchers. Public laws typically contain only the amendments to the statute, not the entire statute. There may be hundreds of cross-references to existing law in a public law. Multiple subject matters are found in a single public law. More useful to the researcher are codifications of legislation. The process of codification is the sorting of parts of public laws by subject matter. As codified law is arranged by subject matter, it is much easier to find a law relevant to one's query. Codified law is found in the United States Code, which is the official publication. Westlaw publishes the United States Code Annotated, one of the products included in its electronic database. In addition to a codification of the code, this product includes commentary, legislative history, and other explanatory information about the law.

The Congressional Record is a record of the daily business of Congress. It is considered the most reliable source for debates and the history of legislation. It is even more accurate than recorded video and audio of House and Senate proceedings because it includes material inserted into the record by members. Members typically ask that a truncated version of amendments to legislation be read to save time. Such requests are almost always granted. The Congressional Record includes the full text.

### Executive materials

Newly proposed federal regulations and adopted versions of new regulations are found in the Federal Register that is published daily. Regulations published in the Federal Register are not codified. In addition to the regulation itself, the Federal Register publication will include explanatory information that can be quite helpful in understanding the regulation. After a regulation is adopted by a federal administrative agency, it is codified and published in the Code of Federal Regulations, which is arranged by agency and subject matter. For state administrative agencies, one must determine where newly proposed regulations and adopted versions of new regulations are published, as this varies from one state to another. Each state generally has a codification of state regulations that varies somewhat from one state to another.

Executive orders of the president are recorded chronologically in the Federal Register (not codified). They are published annually by subject matter in Title 3 of the Code of Federal Regulations. Executive orders of the governors are generally handled less formally than executive orders of the president. Some states do not codify executive orders of governors. The official websites of state governors are a good starting point to find the executive orders of governors.

## Case law

Case law, which comes from the judicial branch, is contained in various reporters, depending upon the specific court. Decisions of the three levels of Article III courts (U.S. Supreme Court, U.S. Courts of Appeals, and U.S. District Court) are published in chronological order. A useful reference for citation style is The Bluebook, published by the Harvard Law Review Association.[8] Example 2.1 illustrates a citation to a U.S. Supreme Court decision, and Example 2.2 discusses how to use that citation.

---

**Example 2.1** *Bates v. Dow AgroSciences*, LLC, 332 F.3d 323; 2003 U.S. App. LEXIS 12012 (5th Cir. 2003) is a citation of the same case used in Example 2.2 from a court below the U.S. Supreme Court, the U.S. Court of Appeals for the Fifth Circuit.

---

**Example 2.2** *Bates v. Dow AgroSciences*, LLC, 544 U.S. 431, 125 S. Ct. 1788, 161 L. Ed. 2d 687, 2005 U.S. LEXIS 3706 (2005) is a citation to a U.S. Supreme Court decision. To understand what this citation means, we will begin with the case name. Bates is the name of the first plaintiff. As he is an individual plaintiff, one uses only his last name. Dow AgroSciences LLC is the name of the defendant. As the defendant is not a natural person, we use the name of the company. The company is a limited liability company, which may be abbreviated in the title LLC. '544 U.S. 431' is the citation to the decision in the official reporter (the United States Reports). It is the preferred citation because it is the citation to the official reporter. The other citations are to various private providers. The number, 544, is the volume number of the United States Reports in which the decision is found. The number, 431, is the page number in that volume on which the first page of the decision is found. The abbreviation U.S. indicates that this is a Supreme Court decision. The year that the decision was reported is found in parentheses. That there is no abbreviation for U.S. Supreme Court within the parentheses is unique to Supreme Court decisions. For all other courts, there will be an abbreviation of the court name within the parentheses that contains the year.

Decisions of the U.S. Supreme Court are found in the United States Reports and other private services. Opinions of the U.S. Court of Appeals are published in the Federal Reporter and other private services. The Federal Reporter is a Westlaw publication; however, it has become the preferred citation among lawyers and courts. Federal District Court opinions are located in the Federal Supplement and other private services. The Federal Supplement® is the preferred citation. The Federal Supplement is a Westlaw publication. The websites of the U.S. Supreme Court and those of lower federal courts are a rich source of information about the day-to-day decisions of the courts in the cases before them.

Decisions of state courts, if published at all, are published in bound volumes called reporters and are available through online databases. Many states do not publish the decisions of trial courts. Unpublished decisions have no precedential value. With the widespread availability of online resources, copies of unpublished decisions may often be readily found. Unpublished decisions are not law and should not be relied upon. The header to an unpublished decision will usually state that it is unpublished. Some states have official reporters that are published by the states. Many designate a private service that published the cases in serial form as the official reporter.

## Reading judicial decisions

Reading a judicial decision is an art form. It is not unusual for reports in the press of an important judicial decision to misstate what the court actually ruled. That is why it is important to be able to read cases that pertain to one's business and understand them. Much of the verbiage that is published about judicial decisions in the press and other secondary sources is inaccurate.

The opinion is that part of the published case that was written by a judge. In addition to that part, a typical publication of the case will include the title, the parties (plaintiffs and defendants), attorneys for the parties, citations to various reporters, the prior history of the case, and explanatory materials. Explanatory materials are usually added by private services as aids to understanding the case. Though these materials are often useful, care must be taken in using them because they occasionally misstate the holding in the case. The Supreme Court includes a syllabus that summarizes the case in their decision in it. The syllabus is not part of the opinion and is not law. Like explanatory materials prepared by private services, the syllabus is often useful to understanding the decision but occasionally contains errors.

The opinion usually contains a discussion of the facts that gave rise to the dispute. The opinion will also discuss what lower courts and administrative agencies decided when they addressed the dispute. Most opinions also state the questions that the opinion will address. The Supreme Court's grant of a writ of certiorari always states the questions that the Supreme Court will address. Orders granting writs of certiorari are published on the U.S. Supreme Court website and are also available through the major private databases. When multiple questions are presented, the opinion will usually be divided according to the questions presented. Each judge or justice has his or her own style so the structure of opinions varies substantially.

The legally operative part of the opinion is the holding. If there is more than one question presented, there will usually be a holding corresponding to each question. Sometimes, an answer to one question makes it unnecessary to answer the other questions presented. If the Supreme Court can decide the dispute by interpreting a statute, it will not address constitutional questions raised in the dispute. Sometimes, courts begin the holding by stating, "We hold . . ." This makes finding the holding easy; however, not all judges write their opinions in this manner, so finding the holding is not always easy. Sometimes, judges state their opinions on other issues. This matter is not legally operative and is called "dicta." When an opinion is not written clearly, lawyers may argue about what is the holding of the case and what is dicta. Decisions will also include an order. This may be that the lower court decision is upheld, or it may be that the lower court decision is reversed. If the decision of the lower court is reversed, there will usually be directions to the lower court as to how to proceed. It is not unusual for an appellate court to uphold the decision of the lower court in part and reverse in part.

If the decision is that of a trial court, there will be an order, a judgment, or both. An order contains the court's grants of injunctive relief. An injunction is a court order that requires a party to take some action or refrain from some action. A judgment is made where the defendant is ordered to pay the plaintiff the sum of money. If the defendant wins, the case is usually dismissed with prejudice, which means that the case is over.

---

**Example 2.3** John kept a few horses in his back yard. As John traveled for his work, the horses were often left without care. John ignored repeated warnings from the county animal control officer that he was in violation of the county ordinance that forbids neglect and cruelty to animals. The county animal control officer issued an order that required John to sell his horses within thirty days. The order prohibited him from keeping horses on his property. John ignored the order. The county brought a lawsuit seeking injunctive relief. The court issued an injunction that required John to sell or give away the horses within thirty days and keep no more horses on his property. John ignored the court's order. Upon motion by the attorney representing the county, the judge ordered John to attend a contempt hearing. At the contempt hearing, the judge ordered John immediately jailed for civil contempt. With assistance from his family, John gave the horses to a horse rescue society. John's attorney provided the attorney for the county and the judge with proof of compliance with the judge's order. The attorney for the county consented to John's release, whereupon the judge ordered him released.

## Notes

1  W. Page Keeton et al., *Prosser and Keeton on the Law of Torts* (5th ed. 1984).
2  Law Library of Congress. Retrieved May 22, 2018, www.loc.gov/law/.
3  U.S. Government Publishing Office. Retrieved May 22, 2018, www.gpo.gov/.
4  USDA Office of the Administrative Law Judges. Retrieved May 22, 2018, oalj.oha. usda.gov/.
5  The National Agricultural Law Center. Retrieved May 22, 2018, nationalaglawcenter. org/.
6  Legal Information Institute (LII). Retrieved May 22, 2018, www.law.cornell.edu/.
7  Congress.gov. Retrieved May 22, 2018, www.congress.gov/.
8  The Bluebook. Retrieved May 22, 2018, www.legalbluebook.com/.

# Chapter 3

# Torts

## Introduction

### *Definition*

When one person does harm to the person, property, or reputation of another, it is likely that a tort has been committed. Either monetary damages, injunctive relief, or both may be available. A tort generally does not include the breach of an agreement (a contractual duty). Not all harms to the person, property, or reputation of another are torts. Generally, only serious harms are torts. A tort may also be a crime if the conduct that caused the harm is so unacceptable that it interferes with the welfare or morals of the public in addition to the interest of a private party. The elements of crimes and torts are usually different. A tort action must be brought as a civil action separate from the criminal prosecution brought by the government.

---

**Example 3.1** Freddy Farmer grew and sold cantaloupes. Due to Freddy's negligence the cantaloupes were contaminated with a pathogen that causes serious cases of food poisoning, and even death. Ursula Unlucky bought and ate one of Freddy's cantaloupes. The pathogen in the cantaloupe caused a severe case of food poisoning in Ursula that rendered her pancreas permanently unable to produce insulin. She must wear an insulin pump for the rest of her life. The jury in Ursula's state court action found Freddy liable in negligence and awarded economic damages for her past and future medical expenses (discounted to present value), lost income due to months away from work, and pain and suffering. Since the outbreak associated with Freddy's cantaloupe sickened an additional 500 or more people and caused at least 17 fatalities, the federal district attorney successfully obtained an indictment against Freddy for multiple counts of the strict liability crime of introducing an adulterated food product into the chain of commerce in violation of the Federal Food Drug and Cosmetic Act. Under the terms of

---

the plea agreement that his attorney negotiated with the district attorney, Freddy pled guilty before a federal district court judge to one count of a federal misdemeanor. The judge sentenced him to six months of unsupervised probation.

At common law, tort actions to recover for the death of a person were not recognized. All states have enacted wrongful death statutes that allow recovery for the wrongful death of a person. The provisions of these statutes vary widely. They govern when recovery is available, by whom, and limitations upon amounts recoverable. A discussion of these statutes is beyond the scope of this book.

## Burden of proof

The evidence presented to the jury or the judge by the parties to a tort case must favor the plaintiff by more than 50 percent. Ties go to the defendant. This burden of proof is called a preponderance of the evidence. This is in sharp contrast to the burden of proof that the government must meet to prove a crime. That standard is beyond a reasonable doubt. If the jury has any reasonable doubt that the defendant committed the crime, it must find the defendant not guilty. It is not uncommon for a criminal defendant to be acquitted but found liable in a civil tort case where both actions arose from the same facts.

## Relief

For most torts, the relief that plaintiffs typically seek is money damages. Monetary damages are the measure of the economic loss that the plaintiff has experienced as a result of the defendant's tort. Where, for example, a car is rendered a total loss in an accident, we can get an estimate of the value of the car and that will be the measure of damages. Where there are medical expenses resulting from a personal injury, the costs associated with those are also relatively easy to measure. The cost of future medical care may also be recovered if it can be reasonably anticipated. For loss of quality of life and pain and suffering, the value of these damages is generally left to a determination by a jury. There is generally no compensation for purely emotional injuries, with a rare exception for extreme emotional distress.

For certain torts, a jury may also award punitive or exemplary damages. These damages are unrelated to the economic loss and are intended to punish the defendant. Unlike a criminal sanction, the money is paid to the plaintiff, not to the state. A jury, or judge in the case of a bench trial, is never required to grant punitive damages, except where the damages are mandated by statute. An example of punitive damages required by statute is given in Example 3.2.

---

**Example 3.2** Nada Feckless decided that it was time to introduce his son, Junior, then seven years of age, to a family tradition: cutting "wheelies" in some hapless farmer's field. He picked John's wheat field because it had developed such a wonderful shade of green after a long winter. Junior became quite proficient at cutting wheelies with Nada's four-wheeler. He tore up most of John's wheat field. Nada proudly posted pictures on his Facebook page. John sued both Nada and Junior Feckless for trespass. John sought actual damages of $30,000 and an additional $30,000 in statutory punitive damages. The state where John's farm is located has a statute that requires that judges double damage awards for willful destruction of crops. The court appointed a guardian *ad litem* to represent Junior due to his age and interests adverse to his father. Junior's attorney argued that he was too young to understand the nature of his actions. After deliberation, the jury found Nada liable for trespass but declined to find any liability in Junior. The jury found actual damages of $29,000 for damage to the wheat crop. The judge doubled the amount of damages found by the jury and entered a judgment for $58,000. The judge also ordered Nada to pay $7,835 to the guardian *ad litem* for her fees and expenses.

---

As a remedy for certain torts, the plaintiff may want the defendant to cease or modify the offending activity. In that event, the plaintiff will seek injunctive relief. An injunction is a court order requiring the defendant to either quit doing something or take some affirmative step. A defendant's failure to follow a court's order is punishable as civil contempt.

## Types of torts

There are three types or theories of tort: intentional, negligence, and strict liability. Torts based upon a negligence theory are overwhelmingly the most common.

### Intentional torts

The key element of an intentional tort is an intent to do a voluntary act that constitutes the tort. There is often confusion among the public as to what constitutes an intentional tort. An intentional tort occurs when the defendant voluntarily does the act that constitutes the tort. The plaintiff does not have to prove that the defendant intended to commit a tort. It is sufficient to prove that the defendant intended to commit the acts that constitutes the tort. As illustrated in Example 3.3, the intentional tort of trespass is defined as the wrongful entry onto the real property of another without permission. The reason why the defendant entered the property without permission is generally irrelevant to determining whether the tort occurred, although it may be relevant to the measure of damages.

**Example 3.3** Robert had his property surveyed prior to siting his new house. The surveyor that he hired made a serious error when he surveyed the property. The survey showed the eastern boundary of Robert's property to be fifty feet farther east than the boundary actually was. Robert began land clearing on land that he mistakenly thought to be his. He then built his dream house on the cleared land. Some months after Robert had moved into his dream home, his neighbor, Ian, came to visit his property. Ian was shocked at what he saw. He asked Robert to immediately remove the house and restore the property to its original condition. Robert laughed, "The house is built. There is nothing that I can do." Ian hired an attorney and sued Robert for the tort of trespass. Ian demanded that Robert immediately remove the house at his expense. He also asked for economic damages that included the cost of reforestation, triple the value of the trees removed, and loss of value of the property caused by removal of the trees. After a bench trial, the judge ordered that Robert remove the house from Ian's property within sixty days. He also awarded damages equal to the reasonable cost of reforestation and double the market value of the timber at the time that it was removed. The judge refused to award damages for the diminished value of the property, holding that awarding damages for the lost timber and damages for loss of value of the property would be double counting of the economic damages. A state timber theft statute that mandates punitive damages as double the value of the timber taken left the judge without discretion to award less than double damages for the timber. He declined to order the triple damages that the plaintiff sought. That the survey was incorrect and that the error was the fault of the surveyor are both irrelevant to the question of whether Robert trespassed upon Ian's property. Robert's refusal to leave Ian's property after Ian's demands that Robert do so leaves no doubt as to Robert's intent.

To reiterate, the elements of intentional torts consist of certain intentional acts. One need not be aware that one is committing an intentional tort. If such were the case, "I didn't know" would be a defense. Other examples of intentional torts include battery (unwanted touching of another), assault (a credible threat to commit a battery, e.g., pointing a firearm at someone), false imprisonment (illegal confinement), intentional infliction of severe emotional distress (acts or words intended to shock), defamation (libel or slander), and invasion of privacy (using a person's name without authorization or publicizing a private life). Discussed in Chapter 4 will be the torts of nuisance and trespass, the two most important intentional torts relevant to agriculture.

## Negligence

At its simplest, negligence is the failure to act as a reasonable person would act under similar circumstances. Negligence can arise from some act that a reasonable person would not have done under the same circumstances. The law of negligence is based on society's expectation that everyone will exercise due care in his or her conduct toward others where it can be foreseen that the conduct might result in an injury. Negligence results from carelessness, thoughtlessness, or oversight rather than from willfulness.

The tort of negligence has four elements: duty, breach of duty, proximate causation, and actual damages. Each of the four elements must be proven by the plaintiff to establish a cause of action based upon a negligence theory. The failure to prove any element will result in dismissal of the case. To survive a pretrial motion to dismiss, the complaint must clearly state all four elements of the tort of negligence. It is not necessary at the commencement of an action that the plaintiff be in possession of all of the facts necessary to prove a tort in negligence. Evidence in the possession of the defendant needed to prove one's case may be obtained through pretrial discovery. At trial, the plaintiff must have presented sufficient credible evidence in support of each element to make out a *prima facie* case of negligence by the conclusion of his case in chief. If the plaintiff fails to make out a *prima facie* case, the plaintiff's case will not survive a motion to dismiss by the defendant.

The plaintiff's first step in establishing a *prima facie* case is to prove that the defendant owed him a duty. A duty may be created by law, contract, or assumption of a duty. Common law, legislation, assumption, and contracts between the parties are sources of duty. The duty of operators of slow-moving farm equipment on public highways to ensure that the equipment is visible to other drivers is established both by common law and legislation in most states. In general, the common law created the general duty while the legislation provided additional details such as the requirement of a reflective sign of certain specifications. A contract between two parties may create a duty that was not created by law. A farm that operates an agritourism operation that includes a swimming area may hire a lifeguard to protect its customers. The lifeguard's contract with the farm owner requires her or him to protect her or his employer's customers who use the farm's swimming area. Absent the contract, the lifeguard would have no duty to the customers of the farm. The status of certification as a lifeguard does not impose upon a person a duty to rescue swimmers in a swimming area that does not employ the lifeguard. In general, the law imposes no duty to rescue. The other customers have no duty to rescue a fellow customer in distress in the farm's swimming area. Should a customer attempt a rescue, however, that customer has assumed a duty to rescue competently. The duty is assumed either expressly or implied by actions. A customer of a corn maze that signs a waiver has expressly assumed the normal risks associated with a corn maze. The customer, above, who attempts a rescue has impliedly assumed a duty by his actions. Examples 3.4, 3.5, 3.6, and 3.7 are related examples that explore the question of whether a duty exists.

**Example 3.4** Larry is a certified lifeguard. While on vacation at Agricultural Adventures, a local agritourism operation, he saw a child who had wandered outside the boundary of the kiddie wading area. While he could have easily rescued the child, he simply stood and gawked while the child drowned. The child's parents sued Larry because he was a certified lifeguard who could have easily rescued the child without any danger to himself. The parents' action will not survive a motion to dismiss because Larry was on his own time and had no duty to rescue anyone.

**Example 3.5** Larry the certified lifeguard was on vacation at Agricultural Adventures. He saw a child who had wandered outside the boundary of the kiddie wading area. He successfully brought the child up to the shoreline but dropped the child when he turned to say hello to a friend. The child was severely injured when he hit the ground due to weak bones that were unknown to Larry. By engaging in the rescue, Larry assumed a duty to rescue non-negligently. Dropping the child on the ground is likely a breach of Larry's duty to rescue non-negligently. That a child with normal bones would not have been injured is not a defense.

**Example 3.6** Larry the certified lifeguard was on vacation at Agricultural Adventures. A child who wanted to go out into the deep water of the creek, outside the boundary of the kiddie wading area, persuaded Larry to take him there. As the child appeared to be doing well in the deep water, Larry left the child alone in the deep water to go buy a freshly made certified organic veggie juice. When Larry returned to the creek, the child was still in the deep water and was crying for help. Larry ignored the cries. Larry has a duty to rescue the child because he assumed that duty when he took the child to deep water.

**Example 3.7** Agricultural Adventures operates in a state with a statute that protects agritourism operations by limiting their standard of care to that owed to a trespasser. The statute requires that agritourism operations post signage to make customers aware of the limitation on liability. Agricultural Adventures had posted the signage required to comply with the statute. A customer would ordinarily be classified as an invitee who is owed a duty defined by the highest possible standard of care, to make the property safe or warn of conditions that cannot be made safe. The duty owed to a trespasser requires only a limited standard of care, to avoid maliciously injuring the trespasser. Under this standard of care, Agricultural Adventures would likely have no liability to the next of kin of the child in the previous three examples because it did not breach any duty owed to the child.

Before a court can determine whether duty has been breached, it must establish the standard of care as discussed in Example 3.7. The standard of care is defined by what a reasonable person would do under the same circumstances. Defining what constitutes reasonable care is critical to establishing the defendant's duty. A breach of duty may be the result of either an act or a failure to act. The standard of care for a professional will be established as that used by an ordinary member of the profession. Example 3.8 provides an example of this.

**Example 3.8** The surveyor from Example 3.3 may be liable to Robert under either a negligence theory or a breach of contract theory; however, it is by no means certain that the surveyor will have any liability to Robert. It may be that the surveyor conducted the survey in accord with applicable professional standards, in which case it is unlikely that the surveyor would have any liability to Robert. Professional standards set the "duty of care" for a professional. Professional standards are not designed to prevent all errors because such a standard would render the services of professionals far too costly for clients and the economy to bear.

Proof of duty and breach of duty are often closely tied to regulatory law. Violation of a regulation that was designed to prevent the type of injury that occurred may result in application of the doctrine of negligence *per se*. Under the doctrine of negligence *per se*, the elements of duty and breach of duty will be deemed proven where such a regulatory violation occurred. Sometimes, the defendant is in control of the instrumentalities that caused the injury. In such cases, courts may apply the doctrine of *res ipsa loquitur*. This doctrine allows the plaintiff to avoid pretrial dismissal of the action for failure to prove breach of duty when it is clear that the incident would not have occurred without some form of negligence. It is sometimes used in airline cases where the plane was under the control of the airline at the time of a crash. The doctrine of *res ipsa loquitur* is also used in food poisoning cases.[1]

**Example 3.9** Farmer Larry applied a pesticide on a crop in a manner that was prohibited by federal law. As a direct result of that regulatory violation, he destroyed his neighbor's cotton crop. Under the doctrine of negligence *per se*, it would be sufficient for the neighbor to prove the regulatory violation to establish both the existence of a duty and breach of duty.

There are rules for establishing the duty to protect those entering land. The status of the injured person is a factor in defining the duty owed by the farmer to that person. There are three categories of persons entering land: trespasser, licensee, and invitee.

As noted above, the duty of reasonable care owed to a trespasser (one who enters and remains without permission) is slight. That means that the landowner may not maliciously injure the trespasser. The landowner may not use more force than necessary to evict the trespasser from the premises after the trespasser has been asked to leave. The landowner may not use deadly force. Any person generally has a right to defend himself from the threat of deadly force; however, this is not the same as the right to defend land.

A landowner must also allow the use of his land by one whose use is necessary to prevent bodily injury or death. Such a person is not a trespasser but may be required to pay for any actual damages to the property. A landowner who refuses one who needs to use the land out of necessity may be found both criminally and civilly liable. For example, the owner of a dock may not refuse to allow an exhausted swimmer use of the dock. If the dock owner refuses the swimmer use of the dock and swimmer drowns as a result, the dock owner may be found both civilly and criminally liable.

There is a higher duty owed to a licensee (one who enters the land with permission for his or her own purpose or business rather than for the landowner's or tenant's benefit). An example of a licensee is a social guest. Here, the landowner has the additional duty to warn the licensee of dangerous conditions or dangerous animals on the premises. If the licensee is a hunter, the landowner may also have a duty to warn him or her of other hunters already on the property. Many states have abolished the category of licensee.

The highest level of duty is owed to an invitee (one who is on the land with permission for the benefit of the landowner or tenant). Examples of invitees are a repairman or a hunter who shares his game with the landowner. In the case of an invitee, the landowner has the additional duty to make the premises safe or to warn of any conditions that cannot be made safe.

There is a special theory of liability in the case of young trespassers called the 'attractive nuisance' doctrine. A landowner may be liable for injuries to child trespassers where he would not be liable to adult trespassers under the same circumstances. This doctrine holds that children do not have the same experience or judgment as adults. Though it is not necessary for application of the doctrine that there be something attractive on the property, it is nonetheless the case that they may be strongly attracted to explore certain things, such as farm ponds, animals, or farm machinery. A duty of care similar to that for invitees will be applied where a reasonably prudent person would have foreseen the likelihood that children would trespass on the premises.

Establishing the first two elements of a tort of negligence establishes that the defendant was negligent. It does not establish liability. The plaintiff must prove the third element of proximate causation (sometimes called legal causation) in addition. Proximate causation is related to the foreseeability of the injury resulting from the defendant's misconduct. In the early part of the twentieth century, in a celebrated case, a Mrs. Palsgraf was injured at a railway station when the force of an explosion caused a large clock to tip over and fall on her. The clock was at the other end of the platform far from the site of the explosion. The explosion was triggered when a passenger accidently dropped a package of explosives on the track. The passenger dropped the package because a conductor, employed by the defendant, pushed the passenger onto the train. In the 1928 N.Y. Court of Appeals decision in *Palsgraf v. Long Island R.R. Co.*,[2] the court, in a four to three decision, denied Mrs. Palsgraf any recovery for her injuries because she was not in the reasonably foreseeable zone of danger. That this was a four to three decision of New York's highest court demonstrates that reasonable people can differ on the question of what is foreseeable.

The fourth element, actual damages, is also essential to proving a case of negligence. If there are no actual damages, the plaintiff cannot recover using a negligence theory. Actual damages include any economic losses that may include the fair market value of lost property, repairs to damaged property, and medical expenses. Actual damages also include reduced quality of life and pain and suffering. Future medical expenses that can be reasonably expected may also be recovered at the discounted present value. A spouse may recover for loss of consortium with the injured spouse. Though emotional damages are generally not included within actual damages, the cost of psychiatric care that results from the injury may be recovered.

If a plaintiff proves the four elements necessary to establish a claim of negligence, the defendant may be able to offer a defense that will prevent or limit a recovery of damages by the plaintiff. One common defense is called "contributory" or "comparative" negligence, depending upon the law of the state where the action is brought. Society expects a person to exercise due care for the safety of his or her own person or property. If a plaintiff is negligent in caring for him- or herself in preventing the injury, then he or she may be barred from recovering damages from the defendant even though the defendant was also negligent. The common law rule was contributory negligence. Under this rule, any negligence on the part of the plaintiff means that the plaintiff gets nothing. This rule continues to be followed in a few U.S. states. Most states employ the rule of comparative negligence because a complete bar to recovery is a harsh consequence for a small amount of negligence. The majority of U.S. states have statutes that allow some recovery under a theory of comparative negligence (or comparative fault). The judge or jury compares the negligence of the plaintiff with that of the defendant and divides the damage award between the two parties proportionately. Under the rule of comparative negligence, the jury is asked to assign fault expressed in percentages to both the plaintiff and defendant. The judge then reduces the plaintiff's award by the percentage that the jury has decided was the amount of fault assigned to the plaintiff. Most comparative negligence states bar recovery where the plaintiff's negligence exceeds a certain percentage, typically 50 percent.

A second defense to negligence under the common law is called "assumption of the risk." This can be raised when the plaintiff voluntarily assumes a known risk. All participants in athletic activities assume the normal risks of the activities. For certain activities with known risks (e.g., equestrian activities), participants may sign waivers that absolve the owner or organizer of the activity from liability for the normal risks of the activity. The beneficiary of the waiver is not absolved from liability for risks that are not normal risks of the activity. The beneficiary of the waiver is also not absolved from liability for acts of gross negligence. As a waiver is a contract, a person younger than the age of eighteen cannot sign a valid waiver. The signature of a parent or guardian on the waiver of the child does not prevent the child from bringing a lawsuit when the child reaches the age of eighteen.

Gross negligence is found along the line between intentional torts and negligent torts. Proof of gross negligence requires proof that the defendant acted with reckless disregard for the health or welfare of others. Unlike ordinary negligence, punitive damages may be awarded where gross negligence is proven. In addition to the four elements of a tort in negligence, it must also be proven that the defendant acted with reckless disregard.

---

**Example 3.10** Farmer John irrigated his lettuce with water from a pond to which livestock had full access. Farmer John knew that his livestock defecated in the pond, and that irrigating a crop intended to be consumed raw with water likely to be contaminated with deadly pathogens by such practice would contaminate his lettuce. Farmer John was grossly negligent. Should any of his customers become ill from eating his lettuce, he may be assessed punitive damages and actual damages. In this example, he is also likely to be criminally prosecuted if any serious injuries or death result from consumption of his lettuce.

---

### Strict liability

As discussed previously, there usually must be a finding of fault to establish an intentional tort or negligence. An exception to this is the concept of "strict liability." Under this exception, a person who engages in an "ultrahazardous activity" or an "abnormally dangerous activity" is liable for all injuries proximately caused by her or his activity, even if he or she took the utmost care possible to prevent such injuries. Therefore, this is liability without fault. An activity is considered to be ultrahazardous or abnormally dangerous if it involves a high degree of risk of serious harm and the risk cannot be eliminated even with reasonable precautions. A few states apply a strict liability theory to injuries resulting from aerial application of pesticides. Most states apply a negligence theory.

A majority of states apply strict liability in tort to product liability cases. The allegation in such cases is that there was negligent production or design of the product. This is an important issue for all producers of human food and animal feed.

## Vicarious liability

An employer is generally liable for torts of an employee that were done within the scope of employment. For torts of agents other than employees, the employer generally has no liability. For example, a real estate agent who negligently and incorrectly measures the square footage of a house may be liable to the purchaser of a house for damages. The owner of the house that hired the real estate agent would not be liable for the error in measurement. Likewise, an aerial applicator of pesticides is liable for his torts as illustrated in Example 3.11. The farmer that hired the aerial applicator would not have liability because the aerial applicator is an independent contractor.

---

**Example 3.11** Farmer Jones hired Buzz Buzzard to spray his cotton with a restricted use pesticide. Farmer Jones' due diligence showed no violations of any pesticide law by Buzz or any complaints to pesticide regulators. In the course of spraying Famer Jones' cotton, Buzz neglected to shut off his sprayer while crossing a highway. As a result, he sprayed a rural mail carrier whose window was down as she delivered mail. The rural mail carrier was rendered permanently unable to care for herself. As Buzz is an independent contractor, Farmer Jones has no vicarious liability for his torts.

---

**Example 3.12** Same facts as Example 3.11, except that Farmer Jones did no due diligence. Buzz had twenty-three violations of pesticide laws, and his applicator certification was suspended. While Farmer Jones would have no vicarious liability as Buzz is an independent contractor, Farmer Jones would likely be liable for his own tort—that of negligent selection.

The law of vicarious liability is complex. It varies greatly from one state to another. There are many exceptions to the general rules governing liability for the torts of agents and independent contractors.

## Insurance

Insurance is a contractual method of transferring risk from one person to another. There are two components to every insurance policy. The first is to pay for covered liability. The second is a duty to defend. This second aspect of insurance is at least as important as the first as the cost of defending against tort suits, especially agricultural nuisance suits, can be very expensive. Insurance pays for the costs of investigation, attorney and expert witness fees, and court costs.

Most farms buy farm liability policies to provide protection from tort liability. The typical farm liability policy covers torts that arise from normal farming activities. Agritourism and retail activities are often excluded from coverage. Products liability coverage in a farm liability policy is typically limited to raw agricultural products. Generally, no coverage is provided for injuries or illnesses arising from food or feed products for which the farm provided further processing. Another exception to coverage is for injuries that result from intentional torts or crimes committed by the insured farmer. There are some exceptions to this general rule.

An insurance company is obligated to pay damages only for legal obligations of the insured. An insurance company will not pay moral obligations of the insured. Because an insurance contract is governed by the policy, which is a contract between the insured farm and the insurance company, coverage provided is defined by the policy. Certain events may be excluded from coverage. There is typically an upper dollar limit on coverage and a deductible that the policyholder must pay for each claim. Risks not covered by an insurance policy are self-insured. The deductible, the amount that the policyholder must pay, is one form of self-insurance. Insurance is regulated by state law. Within the limits of state law, insurance companies have a great deal of freedom to define the terms of the policies that they sell.

Most farm liability policies impose an obligation on the insurance company to defend the insured. This aspect of most policies requires the insurance company to provide an attorney at no cost to the insured and pay other associated costs of litigation. Costs associated with litigation include court costs and the costs of experts who serve as consultants and those who testify as experts. This is an often-overlooked reason for obtaining insurance coverage. If the limits on what a policy will pay are too low, the insurance company may simply pay the policy limits to the plaintiff and thereafter refuse to provide a defense. Insurance companies may satisfy their obligation by paying the plaintiff the limits of the policy. After the insurance company has done this, it is no longer under any obligation to defend the insured. It is, therefore, of great benefit to be sure that one has enough insurance. The place to save money is with a higher deductible, not with a lower insurance limit. Per dollar of coverage the cost of insurance generally declines as the amount of coverage goes up.

> **Example 3.13** L. O. Value was pleased with the cost of his general farm liability policy. The trade-off for such a low premium was that he had only $400,000 of coverage. One day one of his cows got out on the highway. It was hit by a driver who was rounding a corner and could not see the cow in time to stop. The driver was seriously injured. Mr. Value was shocked when the jury awarded the plaintiff $750,000. To its credit, Mr. Value's insurance company negotiated the payment down to coverage limits so that Mr. Value had no out-of-pocket costs. Another company might have simply written the plaintiff a check for $400,000 and refused any further involvement in the lawsuit. This would have meant that Mr. Value would have had to find and hire his own attorney for an appeal at his own expense or, alternatively, have paid the remaining $350,000 of the judgment.

### Insurance terminology

There is a lot of terminology in the insurance business. It helps to know the basics. The owner of the insurance policy may be, but is not always, the *beneficiary* of the policy. For example, a farmer who owns a products liability insurance policy may also designate named buyers of his products as insureds. Often, his contract with the buyer will require this. The buyer is said to be a *third-party beneficiary*. A *premium* is what the policyholder pays for insurance coverage.

A *rider* is an additional policy that is added to a standard policy to cover something that was excluded from the standard policy.

> **Example 3.14** Sarah Jean decided that she could sell some of the produce that her husband, Dick, raised. She built a farm store to market produce to their customers. She asked her insurance agent whether their farm liability policy covered this. Her insurance agent said that she did not really know; however, she thought there was coverage for it. That did not satisfy Sarah Jean, so she sent a copy of the policy to her attorney, who read it and determined that there was an exclusion for retail operations. Sarah Jean bought a rider to cover the retail operation.

A *policy* is the contract between the policyholder and the insurance company. Only that which is written in the insurance policy is legally binding. Oral statements by *insurance brokers* or *agents* are not binding upon the insurance company that they represent. Insurance brokers or agents are usually independent business people, whether they are *captive* or *independent* agents. The captive agent represents only one company whereas an independent agent represents many. They are not employees of the insurance company and have no power to contractually bind the insurance company. What they tell the policyholder about the policy is not legally binding on the insurance company. The best way to find out what is covered is to ask for the agent to ask the company's *underwriter*, who is a company employee, and return the response in writing. Responses should be archived off-site where they are safe in the event of a dispute with the insurance company about coverage. Off-site, secure storage of important business documents should be part of every business risk management program. Off-site storage ensures that important records are available in the event that the business is destroyed by a natural or other disaster.

An underwriter is an employee of the insurance company who determines whether a policy will be written, with what provisions, and at what premium. The underwriter has the authority to bind the insurance company. The underwriter works with actuaries that determine the cost of risk. An *actuary* is a statistician who determines the cost of risk. Insurance depends upon the existence of a history of losses. Without a history of losses, the cost of risk cannot be determined. With technological change or change in the legal environment, a history of risk is often lacking, and insurance companies are reluctant to write policies. With the great interest in local agriculture, new farm businesses are arising for which there is no risk history. It is often difficult or impossible to obtain insurance coverages for these farm businesses.

In the insurance business, an *event* is what triggers a *claim*. A claim is made against the insurance company when there has been an insured loss. An *adjuster* is a representative of the insurance company who determines whether the claim is valid and, if valid, the value of the claim. Some adjusters are employees of the insurance company whereas some are independent contractors.

Only an *insurable interest* may be insured. An insurable interest is something for which the insured will experience a loss if an event leading to that loss occurs. As a general rule, an event that would not lead to a loss on the part of the insured is a gambling contract, not an insurance contract. Gambling contracts are regulated under different laws than insurance contracts.

Insurance companies typically sell the risk that they are covering to investors. These investors are called *reinsurers*. One of the largest reinsurance markets is Lloyd's of London.

### Policyholder obligations and other considerations

Motor vehicle coverage is a complicated and important area of insurance for every farm business. One needs to plan carefully for issues that include authorized drivers, authorized uses, and pulled vehicles such as farm equipment and trailers. Losses associated with motor vehicles are the greatest risk that most farm businesses face on a day-to-day basis. It is not unusual for farmers to use personal vehicles for business and business vehicles for personal purposes. It is not unusual for a farmer facing a claim to both be defending the claim and litigating with her or his insurance company over the scope of coverage. This is an unhappy position to be in and can be avoided with planning, careful record keeping, and good communication with one's insurance company. Insurance companies do not like to litigate with their clients and are more than happy to work with their clients to ensure that that does not happen.

Managing one's insurance coverage is very important. An important part of managing one's insurance coverage is to read the insurance policy. Managing one's insurance coverage means having a good understanding of what is covered. It means promptly notifying one's insurance carrier of any significant changes in one's operation. Doubts should be resolved by talking to one's insurance carrier. The information given to one's insurance agent may result in a premium increase. That is greatly to be preferred to discovering that a loss is not covered after an event has occurred.

Most insurance policies require prompt notification of potential claims to maintain coverage. Typically, it can be three or more years after an injury occurs before a potential defendant is served with process in a case. It may even be a substantial amount of time before a potential defendant is notified of the potential claim. Any time a serious injury occurs on one's farm, one should notify his or her insurance company in writing of the potential claim. Insurance companies can help a farm business owner prepare for potential claims. Insurance companies have many resources. Individually and collectively, insurance companies conduct a great deal of research on reducing losses. Most insurance companies provide discounts for using best practices. It is up to the buyer of insurance to inquire about these resources.

Insurance policies should be reviewed carefully before they are purchased to ensure sufficient coverage for the farmer's individual situation. After purchase, they should also be reviewed periodically to make sure that the amounts and types of coverage continue to be appropriate. It is important to work with one's insurance company on one's legal defense if one is sued and on the avoidance of liability in the first place. Even if one's insurance company defends and wins, litigation takes a lot of time that could be better spent on developing one's farm business. No one wants a customer injured when that injury could have been avoided.

## Notes

1 *Stevenson v. Winn-Dixie Atlanta, Inc.*, 211 Ga. App. 572, 440 S.E.2d 465, 1993 Ga. App. LEXIS 1577, 467-469 (Ga. Ct. App. 1993).
2 248 N.Y. 339, 162 N.E. 99 (N.Y. 1928).

# Chapter 4

# Nuisance and trespass

## Introduction

The torts of private nuisance and trespass both involve an offense to the ownership of real property. Trespass and nuisance as they appear in litigation are most often intentional torts. In some states, trespass may also be based upon a negligence theory. Nuisance may also be based on either a negligence or strict liability theory, depending upon the facts in the dispute. There is also a cause of action called a public nuisance that is not a tort. It is not uncommon in nuisance actions for a plaintiff to base his or her complaint upon multiple theories, including both public and private nuisance.

The distinction between a private nuisance and a trespass is that the first addresses the use of real property, and the second addresses the exclusive possession of real property. A nuisance is an unreasonable interference by one landowner with another landowner's use and enjoyment of his or her property. A trespass is the wrongful entry onto the land of another. It is an unexcused interference with a landowner's right of possession. A trespass includes not only a person's physically entering property without permission, but any extension of the person. Extensions of the person may include a vehicle, a bullet, nitrate molecules, and a second person who is serving as the agent or contractor of the first person. In the last example, the second person would also be a trespasser. There is no bright-line rule separating private nuisance and trespass. Some courts of some states have held that nitrate molecules or smoke emanating from the property of one person and injuring the property of another constitutes a private nuisance. The courts of other states have held, with identical facts, that these actions constitute a trespass. It is not uncommon to find conflicting precedents within a state court system.

The Supreme Court of Minnesota addressed the question of whether pesticide spray drift can constitute a trespass in its 2012 decision in *Johnson v. Paynesville Farmers Union Cooperative Oil Company*.[1]

> Our case law is consistent with this traditional formulation of trespass because we have recognized that a trespass can occur when a person or tangible object

enters the plaintiff's land. . . . This distinction between interference with possessory rights and interference with use and enjoyment rights is reflected in the only reported decisions in Minnesota, both from the court of appeals, which reached the question of whether an invasion by particulate matter constitutes a trespass. In both cases, the court of appeals held that such invasions do not, as a matter of law, constitute trespass.[2]

The Supreme Court of Minnesota went on to hold that spray drift can be a private nuisance.[3] Other states that have addressed the issue have taken a contrary view.[4] It is worth noting that nitrate pollution from livestock waste has similarly required courts to choose between nuisance and trespass theories.[5] Most attorneys who bring such suits will raise both theories.

A public nuisance is an action based upon a landowner's interference with the rights of the public by endangering public health or morals. An example is a person who operates a rowdy bar that attracts the criminal element to a neighborhood, thereby endangering the people who live and work in the neighborhood. Operation of a brothel is another land use that many courts have held to be a public nuisance. Public nuisance actions are generally, but not always, brought by governmental entities. A public nuisance may be brought either by criminal or civil action. Only a governmental entity may bring a criminal action.

## Trespass

The definition of trespass is the wrongful entry onto the real property of another without permission. "Wrongful" is not redundant with "without permission." Not all entries without permission are wrongful. A search of property by a law enforcement officer with a valid search warrant is without permission but not wrongful. A person who must enter property without permission to save his own life or that of another has not entered the property wrongfully. An airplane that needs to make an emergency landing in a farmer's field is the classic example of necessity. The pilot of such a plane has not made a wrongful entry onto the property because it was necessary to protect his life and the lives of any passengers. For that reason, there is no tort of trespass, although the pilot may be required to pay for actual damages caused to any crops. When one must make use of another's real property to protect the life or safety of oneself or another, interference with that effort by the landowner may be tortious or criminal conduct.

### Remedies

The remedies for a trespass are either monetary damages, injunctive relief, or both. When a trespass is based on the theory of intentional tort, monetary damages may consist of economic damages, punitive damages, or both. Economic damages are confined to the actual damage caused by the interference with the landowner's right of possession. Punitive damages are designed to punish and are determined by the jury. Unless there is a statute requiring it, juries are never required to award punitive damages. If the trespass is based upon a negligence theory, only economic damages are available.

Injunctive relief is usually in the form of ejectment. Ejectment is the removal of the defendant or the defendant's property from the property of the plaintiff. The plaintiff may also desire an injunction that orders the defendant not to return to the plaintiff's property.

---

**Example 4.1** Beamer was building a new steel building to shelter his new tractor when it was not in use and to allow repairs to be made in any weather. Unbeknownst to Beamer, the survey upon which he based his siting of the building was incorrect. As constructed, half of the building sat upon property owned by his neighbor, Mercedes. Mercedes demanded that Beamer remove the building immediately, at his expense. Beamer balked at this expensive request. Mercedes brought a trespass action demanding that Beamer remove the building from her property and restore her property to its original condition at his expense. The court found a trespass and granted an injunction that ordered Beamer to remove the building and restore the property at his expense. The injunction specified that he was to plant ten 10-inch-diameter trees to replace those that he had cut.

---

The remedy sought can be important to the applicable statute of limitation, a statute that bars a lawsuit a certain number of years after an injury is discovered. The statutes of limitation for monetary damages are typically shorter than the statutes of limitation for ejectment. Statutes of limitation vary greatly from state to state. The statute of limitation for ejectment is generally the same number of years that are required to acquire property by adverse possession. Acquisition of property by adverse possession will be discussed in Chapter 6.

## Nuisance

A private nuisance is a common law tort that is defined as an unreasonable interference by one landowner with another landowner's use and enjoyment of his or her property. The harm suffered must be substantial. Almost all actions that an owner undertakes on her or his property will in some way interfere with the uses that his or her neighbors make of their property. For that reason, nuisance decisions emphasize the extent to which the defendant's actions were unreasonable. Examples of unreasonable interferences with a landowner's use and enjoyment of her real property include smoke, odors, noise or vibration, obstruction of private easements, removal of lateral or subjacent support (causing landslides or subsidence), and interference with riparian rights such as by pollution or diversion of a natural body of water. In most states, if the defendant's interference involves a physical invasion of the plaintiff's property the tort is a trespass and not a nuisance. Plaintiffs often allege both trespass and nuisance in their complaint to give courts the option of determining whether the offending actions were a trespass or a nuisance.

## Theories

A private nuisance action may be based upon one or more of the three tort theories (intentional, negligence, or strict liability) discussed in Chapter 3. Regardless of the theory used, the offending conduct must be the proximate (legal) cause of the interference in the other landowner's interest in the use and quiet enjoyment of his or her land.

Most private nuisance actions are based on an intentional tort theory unless the nuisance was not continuing. What typically happens is that the landowner creating the nuisance is asked to stop and refuses. At that point, the nuisance becomes an intentional tort if the interference was unreasonable. If the activity of the person causing the nuisance is abnormally dangerous, for example, blasting to loosen rock in a quarry, the defendant can be held strictly liable for the resulting injuries, even though there was neither negligence nor intent. If the legal action is based upon a negligence theory, the four elements of any tort in negligence—duty, breach of duty, proximate causation, and actual damages—must be proven. No actual damages are needed to prove a nuisance if an intentional tort theory is used. As with all intentional torts, and those based upon gross negligence (reckless disregard), a jury may award punitive damages.

---

**Example 4.2** Enlightened Power and Light operated the Buena Vista Generating Plant until 1985. The Buena Vista Generating Plant was located along the scenic Buena Vista River, which is navigable. In January 2014, a dam holding back 10,000 tons of coal ash burst, pouring its entire contents into the Buena Vista River. Downstream farmers temporarily had to truck in water for their livestock because the river water was temporarily unfit for consumption. The cause of the spill was rain from a tropical storm and a rusted pipe that ran under the dam. Enlightened Power and Light had negligently failed to inspect the pipe. But for that negligence, the spill would not have occurred. The generating plant is no longer operating and is obsolete and will not be restarted. The entire contents of the coal ash pond flowed into the Buena Vista River. This is an example of a one-time nuisance. It is unlike a factory that continues to pour new pollutants into a river. As it is not a continuing nuisance, the only theory available to plaintiffs, such as these farmers, is a negligence theory. Since riparian owners generally do not own the land under a navigable water, there can be no trespass since there was no entry onto the land of another.

**Example 4.3** Fred Doe operates a large, total confinement of a hog finishing operation. His neighbors in an adjoining subdivision find the stench unbearable. His neighbors hired an attorney who sent Mr. Doe a cease-and-desist letter that demanded that Mr. Doe immediately stop damaging his neighbors' quality of life through an unreasonable interference with their use and quiet enjoyment of their properties. In the letter, the attorney cited the many water quality violations that the state water quality agency assessed against Mr. Doe's operation and a continuing enforcement action. Mr. Doe sent the attorney a nasty letter in which he refused to consider their complaint. Since Mr. Doe's operation is continuing and the nuisance that it creates is continuing, the nuisance action may be based upon an intentional tort theory. Given the water quality violations, Doe's operation will likely fall under an exception to his state's right-to-farm law with the result that it will not provide him with protection.

### Determining unreasonableness

An intentional interference with another's interest in the use and enjoyment of land is unreasonable if the gravity of the harm outweighs the utility of the actor's conduct or the harm caused by the conduct is serious and the financial burden of compensating for this and similar harm to others would not render the continuation of the conduct infeasible. In determining the gravity of the harm, the following factors are important: the extent of the harm involved, the character of the harm involved, the social value that the law attaches to the type of use and enjoyment harmed, the suitability of the particular use and enjoyment harmed to the character of the locality, and the burden on the person harmed of avoiding the harm. There are factors that a court must weigh when balancing the utility of the conduct that caused the harm against the damage to another's interest in the use and quiet enjoyment of land. These factors are the social value that the law attaches to the primary purpose of the conduct, the suitability of the conduct to the character of the locality, and the impracticability of preventing or avoiding the harm.

> The law of nuisance plys between two antithetical extremes: The principle that every person is entitled to use his property for any purpose that he sees fit, and the opposing principle that everyone is bound to use his property in such a manner as not to injure the property or rights of his neighbor. For generations, courts, in their tasks of judging, have ruled on these extremes according to the wisdom of the day, and many have recognized that the contemporary view of public policy shifts from generation to generation.[6]

The question of whether the interference is unreasonable is not a question of law but one of fact for the jury.

It is no defense to a nuisance action that the defendant's land use was first in time. That the plaintiff came to the nuisance may be considered at the remedy phase of the trial, but not in the determination of whether a nuisance exists. At common law, it was no defense to a nuisance action that the offending land use was first in time. The logic of this rule is that the user who is first in time should not be able thereby to determine the uses of land in a locality for all time simply through being first. Most states have by legislation adopted right-to-farm statutes that reverse this rule for certain farm uses. Right-to-farm laws are discussed later in this chapter.

### Remedies

After the court has determined that a nuisance exists, the court must determine the appropriate remedy. There are three possible remedies: money damages, injunctive relief (abatement), or some combination of the first two. Courts have found different remedies for private nuisances, based on the circumstances. One remedy is an injunction (correction of the condition), which is an appropriate remedy when the condition is one that can be changed. This is also called "abatement." If the condition cannot be abated, the plaintiff may be awarded monetary damages for the loss of his or her property value due to the permanent nature of the nuisance. The court has the flexibility to impose both remedies if it finds that to be appropriate for the particular circumstances. In deciding whether to enjoin a nuisance or award monetary damages, the court often balances hardships and benefits. Where the plaintiff is also at fault, it is possible that the plaintiff may be forced to pay part or all of the cost of abating the nuisance.

Where the nuisance is wholly in the past and will not happen again, the only remedy that can be granted is money damages. Aside from that situation, courts apply a balancing process similar to that used to determine whether a nuisance exists to fashion a remedy. Courts balance the "hardships" or "equities" to determine whether to enjoin the nuisance, grant only a judgment for damages, or use some combination of these remedies. The same factors are used to determine the scope of injunctive relief. Injunctive relief may entirely prohibit the offending activity or may require a modification of the activity.

When the court grants monetary damages alone, the offending activity is allowed to continue unabated. This remedy is usually granted when the offending activity has great economic importance, and the neighboring activity of the plaintiffs has much less importance. The damaged landowners are compensated for their losses through a one-time payment of money. In general, future owners of the land are bound by this determination by the court. Where abatement (injunctive relief) alone is used, the offending landowner whose activity constitutes a nuisance may be required to either modify the activity or cease the activity altogether.

The third remedy may be a combination of the first two. The third remedy is unique among tort remedies in that it may be the plaintiff, not the defendant, who pays. When a plaintiff came to the lawsuit with unclean hands (an equitable concept), the plaintiff may be forced to compensate the defendant for the cost of abating the nuisance. When the plaintiff engaged in an activity on his land that was likely to suffer from a known and preexisting activity on the defendant's land, the court has the power to order the plaintiff to pay the defendant's cost of abating the nuisance. *Spur Industries, Inc. v. Del E. Webb Development Co.*[7] is the leading agricultural nuisance case that addresses this issue. Del E. Webb Development Co. (Del Webb) began developing Sun City, Arizona, in 1959 on farmland that it had purchased for that purpose. At that time, the two predecessors in interest that combined to form Spur Industries, Inc. (Spur) were feeding 6,000 to 1,000 and 1,500 head of cattle, respectively, in the area near the land purchased by Del Webb. Spur's predecessors in interest had begun these operations in 1956. By the time that Del Webb brought this suit, Spur, which had purchased these two operations, had 20,000–30,000 head on feed. The Arizona Supreme Court agreed with the trial court that there was no doubt that the odor and flies from Spur's feedlots created a private nuisance for Del Webb and a public nuisance for the citizens of Sun City. It agreed that the trial court properly permanently enjoined Spur from operating the feedlots at that location. It found, however, that Del Webb in "coming to the nuisance" was not an innocent party. It ordered Del Webb to indemnify Spur for the cost of shutting down its operation at that location. It noted that the nuisance was so extensive and affected so many residents of the southern portion of Sun City that it could have been enjoined as a public nuisance. This decision led the legislators of every state to pass right-to-farm laws that reverse the "coming to the nuisance rule" for qualifying farms. As a result of those laws, Spur Industries' activities most likely would not be found to be a nuisance today. The right-to-farm laws of some states go further than reversing the "coming to the nuisance" rule. These laws operate statutes of limitation on bringing a nuisance action without regard to which land use was first in time.

### Public and private nuisances distinguished

As noted above, nuisances may be of two types: public or private. A public nuisance is one that affects members of the public, not necessarily land. Most courts do not consider a public nuisance a tort. It is an action to protect the health and welfare of the public. This is in contrast to a private nuisance that involves a particular injury to a specific individual landowner. An action to abate a public nuisance is usually brought by a government. It may be brought as either a civil suit or a criminal action against the wrongdoer. It is possible for a private party to bring an action to abate a public nuisance; however, a private party is limited to a civil action rather than a criminal claim. There are serious hurdles that usually prevent a private litigant from bringing a public nuisance action. A private litigant may have difficulty proving standing. To prove standing, a private litigant must be able to show a "special injury," whereas a government may bring a public nuisance action under its "police powers." The government's police powers exist to protect the health and welfare of the public. A special injury is an injury specific to a private litigant. In many cases of public nuisance, no such special injury exists. Rather than engage in this analysis, some courts have held that a nuisance may be both public and private if a large group is affected and, in addition, some individual landowners are injured in unique ways. This depends on the facts of the specific case, and because of the difficulty involved in determining those facts, courts and attorneys do not always distinguish adequately between public and private nuisances. As a result, precedents in some states are contradictory and confusing.

### Right-to-farm laws

One of the important factors in deciding a nuisance case is the nature of the area in which the activity is located. In response to urban sprawl, the encroachment of residential development on farmland, and the threat of increased nuisance lawsuits by the new urban dwellers against existing farms, many states have enacted right-to-farm laws. These statutes limit the circumstances under which a farm can be considered a nuisance by requiring the court to consider the change in conditions in the area surrounding the farm before declaring it a nuisance. Many right-to-farm laws reverse the "coming to the nuisance" rule that required courts to ignore which use came first in determining whether a nuisance exists (the courts could always consider which use came first at the remedy stage of the trial).

Right-to-farm statutes generally fall into four types. The first type is the most common and reverses the "coming to the nuisance" rule. Most of these statutes establish some time period that the farm must have been in existence prior to the start date of the plaintiff's use. The second type of statute is a presumption that a farm is not a nuisance. Most of these statutes allow the plaintiff to rebut the presumption. The third type of right-to-farm law is the exclusion statutes that exclude farming operations from the definition of a nuisance. The fourth type excludes certain theories or claims. For example, private nuisance actions against farming operations may be barred, but public nuisance actions may still be brought. In addition, many states require that a plaintiff attempt to engage the prospective agricultural defendant in mediation as a precondition to filing suit. If the attempt at mediation is not made, the suit is subject to being dismissed. Such statutes generally also determine who may be acceptable mediators. Generally, mediators must be court-approved.

The decision by the Iowa Supreme Court in *Bormann v. Board of Supervisors in and for Kossuth County, Iowa*,[8] has cast some doubt on the constitutionality of right-to-farm laws that reverse the "coming to the nuisance" rule. The issue is whether these laws deprive landowners of a property interest in violation of the Takings Clause of the Fifth Amendment. Many right-to-farm laws in effect limit the right of use and enjoyment of property by limiting the right to force the abatement of nuisances. The Iowa Supreme Court held that the statute at issue in Bormann was an uncompensated governmental taking of private property in violation of the Fifth Amendment. No other state court has followed that opinion in the years since it was decided in 1998.

## Notes

1 811 N.W.2d 693, 2012 Minn. LEXIS 380 (Minn. 2012).
2 *Id.*, at 102.
3 *Id.*, at 113.
4 Sarah E. Redfield, Agriculture Law Symposium: Chemical Trespass?—An Overview of Statutory and Regulatory Efforts to Control Pesticide Drift, 13 *Kentucky Law Journal* 855 (1984).
5 *Concerned Area Residents for The Environment v. Southview Farm*, 834 F. Supp. 1422; 1993 U.S. Dist. LEXIS (W.D.N.Y. 1993).
6 *Antonik v. Chamberlain*, 81 Ohio App. 465, 18 N.E. 2d 152 (Ohio Ct. App. 1941).
7 108 Ariz. 118, 494 P.2d 100, 1912 Ariz. LEXIS 214 (Ariz. 1912).
8 584 N.W.2d 309, 1998 Iowa Sup. LEXIS 214 (Iowa 1998).

# Chapter 5

# Contracts

## Introduction

Contracts are the linchpin of any free enterprise system. Contracts allow the participants in any such system to freely agree among themselves with a minimum of government involvement. Most of the great things accomplished by our society have been accomplished by free people that join together through a complex network of interlinked contracts. That most of the contracts are honored without any judicial involvement is a testament to the integrity of the participants and the competence of the attorneys who advise them. Though one hopes that difficulties will not be encountered, skilled attorneys draft contracts to anticipate difficulties and contingencies. A well-drafted contract is one of the best ways to avoid litigation.

A contract is a voluntary agreement between two or more parties that a court will enforce. The rights and obligations created by a contract apply only to the parties to the contract (i.e., those who agreed to them). However, there may be third-party beneficiaries that have enforceable rights under the contract. A life insurance contract is an example of such a contract. Generally a third-party beneficiary must be an intended beneficiary of the contract to have any enforceable rights. Example 5.1 illustrates such a contract.

---

**Example 5.1** Mega Produce Buyer, Inc. includes an indemnification provision within each of its contracts with growers. The provision states, "Grower agrees to indemnify Buyer for the costs of any mandatory or voluntary recalls of product of the same type as that supplied to Buyer. Grower shall provide Buyer with a current certificate of insurance for a policy that covers such recalls and notify Buyer of any changes of insurance coverage within ten (10) days of such change. This provision shall apply even though it is subsequently proven that none of Grower's product was contaminated with the pathogen or other prohibited substance that triggered the recall."[1] Under this clause, Mega Produce Buyer, Inc. is a third-party beneficiary of every such insurance contract of every grower that signs a contract with Mega Produce Buyer, Inc.

---

Most states of the United States follow the principle of freedom to contract. The courts will generally not intervene in contracts that were entered into by competent parties even where the contract is very disadvantageous to one party. There are common law and statutory exceptions to this rule, particularly for consumer contracts.

This chapter covers those contracts that are not for the sale of goods. Contracts for the sale of goods are governed by Article 2 of the Uniform Commercial Code (UCC). Contracts for the sale of goods under the UCC are covered in Chapter 9.

## Elements of a valid contract

For a contract to be valid and enforceable in court, five elements must exist. The parties to the contract must be competent. The subject matter of the contract must be a legally proper subject matter. There must be a meeting of the minds. A meeting of the minds consists of the third and fourth element of an enforceable contract. The third element is an offer, and the fourth element is an acceptance of that offer. The fifth and final element is an exchange of value, sometimes called consideration and detriment. Consideration is the inducement or benefit that causes one to form a contract. Detriment is what one gives up to obtain the benefit.

---

**Example 5.2** Joe sold a horse to Sam for $500. The $500 is the benefit of the bargain to Joe—in contract language, the consideration. The horse that Joe gave up is, in contract language, the detriment. It is the reverse for Sam. The horse is the consideration for Sam. The $500 that Sam gave up is the detriment.

---

### Competent parties

For a contract to be enforceable, the parties must have legal capacity. Those without legal capacity are those that society deems to need extra protection from deception. The party against whom enforcement is sought must have reached the age of majority (eighteen under most state laws) at the time the contract was made. The party against whom enforcement is sought must have had sufficient mental capacity at the time the contract was made to understand the significance of the contract. Those adjudicated incompetent generally cannot form contracts enforceable by the other party.

Minor children are defined as those below the age of majority, usually eighteen. They are deemed by society to need additional protection. If a minor child enters into a contract, that agreement can be voided by the minor but is generally binding on the other party. This is called a voidable contract, which means that it will be valid (if all other elements are present) unless the minor wants to terminate it. The consequences of a minor voiding a contract may be harsh to the other party. The minor need only return the subject matter of the contract to void the contract. If the subject matter of the contract is damaged, the loss belongs to the competent party, not the minor. The rule is also one-sided. The party who is not a minor has no right to void the contract. Indeed, the minor may enforce the contract against that party by affirming the contract when he or she reaches the age of majority. Minors who have been emancipated by a court of competent jurisdiction are treated as adults for the purpose of this rule.

---

**Example 5.3** Richie, age sixteen, went to his local luxury car dealership and bought a luxury car. He intended to use it for joy riding. Just as he pulled out of the dealership, his new car was hit by a large truck. Richie was unhurt, but the car was a total loss. Richie borrowed a broom from the dealership and swept what was left of the car back on the dealership premises. He then told the representative of the dealership that he was voiding the contract and demanded that the dealership return his money. As Richie was a minor and the car was not a necessity, the dealership had to return the full purchase price to Richie.

---

Those with a lack of mental capacity are also deemed in need of protection by society. If the mental capacity of a party is so diminished that he or she cannot understand the nature and the consequences of the transaction, that contract is voidable as a contract with a minor. Furthermore, if the party with diminished mental capacity cannot act in a reasonable manner regarding the contract and if the other party knew of the defect, that contract is void. Mental disease alone does not necessarily mean that a party is mentally incompetent for contractual purposes. A person adjudicated incompetent cannot enter into a contract unless a court determines that person has regained his or her competence. Unless a court has determined that a person is incompetent, there is no bright line between competence and incompetence. This may create serious problems for some elderly individuals who have gradually lost competence over time. It is also a problem for those with a temporary impairment from the use of alcohol or other mind-altering substances. Courts are generally loath to find a person incompetent because such a finding deprives that person of the ability to participate in society. Example 5.4 is drawn from a famous judicial decision.

Given the difficult hurdles required to prove that a person does not understand what he or she has agreed upon, there are unscrupulous individuals that make a very good and entirely legal living taking advantage of the diminished capacity of elderly individuals. In his work, the author has met individuals who work the nursing home circuit. The residents of nursing homes, including individuals with

Alzheimer's disease at an intermediate stage, are competent to sign enforceable contracts, even though their mental capacity is seriously diminished. As our society ages, this will continue to be a serious and unresolved problem. The alternative is to take away the rights of the elderly, something that should give everyone pause.

---

**Example 5.4** W. O. Lucy and J. C. Lucy sued A. H. Zehmer and wife, Ida S. Zehmer, for specific performance to compel the sale of the farm, known as the Ferguson farm, to them under a contract of sale between W. O. Lucy and A. H. Zehmer and Ida S. Zehmer.[2] J. C. Lucy is the brother of W. O. Lucy. He purchased a half interest in the Ferguson farm purchase from W. O. Lucy. W. O. Lucy and A. H. Zehmer wrote a memorandum of sale on the back of a restaurant check while sitting in Zehmer's restaurant. W. O. Lucy brought along a bottle of whiskey for Zehmer to drink. W. O. Lucy also had a few drinks. Under the terms of the agreement, W. O. Lucy agreed to pay the Zehmers $50,000 for the Ferguson farm, located in Dinwiddie County, Virginia, containing about 471.6 acres. Mrs. Zehmer, who had observed the discussion of about thirty to forty minutes that led to the agreement, also signed the memorandum. Mr. Zehmer defended by stating that he was too drunk to competently form a valid contract. He testified at the trial that "I was already high as a Georgia pine, and didn't have any more better sense than to pour another great big slug out and gulp it down, and he took one too."[3] The Supreme Court of Virginia reversed the trial court and remanded, ordering that specific performance be granted. It held that the drunkenness of Mr. Zehmer did not render him unable to understand his actions. It held that he was competent to sign the contract.

---

An exception exists, however, for contracts for necessity. Contracts that a minor or incompetent person makes for necessaries may be enforced by the other party to the contract. Necessaries are the basic requirements of life that include food, clothing, shelter, or transportation. Example 5.5 illustrates this principle.

---

**Example 5.5** Johnny, age sixteen, is the sole support for his parents, who are disabled and unable to work. The bus line that he uses to get to work is being discontinued as a cost-cutting measure. Johnny buys an inexpensive used car from the XYZ Used Car Company. In this circumstance, the car is a necessity for Johnny, and he cannot void the contract should he desire to do so.

---

## Proper subject matter

The purpose of the contract must be both legal and moral for the contract to be valid. Subject matter is not proper if it is contrary to public policy. A contract that lacks proper subject matter is generally void. A contract or a contract provision that is void is completely unenforceable. If the void provision was central to the subject matter of the contract, courts will not reform such contracts. The entire contract will be void. A court may reform a contract where the void provision was not central to the agreement of the parties.

---

**Example 5.6** By statute, North Carolina law prohibits oil and gas leases whose initial exploration and development term is longer than ten years. An oil or gas lease that extends beyond an initial term of ten years might be changed (reformed) by the court to a contract whose exploration and development term ends after ten years.

---

Most states have many examples of improper subject matter. Improper subject matter varies greatly from state to state. Prohibitions on gambling contracts are common; however, some states permit gambling contracts. Contracts to commit a tort or a crime and any agreement in restraint of trade are improper subject matter in most states. Something whose sole use is to further an illegal activity, even though not illegal itself, will be deemed improper subject matter in most states. Improper subject matter often includes contract provisions that limit access to courts, require disputes over real property to be adjudicated in a state other than the state where the property is located, require jury trial waivers, or make unusual designations as to venue or applicable state law.

The distinction between a voidable and a void contract is that a voidable contract is enforceable unless voided by the protected party. A void contract cannot be enforced by anyone. Example 5.7 illustrates the complexity of determining whether a contract is illegal.

---

**Example 5.7** Arnold Stoner established a marijuana farm in Colorado that is legal under state law. While visiting his brother, I. M. A. Stoner, in North Carolina, he signed a contract to sell marijuana to his brother. As neither possession nor sale of marijuana is legal in North Carolina, the contract is void in North Carolina. As the contract was signed in North Carolina, Colorado courts may find that it is governed by North Carolina law and is therefore void. If the Colorado court applied Colorado law, the result would be different.

---

## Offer

An offer is a statement that creates a power of acceptance in the person to whom the statement is made. In contract language, the person who makes the offer is the offeror, and the person to whom the offer is made is the offeree. It does not have to be in a certain form. To be valid, an offer must be communicated to the offeree. It must express an intent or willingness to enter into a contract with serious intent and not as a joke or as merely preliminary negotiations. It must be sufficiently definite and certain (especially with regard to the identity of the parties, the subject matter, the price, and the time and place of performance). It is generally effective when the communication is received by the offeree.

> **Example 5.8** North Carolina law makes certain futures contracts void. These include futures contracts in "cotton, Indian corn, wheat, rye, oats, tobacco, meal, lard, bacon, salt pork, salt fish, beef, cattle, sugar, [and] coffee . . ."[4] There are exceptions for federally regulated futures contracts and contracts made in the ordinary course of business by those who use those commodities.

## Acceptance

The power of acceptance lies only with the offeree. The acceptance must relate to the terms of the offer; no changes to the terms of the offer are allowed. The acceptance is effective when it is dispatched (put out of the offeree's possession). This is called the "mailbox rule." (If use of the mail is a reasonable method of accepting, the acceptance is effective when posted.) This rule is interpreted broadly and not limited just to use of the mail. The acceptance must be made within any time limit and in any manner that is specified in the offer. If no time limit for acceptance is specified in the offer, the offer must be accepted within a reasonable time.

A counter-offer terminates the offer. A counter-offer is treated as if it were a new offer. Any change to the offer by the offeree results in the termination of the offer and the creation of a counter-offer. After the offer is terminated, it cannot be revived. A grudging acceptance by the offeree includes complaints about the oppressiveness of the agreement but no alteration of the terms of the original offer. Grudging acceptances are problematic because they create confusion about whether there has been an acceptance or a counter-offer. This often leads to litigation.

> **Example 5.9** Aimee agreed to paint Arnold's barn for $2,500. They argued for most of an hour before reaching this price. Finally, Aimee said, "You are robbing me. There are acres of painting to do there. The job is worth at

least $4,500. See you next week." When Aimee arrived to paint Arnold's barn the following week, she found another crew busy painting the barn. Aimee demanded that Arnold compensate her for the lost opportunity to work for someone else. Arnold refused: He said that he thought Aimee had made a counter-offer.

### Exchange of value (consideration and detriment)

To be enforceable, a contract must be supported by an exchange of value. It cannot be a gift. A gift is not an exchange because the party receiving the gift provided no value to the party who made the gift. Something of value can include money, labor, goods, or a promise to act or not to act given in exchange for a return promise or a performance. The parties must have intended to make such an exchange. The exchange is that which was bargained for. An exchange of a promise for a promise is a sufficient exchange of value to support a valid contract.

Example 5.10 John agreed to build a house for David on David's lot. David agreed to pay John $200,000 upon completion and inspection of the house. This is an example of a common exchange of promises that is a sufficient exchange of value to support a valid contract.

Example 5.11 John promised his children that he would give them the farm on the river. Instead, he sold it so that he could build a new house for his new bride, who coincidentally was younger than his children. His children sued him for breach of contract. John's children never promised him anything of value for his promise. For that reason, no enforceable contract ever existed.

## Types of contracts

An express contract is one whose terms are specifically stated, either orally or in writing. A contract is bilateral if the offeror and the offeree make mutual promises. The offeror is the one who makes the initial promise. The offeree is the one who then accepts the promise and promises some performance in return. Each party must perform. Each party has a contractual right to expect performance of the other party. Such a contract is called a bilateral contract. Most contracts are express bilateral contracts.

A contract is unilateral if only one party makes a promise. The offeror expects the offeree to accept the offer by actually performing an act, not by making a promise to perform the act. An offer of reward for a lost dog is an example of a unilateral contract. It can be performed only through finding and returning the lost dog.

Newspaper advertisements are generally not offers. Advertisements are considered to be solicitations of offers and do not bind the advertiser. Note that other law such as consumer protection statutes or unfair trade practices statutes may impose additional restrictions on advertisers. Bait and switch advertising is generally prohibited in most states. These laws, although they affect contracts, are part of the rather large body of consumer protection law. The exception is an advertisement of a reward that is treated as an offer to form a unilateral contract. These types of advertisements constitute an offer because they induce certain behavior in response. That response will, in some cases, constitute the buyer's side of an exchange of value. Example 5.12 illustrates a common type of advertisement that constitutes an offer subject to acceptance by an act.

---

**Example 5.12** The Gurkin Department Store offered free large-screen TVs to the first five customers to arrive at their store on the Friday after Thanksgiving. Unfortunately, the manufacturer had no more in stock, so Gurkin never received them. Gurkin refused to honor its promise, telling customers that its promise was an unenforceable advertisement. Gail was the first person in line that morning. She sued Gurkin. She demanded that Gurkin provide her with the large screen TV as promised. This remedy is called specific performance. The court held that the advertisement was an offer to make a unilateral contract, that Gail had accepted it, and ordered Gurkin to provide Gail with a large screen TV. Note that the same result might have been reached under state consumer protection law.

---

An implied contact is one where the terms are inferred, in whole or in part, from conduct and circumstances rather than from written or spoken works. The only legal difference between an implied contract and an express contract is the way that mutual assent is given. An "implied in fact" contract is one where the conduct of the parties and the circumstances of the transaction make it reasonable to assume that the parties had an understanding among themselves. Such a contract is enforceable by a court, despite the absence of spoken or written words of agreement.

In a case where the circumstances are such that one person should have a right and the other a responsibility, in spite of a lack of any intention or agreement for such, the court will find a contract "implied in law." If there is something that someone ought to do, the court will find that she or he has an obligation to do it. This is actually the opposite of an express contract because here the contract did not arise from the mutual intention of the parties. This type of contract is called a "quasi-contract." (See Example 5.13.) It is actually no contract at all. It is an alternative remedy (called restitution) that keeps one party from being unjustly enriched at the expense of the other party.

---

**Example 5.13** House painters in a subdivision began painting the wrong house as the result of their own mistake. The owner of the house was aware that they were actually contracted under an express contract to paint his neighbor's house. Wanting his house painted for free, he failed to stop them from painting his house. He informed them of their mistake only after they had completed the work. The painters may be able to successfully sue him for the value of the work performed under a theory of "quasi-contract." Note that the measure of damages is the value of the work performed, not the contract price that the painters had agreed upon with the owner of the correct house. Their contractual obligation to paint the correct house is not released by their having painted the wrong house. If the owner of the house that was painted by mistake was away at the time the house was painted, it is unlikely that the owner would be required to pay. The owner in this scenario had no capacity to notify the painters of their mistake. The owner in this scenario would have a cause of action in trespass against the painters. Whether such an action would actually be brought depends upon the level of damages. One can imagine an example where the house was historic and the color it was painted violated historic preservation rules. At the very least, the house would have to be repainted. In the first variation of this scenario, the owner could not successfully sue for trespass because he knew the painters were painting the wrong house. His acquiescence constitutes implied permission to enter his property and paint his house.

---

## Statute of frauds

Certain contracts must be in writing to be enforceable. Most states have adopted into their common law the celebrated English law passed by Parliament in 1677 called the Statute of Frauds. As common law is judge-made law, the Statute of Frauds differs from one state to another. The legislatures of most states have further modified the Statute of Frauds by statute. Examples of contracts that must be in writing to be enforceable include sales of goods valued $500 or more; promises to pay the debts of another; promises made in exchange for marriage; promises that cannot be performed within one year from the date of the agreement;

promises concerning a sale of land; leases of mineral rights; promises to revive a debt discharged in bankruptcy; and loan commitments in excess of $50,000.

What the writing must contain to satisfy the Statute of Frauds depends on the type of contract, the applicable law, and the subject matter of the contract. As is discussed in Chapter 9, the required writing for a contract for the sale of goods under Article 2 of the UCC is fairly minimal. Some contracts, particularly consumer contracts, have mandatory components required by statute. At the very least, the writing must contain the signature of the party against whom enforcement is sought, an adequate description of the subject matter of the contract, including the quantity, and a price term where that term cannot be established from extrinsic sources. A writing that satisfies the Statute of Frauds does not need to be in a single document. A contract may be contained in multiple documents.

### Exceptions to the writing requirement

A negative consequence of requiring that certain contracts be in writing is that a person could make an oral promise with the intent of breaking that promise later on the grounds that it was not in writing as required by the Statute of Frauds. To prevent this unfair result, courts will sometimes enforce oral contracts even when the Statute of Frauds would ordinarily require a writing. If there has been partial performance by one party in reliance on the promised performance of the other party and the performing party has relied on the oral agreement to his or her substantial detriment, some courts will enforce the agreement. The purpose of this exception is to prevent serious harm to the performing party. As a person is unlikely to perform contractual duties unless there was an agreement, this exception avoids injustice to the performing party while supporting the policy of the Statute of Frauds of preventing fraud.

A second way that courts avoid strict application of the Statute of Frauds is the doctrine of promissory estoppel. If a promise is made that the promisor should have reasonably expected to induce action by the promisee and it does, the promisor cannot raise the Statute of Frauds as a defense. This prevents injustice arising from a noncompliance with the writing requirement.

---

**Example 5.14** Jones worked for his parents, helping them with their farming. He lived in the barn and accepted minimal wages. His parents promised him that they would give the farm to him in their will. At the death of his parents, Jones discovered that they had made no wills and that he would share the farm with his other nine siblings under the laws of intestate succession. As an oral contract to make a will is unenforceable under the Statute of Frauds, his only option is to plead promissory estoppel. The courts of some states would enforce the promise based upon promissory estoppel whereas the courts of other states would not.

Exceptions to the writing requirement are designed to prevent injustice. If one wishes to avoid expensive litigation, good practice dictates putting all contracts in writing, even for those contracts for which the Statute of Frauds does not require a written contract. Should a dispute arise, this avoids having to bring forth witnesses to prove the terms of an oral contract.

## Parol evidence rule

Even when a written contract exists, questions may arise regarding the meaning of specific terms of the contract. A party to the contract may wish to provide evidence outside of the contract to answer those questions. The parol evidence rule states that the best evidence of the agreement between the parties is the written contract. The parol evidence rule prohibits admission of evidence of prior or contemporaneous agreements or negotiations to contradict a term of a written contract. Oral promises made during the contract negotiations are invalid unless incorporated into the written contract.

---

**Example 5.15** Jones signed a written contract with Durham to purchase ten bred heifers from him for a total of $10,000. They orally agreed that Jones would actually pay $15,000 for the heifers; however, $5,000 of the payment was not included in the written contract. Durham wished to hide the money from his ex-wife to whom he owed child support. Jones tendered a payment of $10,000 and demanded delivery of the ten bred heifers. Durham must deliver the ten bred heifers and forego the additional $5,000 payment. The parol evidence rule bars introduction of the oral side agreement into evidence. For that reason, Durham will lose should he decide to sue. If Durham refuses to deliver, he can be held in breach of contract.

---

An exception to this rule exists where there is an ambiguous term or phrase in the contract. In that case, the court will allow additional evidence to clarify the ambiguous term or phrase in the written contract.

Oral statements or modifications made after the contract was signed may be admitted to clarify or contradict the terms of the contract, unless the contract contains an integration clause. An integration clause prohibits the use of subsequent oral statements to contradict or supplement a written contract. An integration clause requires that all modifications of a written contract must be in writing and signed by the parties.

Subsequent modifications of the contract must be supported by the same five elements that are required for the original contract. Subsequent modifications of contracts often fail for lack of consideration. There must be some exchange of value to support the contract modification just as there was to support the original contract.

Example 5.16 Jones hired Dexter under a five-year written contract to manage marketing for his agritourism operation. Six months later, Jones demanded that Dexter sign a non-compete agreement. Dexter did so. At the end of two years working for Jones, Dexter was fed up with Jones' management style. Dexter quit and went to work for Smith's agritourism operation. Jones sued to enforce the noncompete agreement. It was undisputed that Dexter received no benefit from signing the noncompete agreement because he already had a five year contract. Jones could not have dismissed Dexter had he refused to sign the non-compete agreement because that would have breached his existing five-year employment contract. On Dexter's motion for summary judgment, the court ruled that the non-compete agreement was not supported by consideration and therefore unenforceable.

## Remedies for breach of contract

One of the key distinctions to make is whether the contract was one for the sale of goods under the UCC or some other type of contract. Contractual remedies for breach of contracts for the sale of goods are discussed in Chapter 9.

### Money damages

If one party fails to perform a duty under a contract, she or he is said to have breached the contract. This may relieve the other party from an obligation to perform. It may also entitle the other party to seek damages for its economic loss. The most common remedy is an award of monetary damages in an amount to make the injured party whole. A jury decides what amount of money is an appropriate amount for this purpose on the basis of the facts of the case. Legal rules limit the amount of damages that may be awarded.

When there was performance of the contract but that performance did not meet the requirements of the contract, monetary damages may be measured by the difference between the value of what was received and what was contracted for. If the non-breaching party received no useful performance, we can measure the loss by the contract price subtracted from what it ultimately cost to get the benefit of the contract from someone else. These two alternate scenarios are illustrated in Examples 5.17 and 5.18.

Example 5.17 Jones contracted with Best Steel Buildings to have a farm building constructed. The contract price was $200,000. Unfortunately, the roof leaked, and Best Steel Buildings refused to repair it. As it will cost Jones $20,000 to repair the roof, his damages are $20,000. He may reduce his payment to Best Steel Buildings to $180,000.

> **Example 5.18** Jones contracted with Best Steel Buildings to have a farm building constructed. The contract price was $200,000. Unfortunately, Best Steel Buildings had not even begun construction by the completion date set in the contract. Jones notified Best Steel Buildings that he was holding them in breach and seeking someone else to construct the building. The contract price that Jones was able to get from another contractor was $230,000. He had $500 of incidental costs associated with rebidding the contract. Total damages that Jones may recover from Best Steel Buildings are $30,500.

Example 5.18 also illustrates the concept of incidental damages. When a party to a contract fails to perform, it is reasonable to expect that there will be incidental expenses associated with finding another contractor. These costs may be recovered as incidental damages so long as such damages are reasonably foreseeable.

Expectation damages may be recovered when those damages are foreseeable. When a farmer buys seed or other inputs, there is an expectation that he or she will be able to produce a crop and net return above expenses on that crop. Often, expectation damages far exceed the value of the contract. Expectation damages are subject to a duty to mitigate.

> **Example 5.19** Jones bought cotton seed from XYZ Seeds to plant his 200 acres. Soon after planting, it was apparent that there was a germination problem. Jones made no attempt to replant. He sued XYZ Seeds for his expected profit on the lost cotton crop. At trial, XYZ Seeds introduced expert testimony that Jones had time to replant with a loss of yield that would not have exceeded half a bale per acre. Upon motion by the attorney for XYZ Seeds, the judge limited damages to what Jones had paid XYZ Seeds for the cotton seed plus the net return from an additional half bale per acre on the 200 acres. She held that Jones had wrongfully failed to mitigate damages.

Consequential damages are damages that arise as a consequences of the defendant's breach of contract. Consequential damages may be limited by contract or by state or federal law. For common carriers, Internet service providers, and communications companies, consequential damages are usually limited by federal (and sometimes) state laws. Even when not limited by law, courts are reluctant to award consequential damages because these damages often far exceed the value of the contract. For there to be any chance of obtaining an award of consequential damages, those damages must be clearly foreseeable, or the written contract must provide for them.

> **Example 5.20** Larisa bought disinfectant to use on her lettuce-processing line. Unbeknown to her, the disinfectant was defective, and she shipped lettuce contaminated with a deadly pathogen. The court ruled that she could not recover her costs of recall from the manufacturer of the disinfectant because the manufacturer could not have reasonably foreseen such damages.

Damages available upon breach of a contract can, to a significant degree, be dictated by the terms of a well-drafted, written contract. Consequential damages may be provided for. More commonly, contracts exclude the possibility of recovering consequential damages. In general, a plaintiff may not recover his or her attorney fees, expert fees, and other court costs of an action unless the contract contains a clause, known as an attorney fees and costs clause, that specifically provides for recovery of these litigation costs. Modification of the ability to obtain damages or other relief in a written contract will in all cases be limited by applicable law.

### Non-monetary remedies

When the injured party does not feel that monetary damages are a sufficient remedy, that party may ask the court for an injunction that requires the contract to be performed as agreed. This remedy is called specific performance. Specific performance is usually granted only where the subject matter of the contract is unique in some way. Law deems all parcels of land unique; therefore, specific performance is a common remedy for the seller's breach of a land sales contracts. In such a case, the prospective buyer of the land would ask the court for an injunction requiring the seller to perform the contract as written. Upon tender of the purchase price by the buyer, the seller would be required to execute and record a deed transferring the land to the buyer. If a court's injunction is not obeyed, the court may enforce its order through civil contempt. A person found in civil contempt by the court may be jailed until such time as the person complies with the order of the court. In this situation, compliance would be signing a deed transferring the property to the buyer.

Injunctive relief is a flexible remedy for breach of contract. Injunctions may be fashioned to either restrain the defendant from engaging in an action or to compel a requested action. Injunctive relief is used to enforce nondisclosure agreements and non-compete agreements. These types of agreements are common in employment contracts, business sales, and business relationships involving intellectual property. Nondisclosure agreements may prohibit employees or former employees, potential buyers of the business, and independent contractors from disclosing or using the company's confidential information. Non-compete agreements prohibit employees from taking another, similar position with a competitor in a specified geographic area.

Negative injunctions are the primary remedy available for enforcing non-compete agreements because the Thirteenth Amendment prohibition on involuntary servitude prohibits any injunctive relief that orders an employee back to work with his original employer. Courts tailor negative injunctions as narrowly as possible because such injunctions prevent former employees from finding other work in their field. The law does not require a former employer to rehire the former employee against whom a negative injunction was obtained. Non-compete agreements are also important in the sales of businesses. Non-compete agreements are used to prevent the seller of the business from opening a similar business in competition with the business that he just sold.

### Rescission and restitution

Another remedy for breach of contract is rescission and restitution. This is the typical remedy where the plaintiff was induced by fraud to enter the contract. Where the plaintiff was induced into the contract by fraud, there is technically no contract because there was no meeting of the minds. Nonetheless, there must be a remedy in these situations, and that remedy is rescission and restitution. It is used where an injured party would be more damaged by accepting performance of the contract than by being put in the position he or she was in before the contract was made. Rescission means that the contract is rescinded or canceled. Restitution means that the injured party is made whole. That is usually done by return of the money or the property that the injured party gave to the other party to the contract.

---

**Example 5.21** Joe bought a used car from Buzz's Backyard Autos. Joe paid $500 for the car. Buzz represented that the car was mechanically sound but it in fact had serious, latent mechanical defects known to Buzz. In fact, Buzz had added sawdust to the transmission to conceal the grinding sound that it was making. Rescission and restitution is an appropriate remedy in this situation. Joe gets his $500 back, and Buzz gets his car back.

---

## Defenses to breach of contract lawsuits

Sometimes there is a significant change in circumstances between the time a contract was signed and when performance must occur. Courts usually do not allow intervening events as an excuse for non-performance. However, there are some exceptions to that rule. One is the doctrine of impossibility. Some courts will excuse performance and terminate the contract if they find that, after making the contract, circumstances have changed to an extent that could not have been reasonably foreseen by the parties.

---

**Example 5.22** King's Ransom was a very successful race horse. His owner, Eric, had a contract with Constellation Stables to provide stud service to their prize mare. Prior to the appointed date for breeding the mare, King's Ransom was standing under a tree that was struck by lightning. King's Ransom died instantly. As such a service is unique to that particular stud, there can be no replacement. A contract for stud service is for a particular stud and its unique genetics. Performance of the contract would be excused by impossibility in this situation.

---

Courts also recognize the doctrine of commercial impracticability. Unlike impossibility, performance, even though theoretically possible, would involve extreme and unreasonable difficulty, expense, injury, or loss that could not have been anticipated by the parties. Commercial impracticability is also recognized where performance would be futile. There is no bright line between impossibility and impracticability.

---

**Example 5.23** The facts are the same as in Example 5.22 except that King's Ransom contracted a virus that rendered him completely sterile. Although Eric could go through the motions of taking King's Ransom to Constellation Stables and mating him to their prize mare, the exercise would be pointless. The objective of the contract is to produce a foal, fathered by King's Ransom. Most courts will excuse performance under the doctrine of commercial impracticability.

---

Mutual mistake is another defense available to a defendant in a breach of contract action. Technically, there was no contract because meeting of the minds did not occur due to the mutual mistake as to the subject matter of the contract. The unilateral mistake by one party is not a defense to breach of contract action. *Raffles v. Wichelhaus*[5] is an 1864 British decision that remains one of the best examples of the successful use of the defense of mutual mistake. Unbeknown to either party, there were two ships named *Peerless* involved in the Indian cotton trade. As they had not agreed as to which ship was the subject of the contract, there had been no meeting of the minds and no valid contract.

The passage of time may also be a defense to a breach of contract action. Most states have adopted statutes that require an injured party to file any cause of action within a reasonable time. These laws are called statutes of limitations. They specify time limits for filing breach of contract actions. Three years is a very common time limitation for filing breach of contract actions. In addition to statutes of limitation, the common law doctrine of laches may apply to breach of contract actions where the failure of the plaintiff to timely assert his or her cause of action may have placed the defendant at serious disadvantage. The doctrine of laches is an equitable doctrine that bars injunctive relief.

## Stipulated or liquidated damages

Parties to a contract can specify in the contract the amount of damages in case of a breach. If that amount is not excessive, the court will award the amount stipulated (called stipulated or liquidated damages) rather than the amount of the actual damages. If the amount of stipulated damages is found to be excessive by the court, the court will not enforce the liquidated damages clause. An excessive amount of money is an amount above any reasonable estimate of actual damages. Such an unreasonable amount of money is considered a penalty designed to coerce performance. Penalties are unenforceable. In that case, the court will ignore the amount provided in the contract, as if the contract were silent on the issue, and assess damages itself. Conversely, the court will generally view the stipulated amount as reasonable, rather than an excessive penalty, if it is an honest estimate of probable loss. In deciding whether the amount is reasonable (an honest estimate), the court looks at whether it is difficult to foresee and measure actual damages.

The advantage of a liquidated damage clause in the contract is that it avoids litigating the amount of damages where there is a breach. These provisions are often used in construction contracts when a delay in completion of the contract will result in an amount that may be deducted from the contract price for each day that the deadline is missed. In lay terms, these are often called penalties; however, they are actually liquidated damages. Such damages are a reasonable estimate of the loss caused by the delay in completion.

Punitive damages are a tort remedy, not a contract remedy. Such damages may arise out of a contractual relationship only where a tort in addition to a breach of contract was committed. Such situations are rare. For this reason, penalties in contracts are not allowed. A penalty, such as punitive damages, is designed to punish and is unrelated to the actual damages from the breach of contract. Unfortunately, non-lawyers often use the term penalty when stipulated damages are intended.

## Conclusion

Much of this chapter is focused upon how poorly drafted contracts are interpreted. To an impressive degree, courts will enforce the provisions of well-drafted contracts. There are a number of important characteristics of a well-drafted contract.

First, such contracts are fair to all parties. Given that judges are human, a contract that is blatantly unfair or one-sided will cause many judges to seek ways to avoid its harshness. Second, obviously illegal provisions are to be avoided. Such provisions can quickly unravel any enforcement action. Third, every term should be clear and based upon terms whose meaning has been established by precedent. Fourth, contract language is dictated to an extent by usage in a particular business. The attorney retained to draft a contract should be familiar with the underlying business, or at least willing to learn. In many parts of the United States, particularly outside the Midwest and California, there are often few attorneys with agricultural experience.

## Notes

1 This provision is similar to provisions in contracts in current use that the author has reviewed.
2 *Lucy v. Zehmer*, 196 Va. 493, 84 S.E.2d 516, 1954 Va. LEXIS 244 (Va. 1954).
3 *Id.* at 497.
4 N.C.G.S. § 16-3 (2014).
5 159 Eng. Rep. 373 (Ex. 1864).

# Chapter 6

# Real property

## Introduction: real property distinguished from personal property

Real property and personal property must be distinguished from each other because different legal rules apply to each. For example, law governing inheritance, taxation, and contracts is quite different for real and personal property. Real property is immoveable property, such as land, buildings attached to land, and other things incidental to land such as fences that are permanently attached to the land. Personal property is generally moveable or intangible. Personal property is all property that is not real property. That said, distinguishing personal property from real property is not always easy. As ownership and the security interests of creditors in property is often determined by whether the property is personal or real, the issue is often litigated.

It is possible for personal property to become part of the real property. A fixture is something that was once personal property and has become attached to real property in such a way as to lose its status as personal property and be considered part of the real property. The intent of the owner of the personal property at the time of fixation is the primary consideration in determining whether something is permanently attached to real property. Courts use an objective test to determine the intent of the owner. They look to the actions that the owner took at the time of fixation. One of the important consequences of this classification is that it determines what will be part of a sale or lease of real property. Some items are easy to classify as fixtures, such as items permanently attached to buildings or fences, but others may be harder to classify, such as grain bins, shop equipment, or corral headgates. Whether such items become part of the real property should be specified in the sales contract or lease agreement. A filing under the Uniform Commercial Code may be made to preserve the interest of the tenant or the holder of security interest in the tangible personal property that is attached to the land. This filing will allow for removal of the property. If a lease does not specify whether something that the tenant attaches to the property may be removed, the general rule is that it stays with the property when the lease ends. This rule applies even though the tenant paid for the personal property that was attached to the land. This is also important with the sale of real property so that both buyer and seller understand and agree upon what is included in the sale. As a general rule, things attached to the land are part of the real property and pass with the land. Example 6.1 provides an example of a typical situation.

---

**Example 6.1** Ernie Angus leased land upon which to graze his purebred Black Angus cattle. Ernie bought a lift to add to the barn on the property to make it possible to move baled hay in and out of the second floor of the barn. The barn required substantial modification to install the lift. His lease was silent both as to whether he was permitted to install the lift and whether he was allowed to remove the lift at the end of the lease. Ernie never discussed any aspect of the lift with his landlord—neither installing it nor removing it at the end of the lease. A week before his lease ended, his landlord happened by and found Ernie with saw and wrecking bar getting ready to remove the lift. Alarmed that removing the lift would make the barn unusable, Ernie's landlord forbid him to remove the lift and threatened to take legal action to stop him. Courts of most states would likely side with Ernie's landlord because removing the lift would do substantial damage to the barn. Additionally, the laws of most states would not treat the lift as special purpose property and, absent agreement, would find that Ernie's actions evinced an intent to permanently attach the lift to the real property.

---

There is an exception for special purpose property. For example, a tenant who installs a pizza oven in a rented premises most likely did not intend for it to become part of the real estate. Special purpose property attached to the land does not generally become a fixture. Fixtures are taxed as part of the real property and not as personal property. In most states, personal property is taxed separately, if it is taxed at all. Tax rates and rules are usually quite different for real property and personal property.

---

**Example 6.2** Carya Pecan had a custom nut-shelling business. She leased a steel building on a lot next to her hickory grove. She bought a high-tech, patented nut cracker to increase her throughput. Given the vibrations produced by such a high-volume, unique piece of equipment, it had to be secured to the floor so that it would not move. To do this, Carya, had a concrete floor poured in the building to which she bolted the nut cracker. Her lease is silent about whether she may remove the nut cracker at the end of the lease. She has no agreement with her landlord. Courts of most states would likely treat this as special purpose property that may be removed by the tenant at the end of a lease. It is not of the type of property that most tenants could use. Carya would most likely be liable for any damages to the property caused by removal of the nut cracker.

Not all personal property that is attached to the land is a fixture. To be a fixture, the personal property attached to the land must maintain its identity and character. Construction materials used in real estate development often so lose their original character that they are not fixtures. In its unpublished decision in *Baker Construction Co. v. City of Burlington*,[1] the NC Court of Appeals discussed that building materials used to put underground utilities in the subdivision at issue became merged with the realty such that they could not even be characterized as fixtures.

Confusion as to the character of the property is also common with growing crops, Christmas trees, and timber. On the one hand, plants that grow spontaneously on the land, such as trees, bushes, or grass, are called *fructus naturales* and are part of the land until severed. On the other hand, crops that result from annual planting and cultivation, such as cotton, tobacco, or soybeans, are called *fructus industriales* and are considered to be personal property. The classification of crops determines their ownership. Crops that are not annual, such as perennial forages, tree crops, and Christmas trees, are generally treated as part of the real estate, until severed. Though the parties to a lease may agree that these multi-year crops belong to the tenant, that agreement neither changes the character of the property nor binds all third parties, such as creditors of the landlord with security interests senior to the recorded lease. Timber is generally part of the real estate until it is severed.

## Elements of ownership

Ownership of property can be viewed as a "bundle of sticks." The rights of the owner depend on whether he or she has all of the sticks in the bundle or only part of them, such as a lease or a life estate, mineral rights, or a surface estate. Full ownership rights include the right of disposition and the right to control the property (within the boundaries of the law). The right of control includes the right of exclusion – closely related to exclusion – the right of possession, and the right of quiet use and enjoyment.

The right of disposition means that property, or an interest in property such as oil and gas rights, may be transferred during life by voluntary sale, gift, lease (at the termination of which the owner regains possession), or an inter vivos transfer to a trust. An owner may also use real estate as collateral for a loan that may ultimately result in an involuntary disposition. In addition to an involuntary foreclosure sale to satisfy a loan, an involuntary sale may also result from foreclosure for taxes due, involuntary sale as the result of execution of a judgment, or a court order such as one arising from a divorce action. Property may be transferred at death by will, intestate succession, automatically by right of survivorship to a joint owner, by gift *causa mortis*, or transfer to a trust. Property may also be transferred by one who never owned it pursuant to a power of appointment.

A property owner has a right of possession defined as the right to exclude others from the property. This right may be protected by bringing an action for the tort of trespass to regain possession and eject the trespasser. A property owner has a right of use and quiet enjoyment defined as a right to be free from unreasonable interferences caused by the uses that neighboring property owners make of their land. This right may be protected by bringing an action for private nuisance. Use includes the right to destroy the property. There may be regulatory limits on the right to destroy one's own property.

## Types of ownership

### Freehold estates

A freehold estate is an interest in land or that attached to it that is of indeterminable duration. Freehold estates are categorized in terms of duration and can be divided into fee estates and life estates. A freehold estate has a potentially infinite duration or an unpredictable length. Freehold estates are distinguished from leasehold estates where the lessee has the possessory right and use of the estate for a limited time of fixed duration.

The most common free estate is the fee simple (sometimes called "fee simple absolute"), which encompasses all the ownership rights. Property owned as a fee simple estate has fewer restrictions placed upon it than any other way to hold real property.

There are two freehold estates that the owner or her or his heirs may lose if certain events occur: fee simple determinable estate and the fee simple subject to a condition subsequent. A fee simple determinable is a fee simple estate that continues until automatically terminated by the occurrence of some specified event, after which the land reverts to the grantor or his or her heirs. The interest retained by the grantor in this type of ownership is called the possibility of reverter. A similar estate is called a fee simple subject to a condition subsequent. Here the fee simple estate may be terminated (but not automatically) by the grantor or her or his heirs upon the happening of a named event. This future interest of the grantor is called a right of entry for condition broken or a power of termination. Lest the reader think that these two types of freehold estates are irrelevant remnants of some medieval past, Example 6.3 is a real life example.

Example **6.3** In 1881, Richard Stanhope Pullen gave two parcels of land— one to the Trustees of North Carolina State University and one to the City of Raleigh. Both were fee simple determinable estates. The grant to the Trustees of North Carolina State University was conditioned on the continued use of the property for educational purposes. The grant to the City of Raleigh was conditioned on the continued use of the property for park purposes. The two properties are separated by the rather narrow, curving Pullen Drive. The reverter in both deeds is to Richard Stanhope Pullen and his heirs. The heirs of Richard Stanhope Pullen have preserved his vision for the properties and resisted any attempt to straighten and widen Pullen Drive by periodically reminding the City and the University that such an endeavor would violate the terms of both reverters, triggering reversion of both properties to Richard Stanhope Pullen's heirs.

A life estate is a freehold estate whose duration is measured by the life of a person whose life is called the measuring life. The measuring life may either be that of the holder (life tenant) of the life estate or a third person. Life estates are usually created either by deed or will. The life tenant has the right of possession and use of the property and may generally convey his or her interest by sale or gift. The life tenant may lease his or her interest. The reversioner or remainderman has a vested, future interest in the property that may also be conveyed but not leased. As the reversioner or remainderman has only a future interest and no current right to possession, there is nothing to lease. At the death of the measuring life, the property belongs to a reversioner if no disposition of the fee was made at the time the life estate was created. A reversioner would be the grantor or his heirs, who held the fee during the life estate. Alternatively, at the death of the measuring life, the property may belong to a remainderman or remaindermen if the person who created the life estate designated one or more persons to take possession at the termination of the life estate.

Example **6.4** Aimee transferred a life estate to her daughter, Cheryl, with Cheryl's life as the measuring life. She also transferred a life estate to Fred, her son, with Fred's life as the measuring life, with the remainder interest at Fred's death to the United Methodist Church. At Cheryl's death her life estate will revert to her mother or, if her mother is deceased, her mother's estate. Contrast this with what happens at Fred's death. His property will pass into the possession of the United Method Church because Aimee designated the Church as the holder of the remainder interest.

A life tenant owes a quasi-fiduciary duty to the reversioner or remainderman. The life tenant has a duty to protect and preserve the property, called a duty to avoid waste. There are three types of waste that include deliberate destruction, loss through negligence, and improvements to the property. A reversioner or remainderman is entitled to receive the property in the same condition that existed when the life tenant received it. A life tenant may make improvements to the property only with the permission of the reversioner or remainderman. The duties of a life tenant include paying taxes on the property, including local assessments; making or paying for repairs; and paying interest but not principle on encumbrances such as mortgages. Although the life tenant has a duty to make repairs, this does not, in most states, include a duty to insure the property. The duty to pay interest on encumbrances is generally limited to the income generated by the property or the fair rental value of the property. A life tenant has a right to estovers. A right to estovers entitles the life tenant to cut timber for personal use as fuel, for fencing the property, and for use in making repairs to structures on the property. In general, commercial timber operations are not permitted unless the property has a history of commercial timber operations prior to the creation of the life estate or the documents creating the life estate permit timbering. A life tenant may neither make improvements to the property nor change the use of the property. To do so is waste for which the remainderman or reversioner may obtain an injunction to prevent. The remainderman or reversioner has no current right to enter the property while the life tenant is in possession. To do so may constitute a trespass.

Life estates that are expressly created are usually done so by deed or will. It is possible for the grantor to create a life estate with him- or herself as the life tenant. Such a life estate is called a retained life estate. Retained life estates are commonly used in some regions of the United States as inexpensive will substitutes. A granted life estate is one that is created by a grant from the grantor to another person, either during life by deed, or at death by will. Life estates may also be created by operation of law. Some states provide a surviving spouse with a right to claim a life estate in real property owned by the deceased spouse during the marriage. For this reason, it is considered good practice in many states to have the spouse of the seller sign the deed to waive marital rights. This is needed even though the spouse of the seller was not an owner of the property.

Life estates are, unfortunately, used for estate planning purposes by many farm families in some regions of the United States. There are serious problems that can result from using life estates as an estate planning tool. For example, most life estates do not have sufficient flexibility to provide an adequate income to a surviving spouse in the face of unexpectedly high inflation. The lack of flexibility in the uses of the property that may be made by the life tenant is another of these problems. The lack of case law that defines the relationship between life tenant and remainderman or reversioner is yet another. These provisions can be provided in the instrument that created the life estate; however, this is seldom done.

Retained life estates are particularly problematic. The retained life estate is one where the grantor retains the life interest and transfers the remainder interest to someone else, usually a child. The grantor may be shocked to discover that her or his child can now prevent her or him from changing the use of the property or improving it. If the intent in creating a retained life estate was to remove it from the federal taxable estate so that appreciation of the property from the date of the grant to the death of the grantor will not be in the taxable estate, this attempt will fail. Under federal tax law, a retained life estate is considered an incomplete transfer. As such, the entire property will be valued in the grantor's estate at the date of the grantor's death.

---

**Example 6.5** Husband, shortly before his death, granted a life estate in his farm to his wife, with a remainder interest to their adult child. The deed that created the life estate said nothing about whether his wife, as life tenant, could sell timber from the land. The husband had a $1 million life insurance policy on his life with their child as beneficiary. Before his death, the husband told his wife and their child that the purpose of the insurance was to give their child enough money to pay off the mortgage on the farm. The husband also expressed his desire that his wife sell the timber on the farm to pay for her support, with additional funds for her support provided by rental payments on the farm, paid to her by their child, who was expected to rent from his mother and cultivate it. All of these desires were expressed orally by the husband without being incorporated into any document. After his father's death, their child used the funds from his father's life insurance policy to buy another farm. For that reason, he refused to pay rent for his use of the farm in which his mother had a life estate. He stated that he needed the money to make principal payments on the mortgage. When his mother proposed a timber sale, he directed his attorney to send her a cease and desist letter. The attorney for the wife of the decedent sent her own child a notice to quit, purporting to terminate the lease of the farm. Her child claimed that he was rightfully on the property and refused to leave. He also stated that his mother had no right to terminate his lease. His mother filed an eviction action against him with a demand for past due rent and, in the alternative, an action for trespass, damages, and injunctive relief. Mother and child now communicate solely through their respective attorneys.

---

## Co-ownership of freehold estates

A tenancy in common is joint ownership of property where each owner holds an undivided, separate, and distinct share in the property. Each tenant in common has an equal right of possession and enjoyment of the property with all of the co-owners. Each owner's interest is inheritable either by will or intestate succession:

There is no right of survivorship. Each owner has a right to sell or bequeath his or her share without the consent of the other co-owners. The interests of tenants in common may or may not be equal. The creditors of a co-owner may execute against that owner's interest in the property. A fiduciary relationship exists between co-owners, meaning that one owner cannot benefit from the property to the detriment of the other owners. If one co-owner pays the property taxes or mortgage interest, he or she has the right to compel pro rata contributions by the co-owners. There is also a right of contribution for repairs, unless they are made by the co-owner in possession. In many states, a co-owner in possession has no right to contribution for repairs. Some states allow a judicial action for waste to force a possessory co-owner to protect and preserve the property. This action was not available under common law. Each co-tenant has the right to possess all portions of the entire property. If there has been an ouster (a wrongful dispossession or exclusion from the property) by the owner in possession, a non-possessory owner can bring an action for ejectment to regain possession. A tenancy in common can be terminated by partition. In a partition action, the court divides the land held by the tenants in common into distinct portions that are then held separately, if possible, or else sells the property and divides the proceeds among the owners. Joint tenancy is the joint ownership of property where each owner owns an undivided equal interest in the entire property. Four unities are required to create a joint tenancy: (1) time—all interests are created at the same time; (2) title—the interests all come from the same source (e.g., deed or will); (3) interest—each owner has an identical type and duration of interest; and (4) possession—all interests have identical rights of enjoyment. Under common law, joint tenants had a right of survivorship. The statutes of most states now require that the language of the conveying document (e.g., written contract or deed) specifically expresses the intention to create a joint tenancy with right of survivorship for the right of survivorship to exist. Otherwise, the law presumes that the joint ownership is a tenancy in common.

Tenancy by the entirety is joint ownership held by a husband and wife (considered to be one unit). Since the decision of the Supreme Court that found a constitutional right for same sex couples to marry, states are required to extend the right to hold property as tenants by the entirety to same sex couples. Five unities are necessary to create a tenancy by the entirety—the four mentioned above for a joint tenancy plus the unity of the person (husband and wife). The laws of many states presume this type of ownership, a conveyance of real property, is made to spouses. To create any other type of ownership, the conveying document must contain specific language. Tenancy by the entirety is generally applicable only to interests in real property. Neither spouse has the right to convey his or her interest without the agreement of the other. Creditors of an individual spouse may not force the sale of property owned as a tenancy by the entirety to satisfy a debt or judgment. Real property acquired before marriage does not automatically become property owned by the couple as tenants by the entirety. Divorce severs a tenancy by the entirety, rendering it a tenancy in common.

**Example 6.6** Henry and Henrietta owned a farm as tenants by the entirety. Henry was in an auto accident that was his fault. The court awarded a $1 million judgment against him. As the farm was owned as tenants by the entirety, the judgment creditor could not execute against the farm to satisfy the judgment. Henry and Henrietta sought a divorce. Under the terms of the property settlement, Henrietta was to receive the entire farm. Henrietta's attorney neglected to effect the transfer of Henry's interest in the farm until after the judge signed the divorce decree. Henry's creditors claimed, correctly, that the divorce decree converted the tenancy by the entirety into a tenancy in common. As a result, the $1 million judgment against Henry attached to his half interest in the farm. The result was that Henrietta could not keep the farm because Henry's creditors could reach the half interest that Henry formerly owned. Henrietta quickly converted her distress into a malpractice claim against her attorney.

### Trusts

Real property, as well as personal property, may be owned by a trust. A trust is a fiduciary relationship among a trustor (also called a grantor or a settlor and defined as the one who transfers the property into the trust), the trustee (defined as the one who manages the property for the benefit of the beneficiary), and the beneficiary (defined as the one who receives the benefit of the property transferred into the trust). A trust is a variation on joint ownership because the legal title to the property is held by the trustee, and the beneficial (equitable) interest is held by the beneficiary. Because the terms of the trust are up to the trustor, a trust is a much more flexible device for transferring property than some other methods, such as a life estate.

**Example 6.7** Lawrence Johnson owned a farm that his ancestors purchased from the Tuscarora in 1660, prior to the establishment of the colony of Carolina by the Lord Proprietors. Although he dearly loved his wife, Mindy, the thought that the farm might pass out of his family's ownership caused him unbearable pain. He wanted any income from the farm, beyond that needed to retain it, to be used for Mindy's benefit. He set up his will with a testamentary trust to take ownership of the farm at his death. He appointed Mindy as trustee and co-beneficiary with their son, Luke. As trustee, Mindy had no power to sell or otherwise convey the farm. Income generated by the trust was first to be applied to pay taxes and any other obligations associated with the farm. Mindy was authorized to pay any remaining income to herself. At Mindy's death, the trust terminated, with Luke taking title to the farm real estate.

## Acquisition and disposition of real property

### Contracts for the sale of land

A contract of sale is an agreement to acquire or to dispose of property at some specified time period. Both parties are bound by the terms of the contract. The Statute of Frauds requires that all contracts for the sale of real property be in writing. There are four basic types of sales contracts. These are an option contract, a preemptive right, an interim sale contract, and a long-term sale contract.

### Options

An option contract is one by which the owner of property (the optionor) agrees with another person (the optionee) that the optionee shall have the right to buy the optionor's property at a fixed price within a certain period of time. The optionor is not bound to make the purchase. Subsequent negotiations and counter-offers do not constitute a rejection of the option by the optionee. When the option is properly exercised, the option contract becomes a contract to sell. The option contract must be recorded to give the optionee priority over subsequent lien holders and purchasers for value. An optionee at the execution of an option contract pays the option price to the owner of the land. The option price is usually calculated as some percentage of the purchase price. If the optionee chooses not to purchase the property by the deadline in the option contract, the optionee forfeits the money paid as the option price. The optionee has no other obligations. Option contracts are often used to facilitate real estate development. Option contracts allow developers to assemble tracts of land sufficiently large for their development objectives. Many lenders will not provide construction loans until the land for the development is acquired. Option contracts can serve as an alternative to buying all the land outright.

### Preemptive rights

The owner of property may grant preemptive rights to a prospective buyer by contract (called right of first refusal). The owner is not bound to sell but, if he does, he must give the other contracting party the first right to buy. A contract of preemptive rights must contain a reasonable price provision linked to a fair market value or price that the owner is willing to accept from a third party. Though preemptive rights may last for decades, most states limit the total duration of preemptive rights by either statute or common law.

### Interim or long-term sales contracts

Real estate contracts can be classified as either interim or long-term. The interim contract is typically of short duration, maybe several months or less, and results in a transfer of legal title and possession at a specified future date. Under the

Statute of Frauds, a contract for a sale of real property must be in writing to be enforceable. No particular form is required, and the writing will be sufficient for this purpose if it is signed by the party to be charged (the defendant in a breach of purchase contract action), there is a description of the subject property (a legal description is not required but is preferred), and all elements of the contract are present. The basic requirements for a real estate contract are described in *Rawls & Assoc. v. Hurst*.[2] "[A] contract for the sale of real property must meet the following requirements: be in writing; signed by the parties; contain an adequate description of the real property; recite a sum of consideration; and contain all key terms and conditions of the agreement."

As most real property is transferred under general warranty deeds, it is necessary that the seller provide marketable title. To ensure this, the closing attorney prepares an abstract of title that is a history of the property complete with any encumbrances or other title defects listed. Title is considered to be marketable if a title insurance company will cover the property without significant exceptions. There are two types of title insurance: lenders and owners. The former protects the lender for the balance of the loan remaining, and the latter protects the purchaser for the amount of the purchase price. The title insurance company also agrees to pay for the cost of defending the title against a lawsuit by another claiming title. Title insurance does not protect appreciation in the property after the date of purchase.

It is important that all important terms be in the written contract. Under the parol evidence rule, evidence outside the four corners of the contract is not admissible unless it is offered to show fraudulent inducement, mutual mistake, or to resolve an ambiguity.

A long-term contract for sale, often called an installment land contract, is used primarily as a financing device. The buyer becomes the beneficial owner and takes possession of the property, but the seller retains legal title, usually for many years, until the final installment payment is made. The seller may get an income tax advantage by stretching out the payments over an extended period of years. For this and other reasons, the buyer generally cannot pay off the debt owed early without permission of the seller. While the land is in the buyer's possession, he must not allow waste of the property, and he is obligated to pay the property taxes. If the buyer departs substantially from the terms of the contract, the seller can declare the buyer's interest forfeit and retake possession of the property. With a forfeiture, the seller not only gets the land back but gets to keep all payments made. At common law, no legal action in court was required for the seller to declare forfeiture and take possession of the property. This is a harsh result, and the right to declare a forfeiture was often abused. To mitigate the harshness of forfeitures under installment contracts, most states have passed laws that require some minimal level of judicial involvement to prevent overreaching by the seller. A few states have gone further and abolished the long-term sales contract. These states treat long-term sales contracts as mortgages. Remedies for breach of a real estate sales contract are governed under the rules contract law discussed in Chapter 5.

## Deeds and other evidence of title

A deed is an instrument of writing that has been signed, sealed, and delivered and serves to transfer an interest in real property from a grantor to a grantee.

A general warranty deed not only conveys the land, it also contains assurances that the seller owns the property, the title is free from defects and encumbrances, and the grantor will protect the grantee from any title claims that may arise. A special warranty deed promises that the title is free from defects and encumbrances that may have arisen since the grantor acquired title. A special warranty deed does not promise that anyone else, other than the grantor, has not caused defects in the title.

A quit claim deed conveys only the interest that the grantor has in a specific property. If the grantor has no interest in the property, the quit claim deed conveys nothing. There are no promises made in a quit claim deed regarding the title. Quit claim deeds are primarily used to clear titles. All who have even remote interests in the property, even if too small to have value, can relinquish that interest by means of a quit claim deed. Quit claim deeds are particularly useful for settling boundary disputes and facilitating property settlements in divorce. Unlike a transfer under a warranty deed, the grantee under a quit claim deed has no legal action against the grantor if the title is later found to be defective or non-existent.

To have a valid deed, there must be a competent grantor and a grantee capable of holding title. In addition to the names of the grantor and the grantee, the deed must also contain a sufficient description of the property, the operative words of conveyance, and a proper execution by the grantor, including his signature and seal. The final requirements for a valid transfer are delivery of the deed to the grantee and the grantee's acceptance of the deed. Most states have added as an additional requirement the payment of a transfer tax and recording fees.

---

**Example 6.8** Some months after his friend Bob's death, Larry received a mysterious envelope in the mail. In the envelope was a deed to Bob's farm that Bob executed before his death. The deed purported to transfer Bob's farm to Larry. The attempted transfer was ineffective because Bob did not deliver the deed to Larry during his lifetime.

---

Many states recognize a probated will as evidence of title equivalent to a deed. It is good practice when an estate is settled to have new deeds recorded. This can save expense and delay when property is sold. Some states use an alternative to the system of deeds that is called the Torrens system. It is a property registration system done through the court system.

## Security interests

A mortgage is a security interest in real property that guarantees the payment of a debt. Always in writing, it is a contract between the mortgagor (the borrower/ debtor) and the mortgagee (the lender/creditor). The borrower, who owns the land, gives a mortgage to the lender to secure a debt. The underlying debt is evidenced by a promissory note. The security interest is perfected by recording the mortgage in the place where property records are recorded.

Many states also recognize a deed of trust as a real property security instrument. A deed of trust is an instrument by which a debtor transfers title in real property to a disinterested third party (the trustee) to be held in trust for the beneficiary (the creditor) as security for the performance of an obligation (the payment of a debt). If the debtor defaults on the loan, the trustee can sell the property at a foreclosure sale, and the creditor can bid on the property at that sale. A deed of trust arrangement is a three-party security interest in real property whereas a mortgage is a two-party arrangement.

In a title theory state, the mortgagee holds legal title to the property. The holder of legal title is forbidden to bid at a foreclosure sale. For this reason, deeds of trust are commonly used in title theory states so that the lender can bid at the foreclosure sale. Quite often, the lender is the only bidder at the foreclosure sale. Foreclosed property does not have the same market value as property that has been voluntarily traded. Foreclosed property may have hidden title defects such as the use of a defective foreclosure process. The potential for hidden defects depresses the value of property that has been through a recent foreclosure.

A mortgage is drafted as either a conveyance of the property to the mortgagee (the title theory) or as a lien to secure payment of a debt (the lien theory). Even in title theory states where the mortgagee (lender) acquires legal title, the mortgagee does not acquire the right of possession. The mortgagor retains possession and has beneficial use of the property.

Security interest may be enforced in the event of default by foreclosing on the property. For a foreclosure to proceed there must be a default by the borrower. The default may be either monetary or non-monetary. A monetary default is a failure to make payments as they come due. It is the most common type of default that can trigger a foreclosure. Non-monetary defaults are based upon some other violation of the financing agreement. A borrower is typically expected to maintain the property and maintain casualty insurance coverage. The failure to do so is a default.

To avoid the harsh result of a strict foreclosure, the mortgagor has an equity of redemption after he defaults on his or her debt. This means that a defaulting mortgagor may prevent foreclosure by paying the full amount of the mortgage debt plus interest and costs before the foreclosure sale, including the expiration of any upset bid period. In some states, after the upset bid period is over, this right is extinguished. In other states, the equity of redemption may extend for as long as two years after the conclusion of the foreclosure sale. Some of these states also extend the right to redeem the property beyond the debtor to persons related to the debtor.

A debt payable in installments usually contains an acceleration clause that states that the entire debt (including interest due) will be due and payable immediately if the mortgagor fails to pay any installment when due. Similarly, a due-on-sale clause is an acceleration clause that authorizes a mortgagee or deed of trust beneficiary to accelerate the due date of the entire loan balance if the mortgagor transfers the property and the mortgage (or deed of trust) without the permission of the mortgagee.

A foreclosure sale can result from a judicial action brought by the mortgagee or trustee where, if the court finds a default, it orders a judicial sale of the property. Judicial foreclosures are also called foreclosures by action. The debt is satisfied from the sale proceeds, and the excess, if any, is paid to the mortgagor. If the proceeds are insufficient to pay the debt, the mortgagee can obtain a personal judgment against the mortgagor for the deficit. This is called a deficiency judgment. Some states do not allow deficiency judgments.

Another way to foreclosure is through a power of sale clause in the mortgage contract or deed of trust. That clause permits the mortgagee or trustee to sell the property without a court proceeding, upon default by the mortgagor. To protect borrowers from overreaching by creditors, the laws of most states require that foreclosures by power of sale be conducted under judicial supervision.

## Methods of sale

Buyers and sellers can be brought together in several different ways. This section discusses methods commonly used.

### Private agreement

A buyer and seller may always use a private agreement. A private agreement is a contract between two individuals without the intervention of a third party. The buyer and the seller must decide on a price that is mutually acceptable.

### Licensed brokers

Another method of transferring land is through a licensed broker. Here the price is determined by mutual agreement of the buyer and seller, but many potential buyers may look at the property, and offers from several people may be made. Because of his or her expertise, the broker can advise the seller about what is a reasonable price.

A typical real estate sales office is supervised by a broker (also called agent) who may employ many sub-brokers who work for her or him as independent contractors. Brokers are generally licensed and regulated by the state in which they work. The real estate agents are, in legal terms, agents of the broker. The arrangements under which a broker works include seller agency, buyer agency, and dual agency. A broker who is a seller's agent works primarily for the seller and is under a duty to inform the seller of any material information that is revealed to her by the buyer. The seller's agent is also under a duty not to reveal such information about the seller to the buyer. With a buyer's agent, the situation is reversed, and the buyer's agent is representing the buyer. In dual agency, the broker may not reveal either the buyer's or seller's confidential information. Detailed discussion of agency arrangements is beyond the scope of this chapter.

Real estate brokers are usually compensated by a commission based upon a percentage of the sale price of the property. The contract between the seller and his broker defines what the broker must do to be paid. The failure of a seller to understand what triggers payment is a common source of disputes and liability. Brokers who sell farm real estate typically charge higher commission rates than brokers who sell residential properties because farm real estate has a smaller pool of potential buyers, making it more difficult and costly to sell.

## Auctions

An auction is a public sale of property to the highest bidder. Auctions are often used when competition for particular land already exists, when the sale must be made by a certain date, or when the value of the property is difficult to determine. Auctioneers, like real estate brokers, must be licensed by the state in which they practice. Typically, an auction is conducted with ascending bids, with the highest bidder buying the property. Such auctions may be conducted "with reserve" or "without reserve." When an auction is conducted with reserve, the property does not sell unless a minimum reserve price is reached. Whether the auction is with reserve or without reserve must be announced to the bidders in advance. Another type of auction is a reverse, or Dutch auction, where the auctioneer starts with a high price and lowers it until a buyer is obtained.

---

**Example 6.9** Morris decided to sell his farm. He signed a brokerage contract with broker Bob. The contract gave Bob an exclusive right to sell the farm for a period of two years from the date the contract was signed. The contract included a provision providing that in the event of breach, the breaching party would be liable for court costs and reasonable attorney fees in addition to damages. After a year, Morris gave up on Bob and sold the farm to Earl without any involvement from Bob. Bob's attorney sent a demand letter to Morris that demanded full payment of the commission on the sale to Earl. Morris' attorney advised him to let him negotiate a settlement of payment of the commission. He advised Morris that if he went to court he would be liable for court costs and reasonable attorney fees in addition to the full commission.

---

## Sealed bids

Another method of bringing together a buyer and a seller is by sealed bid. The potential buyers bid only once and without any knowledge of competitors' bids. Many prospective buyers do not like this method as they are operating without full knowledge.

# Rights, limitations, and taxation

## Easements

An easement is the right of one person to legally enter and use the land of another. Easements are classified in two types: (1) an easement appurtenant and (2) an easement in gross. Easements appurtenant are often called rights of way. Rights of way always involve two adjoining pieces of land. The legal term for the property served by the right of way is the dominant tenement. The property over which the right of way passes is called the servient tenement. In some cases, a right of way does not allow access to a particular parcel. The purpose of the right of way is to provide a place for power transmission lines or a natural gas pipeline. This type of right of way or easement is called an easement in gross.

The law treats these two types of easements quite differently. Easements appurtenant generally run with the land. This means that when the servient tenement is sold or passed at death by will or intestate succession, it remains subject to the easement. Likewise, the right of way that provides access to the dominant tenement, unless limited by the terms of the grant or abandoned, has the potential to last forever. The terms of all types of easements are very import as they trump general principles of law.

---

**Example 6.10** Theo divided his eighty-acre farm between his two children, John and Emily. John got the front forty acres, and Emily got the back forty acres. To ensure access to the back forty acres, both deeds provided for a perpetual easement to provide access to the public road that runs along the front forty acres. John failed to pay his taxes, and the property was sold in a tax foreclosure auction to Ima Speculator. Ima purchased subject to the easement and must continue to allow Emily to use it.

---

**Example 6.11** The facts are the same as Example 6.10 except that Emily purchased John's property at the tax foreclosure auction. As she owns both properties, the easement is extinguished by merger and no longer exists.

Easements in gross are usually personal and are extinguished with the death of the holder; they are generally not transferable. Utility, railway, natural gas pipelines, and similar right of ways last a very long time only because their corporate owners last a very long time. Should a corporation be liquidated, these easements would cease to exist. Terms of these easements are very important. Such easements are limited to the uses that are expressly listed in the instrument that created the easement.

---

**Example 6.12** Jason owns a farm through which a railroad passes. The easement to the railroad was granted in 1851. One day Jason saw men with trenching equipment placing fiber optic cable parallel to the railroad line. Jason hired a lawyer to sue the cable and the railroad companies for trespass. The cable and the railroad companies defended by reference to the railroad company easement. Jason's attorney responded that the 1851 deed of easement did not list fiber optic cable as a permitted use of the easement. The court agreed that the railroad company had no right under the easement to grant the cable company the right to place a fiber optic cable on Jason's land. The terms of the railroad company's easement limited it to using the right of way for railroad purposes. Jason's attorney negotiated a hefty payment in return for Jason's agreement to amend the terms of the easement to include fiber optic cables.

---

Easements may be created by express grant in a deed, express reservation in a deed, prescription, and implication. Creation by express grant in a deed occurs when the owner of the property subject to the easement grants another person the easement. The easement is evidenced by a recorded deed. A reservation in a deed is made where a property is subdivided and a right of way for the use of the remaining property is reserved. Sometimes property is subdivided, leaving a parcel landlocked. Here the owner of the property neglected to reserve an easement for the landlocked property. As no rational person would intentionally landlock his or her own property, courts will find a right of way created by implication. Finally, one person may use the property of another for access without permission. As there exists in most states a statute of limitation on bringing a trespass action, a person who uses a right of way without permission will eventually own the right of way. This may even apply to the public at large.

---

**Example 6.13** For more than a century, members of the public walked across a vacant parcel of land from the public highway on Brilliant Island to get to the beach. When a developer attempted to close the path, affected members of the public sued, claiming an easement by prescription. The court held that the state's twenty-year statute of limitation to bringing a trespass action had long passed. The court forbade the developer to bar public access to the beach.

Some states have statutory provisions to protect owners of landlocked property. In such states, a person may petition the court for the creation of a right of way over his or her neighbor's property. This is an exercise of the government's power of eminent domain. A successful petitioner for a right of way must pay the landowner over which the right of way passes a sum determined by the court to be the fair market value of the right of way.

### Covenants running with the land (restrictive covenants)

When parties convey land, they can make agreements regarding its use. If the agreements are part of the deed or in a subdivision map filed with the real property records office, they are binding on subsequent owners and are called covenants running with the land. These covenants are generally classified as (1) express covenants (those explicitly stated in a deed) or (2) implied covenants (those not stated in writing but implied by the language of the deed and existing conditions). A covenant running with the land confers a burden or a benefit on the owner of the land to which it attaches. Such covenants may be enforced only by landowners with standing to sue. Determining standing is complex and varies from state to state.

**Example 6.14** Alex owned two adjacent lots in a subdivision. The deed for each lot contained a restrictive covenant that limited the use of each lot to a single family home. Each home was allowed one auxiliary outside storage building. Alex built his home on one lot and a storage building on the neighboring lot. Alex had a neighbor whose property was in the same subdivision, subject to the same covenants. Alex's neighbor objected to the storage building and demanded that Alex remove it. When Alex refused, the neighbor sued for an injunction to force the removal of the building. The court held that the storage building was auxiliary to the use of the lot as a single family home. Without a single family home on the lot, the storage building was the primary use of the lot, a use that violated the restrictive covenant. Alex was ordered to remove the storage building at his own expense.

## Zoning and land use controls

The government may use its police power to promote the safety and general welfare of society within constitutional limits. Zoning is an exercise of police power to regulate the use of private land for an acknowledged public interest. That interest is in preventing nuisances by separating incompatible land uses. Most zoning occurs at the municipal or county level, and it must relate substantially to the public health, morals, safety, or welfare. As a technique for regulating land use, zoning is based on the idea that in a given area, certain uses are expressly permitted and, consequently, all other uses are prohibited.

## Agricultural districts and tax abeyances

Many states have adopted programs to protect areas of qualifying farm, forest, and horticultural land. Except for programs based upon zoning, most of these programs require that owners agree to participate. Benefits of participation include property tax reductions, protection from private nuisance suits, and recognition by local government. Many states require that taxes forgone be repaid, at least to some extent, if the land is no longer used in the qualifying use.

Under certain circumstances, the valuation of real property for tax purposes may be eligible for a reduced amount based on its present use rather than on its highest and best use (present use valuation). For example, agricultural lands that meet certain income and ownership requirements may be valued based on use as a farm rather than on use as a developed residential area or shopping mall, allowing the owner to pay lower taxes than he or she would if the land were valued at its highest and best use. Such programs are subject to many limitations, and failure to comply with statutory provisions will result in recapture of some of the tax that was foregone. Participation in the program in most states is not automatic. Typically, an application must be made. In many states, these tax benefits are available only in qualifying agricultural districts.

## Lateral and subjacent support

Under the common law, a real property owner has an absolute right to have her or his land supported on the sides (lateral support) and from beneath the surface (subjacent support) by adjacent real property, if the land is in its natural state. The right of lateral support is effective against acts such as excavation or the cutting of road grades. The right to subjacent support is important where there is underground mining. A landowner is strictly liable for the damage to the land if his or her excavation causes adjacent land to subside. However, if there are structures on the land, he or she is liable for the damage to the structures, and the land, if he or she is found to be negligent. Particularly in mining states, some of these rights have been modified by statute. These rights are usually protected by bringing a suit based upon a private nuisance theory.

## Taxation

If a property owner fails to pay his property taxes, the taxing authority (city and/ or county) can place a lien on the property. A tax lien on the property makes the title to the property unmarketable until the tax is paid and the lien released. The taxing authority can either file an action to foreclose a tax lien or can obtain a judgment against the property owner by docketing a certificate regarding the unpaid taxes. After proper procedures are followed as provided by statute, the property may be sold in fee simple, free and clear except for the tax lien, at a foreclosure sale for the amount necessary to satisfy the unpaid taxes, penalties, interests, and costs.

## Adverse possession

The doctrine of adverse possession (also called squatters' rights) permits a person in possession of land for a statutory length of time to acquire title to that property. It is distinguished from the government's exercise of eminent domain because here one private citizen can take land from another without compensation. Adverse possession is best thought of as a statute of limitation on bringing action for ejectment based upon a trespass theory. Though a person may acquire title through adverse possession, the title acquired is not a marketable title. No title insurance company will write a title insurance policy on land whose title is based upon a claim of adverse possession. A quiet title or other legal action is required to render title acquired by adverse possession marketable. As the result of such an action, a judge will require that a new deed be recorded that accurately reflects the ownership of the property.

Certain elements must be present for acquiring title by adverse possession. First, possession must be actual and is not applicable to concurrent ownership with a co-tenant unless there has been an ouster. Where a property includes waste land, forest land, and other land that would not normally be in active use, the possession will still be of the entire property where it is employed in its normal use. Second, possession must be open and notorious, not secret or clandestine. Third, possession must be hostile. This means that the possession was without permission. It does not mean that the one in adverse possession was required to use violence to defend possession. Permissive use never gives rise to ownership by adverse possession. Fourth, possession must be continuous without interruption for the statutory period of the years required to establish adverse possession. The number of years required varies from one state to another, by the type of land and by whether the one in adverse possession had indicia of title. Most states distinguish between privately owned land and state-owned land. Land owned by the U.S. government is never subject to adverse possession. If one has indicia of ownership that purports to confer ownership but does not, most states reduce the period of years required. One common problem is a deed that was not signed by the seller's spouse to release marital rights in the land. Such defective deeds and other instruments that purport to grant title, but do not, are referred to under the rubric of "color of title." One occupant's period of adverse possession may be "tacked" on to the uninterrupted years of adverse possession by prior occupants to meet the statutory period required by the applicable statute. Where the normal use of the property is only seasonal, the lack of use during the off season will not defeat a claim of continuous use. Fifth, exclusive possession must be had by the one claiming property on the basis of adverse possession. Property shared with the true owner will generally bar a claim of ownership by adverse possession. In most states, payment of taxes is not an element of adverse possession because many permissive relationships such as long-term leases also include payment of taxes.

---

**Example 6.15** Jake and Johnny agreed to jointly put up a fence between their two properties. They did not obtain a survey of the boundary before they put up the fence. Ten acres of prime corn land that belonged to Johnny was on Jake's side of the fence. Forty years later, Johnny died, and his executor sold his farm to Ag Land Mutual Investors, LLC, a company that buys and leases agricultural land on behalf of investors. Based upon a current survey, Ag Land Mutual Investors sued Jake for trespass. Ag Land Mutual Investors demanded an injunction to require Jake to move the fence at his expense and pay damages equal to forty years of fair market rental payments on the ten acres. Jake counter-claimed that he owned the ten acres by adverse possession and asked that the court cause a deed in his name to be recorded for the ten acres. The court dismissed the Ag Land Mutual Investors claim and granted the relief requested by Jake.

---

The policy reasons for adverse possession, even though it may seem unfair, are to encourage full use and improvement of real property, to aid in settling boundary disputes, and to aid in clearing titles. The statutory periods of limitation during which claims to land may be pursued in court prevent some of the confusion that can exist with real property titles and encourage the timely resolution of disputes. Adverse possession not only clears the record of many old claims, it often results in the passing of land from the record title holder to the one who has used and claimed the land for many years. It is particularly useful for settling disputes between agricultural landowners.

## Notes

1  2009 N.C. App. LEXIS 1647 (N.C. App. 2009).
2  144 N.C. App. 286, 550 S.E.2d 219; 2001 N.C. App. LEXIS 448 (N.C. App. 2001).

# Chapter 7

# Landlord-tenant law

## Introduction

About half of the agricultural land in the United States is not owned by those farming it. That land is leased. For that reason, landlord-tenant law is a critical component of agricultural law. The landlord is also called the lessor. The tenant is also called the lessee.

## Elements of a landlord-tenant relationship

There are six essential elements of the landlord-tenant relationship. First, there must exist a contract between the landlord and the tenant. (The five elements of an enforceable contract are discussed in Chapter 5.) Second, there must be provision for the payment of rent. If there is no rent paid, the relationship is not a landlord-tenant relationship. Third, there must be a transfer of the estate to the tenant. The estate is the land that the tenant is renting from the landlord. Fourth, possession and control must be with the tenant, not the landlord. Unless the lease or provisions of law allow it, the landlord may not enter the property without the permission of the tenant. A landlord who enters property of his tenant without either legal right or permission may be sued by the tenant for the tort of trespass. Fifth, there must be a reversionary interest for the landlord. Sixth, real estate or an interest in real estate must be the subject matter of the lease. There is no landlord-tenant relationship in a lease of tangible personal property. Leases of tangible personal property are governed under Article 2A of the Uniform Commercial Code rather than landlord-tenant law.

## Classification of tenancies

A tenancy from period to period is a periodic tenancy that can last indefinitely. For agricultural tenancies the period is typically a crop year. It is deemed to automatically renew itself unless adequate notice is given by either the landlord or the tenant to end the lease. It can be created by an oral agreement or by a written agreement.

At common law, the notice requirement for termination of a lease is six months for a year-to-year tenancy. The period allowed in the notice to quit is shorter for tenancies of shorter periods. Most states have modified notice requirements by statute. Many states have multiple classifications with different lengths of notice to quit.

A tenancy for years or for a term is a tenancy measured by time. It lasts for a specified time agreed upon in the lease, and the tenant's right of possession automatically terminates at the end of the term, unless it is renewed by mutual agreement. It is usually created by a written agreement.

A tenancy at will can be terminated by either party at any time. This tenancy can be created by express actions of the parties or by implication.

A tenancy at sufferance is the relationship between a landlord and a holdover tenant. A holdover tenant is a tenant whose lease has expired and who has not yet vacated the premises. This condition can exist for only a short period of time, after which the tenant will be considered a tenant from year to year if the landlord allows him or her to retain physical possession of the property.

Crop-share lease agreements, discussed later in this chapter, are a type of lease unique to agriculture. There are often tax issues to consider in crop-share lease agreements. For example, where the landlord shares in the crops as part of the rent, the tax issue is whether there is "material participation" by the landlord, which would result in the landlord's having to treat his or her rental income as earned income for self-employment tax purposes. There are also issues involving the sharing of farm program payment under federal farm programs.

The flexible lease (also known as a "flex cash lease") is another type of lease that provides for risk sharing between the landlord and the tenant. Unlike a crop-share lease, the landlord is not paid in a portion of the crop. However, the rental payment varies as the crop price rises and falls. For income tax and federal farm program purposes, flexible leases are treated more like cash rent arrangements than crop-share lease agreements; however, specific terms of the lease and the law of the state governing the lease may have an impact on those issues.

## Statute of Frauds

The Statute of Frauds is an old English common law rule that requires certain contracts to be in writing. All contracts for the sale of real property must be in writing. Not all leases need to be in writing to be enforceable. Many states allow enforcement of oral leases that are of relatively short term. Many states have enacted statutes that supply some of the terms, such as a standard start and end date, for oral agricultural leases. In most states, multiyear leases must be in writing.

Whether a writing is required or not, the use of oral leases is not advisable. Memories fade over time. People tend to remember that which they wish to remember. If a dispute arises, the judge or jury will be asked to determine which party to the lease is most believable. It is much better for the lease to be in writing. Written leases reduce the likelihood of a dispute. It is, nonetheless, customary in many parts of the United States to use annual oral leases. Obtaining a written lease may be difficult because asking for one may be seen as an affront, implying a lack of trust.

# Recording

Written leases may be recorded in the local land records office. Recording provisions vary somewhat from state to state. Though recording a lease does not prevent property from being sold, it does protect the tenant's leasehold interest for the lease term, unless a provision of the lease allows the landlord a right to sell the property free of the lease. When negotiating a lease, a tenant should ensure that he or she has a right to payment for any improvements that he or she has made, should the property be sold and the lease terminated before the end of its term. The tenant may also wish to make fixture filings to preserve his or her interest (as discussed in Chapter 6).

Recording also protects the tenant from transfers by operation of law. The most common such transfer involves the death of the landlord and the transfer of the property to his or her estate or heirs or legatees. The property may also be transferred as a result of a judgment sale by a creditor of the landlord. Recording will not protect the tenant from interests of creditors that are superior to his or hers; however, recording will protect the tenant from interests of creditors that are junior to his or hers. A junior interest is generally one that arose after the senior interest. Recording is a way to ensure that the interests of the tenant are senior to any interests that arise after the lease is recorded.

# Duties of the tenant

All tenants have a duty to pay rent. Where there is no payment of rent, there is no landlord-tenant relationship.

All tenants have a duty not to commit waste. Voluntary waste results from a decisive action, such as removing topsoil or cutting timber. Permissive waste results from a failure to do something, such as rotate crops or plant cover crops. Ameliorating waste is waste that results from a physical change to the property by an act of the tenant that adds value and improves the property. For the first two types of waste, the tenant may owe the landlord money damages. For ameliorating waste, the tenant is not liable for monetary damages but may be enjoined from proceeding with making the changes that constitute ameliorating waste.

All tenants must make reasonable use of the property. The tenant is expected to conduct the farm business according to well-established customs or usages of the region. What is considered reasonable varies from one part of the United States to another.

All agricultural tenants are expected to farm in a husband-like manner. The tenant has the right to determine the cropping system as long as she or he does not injure the land. Severe erosion is an example of an injury to the land. Nonetheless, the tenant is not required to yield the land at the end of the lease in the same condition it was in when he took possession. Even so, the tenant has a duty to avoid exhaustion of soil through negligence or improper use. Landlord and tenant may want to measure the soil fertility at the beginning of a lease and at its end. An agricultural lease may contain a provision for payment by either the landlord or the tenant reflecting the fertility balance of the soil at the end of the lease.

The tenant has a duty to make repairs. The tenant must keep up any fences and keep buildings on the property in good repair. The tenant must do this at her or his own expense unless a provision in the lease requires the landlord to share in the cost of repairs. This is a major difference between agricultural leases and residential leases that are usually governed by a state's residential tenancy act. An agricultural tenant generally has a duty to comply with all applicable laws such as those that require farmers to control noxious weeds. Lease provisions may also require tenants to avoid activities that could contaminate the property with toxic waste. A tenant may not make use of the property for illegal activities such as the growing or production of controlled substances. If the lease is oral or not well written, it may be difficult to remove the tenant who has engaged in illegal activities. Well-written leases will list illegal activities and violations of regulations such as zoning that are grounds for eviction. Such leases also usually include a savings clause for any violations not listed.

The advent of certified organic production has made for more complicated leases. If a landlord wants property to be used for only certified organic production, lease provisions may require that the tenant maintain certification. A well-written lease should require that the tenant provide at least annual proof that certification has been maintained. The lease can provide that the failure to maintain certification is grounds for termination of the lease.

## Risk of loss

Under the common law, the duty to make repairs means that the tenant insures the condition of the property. Should any structure on the property be destroyed, the tenant has a duty to rebuild it to its original condition. What this means is that a tenant in an agricultural lease should buy insurance against loss. Many states have altered the risk of loss by statute. This varies greatly from one state to another.

## Crop ownership

Generally, a crop belongs to the tenant until it is harvested and divided. In most states, a landlord has a lien against crops for rents, advances, and possibly other expenses. It attaches as soon as the crop starts to grow, and it is generally superior to all other liens. The federal Food Security Act of 1985 provides for centralized filing of landlords' liens because, to prevail against third parties, the landlord must show that the purchaser knew that the crop was grown on rented land.

The common law right to emblements allows a tenant, after the tenant's lease has expired through no fault of his or her own, to return and harvest the crop if it was seeded before notice of termination. Most states have created statutory rights in lieu of the right to emblements. As annual growing crops are tangible personal property, not part of the real estate, growing crops are not transferred when the real estate is transferred. Growing crops remain the property of the tenant, subject to the landlord's lien for unpaid rent.

---

**Example 7.1** Boris leased land from Hilda, who owned a life estate in the land, measured by her life. Boris grew wheat on the land. Three months before the wheat was ready to harvest, Hilda died. The owner of the remainder interest, her son, Henry, came into possession of the property. Henry told Boris to go away and keep off the property or he would sue him for trespass. He told Boris that the wheat was his now. Boris' attorney wrote a demand letter to Henry that asserted Boris' right to enter the property and harvest the wheat under the doctrine of emblements. Boris' attorney also warned Henry that the wheat was the personal property of Boris and that Boris would hold Henry responsible for any damage to the wheat.

---

## Right to sue

The tenant has the exclusive right to a claim for damage to her or his crops, subject to the landlord's lien in the crops and any proceeds. Conversely, the landlord has the right to a claim for damage to her or his land and fixtures. These rights may be allocated differently by express provisions of the lease or by state law.

## Liability for injuries on leased property

Generally, the landlord is not liable to the tenant or to third parties for injuries caused by conditions on the premises. There is an exception to this if the injury is caused by a hidden defect and the landlord knew or should have known about it but failed to disclose it to the tenant.

A tenant's liability is similar to that of an owner in possession. If the tenant knows or should have known of a defect and fails to correct it, he or she will be liable for resulting injuries, even if the landlord has agreed to make repairs. A landlord will not ordinarily be held liable for the negligence of a tenant. Nonetheless, both landlord and tenant should carry liability insurance. Plaintiffs' attorneys are likely to sue both the landlord and the tenant in any personal injury action.

## Assignments and sublets

At common law, a tenant could freely assign or sublet a lease. An assignment of the lease removes the tenant from the agreement and substitutes the new tenant in his or her place. In a sublet, the original tenant becomes landlord to the new tenant, and the original tenant retains his or her obligations to the original landlord. Most written leases prohibit assignments and sublets without permission of the landlord. A lease may specifically permit assignments and sublets. If a valid assignment of the lease is made, the new tenant has the same rights against the landlord as the original tenant had. With the sublet, the new tenant looks to the original tenant for vindication of his rights. The distinction between a sublet and an assignment is that, in an assignment, the original tenant has transferred his or her entire interest in the property, whereas in a sublet, the original tenant has retained some interest and is, in effect, the landlord of the new tenant.

## Eviction

If a tenant fails to vacate the premises after the termination of the lease, fails to pay rent during the term of the lease, or violates some other provision of the lease during its term, the landlord has the remedy of eviction. Though some states allow self-help evictions, most states require that evictions be supervised by the judiciary. A tenant who is evicted is liable for all the remaining payments due under the lease subject to the landlord's duty to mitigate. The landlord's duty to mitigate requires that the landlord attempt to lease the property to another tenant as soon as possible.

## Right of tenant to remove fixtures

A tenant may remove from the premises any items that were erected by the tenant if they are not so physically attached to the land or buildings that severance would be impractical or that severance would cause permanent damage to the remaining property. Removable personal property, such as sheds and grain bins not in concrete foundations, are distinguished from improvements such as fences. The tenant may remove any fixture for which the landlord grants permission or for which the lease provides a right of removal.

## Farm program payments

In reaching the terms of a lease agreement, the tenant and the landlord should consider any effects on eligibility for federal farm program payments. The lease may require that the tenant raise crops such that eligibility for farm program payments is maintained. Provisions of federal farm programs change with each federal farm bill; however, it is often the case that federal law dictates how farm program payments are to be shared between landlord and tenant. The current trend is away from such rules.

## Residential leases

Residential leases are quite different from agricultural and commercial leases. Agricultural and commercial leases, on the one hand, are generally governed by the principle of freedom to contract. Under the principle of freedom to contract, each party to such a lease is deemed sophisticated and capable of negotiating proper lease provisions. These will generally be enforced as written. Residential leases, on the other hand, are in most states governed by detailed landlord-tenant statutes. The statutes presume a lack of sophistication on the part of residential tenants. Typically, most of the risk of loss is allocated to the landlord. Landlords are generally not allowed to make a retaliatory eviction if the tenant adheres to the provisions of the lease. An eviction is retaliatory if made in response to a tenant's assertion of a legal right.

Among the duties assigned to landlords under state residential tenancy laws are duties to provide fit and habitable premises, comply with all building and housing codes, make repairs necessary to keep the property in a habitable condition, keep the common areas in good condition, maintain all equipment (e.g., electrical, plumbing, and sanitary), and provide smoke detectors, fire extinguishers, and other safety equipment. Among the duties assigned to residential tenants under state residential tenancy laws are duties to keep the tenant's part of the premises clean and safe, dispose of waste properly, avoid deliberate destruction of the property, comply with building and housing codes, be responsible for damage occurring in the areas of exclusive control, maintain safety equipment (e.g., replace smoke detector batteries), and notify the landlord of malfunctioning safety equipment (e.g., inoperative smoke detectors).

Residential tenancy acts typically govern tenant security deposits. These acts typically set limits on the amount of security deposits and may require the deposits be held in escrow. Typically, these acts have provisions governing the return of the deposit at the end of the tenancy. Certain deductions may be made for damages that are the tenant's fault. Federal law gives members of the armed forces certain rights that are not available to the civilian population. This includes a right to terminate the tenancy if the tenant is transferred to a new duty station by military order. In addition to residential tenancy acts, most states have acts prohibiting unfair and deceptive trade practices that apply to a wide variety of transactions, including residential tenancies.

## Other arrangements distinguished from landlord-tenant relationships

There are other arrangements that are sometimes confused with a landlord-tenant relationship. It is important to distinguish these from a landlord-tenant relationship because these other relationships are governed by other bodies of law.

### License

A license is one such arrangement. A license is a right to use property that does not rise to the level of a landlord-tenant relationship. The licensee typically lacks both possession and an interest in real property. The classic example of a license arrangement is a parking space rental in a public parking facility.

In *Lee v. North Dakota Park Service*, the Supreme Court of North Dakota held:

> After reviewing and examining statutes, case law, authorities, and texts, it appears in the major differences between a "lease" and a "license" are that a lease confers exclusive possession against the world and owner, unless otherwise provided, grants exclusive possession and profits, grants a corporeal hereditament or an estate in the land; whereas a license merely grants permission to use the land under certain conditions and restrictions.[1]

In this case, the North Dakota Park Service eliminated a road to the plaintiffs' resort, leaving only a much longer road as their access. It was undisputed that elimination of the road reduced the value of the plaintiffs' resort. The Supreme Court of North Dakota held that unlike leasehold interests in real property that are protected by the Takings Clause of the Fifth Amendment, licenses have no such protection. A government may revoke a license to use real property without any constitutional obligation to pay compensation.

### Employment

Employment relationships, particularly in agriculture, may be confused with leases. This is particularly the case with crop-share lease arrangements. Under a crop-share lease arrangement, both the tenant and the landlord share in the risk of production. The tenant typically provides labor and some of the inputs. The landlord provides land and other inputs. For the arrangement to be a lease, the tenant must have significant management control of the farming operation. The tenant owns the crops produced subject to the landlord's lien in the crops. The landlord's lien ensures payment of rent. Typically, in a crop-share lease arrangement, the buyer of the crop remits the tenant share to the tenant and landlord share to the landlord. By doing so, the buyer ensures that he does not have to pay twice in the event that the tenant fails to remit the landlord share to the landlord.

A share-crop or cropper relationship, distinguished from a crop-share lease arrangement, is an employment relationship. Often agreements do not adequately distinguish between these two very different types of relationships. The Court of Appeals of North Carolina, in its unpublished decision in *Mabe v. Montague*,[2] discussed the distinction between a cropper and tenant under a crop-share lease. Holding that a landlord-tenant relationship existed, the Court of Appeals further held that the defendant had breached her lease agreement by leasing the land to another person. A tenant owns the crops growing on the land as personal property (that is discussed in Chapter 8). By contrast, a cropper is an employee and has no rights in either the land or the crops growing on it. In *Mabe v. Montague*, the tobacco was the property of the plaintiff as a tenant, subject to any landlord's lien for unpaid rent. Unlike a tenant, an employee (or cropper) does not own the crop and may not sell it.

By contrast, an employee is paid a wage to produce a crop and has no legal interest in the farm and no ownership interest in the crop produced. It is possible for an employee to be paid a share of the crops rather than cash. An employee has no legal interest in the crops until his or her share is set aside at harvest as his or her wages. If the employer fails to pay wages due, generally the employee's only remedy is to sue for breach of the employment contract. For an employee, the employer is responsible for proper withholding of taxes from wages. The wages are considered "earned" income for tax purposes. The employer must withhold from the employee's wages and remit that withholding to the IRS even if the wages are generally paid as his or her share of the crop.

In some share lease arrangements, the landlord exercises so much control over the tenant that the relationship ceases to be a landlord-tenant relationship. Courts and the IRS may successfully recharacterize a share lease agreement as an employment agreement. This usually has serious legal consequences for the landlord who was not really a landlord. It increases the landlord's liability exposure in the event of a tort action arising from any injury on the property. It may make the landlord liable for the tenant's injuries as the tenant is an employee and not a tenant. The tax consequences to both the landowner and the tenant are usually disastrous. This danger is particularly great with oral share lease agreements that have not had professional review by an attorney or a tax advisor.

There are a number of characteristics of a tenant that are not characteristic of an employee. A tenant is entitled to exclusive use and possession of the real estate. A tenant may sue the landlord for trespass if the landlord wrongfully enters the property. The crops belong exclusively to the tenant until divided for payment of rent. If applicable, the landlord may have a lien in the crop. A tenant can deduct his expenses from his income in calculating his taxable income. A tenant pays self-employment tax, in lieu of withheld taxes. Depending upon how much money he or she is making, a tenant may be responsible for making withholding payments to the IRS. The tenant is responsible for injuries to invitees if they are injured due to his poor upkeep of the property.

### Partnership

A share lease agreement may also be recharacterized as a partnership if the landlord exercises too great a role in the management of the farm. This is very similar to recharacterization of a poorly structured crop-share lease as an employment agreement. Whether a faulty share lease agreement is recharacterized as an employment agreement or partnership depends upon the facts in context. The distinction between a share lease agreement and a partnership is important. In a general partnership, all partners are individually liable for all debts and obligations of the partnership. There is also special tax treatment of a partnership (e.g., income and losses of the partnership are passed through to all partners). Oral lease agreements, in particular, raise the danger of recharacterization because obligations of the parties are not clearly spelled out. It is not uncommon for bankruptcy courts to recharacterize share lease agreements as partnerships. This allows the bankruptcy creditors to reach the landowner's assets.

## Inns

Most states do not treat rentals of hotel and motel rooms and short-term vacation rentals as leases under landlord-tenant law. These rentals are usually covered under state innkeeper laws.

## Notes

1  262 N.W. 2d 467, 472-473, 1977 N.D. LEXIS 186 (N.D. 1977).
2  2005 N.C. App. LEXIS 1218 (N.C. Ct. App. 2005).

# Chapter 8

# Personal property

## Introduction

Personal property includes every kind of property that is not real property. The two primary classifications of personal property are tangible and intangible. Items of tangible personal property are called the chattels. Examples of tangible personal property include furniture, livestock, and tractors. Examples of intangible personal property include stocks, bonds, notes payable, patents, copyrights, intellectual property rights, and court judgments. In the United States, the value of intangible personal property exceeds the value of all of real property. Most intangible personal property is derivative of some other property interest, either real property or tangible personal property. The first derivatives traded in the United States were futures contracts in agricultural commodities. These contracts became widely traded in the nineteenth century in the years after the Civil War.

An important distinction between personal property and real property is the ease with which a lender with a security interest in personal property may take the property for nonpayment or other breach of a financing agreement. As is discussed later, a security agreement gives a lender an interest in specific property of a debtor. If the debtor fails to pay, the lender with a secured interest in that property may either take the property or force the sale of property to satisfy the debt. In most states, real property that is security for a debt cannot be taken or sold without some involvement of the judicial system. Personal property that is security for a debt may generally be either seized or sold by the creditor without judicial involvement, unless recovery of the property would create a breach of the peace. Example 8.1 illustrates three scenarios.

Money is a special form of intangible personal property. It is special in the sense that its use as a currency is officially sanctioned by a government. As such, the taxes that apply to sales of intangible personal property do not apply to currency transactions. Bitcoin, despite its name, is not currency since the IRS has ruled that it and other cryptocurrencies are not money.[1] Most money today exists in electronic form in owners' accounts. Coins and paper bills are not themselves money. Coins and paper bills represent certain quantities of money. The metal or paper and ink of which coins and bills are made is tangible personal property. The value in coins and paper bills comes from the money represented by those coins and bills.

**Example 8.1** X State Bank (the Bank) made a farm real estate purchase loan to I. M. A. Deadbeat. It also loaned him money to buy a new four-wheel drive pickup truck and a tractor. Mr. Deadbeat never made a single payment on either loan. To execute on the power of sale under its real estate loan to Mr. Deadbeat, X state law required the Bank to go before a magistrate judge to seek an order allowing the sheriff to sell the property in a foreclosure sale on its behalf. X state law allowed the Bank to seek a deficiency judgment in the same action if the sale did not satisfy the full amount owed to it. As Mr. Deadbeat kept the truck in a locked garage at his personal residence, the Bank also had to go before a magistrate judge to obtain an order to allow the sheriff to open the garage so that it could seize the truck. The tractor was in an open field so the Bank could send its employee with a flatbed trailer to pick it up. If the Bank could not resell either the tractor or the truck for the total amount of the loan plus interest and penalties, it could either privately attempt to collect the remaining debt or go to court to seek a deficiency judgment. Without judicial action, the Bank could not compel Mr. Deadbeat to pay.

Tangible personal property can also be categorized as titled and untitled. Motor vehicles are the classic example of titled personal property. All states require that most motor vehicles be registered with the state and have a title. A proper transfer of such property generally requires that the transfer be registered with the state's department of motor vehicles and a new certificate of title be issued to the buyer of the vehicle. The system ensures that the applicable transfer taxes are collected, vehicle property tax bills are sent to the current owner, and vehicle theft is discouraged. Most farm vehicles such as tractors, combines, and other self-propelled farm vehicles that are not intended for use on roadways are untitled tangible personal property. The value of modern farm equipment often runs into the mid to high six figures. The lack of recorded titles, relative isolation, and lack of security of most farms make farm equipment a tempting target for theft. It is important for farm equipment owners to keep good records of serial numbers and other identifying information to aid recovery of stolen farm equipment.

## Personal property under the Uniform Commercial Code

The Uniform Commercial Code (UCC) deals with the law of commercial transactions involving personal property. It contains eleven articles that deal with the multiple aspects of personal property. This section briefly summarizes the UCC.

Article 2 of the UCC deals specifically with the sale of goods. Goods are items that are tangible, moveable, and identifiable. It may or may not apply to goods associated with real property. For example, if a building or mineral deposit is to be removed by the seller from real property prior to the sale of the real property, the severed building or mineral deposit is covered by Article 2. If the same is to be severed by the buyer, its sale is considered to be included in the sale of the real property. As neither the building nor the mineral deposit has been severed from the real property at the time of the sale of the real property, the building or mineral deposit conveys with the real property. Contracts for the sale of goods under Article 2 of the UCC are covered in Chapter 9.

As discussed in Chapter 6, a fixture is tangible personal property that has become part of the real property by attachment to that property. Some of the characteristics of that personal property may be preserved by making a fixture filing under UCC. A fixture filing ensures that the security interest of a lender in personal property that is to become attached to the land will have priority over the security interest attached to the real property. Example 8.2 illustrates this principle.

---

**Example 8.2** ABC Co. sold a cooling unit to Bob who plans to bolt it to a concrete pad outside his vegetable packing facility. ABC Co. financed the purchase of the unit and required Bob to execute a financing statement. The ABC Co. made a fixture filing with the correct government office in the state and county where the cooling unit was affixed. The XYZ Bank holds a security interest (deed of trust) in Bob's real property, including the building. Bob failed to make his payments to the ABC Co. The ABC Co. sent a truck out and removed the cooling unit from Bob's concrete pad. ABC's employees exercised reasonable care to ensure that the property was not damaged by their removal of the cooling unit. The XYZ Bank immediately demanded that ABC return the cooling unit to the concrete pad outside Bob's building. The XYZ Bank asserted that its security interest in the real property prevented ABC from removing the cooling unit. ABC sent XYZ a copy of its fixture filing. XYZ's attorney confirmed that ABC was within its rights to remove it. Had ABC not made the fixture filing, it would not have been able to remove the cooling unit in response to Bob's nonpayment. Absent the fixture filing, the cooling unit would have become part of the real property, subject to the XYZ Bank's security interest.

---

Article 2A governs leases of goods. Like real property, personal property may be leased. The law that governs leases of personal property is quite different from the law that governs leases of real property. Though Article 2A governs leases of tangible personal property, it is not the only law that governs such leases. State registration and titling laws apply in addition to Article 2A. Titling laws vary greatly from one state to another both in terms of the property covered and in terms of procedure. The manner by which tangible personal property is titled affects how it may be leased. State laws governing consumer transactions and prohibiting unfair trade practices also apply to leases of goods. Goods may be leased by the person who supplies the goods or by a third-party financer. Where the lease is a finance lease, it is typically the case that the right to payment will be sold to someone else. This right to payment is a form of intangible personal property.

Article 3 covers negotiable instruments, a form of intangible personal property. Negotiable instruments are often called commercial paper. The 2002 amendments to Article 3 converted the terms "writing" or "written" to "record" to be consistent with the Uniform Electronic Transactions Act. The 2002 amendments did not authorize electronic negotiable instruments or checks. A bearer instrument is a form of negotiable instrument that may be exchanged for cash by any person who holds it. Some negotiable instruments may be negotiated only by a named person.

Article 4 covers bank deposits, and Article 4A covers funds transfers between banks. Bank deposits are intangible personal property. Bank deposits represent a huge proportion of the wealth in the United States.

Article 5 covers letters of credit. Letters of credit are a form of intangible personal property that are used to facilitate transactions when buyers and sellers do not know each other well or do not trust each other. Letters of credit are often used in international transactions. The buyer of goods will purchase a letter of credit from his bank in favor of the seller of the product. The seller consigns the product to a shipper in return for a bill of lading. The seller then takes the bill of lading and gives it to the bank in return for payment. The bank then takes the bill of lading to the buyer and exchanges it for payment. Letters of credit allow the use of a trusted financial intermediary to facilitate transactions.

Article 6 governs bulk transfers and bulk sales. These are the mass transfers of goods that typically occur upon the liquidation of a business.

Article 7 governs warehouse receipts, bills of lading, and other documents of title. Warehouse receipts are important for transactions in agricultural commodities because warehouse receipts serve as documents of title for those commodities. As agricultural commodities are fungible, warehouse receipts allow owners to track the agricultural commodities that they own that are commingled in large warehouses. Some warehouse receipts are negotiable instruments. This means that the person who holds the warehouse receipt can exchange it for cash. Most documents of title now exist in electronic form and are transferred electronically. Article 7 governs the law by which this is done. Article 7 to a significant degree replaces the common law of bailment. A bailment is a transfer of tangible personal property to the care of another without transferring title. The person who transfers the property is called the "bailor." The person who receives the property is the "bailee." The property is said to have been "bailed." A bailor owes a duty of care to the bailee. Though Article 7 has partially replaced these common laws, many pre-UCC precedents remain viable. This law is closely intertwined with the law of tort. The complexity of this law renders those who would draft their own documents foolish. Those who enter these arrangements with oral agreements are even more foolhardy. Unfortunately, such agreements are common in the agricultural sector. Over the course of his career, the author has seen many farmers incur unnecessary losses as the result of such agreements.

Article 8 governs investment securities. Investment securities include stocks and bonds. Much of the world's wealth is held in this form of intangible personal property. Almost all investment securities are now held in electronic form.

Article 9 governs secured transactions. When the seller sells goods, the seller will often finance the transaction. If the seller does not finance the transaction, the transaction may be financed by a bank or other financial institution. Whoever holds the right to be paid will want to be able to recover the property that was financed if the debtor fails to pay. Article 9 allows for security interests in goods. These goods that serve as security for a debt are called collateral.

Some securities interests such as a landlord's lien for unpaid rent attach to farm products by operation of law. Some financing agreements contain after-acquired property clauses that cause the lender's lien to attach to property acquired after the date upon which the financing agreement was executed. The key to understanding these relationships is understanding when a security interest attached to particular property. That is the point at which the creditor can look to that property to satisfy a debt.

The next step in the analysis is to determine when the security interest was perfected. Perfection of a security interest is necessary to establish priority. Often, when a debtor fails to pay his or her debts, he or she has pledged the same property to more than one lender. If there is not enough money to pay all creditors, existing funds will be allocated to the creditor who perfected first. Article 9 governs how security interests may be perfected. Perfection is usually accomplished by filing a document with the appropriate state, county, or other governmental agency that keeps records. These records are public and are indexed so that other lenders may search them before accepting property as collateral for a debt.

For most goods, the buyer in the ordinary course of business was protected from these security interests. There is an exception for agricultural products: the farm products rule. It is quite possible for the buyer of agricultural products to pay twice—once to the farmer and again to the holder of the security interest. To address this problem, Congress enacted a law that preempts Article 9 and other state law if certain procedures are followed.[2]

---

**Example 8.3** The Wholesome Bread Company bought 5,000 bushels of wheat from Larry Farmer. Unfortunately, Larry was insolvent and could not pay his landlord from whom he rented the land where he grew wheat. Larry's landlord asserted a farm product lien and sought payment of the rent from the Wholesome Bread Company. The Wholesome Bread Company is in a state with a central filing system. It failed to file the required notice with the state's Secretary of State. The landlord had filed an effective notice. The Wholesome Bread Company will be required to pay the landlord.

## Commodity futures and option contracts

Futures contracts and options contracts are regulated by the Commodity Futures Trading Commission (CFTC), a federal agency. It regulates publicly traded commodity futures contracts and option contracts. A futures contract is a form of financial derivative. Options contracts include both puts, the right to sell a futures contract, and calls, the right to buy a futures contract. Futures contracts have been traded for many years; however, publicly traded options contracts have only been allowed by the CFTC since 1982. Agricultural futures contracts were created shortly after the Civil War and were the first derivatives to be publicly traded. These contracts allow a producer to sell a commodity at a fixed price before the harvest date. These contracts allow producers and end users of agricultural commodities to set price ranges that they find acceptable through a process called hedging.

---

**Example 8.4** In November, Mary Farmer was impressed that futures contracts for wheat for July delivery were listed for $5.00 per bushel. She sold July contracts for 10,000 bushels, half of her expected production. Mary's farm is in a dry land wheat region, where rainfall varies greatly from one year to the next. Yields often drop by as much as 50 percent in dry years. By July, it was evident that there was a bumper wheat crop. Cash prices were $2.50 per bushel. Mary delivered the wheat subject to her futures contract and sold the rest of her production for $2.50 per bushel.

---

In Example 8.4, Mary hedged half of her expected crop. She did not hedge the other half because she would have been speculating on a normal crop year. Had she had a crop failure, she would have had to go into the market and buy expensive wheat to meet her contractual obligations. Only producers and end users of commodities can hedge. Other market participants are speculators. Note that the party or parties to the other side of Mary's contracts were speculators who were betting that the price of wheat would rise even further. Because it dropped, they lost money. Speculators make futures markets. Hedging would be impossible without speculators. Most speculators do not take delivery of the commodities in which they speculate. Usually, speculators close out their positions prior to the delivery date, as in Example 8.5.

---

**Example 8.5** Dan Daring bought July futures contracts for $5.00 per bushel in November. That meant that he agreed to pay $5.00 per bushel for wheat for July delivery. As wheat dropped to $2.50 per bushel, he lost $2.50 per bushel when he closed out his position prior to the delivery date.

---

# Intellectual property

## Utility patents

Intellectual property is a form of intangible personal property. With the advent of genetically engineered (GE) crops, intellectual property has taken on great importance for agriculture. The U.S. Supreme Court held in 1980 that patentable inventions may be embodied in living organisms.[3] A crop need not be GE to be protected by a utility patent.[4] Utility patents are very important for companies that sell seed of GE crops. Typically, GE crops contain one or more patented genes.

To obtain a utility patent, the inventor must apply to the U.S. Patent and Trademark Office (USPTO) for a patent on the invention. For a patent to be issued, the invention must be novel and nonobvious. Novel means that the invention is for something new. Nonobvious inventions are those that are not merely trivial improvements over what existed before. Patentable subject matter for utility patents includes processes, machines, articles of manufacture, compositions of matter, and improvements to any of those. Laws of nature; physical phenomena; abstract ideas; works of literature, drama, music or art; and inventions that are either not useful or are offensive to public morality cannot be patented. Commercial use of the invention prior to applying for a patent may make it impossible to obtain patent protection. The United States has a one-year grace period; however, most other countries have no grace period.

The patent application must list what is claimed in clear and definite terms. A typical application for patent on an invention will include multiple claims to cover multiple variants of the invention. The invention must be fully disclosed in the application so that one skilled in art may practice the invention. Utility patents give inventors the exclusive rights to make, use, offer for sale, or sell anything that embodies the patented invention for a period of twenty years from the date of first application. A U.S. patent applies only within the territory of the United States. An inventor who wants patent protection in other countries must apply in each country in which patent protection is desired. The United States is party to the Patent Cooperation Treaty that facilitates this process with participating countries with the common application process.

Utility patent protection is available for GE crops because the company holding the patent created a crop with a genetic makeup that did not exist in nature. *Bacillus thuringiensis* (Bt) is a bacteria found in soil that produces toxins that kill certain insects. Bt genes have been transferred into crops such as corn and cotton where those genes are not naturally found. As this represents an invention that is both novel and nonobvious, it may be protected by a utility patent in its manifestation in corn or cotton. The patent does not prevent an organic farmer from continuing to use Bt as a spray on his corn to control insects.

A person who uses the patented invention without a license from the owner of that invention is liable for infringement of the patent. A person who assists or induces another to infringe a patent may also be liable for patent infringement. In an action brought in federal district court, the owner of the patent may obtain an injunction to prevent further use of the patented invention, including destruction of any infringing goods and equipment used to make those infringing goods. The court is also required to award damages at least equal to a reasonable royalty. In exceptional cases, the court may award attorney fees.

### Plant patents

A person who has either invented or discovered a distinct and new plant variety may apply to the USPTO for a plant patent. Plant patents have been available since Congress enacted legislation creating them in 1932. The inventor must have a clone—an asexually reproduced plant variety—and demonstrate that it can be successfully reproduced by asexual reproduction. Plant patents are used in the horticultural industry where most plants are reproduced from cuttings. Unlike a utility patent, invention is not required. Protection is available for "sports" that occurred naturally so long as those sports were discovered in the cultivated area. Plant patent protection may not be obtained for plants that are not found in cultivated areas. Plant patents are not available for tuber-propagated plants such as potatoes and Jerusalem artichokes. The variety for which plant patent protection is claimed must not have been sold or released to the public more than a year prior to the date of application. Although algae and macro-fungi are considered plants for which plant patent protection is available, bacteria are not considered plants for the purposes of plant patent protection. Like a utility patent, a plant patent provides exclusive protection for twenty years from the date of first application. Plant patents may not be obtained in varieties that are reproduced by seed (that is, sexually).

### Design patents

The USPTO issues design patents for ornamental designs. The design may be for a part of the object or the entire object. A design patent is different from a utility patent in that a design patent protects the way something looks rather than the use or function of the object. A design that is dictated primarily by the function of the object may not be patented using a design patent. Design patents are granted for fourteen years from the date of grant. The design of farm equipment, to the extent not primarily functional, may be protected by design patents.

### Plant variety protection

The Plant Variety Protection Act (PVPA) provides protection for varieties of sexually reproduced or tuber-propagated plants that are novel and distinct. Protection is provided to whoever breeds, develops, or discovers those varieties. Certificates of protection are issued by the Plant Variety Protection Office of the Agricultural Marketing Service, an agency of the U.S. Department of Agriculture. To qualify for protection, the variety must be distinct from other varieties. It must be true breeding through successive generations.

Unlike varieties protected by utility patents, for which the plant may not be reproduced at all, a farmer may save enough seed to plant her or his own farm. However, he or she may not sell excess seed of protected varieties. A grain handler who cleans seed of a protected variety on behalf of a farmer who is not authorized to plant it may, along with the farmer, be liable for infringement. Protection under the PVPA is enforced through both injunctive relief and monetary damages. The court may award attorney fees to a successful owner of a protected variety.

---

**Example 8.6** John grows a variety of corn that is protected by a certificate of protection under the PVPA. Each year, he saves enough seed to plant his farm the following year. Joe grows a variety of corn that is protected by a utility patent. Joe asked John why the seed company did not sue him for saving seed. John said, "No problem, it's legal to save seed for your own farm." Joe saved seed to plant on his farm the following year. The seed company sent him a letter demanding that he immediately plow under the corn grown from saved seed or be sued for willful infringement. Joe spent $500 per hour getting educated by his intellectual property attorney about the difference between certificates of protection under the PVPA and utility patents. He plowed up his corn to comply with the demand letter and avoid a lawsuit.

---

## Trade secret

A trade secret is another form of intellectual property. A trade secret is anything of value to a business that is not generally known by the public. To maintain a trade secret, a business must take steps to keep it secret. This may include limiting the number of employees with access to the information and requiring those employees to sign nondisclosure contracts or agreements. Some trade secrets are quite famous, such as the formula for Coca Cola®. Unlike patents and protection under the PVPA, trade secret protection is primarily a matter of state law. Trade secret law varies significantly from one state to another. So long as trade secrets are kept confidential, they last forever. The formula for Coca Cola has been kept as a trade secret for more than a century.

## Trademark

A trademark is the name under which a product or service is sold. Both federal and state trademarks are available. State trademarks are much easier and cheaper to obtain than federal trademarks; however, state trademarks provide protection only in the state that issued them. Federal trademarks provide protection throughout the territory of the United States. Federal trademarks are granted by the USPTO. As with patents, if one wants protection in another country, one must apply for trademark protection in that country. Closely related to trademarks are service marks. Service marks protect the name under which one does business rather than the name of one's product or service.

A trademark keeps a competitor from using one's name. To receive trademark protection, one must demonstrate that the name for which one is seeking protection is identified in the public's mind with the product to which it is connected. Particularly when seeking federal trademark protection, it may be necessary to provide the opinion of an expert who is able to prove the association between the name and the public. This is often done through consumer surveys. A trademark may be a word or words, a picture or logo, a symbol, design, even a sound, or a combination thereof. Trademarks are not allowed in names that are merely descriptive of the product. There are limitations on the ability to use surnames and geographically descriptive terms as trademarks. Surnames and geographically descriptive terms may be allowed as trademarks with a proper showing of association with a product or service. Names that are obscene may generally not be used as trademarks. A trademark that is likely to cause confusion with other marks will not be registered.

Unlike patents, trademarks have potentially infinite life. For federally registered trademarks, there are maintenance documents that must be periodically filed with the USPTO. If the documents are not filed, the trademark will be cancelled by the USPTO. As long as the trademark continues to be used, it remains valid and enforceable. It is up to the trademark owner to defend it by stopping infringement and dilution. This is done by first asking the party infringing or diluting the trademark to stop. If the party infringing or diluting the trademark refuses to stop, it may be necessary to bring a lawsuit against that party to obtain an injunction to stop their infringement or dilution. There are some actions or inactions on the part of the trademark owner that can invalidate the trademark. If the owner of the trademark quits using it, it may be lost through disuse. If the trademark comes to be used generically to mean a particular class of products, the trademark can be lost as well. For this reason, trademark owners often send cease-and-desist letters to those using their trademarks generically.

Infringement of a trademark occurs when one who is not the owner of the trademark uses the trademark on goods similar to those sold by the trademark owner. Injunctive relief and damages are both available for infringement. It is possible for two different companies to use the same name without infringement if the companies are in different lines of business.

**Example 8.7** Toyota® made automobiles and sold them under the name Lexus. Mead Data Central operated an electronic database service for attorneys and accountants that was named Lexis. Mead Data Central®

sued Toyota for trademark dilution. The U.S. Court of Appeals for the Second Circuit reversed a finding of trademark dilution by the district court.[5] The Second Circuit held that, given the great difference between the products covered by the marks, the sophistication of Mead Data Central's customers, and the lack of predatory intent, a blurring of the marks in the minds of members of the public was unlikely.

## Copyright

Copyright protection is a form of intellectual property in written words, lyrics and music, works of drama, and art. Copyright along with utility patent protection is also used to protect different aspects of computer software. The U.S. Copyright Office is a unit of the Library of Congress. It is not necessary to register a copyright with the Copyright Office to have copyright protection. An author or creator of a copyrighted work has copyright protection as soon as the work is fixed in a tangible medium of expression, such as written on paper or typed on a computer.

Registration is, however, important if one wishes to sue an infringer. Copyright infringement consists of copying a copyrighted work. Works that are independently created, even if similar to a copyrighted work, do not infringe the copyright in that work. Copyrights have a very long life. Copyrights generally last seventy years beyond the life of the person who created the work.

**Example 8.8** When you buy this book (if you buy a paper copy), you will own your copy. You can read it, mark in it, give it away, and even sell it. What you may not do is copy it and distribute it, either in paper or on the Internet. I own the copyright in the work itself and have licensed it to the publisher. If you do so, the publisher will very likely sue you for copyright infringement.

**Example 8.9** Durwood bought a state-of-the-art tractor that is fully computerized. He would like to fix it himself. He copied the software that operates it so that he could interface his own diagnostic software with it. By doing so, he has very likely infringed the copyright that the tractor manufacturer holds in its software.

## Derivative interests in subsurface real property

A mineral right or right to oil and gas is an interest in real property. Ownership of these interests in subsurface rights is typically transferred by deed, just as ownership of the entire parcel would be transferred. Though these are transfers of interest in real property, most transfers of interests in the subsurface are derivative of the real property. What is created is some form of intangible personal property. Though this sounds rather theoretical, it has very important practical consequences. Enterprises engaged in the extraction of minerals and oil and gas are often subject to severe financial gyrations. How the subsurface is owned by those enterprises will determine whether the minerals or oil and gas are an asset of the bankruptcy estate or whether they remain an asset of someone else. This determines who gets the property when someone goes into bankruptcy.

In contrast to sales of the subsurface as evidenced by a deed, a lease of the subsurface through an oil and gas lease creates only an intangible personal property right. In most states, the oil and gas is owned by the lessor until it is severed. Should the oil and gas production company file for bankruptcy protection, only the lease, not the oil and gas itself, would be part of the bankruptcy estate. In the oil and gas industry, leases are routinely bought and sold. Some interests in the subsurface are intangible personal property that do not even rise to the level of a lease. Some interests in the subsurface are merely the right to profits should the minerals or oil and gas ever be extracted. These rights are sometimes called a profit à prendre.

## Notes

1  IRS. *Notice 2014-21*. Retrieved June 8, 2018, www.irs.gov/pub/irs-drop/n-14-21.pdf
2  7 U.S.C. § 1631 (2014).
3  *Diamond v. Chakrabarty*, 447 U.S. 303 (1980).
4  J. E. M. *Ag Supply, Inc. v. Pioneer Hi-Bred International, Inc.*, 534 U.S. 124 (2001).
5  *Mead Data Central, Inc. v. Toyota Motor Sales, U.S.A., Inc.*, 875 F.2d 1026, 1989 U.S. App. LEXIS 6644 (2d Cir. 1989).

# Chapter 9

# Contracts for the sale of goods

## Introduction

Article 2 of the UCC governs the sale of goods. "Goods" means all personal property that is tangible and moveable at the time of identification in the contract for sale. This includes unborn animals, growing crops, and other identified things attached to realty.[1] Identified things attached to the realty include minerals, and oil and gas, to be severed by the seller.[2] Those things not described in the UCC (2002) § 2-107(1) that are to be severed by either the buyer or the seller, without serious damage to the land, and timber to be cut, are also encompassed within the sale of goods under UCC (2002) § 2-107(2). Although these things attached to the land are sale of goods and not a sale of an interest in the realty, the sale is not effective until the thing attached to the land is actually severed from the land. As adopted by the states, Article 2 varies somewhat from one state to another. Example 9.1 illustrates property that currently exists and is, therefore, a good.

---

**Example 9.1** Eric signed the contract to buy a foal from Constellation Stables. The foal was conceived three months earlier but has not yet been born. Because the foal exists, albeit unborn, it is a good. For that reason, this is a contract for the sale of goods under Article 2 of the UCC.

---

Article 2 is limited in scope. Article 2 does not apply to contracts to sell. A present contract to sell "future" goods, defined as goods that are not both existing and identified at the time of signing the sales contract, is considered a contract to sell, not a contract for the sale of goods. Article 2 does not apply to the transfers of property resulting as gifts, security interests in property, or leases or bailments. These are not sales. Example 9.2 illustrates property that is identified but does not yet exist. Annual crops are considered existing once the seeds are deposited in the ground.

> **Example 9.2** Eric signed the contract to buy a foal from Constellation Stables. The contract specifies that the foal will be the offspring of Gracious Mare and the stallion, King's Ransom. Gracious Mare has not yet been bred to King's Ransom. As the foal does not yet exist, it cannot be a good. This is not a contract for the sale of goods under Article 2 of the UCC.

## Statute of Frauds

The UCC Statute of Frauds requires that a contract for sale of goods for an amount of $500 or more be in writing to be enforceable. The writing required is minimal. The requirement consists of the identity of the goods, the quantity term, and the signature of the party to be charged. The party to be charged is the party against whom enforcement is sought. Other terms such as price may be established from extrinsic sources. For regularly traded agricultural commodities, that is easy to establish by reference to market prices. It is even possible to have a contract with an open price term so long as there is a mechanism for establishing the price. The contract is not enforceable beyond the quantity shown in the writing. Example 9.3 illustrates a contract with an open price term.

> **Example 9.3** The Big Milling Company contracted with the Big Grain Company to buy 100,000 bushels of spring wheat for delivery on June 15. The contract stated that the price was to be spot price, Minneapolis, on the date of delivery. As there is an adequate mechanism for setting the price, the contract is enforceable.

Quantity can be defined in the contract as output and still meet the requirements of the Statute of Frauds. This is a common type of contract between agricultural producers and their buyers. It is often called an "acre contract." Under an acre contract, the buyer agrees to buy and the seller agrees to sell all the output of a particular crop from a particular acreage or field. This type of contract is beneficial to farmers because the buyer bears the risk of a crop failure. If there is a crop failure and nothing is harvested, the farmer has not breached her or his contract. This is in contrast to a contract for a particular number of bushels. This type of contract is often called a "bushel contract." Should the farmer have a crop failure, it is the responsibility of the farmer to go into the market and buy a sufficient quantity of the crop to meet his contractual obligation to the buyer. If the crop failure was widespread, this can be quite costly for the farmer.

Course of dealing and usage of trade may be used to supplement or explain the terms of the written contract. The course of dealing is the history of dealings between the parties. Usage of trade is the general practice in a particular line of business. Use of course of dealing and usage of trade to supplement or explain contract terms may be barred by specific terms of the written contract that explain a different meaning or intent of the parties.

---

**Example 9.4** Bill signed a contract with the Kisco County Elevator to deliver 5,000 bushels of wheat on June 15. That year, wheat production exceeded all previous records. No elevator within 750 miles of Bill's farm had any capacity to receive additional wheat, and the railroad had a three-month backlog due to its oil hauling business. The Kisco County Elevator had no space and refused delivery when Bill tendered 5,000 bushels. As a result, Bill had to store his wheat on his farm where it lost quality due to his lack of adequate storage. When he finally sold, he sold it for substantially less than the market price on June 15. He sued the Kisco County Elevator for breach of contract. Kisco defended by arguing that the contract was not valid because it contained no price term. The court ruled that the price term could be supplied as a publicly reported market price and held Kisco in breach of contract. Damages were calculated as the difference between what Bill sold his wheat for and what he would have received on June 15 had Kisco honored its contract, plus incidental damages that include added transportation and storage costs.

---

Under certain other circumstances, a contract for sale of goods will be enforceable even if it does not meet the formal requirements of the Statutes of Frauds. If there is a completed transaction for which payment has been made and accepted or the goods have been offered and accepted, the Statutes of Frauds does not apply. There is also an exception to the Statute of Frauds for specially manufactured goods. For the exception to apply, the goods must not be suitable for sale to another buyer in the ordinary course of business, and circumstances must reasonably indicate that the goods are for a particular buyer. The seller must have made a substantial beginning on manufacture of the goods.

Any contract that is admitted in pleadings or otherwise by the party against whom enforcement is sought is enforceable even if not in writing. However, that contract will not be enforced beyond the quantity of goods in the defendant's admission.

### Exception to the Statute of Frauds for contracts between merchants

If there is a sale between merchants, the requirements of the Statute of Frauds are met if, within a reasonable time, there is a written confirmation to the party to be charged, the party to be charged has reason to know the contents of the confirmation, and the party to be charged fails to object to the confirmation within ten days of receiving it. A merchant is a person who regularly deals in a specific type of good. That person is a merchant for that good only. This exception to the Statute of Frauds requirement of a written contract is called "the merchant's exception." If one merchant sends a written confirmation of an oral agreement to another merchant within a reasonable time and the other merchant does not object within ten days, the oral agreement is enforceable according to the terms in the confirmation. The UCC defines "merchant" as a person who deals in goods of the kind or otherwise, by his or her occupation, holds him- or herself out as having knowledge or skill peculiar to the practices or goods involved in the transaction. States vary as to whether a farmer is considered a "merchant" under the UCC.

---

**Example 9.5** In December, a representative of the Kisco County Elevator called Arthur, a wheat farmer in a state that considers farmers to be merchants, and negotiated a contract to buy 50,000 bushels of Arthur's wheat for $3.50 per bushel for June delivery. In May, five months after making the oral contract with Arthur in December, the Kisco County Elevator mailed Arthur a confirmation by first class mail that included all of the contract terms. Arthur received the confirmation but tossed it in the trash without opening it. By June, the market price of wheat had risen to $5.00 per bushel. Arthur sold his wheat to another elevator. Kisco sued Arthur for the difference between the market price and the contract price. In his defense, Arthur argued that he never read the confirmation and that the phone call was a mere inquiry that resulted in no agreement. He also argued that five months was an unreasonable period of time to wait to send a confirmation. Most courts would hold that whether Arthur opened the confirmation or even actually received it is no defense so long as the confirmation was correctly addressed and delivered by a reliable means. First class mail is presumed to be reliable unless there is actual proof of misdelivery. However, five months is probably an unreasonable time for a merchant to wait to send a confirmation. The Statute of Frauds in most states, under these facts, would bar enforcement of the contract. Note that had Arthur admitted to the contract in his pleadings or by any other means, Kisco could have enforced the contract for whatever quantity he admitted to.

---

## Merchants

The policy considerations for the special rules for merchants are that the rules governing merchants should reflect the manner in which merchants actually conduct their business. For that reason, there are other provisions specific to merchants that are discussed in this section.

In addition to the merchants' exception to the Statute of Frauds, there are other special rules in Article 2 of the UCC governing merchants. A merchant may make a firm offer. A firm offer is an offer that is held open for either a period of time specified by the merchant in the offer or, if no time is specified in the offer, for no more than three months. What makes this unique is that the offer need not be supported by consideration of value. For non-merchants, consideration would be required to keep an offer open for a specific period of time.

As discussed in Chapter 5, the general rule is that the addition of terms to acceptance terminates the original offer and renders the acceptance a counteroffer. No contract is formed unless the counter-offer is accepted. This is not the case for dealings between merchants. Additional terms and acceptance in dealings between merchants is treated as a conditional proposal for additional or different terms. The additional or different terms become part of the contract unless the original offer was limited to the terms of the offer, the new or different terms materially alter the original offer, or the maker of the original offer makes notice to the other party within a reasonable time that the new additional terms are unacceptable. Conduct by merchants is sufficient to establish a contract for the sale of goods even though the writings themselves do not firmly establish a contract.

In Chapter 5, it was noted that contract modifications require consideration in the same manner as the original contract. This is not true for modification of contracts for the sale of goods between merchants. There are limitations on this where the original contract prohibited modification or rescission except by a signed writing.

## Other features of contracts for the sale of goods

A party to the contract for the sale of goods may delegate his or her duties under the contract to another person. This does not relieve the original party of his or her responsibilities. Contracts for the sale of goods may contain terms prohibiting such assignments or delegations. The non-delegating party to the contract may demand assurances from the assignee. If adequate assurances are not provided, the non-delegating party may treat the contract as breached.

There are two implied warranties—a warranty of merchantability and a warranty of fitness for a particular purpose—found in contracts for the sale of goods. The implied warranty of merchantability warrants that the goods are of the type generally acceptable to the trade. To be merchantable, the goods must be of the type and quality that are generally traded in the particular line of business. In agriculture and food businesses, any food or feed product that is adulterated as defined by the Federal Food, Drug, and Cosmetic Act[3] is not a merchantable product. The Federal Food, Drug, and Cosmetic Act prohibits disclaiming this warranty. Article 2 provides alternative language that states may use to extend these implied warranties to third-party beneficiaries. The narrowest alternative limits application of these implied warranties to the buyer's immediate family or household. The other two alternatives are considerably broader. The implied warranty of fitness for a particular purpose applies if the party providing the goods has reason to know that the other party has a particular purpose for the goods. Given such knowledge, the party providing the goods impliedly warrants that the goods are suitable for that purpose.

In general, both of the implied UCC warranties may be disclaimed if disclaimed by clear language. Such a clause sometimes states that the goods are sold "as is." As noted above, there is an exception for adulterated food and feed products. Federal law prohibits the sale of adulterated food and feed products.

There may also be express warranties in a contract for the sale of goods. In agricultural transactions, these warranties are often for a specific grade or variety of agricultural products. There may also be warranties that the product meets certain standards such that it meets the requirements for being labeled as "certified organic."

---

**Example 9.6** MegaEgg sold surplus fresh eggs to an egg breaker that made dried, powdered eggs for use in university cafeterias. MegaEgg knew that the eggs would ultimately be used in university cafeterias. MegaEgg made an implied warranty of merchantability that the eggs were not adulterated. As MegaEgg was aware that the eggs were intended for use for human rather than animal consumption, it also made an implied warranty of fitness for a particular purpose that the eggs contained no off-flavors that would be objectionable to humans. Off-flavors are not adulteration that would violate the warranty of merchantability. Off-flavored eggs are perfectly salable if used in animal feed.

---

Other provisions of Article 2 govern the respective obligations of buyer and seller for transportation of goods between them. These terms govern who bears the risk of loss of the goods while they are in transport. The party with the risk of loss is the party with the insurable interest in the goods. The party with the insurable interest is the party with the obligation to buy insurance that covers the possibility of loss of the goods.

## Remedies for breach

When the non-breaching party is the seller, the UCC allows her or him several options for seeking damages from the buyer. First, if the buyer breaches before the seller has delivered the goods, the seller may resell the goods and then sue for the difference between the original contract price and the resale price plus adjustments for net expenses incurred in the resale. Second, the seller may choose not to resell the goods and bring an action for damages against the buyer based on the difference between the contract price and the market price for such goods at the time and place of tender (plus expenses). Third, in cases where damages would be inadequate to place the seller in as good a position as he or she would have been had the contract been performed, the seller may sue to recover lost profits from the buyer. This remedy is often used by "volume sellers." A volume seller is a person or company that is in the business of selling large quantities of the commodity that is the subject matter of the contract. Typical grain dealers would be volume sellers.

There are remedies available to a buyer in the case of non-delivery or non-conforming goods. First, the buyer can "cover," which means that he or she can buy substitute goods from another source and then seek as damages the difference between the original contract price and the cover price plus incidental expenses. To cover, the buyer must first have rejected the nonconforming goods. Second, if the buyer decides to accept nonconforming goods, he or she may give notice of nonconformity, keep the goods, and then sue for damages based on breach of warranty. If the time for making delivery has not expired, the seller must be given an opportunity to cure the breach by substituting conforming goods.

The "perfect tender" rule applies to contracts for the sale of goods. There is an important distinction between contracts for the sale of goods and other types of contracts. Substantial compliance is all that is required for contracts that are not for the sale of goods. The perfect tender rule means that the goods the buyer provides must exactly meet the definition of the goods as stated in the contract. If the seller provides nonconforming goods, the buyer is entitled to treat that as a breach of contract. That is true even though the seller provided more valuable goods as a substitute for the goods specified in the contract. If the seller does not have the goods specified in the contract and needs to make a substitution, the seller must obtain permission from the buyer to do so prior to making delivery. This is very important in markets such as those for produce where the commodity is perishable and prices fluctuate widely over a short period. There are considerable incentives for buyers to avoid contracts where the price has changed adversely to them. Nonconforming goods give buyers that opportunity.

---

**Example 9.7** Ian Builder ordered ceramic floor tiles for a house that he was building. He noticed that the tile that arrived were of a different shade of blue than the tiles required in his contract with Neal Nitpicky, for whom he was building the house. As a buyer of goods, the perfect tender rule entitled Ian to reject the shipment of tiles and hold the seller in breach. If Ian had accepted the shipment and included them in the house, he would not have been in breach of his construction contract with Neal. A construction contract is a service contract that requires only substantial compliance.

## Products liability

There are several legal theories that plaintiffs use to sue in products liability cases. If the theory focuses on the product and its characteristics, the theory is breach of warranty, which is a contract-based remedy. If the action focuses on the conduct of the seller or manufacturer, the theory is negligence or strict liability, which are tort actions.

Most products liability actions are based upon the implied warranties discussed earlier: warranties of merchantability and fitness for a particular purpose. No statement of any kind is required to create these implied warranties. A warranty that goods are merchantable is implied in every contract for the sale of goods, if the seller is a merchant in those goods. An implied warranty can also arise from usage of the trade. In addition, when the seller knows that the buyer is relying on the seller's knowledge and knows the purpose for which the buyer is seeking the product, the seller warrants that the goods are fit for the particular purpose for which the buyer intends to use them. As noted above, a food or feed product that is adulterated under the Federal Food, Drug, and Cosmetic Act violates the implied warranty of merchantability.

There are certain contract defenses that a defendant in a products liability case can make when the claim sounds in contract rather than in tort. Possible defenses to a contract claim of breach of warranty include lack of privity of contract, disclaimer of warranties, and obvious defects. Historically, privity of contract—the contractual relationship between the buyer and seller—was a significant barrier to suits by consumers against manufacturers. At common law, consumers were required to have a contractual relationship with the manufacturer as a precondition for bringing a products liability suit against the manufacturer. Typically, the consumer purchased the product from a retailer and had no contractual relationship with the manufacturer. Third parties, such as children and guests, injured by a product they did not personally buy, had no contractual relationship with either the retailer or the manufacturer. As noted above, Article 2 of the UCC provides alternatives to states for extending the reach of those protected by implied warranties to third-party beneficiaries. At the narrowest, all states have extended protection of these implied warranties to immediate family members and members of the household of the person who bought the product. The person who bought the product does not have to be in privity of contract with the manufacturer so long as he or she bought the product from somebody in the chain of commerce.

Regarding the breach of warranty theory, two kinds of warranties accompany the sale of goods. An express warranty results from plain statements made by the seller about the goods. It may be oral or written, but it does not include representations made during the sales process that may not be totally true but are not stated strongly enough to constitute a warranty. This sort of sales talk is called "puffing" and cannot be the basis for claims of breach. Unfortunately, what is puffing and what is a warranty is not always clear.

**Example 9.8** The XYZ Feed Company sold dairy cattle feed. Its sales people were fond of telling customers that their feed resulted in higher butterfat milk than any other feed on the market. Larry's neighbor had cows that produced higher butterfat milk using feed produced by a different company. Furious, Larry demanded that the XYZ Feed Company pay him for profits lost over the two years that he had used their feed. Larry has no basis for a lawsuit because the statements of the sales people were puffing, not an express warranty.

A seller can attempt to limit or modify the implied warranties by disclaiming with language such as "as is" or "with all faults." To be effective, such disclaimers must be conspicuous but will not be effective if the limitation is unconscionable. A disclaimer of liability for personal injury from consumer goods is "prima facie unconscionable." A disclaimer is also an ineffective defense against fraud (e.g., concealment of a material defect). As noted above, the warranty of merchantability for an adulterated food or feed product cannot be disclaimed. Such an adulterated food or feed product cannot be sold and should be handled in a manner that ensures its destruction.

Obvious defects are generally not subject to implied warranties. The UCC provides that if the purchaser has examined the product or refused to inspect it after requested to do so by the seller, no implied warranty is created regarding defects that would have been discovered by such examination. This is a very important exception to the warranties implied in UCC contracts for the sale of goods. This exception provides important protection to sellers of used equipment and other used goods.

**Example 9.9** James Eggs sold eggs contaminated with a deadly strain of *E. coli*. Such eggs are considered adulterated under the Federal Food, Drug, and Cosmetic Act and, as an adulterated food product, violate the warranty of merchantability. The eggs were purchased by a wholesaler that resold them to a retail grocery chain. James Eggs, the wholesaler, and the retail grocer are all liable under products liability principles.

## Notes

1  UCC (2002) § 2-105(1).
2  UCC (2002) § 2-107(1).
3  21 U.S.C. §§ 1–2201 (2013).

# Chapter 10

# Secured transactions in real and personal property

## Introduction

A security interest in property is an interest that allows the holder of that interest to either take the property or cause the property to be sold in the event that the owner of the property fails to pay a debt. The law of secured transactions is extremely complex. The purpose of this chapter is to acquaint the reader with some of the issues and questions that anyone involved in these transactions should ask his or her attorney.

The first important division in the law of secured transactions is between those interests in real property and those in personal property. As one would expect, security interests in real property tend to be of longer duration than those in personal property. The second major division in secured transactions is between those that arise automatically by operation of law and those that are created by formal means. These divisions are found in the security interests that exist in both real and personal property.

## Security interests in real property

### Formal security interests

Formal security interests in real property are intended to secure repayment of the debt based upon the value of the real property. The first document is likely to be a financing statement that is the contract between the lender and the debtor. The financing statement contains both monetary and nonmonetary terms of the arrangement. Monetary terms include the amount owed, the interest rate, the due date, and amount of each payment. Typically, payments are made monthly or annually. For residential loans, monthly payments are customary. For farmland, payments are usually annual, with the payment date set to follow the expected sale date of the crop. For certain farmers, particularly dairies that sell on a regular basis to one buyer, the buyer of the milk may deduct the amount due from the farmer's milk check and remit it directly to the lender. For dairies, the farm loan payments are set to coincide with the dates of milk checks. Nonmonetary terms in a financing statement often include obligations of the debtor to maintain buildings and fences, to maintain soil fertility, to farm in a husband-like manner, to control noxious weeds, to maintain insurance coverage, to pay taxes, and to take all other measures necessary to maintain the lender's value in the collateral. Breach of any of these nonmonetary terms is called a nonmonetary default. Most financing statements for secured transactions involving both real and personal property contain an acceleration clause that makes all payments under the financing statement due and payable immediately upon either nonpayment, a transfer of the collateral, or other nonmonetary default. Some financing statements also contain penalties for early repayment. Some of these provisions may be restricted or limited by federal or state law, particularly for residential transactions. Some provisions in financing statements may be required by federal or state law.

The second document in a secured transaction is a document to be filed with the land records office that provides evidence of the security interest in the property. It is this filing that gives the lender its priority. This document must meet the requirements for filing. At the closing of any loan on real property, there are typically many other documents in addition to those described above; however, they do not create a security interest in real property. A properly filed document that evidences a security interest gives the lender a security interest that is senior and superior to most subsequent creditors.

Most formal security interests in real property are evidenced by a mortgage or a deed of trust. A "mortgage" is a two-party security interest in real property. The "mortgagor" is the borrower and owner of the property. The "mortgagee" is the lender. A "deed of trust" is evidence of a three-party security interest in real property. The borrower is the "grantor." The lender is the "beneficiary," and the third party is the "trustee." Both types of security interests in real property are commonly called mortgages. Which type of security interest is used depends upon whether the state where the property is located is a title theory state or lien theory state. In a lien theory state, the borrower retains both legal and equitable title, and the lender has a lien on the property. In a title theory state, the borrower transfers legal title to the lender. The practical consequence of this esoteric body of law for the lender is that title theory states do not allow the owner of legal title to bid at the foreclosure sale. As the only bidder at most foreclosure sales is often the lender, that means that many foreclosures would fail for lack of a bidder if the lender could not bid. To solve this problem, a third party is introduced into the transaction to hold legal title to the property. This third party is a trustee who exercises the right of foreclosure in the event of the borrower's default. This allows the lender who is the beneficiary of the deed of trust to bid at the foreclosure sale.

In a slight majority of states, mortgages and deeds of trust may contain a "power of sale" clause. In the absence of such a clause, the only way to foreclose on the property in the event of a default is to bring a formal judicial action before a court. A power of sale clause allows the lender to foreclose and conduct the sale without judicial involvement. Some states that allow use of this procedure require that a magistrate or other official review the foreclosure before it can proceed. The purpose of interposing a magistrate in the process is to prevent fraud and overreaching by the lender. Foreclosures under powers of sale are much faster than judicial foreclosures.

---

**Example 10.1** Harry bought a farm using credit. His mortgage contained a power of sale clause. Through a clerical error, his lender failed to credit his account with his annual payment. Pursuant to state law, his lender published a notice of sale in the legal paper of record for the county in which Harry's farm was located. Harry never read the notice of sale. In accord with the terms of the notice of sale, his lender conducted a public auction of Harry's farm. Under state law, Harry's equity of redemption expired when the hammer fell. Though Harry may have a tort action against his lender, his farm along with all improvements to it is gone forever.

---

Reasons why landowners borrow money vary greatly. Most initial purchases of land require borrowing money to complete the purchase. Landowners may also borrow money to finance improvements to the property or to use the money in other areas of their operation. It is not uncommon to find properties that are subject to second and even third mortgages. The first mortgage has the highest priority, the second is below the first, and so on. In the event that the foreclosure sale produces insufficient funds to pay all the creditors, the creditors with the highest priority get paid first. The costs of sale such as sheriff's fees and the auctioneer's fee are considered priority items and are paid before any creditors are paid.

Some landowners secure lines of credit with their lenders to finance operations. The amount owed on a line of credit will go up and down as a landowner borrows and repays. Lines of credit typically contain provisions that put caps on the total amount of money that can be borrowed. Lines of credit often contain a demand clause that allows the lender to require that all money owed be paid immediately. During economic recessions, it is not uncommon for banks to call in their lines of credit. This is often a reason why farms are forced to file bankruptcy during times of economic stress. Lines of credit are secured in the same way as any other real estate debt, through mortgages or deeds of trust.

Law applicable to secured transactions in real property varies greatly from one state to another. Many states provide borrowers with more rights where the interest in the property is a purchase-money security interest. This means that the money borrowed was used to purchase the property. States also vary greatly as to whether a "deficiency judgment" is allowed after foreclosure. It is common that the money received from a foreclosure is insufficient to repay the money owed. Some states allow a lender to seek a judgment for any money that remains unpaid after the foreclosure. Some states do not allow a deficiency judgment if the seller who was the previous owner of the property financed the sale. Other states do not allow deficiency judgment where the property is the debtor's principal residence.

### Other priority interests in real property

In addition to security interests formally created in real property, some interests may attach by operation of law. For example, judgments in legal actions against the landowner and unrelated to the property may attach to the property, giving the judgment holder a priority claim. Some states require a filing before a judgment attaches to real property. Trades people who do work on the property often have an automatic lien for any unpaid amounts due them. Filing to perfect the lien may eventually be necessary; however, for some period of time, the lien affords priority without filing. As such liens are not in the public record, it may be difficult to know that they exist.

---

**Example 10.2** Harry hired Donny to make extensive repairs to the barn on his farm. The total bill was $20,000, none of which Harry paid. Harry sold the farm to Betty three weeks after the work on the barn was complete. Under state law, Donny had 180 days after he completed the work to make a filing to perfect his workman's lien in the farm. He filed three months after he completed the work. For that reason, Betty's closing attorney failed to find the lien. Betty purchased owners' title insurance. When Donny threatened to bring a judicial action to force a sale of the farm to obtain payment, Betty referred the matter to her title insurance carrier. Her title insurance carrier paid $20,000 to Donny to release the lien on the farm. If Betty's title insurance carrier can find Harry, it can sue him to recover the money as Harry violated the warranty against encumbrances under the general warranty deed that he signed.

---

## Security interests in personal property

Creating a security interest in personal property has similarities to creating a security interest in real property. As noted in the section on security interests in real property, many of the provisions of the financing statements are the same. First, there is a contract between the borrower and the lender that is evidenced in a financing statement. Second, there is some filing (a UCC-1) that provides evidence and public notice of the security interest that was created in the personal property. The UCC-1 is used exclusively for security interests in personal property. The UCC-1 contains the debtor's name and address, the creditor's name and address, and a description of the collateral. The description of the collateral can be very general and may even include property acquired after the date of the

UCC-1. Security interests under Article 9 of the UCC often contain an "after-acquired property" clause. An after-acquired property clause gives the lenders security interest in a property that the business acquires after the original loan was made. Such clauses can complicate borrowing from a different lender.

---

**Example 10.3** Harry decided to add a retail local food store to his farm operation. To obtain operating capital, Harry obtained a line of credit from the XYZ Bank. The line of credit was secured by a mortgage that included an after-acquired property clause that included all subsequently acquired real and personal property. Harry later bought a tractor, the purchase of which was financed by the ABC Finance Company. The ABC Finance Company made a UCC filing to secure its collateral in the tractor. Unfortunately, the filing was, in error, made in the wrong county. As the ABC Finance Company failed to establish priority, the security interest of the XYZ Bank attached to the tractor. Should Harry not be able to pay his debts and the available funds are less than required to pay both XYZ Bank and the ABC Finance Company, the XYZ Bank will be paid first out of any proceeds from the sale of the tractor.

---

Article 9 of the UCC governs secured transactions that involve collateral. Collateral is any property subject to a security interest. Collateral may be literally any type of property. Real property and both tangible and intangible personal property can be collateral. A secured party is the person who has a security interest in collateral. There are some types of personal property that cannot serve as collateral. Such property is usually intangible personal property that contains provisions under the instrument that created it that prevents assignment of the property. Many smaller businesses organize as limited liability companies (LLCs). LLCs are discussed in Chapter 14. Many LLCs contain an anti-assignment clause in the operating agreement. Some courts have held that those anti-assignment provisions prevent security interests from attaching to ownership interests in LLCs.

One of the difficulties that arises with financing statements is ensuring that the correct name of the debtor is listed on the financing statement. This is a particular problem where a business is operated under a corporate name. Having the incorrect name on the financing statement may cause the lender to be an unsecured creditor. Whether the creditor is actually rendered unsecured depends upon the extent of the error and state precedent.

One way to divide security interests is on the basis of whether the interest is a purchase-money security interest. A purchase-money security interest arises when the seller of goods or software[1] provided part or all of the financing for the buyer's purchase. The consignor in a consignment arrangement is considered to have a purchase-money security interest in the consigned property. Consignment is a common way to sell used farm equipment and other property. Typically, the consignor transfers possession of the property to the consignee who holds the property either until it is sold or, in the absence of the sale, returned to the consignor.

---

**Example 10.4** Arnold owned a tractor. He decided it no longer fit his farming operation. He consigned it to the XYZ Equipment Company to sell. Under his arrangement with XYZ, he agreed to pick up the tractor in three months if it did not sell. At the time of the consignment, Arnold owed $50,000 of the original purchase price on the tractor to the Relentless Finance Company. The tractor served as security for the debt. Unbeknownst to Arnold, the Relentless Finance Company had incorrectly filed the security interest in the tractor. XYZ filed for Chapter 7 bankruptcy one month after Arnold consigned his tractor to them. The bankruptcy court ruled that the tractor was property of the bankruptcy estate and ordered it sold. Arnold was an unsecured creditor in the bankruptcy and ultimately received $2,000 for his interest in the tractor. As the Relentless Finance Company had failed to perfect its security interest, it had no security interest in the tractor. Therefore, it had no secured claim in XYZ's bankruptcy. XYZ received no notice of the bankruptcy and filed no claim. Under its financing statement with Arnold, the Relentless Finance Company demanded that Arnold repay the $50,000 that he owed them. Arnold's attorney told him that he owed the Relentless Finance Company the money even though he no longer owned the tractor.

---

An Article 9 security interest can also attach to intangible personal property. Banks often require a deposit account be maintained as part of the collateral that the borrower provides for a loan. Courts have often been called upon to determine whether sufficient control of the deposit account was exercised to perfect the bank's collateral in the deposit.

## Common financing statement provisions

A common financing statement provision is a choice of law clause. A choice of law clause determines which state's law applies to the contract. The financing statement may also have a choice of forum clause. A choice of forum clause determines the designated court before deciding a dispute that arises under the contract embodied in the financing statement. The financing statement may also contain an arbitration or mediation clause. Arbitration is a nonjudicial means of resolving any dispute that arises under the contract. In arbitration, a neutral third party acts much as a judge would act to resolve the dispute. If the arbitration is binding, the arbitrator's decision is enforceable by either party. Courts will generally not overturn an arbitrator's decision even if the arbitrator did not follow the applicable law. Those signing financing statements that contain binding arbitration provisions should consider how the arbitrator is to be selected and how the arbitrator and other costs of arbitration are to be paid. The location of arbitration is also an important consideration. It is not unusual for arbitration clauses in financing statements to be very one-sided. Mediation also involves a neutral third party. The role of a mediator is, however, quite different from that of an arbitrator. A mediator attempts to help the parties reach their own resolution of their dispute. A mediator does not decide any issues, and a settlement is reached only if both parties agree.

Another common provision is a subordination clause. A subordination clause subordinates the security interest in one debt to another. It is used to facilitate coordination of multiple security interests in the same collateral. As Example 10.5 illustrates, such clauses are often part of commercial lending arrangements. Such clauses ensure that subsequent financing, necessary to the success of a project, can be obtained.

---

**Example 10.5** Wilson planned to grow blueberries commercially. Wilson bought a suitable farm that was financed by the XYZ Bank. The XYZ Bank's security interest was secured by a recorded mortgage. As Wilson knew that it takes three years for transplanted blueberry bushes to come into production, he had no wish to incur the cost of building a packing facility until it was needed. To ensure that he could obtain financing to build the packing facility, he negotiated a clause in his financing agreement with the XYZ Bank that it would subordinate its security interest in the farm to the lender, unidentified at the time of signing the financing agreement, which provided financing for construction of the packing facility. This subordination clause in Wilson's financing agreement with the XYZ Bank was designed to allow him to give a priority security interest to the lender that financed construction of the packing facility.

---

## Buyer in the ordinary course of business

A buyer in the ordinary course of business (buyer in the ordinary course) is a person who buys a good in the ordinary course of the seller's business. A buyer in the ordinary course may generally expect that no security interest will attach to such goods when he buys them. This rule is essential to support inventory financing for retailers. The buyer in the ordinary course rule is the default UCC rule.[2] For titled personal property, statutes that require titles add another layer of complexity to determining who maintains a security interest in personal property. Many courts have held that who holds the title does not necessarily determine who has the security interest with priority in that property.

## Farm products rule

Under the UCC, a buyer of farm products who buys from the farmer who grew the products may not assert the buyer in the ordinary course defense.[3] Federal law has preempted this UCC rule except for holders of security interests that follow the federally prescribed procedure.[4] Federal law provides two options for states that allow holders of security interests in farm products to preserve those interests in the hands of buyers in the ordinary course of business. States are permitted under federal law to set up a central filing system that will preserve the security interest against a buyer in the ordinary course of business. In states that have not set up central filing systems, federal law provides that holders of security interests may preserve those interests by direct notice to the buyers. Notice provided to buyers through a pre-sale notification system (PNS) must provide notice to potential buyers within one year prior to the sale of the farm products.

***

**Example 10.6** Jones bought a tractor from the ACME Implement Company. ACME financed its inventory with a line of credit from the Relentless Finance Company. The line of credit was secured by ACME's inventory. ACME filed for bankruptcy the day after Jones purchased the tractor. There was almost no inventory left because ACME's manager had sold most of the inventory and embezzled the funds before fleeing to parts unknown. Should Relentless attempt to recover from Jones based upon its security interest in the inventory, Jones may assert that he was a buyer in the ordinary course of ACME's business as a complete defense.

***

The PNS notice must contain the name and address of both the creditor and debtor. It must contain the Social Security number or other approved identifier of a flesh-and-blood debtor. For a business entity debtor, it must contain the IRS taxpayer identifier number or other approved identifier. It must contain a detailed description of the farm products subject to the security interest that includes the amount of product, if applicable, the crop year, and the name of each county or parish where the farm product is to be produced. Similar information must be provided to the central filing system in those states that have established such a central filing system. The farm products rule continues to be a source of confusion and litigation.

**Example 10.7** Bernie grows wheat in a state with a centralized filing system. His wheat is subject to the security interest of the Growers Bank that provides him with his annual operating loan. Growers Bank filed a proper notice with the centralized filing system in the state where Bernie sold his wheat to the Local Bakery. The Local Bakery was not registered with the state centralized filing system. Bernie, who is insolvent, took all the money from the sale of his wheat and fled to a country without an extradition treaty with the United States. Growers Bank may bring a successful lawsuit against the Local Bakery to recover the money that they paid Bernie for his wheat. The Local Bakery will pay for the wheat twice.

## Enforcement

Unlike security interests in real property, almost all states allow security interests in personal property to be enforced without resorting to the judicial system. For tangible personal property, such as automobiles, all the holder of the security interest needs to do is take the property and sell it. The lender will usually be required to provide an accounting to the borrower once the property is sold. Should there be excess proceeds beyond that needed to pay the debt and expenses of sale, any remaining funds are given to the borrower. In most cases, there will be a deficiency, and most states allow the creditor to sue the debtor for a deficiency judgment. Judicial involvement and enforcement will be needed where acquiring the property would require either a breach of the peace or breaking and entering. To acquire the property under such circumstances will usually require a court order and the involvement of law enforcement.

## Statutory trusts

Statutory trusts are not secured transactions; nonetheless, their application has some of the characteristics of secured transactions. Statutory trusts are based on the assumptions that farmers selling perishable products are relatively unsophisticated and in a bargaining position inferior to those buying their products. Statutory trusts are designed to improve the position of farmers in these transactions. A statutory trust is a legal fiction designed to segregate funds generated by selling agricultural products from a company's other assets. When a buyer of agricultural products sells products purchased from farmers, the funds generated by selling those products remain in trust for the farmers until the farmers are paid. A statutory trust is not a trust in the sense that no separate legal entity is set up to hold the funds. Should a buyer of agricultural products file for bankruptcy, the funds in the statutory trust are deemed to remain the property of the farmers who produced the products. As these funds remain the property of the farmers who produced the products, those funds are not part of the bankruptcy estate and may, therefore, be returned to those farmers.

There are two important federal laws that create statutory trusts in agricultural commodities: The Perishable Agricultural Commodities Act (PACA)[5] and the Packers and Stockyards Act (PSA).[6]

PACA creates a statutory trust for the benefit of farmers who produce fresh fruits and vegetables, whether frozen or packed in ice. Also covered by PACA are cherries in brine. All dealers in these products must obtain a license under PACA.[7] As the trust created by PACA is a statutory trust, a farmer making a claim for amounts due for perishable agricultural commodities must follow the steps required by PACA or lose the claim.[8] That the funds from produce sales were co-mingled with funds from non-produce sales—not protected by PACA—does not prevent a successful PACA claim. The PSA provides similar statutory trust protection to livestock producers. Farmers who raise poultry and swine under contract receive the benefit of the statutory trust created by PSA even though those farmers do not own the poultry and swine. A wide variety of poultry and livestock species and their products are covered under the PSA.

## Conclusion

It should be evident from the foregoing discussion that using and managing credit is complex. Too often, farmers keep poor records, respond to serious situations too slowly, and lack adequate legal advice. Modern farming requires as much or more credit as other businesses of similar size. The volatility of farm income due to weather, crop and livestock diseases, and market price fluctuations makes managing credit more difficult for farm businesses than for many other businesses. As the examples in this chapter should make clear, there is no longer a place in U.S. agriculture for farmers who do not understand credit and the legal means by which that credit is secured.

## Notes

1  UCC (2010) § 9-103(b)(3).
2  UCC (2010) § 9-320(a).
3  *Id.*
4  7 U.S.C. § 1631 (2013).
5  7 U.S.C. §§ 499a–499s (2013).
6  7 U.S.C. §§ 181–231 (2013).
7  7 U.S.C. § 499c (2013).
8  7 U.S.C. § 499e (2013).

# Chapter 11

# Estate planning and farm transition

## Introduction

Most farms in the United States are family-owned, and many are multigenerational enterprises. Planning for transition from one generation to another is an important part of maintaining viable farm businesses. Estate planning is an important part of this process. An estate plan for a farm may include both lifetime transfers and transfers at death. Property may be transferred voluntarily during one's life by sale or gift. Some of these lifetime transfers may also include transfers of management control over all or part of the farm business. Farm transition includes more than estate planning. Planning for transfers of management control is an important part of this. Obtaining tax and legal expertise prior to making irrevocable transfers is key to successful farm transition planning.

In some ways, the legal part of estate planning is the easy part. The other part that involves control of assets, retirement, emotions of family members, long simmering family feuds, illness, and facing mortality are the hard parts of estate planning. If these aspects of estate planning and farm transition are not handled well, these issues can manifest themselves in the legal process and result in painful and costly litigation. Estate planning is the orderly accumulation, conservation, and transfer of one's property to one's desired heirs. There is a popular misimpression that estate planning is only for the old or the rich. Nothing could be farther from the truth. A young family with small children, moderate investments, and sizable debt has more need for an excellent estate plan than many older rich people. In the event of the death of both parents, provisions for minor children need to be sufficient to provide for the physical, emotional, and financial needs of those children.

## Initial analysis

The initial analysis begins with the family situation. Who are family members with an interest in the estate? Who are family members with an interest in the farm business as a going concern? It is very often the case that the two sets of family members will not be the same. Typically, the set of family members interested in the estate is larger than the family members interested in the farm business. Most states provide some family members with a right to share in the estate. The surviving spouse almost universally has a right to share in the estate. The surviving spouse's right to share in the estate may have been restricted or modified by a prenuptial agreement or other marital contract. Most states allow prenuptial agreements in which a surviving spouse's right to the estate may be defined. Some states also allow post-nuptial agreements, which are contracts between spouses that have the same effect but which are created during the marriage rather than before it. There may also be surviving ex-spouses who have a contractual right arising from a property settlement or a court order that entitles them to share in the estate of the decedent. In some states, children also have a right to share in the estate. The law governing the right of family members, spouses, and ex-spouses to share in the decedent's estate are complex and may extend beyond the probate estate. The probate estate is usually limited to those assets that are distributed under the terms of a will or, in the absence of provisions in a will, under the laws of intestate succession. Some states allow the rights of a surviving spouse, and sometimes other family members, to extend to assets of the decedent held in a living trust. A living trust is a will substitute that was revocable by the decedent during his lifetime. Example 11.1 illustrates an attempted use of a living trust to prevent a surviving spouse from exercising her spousal rights. In a community property state, title to property is vested in both spouses, making the initial transfer to a living trust impossible without the signature of both spouses on the document transferring title to the trust.

---

**Example 11.1** Mr. Jones lived apart from Mrs. Jones, whom he loathed. For reasons of religious belief, neither Mr. nor Mrs. Jones was willing to pursue a divorce. When Mr. Jones learned that he suffered from an illness from which he was likely to soon die, he directed his attorney to place his assets in a living trust. Mr. Jones then shuffled off this mortal coil. The attorney for Mrs. Jones filed Mr. Jones' estate for probate together with a motion to compel the trustee of his living trust to transfer to the estate those assets of the trust to which Mrs. Jones was entitled under state law. Had Mr. Jones created an irrevocable trust rather than a revocable trust, he could have reduced the scope of his assets within the reach of his surviving wife. Many states put personal property in an irrevocable trust beyond the reach of a surviving spouse. Real property is a different matter. Without a spousal waiver, real property typically remains within the reach of a surviving spouse. There are important reasons why Mr. Jones would not wish to put his property in an irrevocable trust. These reasons include loss of control of the property, inability to take the property back, and tax considerations.

With the complex family situations that exist today, it is not unusual that the family member with an interest in continuing the farm business is a family member without any statutory right to share in the estate. For the farm business to continue, the estate plan must be able to satisfy family members with statutory rights while leaving enough farm assets in the business for it to continue.

The next step in the analysis is a detailed examination of how property is owned. This is important because how property is owned and what is owned act as limitations on the freedom of the person planning his or her estate to distribute the property as he or she wishes. If the character of ownership is misunderstood, the wishes of the decedent as to who receives the property at his or her death may not be carried out. Different types of property ownership are discussed in Chapters 6 and 8. Example 11.2 illustrates the problems that may arise from misunderstanding how property is owned.

---

**Example 11.2** Jeremiah and his identical twin brother, Jason, owned Blackacre Farms as joint tenants with a right of survivorship. Jason never married and had no children. Jeremiah had a daughter, Alice, who was actively engaged in the farm business and wished to continue it after her father and uncle died. Other than Alice, the only relative of Jeremiah and Jason was their nephew, Hyde, the son of a deceased sister, Shirley. Hyde lived in London and had no interest in the farm. Under the terms of his will, Jeremiah gave his entire interest in Blackacre to Alice. Jason had hired an attorney to draft a will that would have given Alice his entire interest in Blackacre; however, he never returned to his attorney's office to sign the will. Jeremiah died instantly when a tractor rolled over on him. Jason, upon seeing his brother pinned under the tractor, had a heart attack and later died from a surgery-related infection. Jeremiah's interest in the farm passed by operation of law as survivorship property to Jason. Jeremiah had no interest in the farm to give to Alice under the terms of his will because, upon his death, his entire interest passed as survivorship property to Jason. In the interval between Jeremiah's death and Jason's death, Jason owned all of Blackacre. As Jason never signed his will, he died intestate, and his estate was subject to the laws of intestate succession. Under the laws of the state where Blackacre is located, Hyde and Alice each received a one-half undivided interest in the farm. Hyde wanted a cash payout of his share and successfully compelled the sale of the farm.

---

All estate planning documents, particularly existing wills, should be reviewed at least annually to make sure that those documents are up to date. A will has no legal effect until the death of the person that made it. It is interpreted as of the date of death even though made years earlier. During the intervening period, a spouse may have died, and the person who made the will may have remarried. Divorces are also common. In most states, a divorce revokes provisions in the will that gave property to the now ex-spouse. Nonetheless, it is very poor planning to leave these things to chance when analysis of existing estate planning documents could easily correct any problems. Beneficiaries of contractual arrangements such as life insurance are not changed by divorce. The owner of the policy must contact the insurance company to change the beneficiary. Example 11.3 illustrates problems that may arise when wills are not revised after a divorce.

---

**Example 11.3** Alyssa owns a farm, Windacres, with her husband, Bob. They both made "kiss me" wills with reciprocal provisions giving everything owned by the predeceasing spouse to the surviving spouse. Spouses were not named in either will. Instead, surviving spouses were referred to as "my husband" and "my wife," respectively. Alyssa and Bob had two children, Alyssina and Bobby. It was their intention that Alyssina and Bobby should each receive half of their combined estate at the death of the last to die. Alyssa caught her dress in farm equipment from which the guard had been removed. She died instantly. Bob inherited the entire farm under the terms of her will. Bob remarried to Goldie. Tragically, Bob died on their honeymoon when he slipped on a banana peel Goldie had dropped while they were viewing the Grand Canyon. As Bob's wife at the time of his death, Goldie owns Windacres to the exclusion of Alyssina and Bobby. In most states, it is irrelevant to the analysis that the will was written years before the marriage to Goldie. Bob had not changed the beneficiaries of his life insurance policy. It listed Alyssa as beneficiary with Alyssina and Bobby as contingent beneficiaries. As Alyssa was dead, Alyssina and Bobby received the proceeds of the policy.

---

A thorough analysis of the family situation will include an analysis of insurance coverage. Life insurance is a key component of many estate plans. Other types of insurance that are important to estate planning include disability insurance and long-term care insurance. Disability insurance provides income when a person is unable to work, whether the disability is temporary or permanent. Long-term care insurance covers the cost of care should the insured no longer to be able to care for him- or herself. Life insurance can provide a fund to pay taxes and other expenses of settling the estate. Other expenses of settling the estate may include existing debts of the decedent, medical expenses, funeral expenses, and estate settlement costs that may include court costs, administrator or executor's fees, appraisal fees, and attorney fees. Life insurance can also create an estate for children who are not involved in the farming operation. This can ensure equitable treatment of all children and reduce the likelihood of litigation. Insurance is governed by contract law. As noted above, an insurance policy is a contract between the owner of the policy and the insurance company. The owner of the policy has a contractual right to change the beneficiary. The beneficiary of an insurance policy is governed neither by terms of the will nor by the laws of intestate succession. Example 11.4 illustrates this principle.

---

**Example 11.4** Duane was proud of how he had provided for his wife. He had purchased a $2 million life insurance policy that named her as the beneficiary. Time changes everything, and what was once a loving relationship ended in bitter divorce. Duane remarried and vowed that his first wife would never get a penny more of his property than the court had ordered. Duane never reviewed his life insurance policies. When he died, his first wife filed a claim as beneficiary of the $2 million life insurance policy. Outraged, his second wife to whom he was married at his death filed a lawsuit against the insurance company demanding an injunction that would require the company to pay the death benefit to her. Duane's first wife counter-claimed, demanding that the insurance company pay her the death benefit. The court ruled that the insurance policy, being a contract, listed Duane's first wife as the beneficiary. It ruled that as the beneficiary, Duane's first wife was entitled to the $2 million death benefit.

---

Lifetime transfers of property require review to ensure that complete transfers have been made and that all requirements of tax law have been met. Lifetime transfers of property without consideration or at sale prices of less than fair market value are gifts of the value transferred without consideration. The federal government and some states charge gift tax on these transfers. Even if gift tax is not owed, there may be a filing requirement. If no gift tax return has been filed, no statute of limitation applies, and federal or state taxing authorities may inquire about gift tax obligations even after the death of the person who made the gift. In addition to tax due, there may also be penalties and interest due if tax requirements were not met. Gifts, particularly of real property, may also be subject to requirements designed to ensure that the gift was intended and completed. Example 11.5 illustrates the consequences of making an incomplete gift.

---

**Example 11.5** John decided to give his farm to his son, Larry. He did not want Larry to have control of the farm until after his death. To accomplish this, John had his attorney draft an undated deed to his son, Larry. He directed his attorney not to record the deed and to give him the original.

---

John kept the deed in his top desk drawer where his daughter Alice found it at his death. She resisted the temptation to burn it and instead hired an attorney to contest its validity. The court ruled that John's gift to Larry was incomplete as the deed was neither dated nor recorded. Because John failed to complete the gift before his death, the court ruled that the farm was part of John's estate.

The initial analysis should include discussion of family goals. Decisions governing the disposition of property at death are solely decisions of the person who owns the property unless those decisions are constrained by law or contract as discussed above. Common goals include financial security for oneself and one's spouse in retirement. It is not unusual for there to be very little estate left when a person dies, because retirement is expensive. This can be a serious problem where a family goal is also continuing the farm business into the next generation. Unless there are other major assets separate from the farm business, the goals of the financially secure retirement and transferring the farm business to the next generation are often in serious conflict. Many parents also say they wish to treat their children equally. This goal is also typically in serious conflict with the goal of continuing the farm business. It is often better to think of this goal as treating all the children equitably. This means that everyone gets something, but the goal of continuing the farm business remains paramount. Making this work requires excellent communication within families and creative structuring of the estate plan. Many families have found that hiring an outside facilitator to help with this process is well worth the money spent. It is certainly cheaper than going to court over the estate after the patriarch and matriarch have died.

## Transfers of property at death

There are several ways that property may be transferred at death. The owner of the property may decide which methods are used to transfer her or his property by either an affirmative decision made during his or her lifetime or through inaction. At death, all of the decedent's remaining property will be transferred. Dead people do not own property, not even their own bodies or the cemetery plot in which it is placed. Disposition of the decedent's body is the right of the decedent's next of kin. Disputes over who has the right to make funeral arrangement is not an uncommon source of litigation It is best to make one's wishes clear to one's close relatives while alive and able to communicate.

One way to transfer property at death is through ownership of survivorship property that passes by operation of law to the surviving owner or owners. A second way to transfer property at death is by testate succession under provisions of a will. A third way to transfer property is through inaction that results in intestate succession. If a person dies without a will, the law of the state of residence determines who receives the property. A fourth way to transfer property is through indirect ownership in a trust. The provisions of the trust control how the property will be distributed. A fifth way that property can be transferred is pursuant to the "beneficiary designations" in contractual vehicles such as life insurance policies and retirement plans. One may even transfer property that one does not own with a "power of appointment." These methods of transfer are mutually exclusive. Occasionally, more than one method is attempted. If the competing methods give the same property to different people, litigation is likely. A common example is survivorship property or remainder interests that are also purportedly distributed under a contrary provision in a will. Example 11.2, earlier, illustrates this problem.

### Survivorship property

When more than one person owns property, the ownership rights of each are limited by the rights of the other owners. These rights are created by either the document of ownership or by operation of law.

If a married couple owns real property and, in some states, a mobile home, the ownership is called "tenants by the entirety." Based on the common law theory that husband and wife are one unit, the law considers that the spouses together hold title to the entire interest in the property. Neither spouse can sell, lease, or mortgage the property without the written consent of the other. Creditors cannot take property held as tenants by the entirety for a debt owed by only one spouse. The property automatically passes to the surviving spouse at the death of the deceased spouse. It is subject neither to probate nor the provisions of the first spouse's will, so transfer of ownership is simplified. Joint owners of real property who are not married to each other hold the property as "joint tenants," with each owning an undivided interest in the whole property. It is similar to tenants by the entirety for married couples, but it must be created by an express agreement for a right of survivorship rather than being created automatically by a marital relationship as in tenants by the entirety.

Unlike a tenancy by the entirety, the joint tenancy may be used to own both real and personal property. Some joint tenancies have a right of survivorship, and some do not. In some states, the creation of a joint tenancy without any statement to the contrary automatically creates a right of survivorship, whereas in other states, the right of survivorship must be specifically created in the document that created the joint tenancy.

Personal property, such as bank accounts, certificates of deposit, or stock certificates, can also be owned by joint tenants with or without a right of survivorship. The right to survivorship should be specified in the document of ownership. It should never be assumed even if state law allows survivorship by implication. At the death of the first joint owner, the property passes automatically to the surviving owners. It is not subject to probate; however, it is part of the federal taxable estate. A downside of joint accounts is that any owner may freely withdraw all of the money in the account. If the owner of an account wants the funds in the account paid to a particular person upon their death, the owner can set up the account as a pay on death account. This accomplishes the owner's objective of transferring the funds at death while preventing the earlier withdrawal of the funds. As the Internal Revenue Service presumes that the first joint tenant to die contributed all of the funds for the entire account, it is important to keep good records of money in and money out of the account. Failure to do so can lead to inclusion of the entire amount in the account in the taxable estate of the first joint tenant to die.

## Testate succession

A will is a legally enforceable declaration of how the testator wants his or her property to be distributed. There are three types of wills. Attested, written wills are the preferred practice. These are formal wills, signed at the end, with witnesses that signed to attest that it was the testator that signed the will. Though not required in all states, the signatures of witnesses to a will should be witnessed by a notary to make proving their signatures easier when the will is probated. Many states recognize holographic wills. Holographic wills are handwritten and lack witnesses to the testator's signature. Different states have different requirements for handwritten wills. Using holographic wills is poor practice as these wills are often found to be invalid or, if valid, their provisions are found to be ambiguous. Nuncupative wills are oral wills made when death is near or, as is sometimes quaintly said, when the testator can "hear the beating of the wings of the angel of death." For a nuncupative will to be valid, most states that recognize them require that death be imminent, that the testator die, and that the will be witnessed by two neutral people who do not take under the will. Nuncupative wills are sometimes called soldiers' wills.

For a will to be valid and enforceable, the testator must be at least of legal age, usually eighteen years of age, and of sound mind. The testator does not have to be competent for all purposes but must understand who he is, what his assets are, who are the natural objects of his bounty, and the consequences of his desired distribution. The natural objects of one's bounty are one's children, spouse, and other relatives, including stepchildren. The will must be made without duress or undue influence. Duress is force, the threat of force, or more subtle coercion such as a threat to cease caring for an elderly testator with limited physical and mental capacity. Undue influence involves no threats. It is more subtle than duress and is proven by the totality of the circumstances in each individual case. Undue influence is a serious issue in estate planning for farm families because there is typically one child who remains on the farm, continues the farm business, and receives most or all of the estate at the death of the children's parents. If the other heirs choose to challenge the validity of the will in probate court, undue influence is a common argument. The issue is whether the child who remained on the farm exercised undue influence over his or her parents or whether the decision to give the bulk of the estate to that child was an expression of the free will of the parents. These cases are heart-wrenching and leave wounds that may take a generation or more to heal.

A will serves purposes in addition to the distribution of property at death. It allows the testator to choose a person or institution to administer her or his estate. This person is called an executor. The testator may choose a guardian for his or her minor children and provide for the management of his or her assets for the benefit of any children. The testator may also push decisions about property distribution into the future through the creation of testamentary trusts and powers of appointment under the terms of his or her will. Funeral instructions should not be part of a will. The will may not be located quickly enough, or the testator may change her or his mind several times about his or her wishes. Rather, funeral instructions should be put in a letter of last instruction to the relative with the statutory right to make funeral arrangements.

Most states require that an executor be bonded before she or he can serve. The purpose of bonding is to protect the beneficiaries of the estate from the malfeasance of the executor. Bonds are purchased from bonding companies that charge a percentage of the face value of the bonds as their fee. The expense of bonding is an expense to the estate that reduces the amount that beneficiaries of the estate will receive. In the case of an only child and sole heir of his or her parents' estates, purchase of a bond to protect him or her from taking money that is already his or hers is an absurd waste of money. For any estate where fraud by the executor is unlikely, an additional provision of the testator's will should be a waiver of the bonding requirement.

For a written will to be valid, most states require that the will be signed by at least two witnesses; however, a few states require three witnesses. Three witnesses are preferred both because a witness may be disqualified or unavailable in the event that they are called upon to testify as to the decedent's wishes. Three witnesses are also preferred because the testator may have moved to a state that requires three witnesses without changing his or her will. It is worth noting that most states will now accept a valid will from another state as being valid.

Some states allow for "self-proved" wills. In such states, the witnesses sign a separate affidavit attached to the will. In this notarized affidavit, the witnesses attest to the validity of their signatures on the will. Through introduction of the affidavit in probate, the necessity of the witnesses appearing to verify their signatures is avoided. This solves the delay-producing and costly process of proving the signatures of witnesses who are dead or unavailable at the time the will is probated. If the testator's family situation is contentious and the probability of fraud high, the option of a self-proved will should not be used because it makes fraud easier.

Once a will has been executed, it can still be changed up until the time of death. One way to make changes is by means of a codicil, which is an addendum executed with the same formalities as a will. Handwritten changes to a will are usually ineffective for lack of proper execution. Handwritten changes may also result in the entire will being declared revoked. Most attorneys will keep a testator's will in electronic form, making it easy to draft a new will. For that reason codicils are seldom used. It is good practice to destroy all copies of old wills to avoid confusion. The person or persons designated to serve as executor under the will should know where the original of the will is kept. The will should be in secure storage with the attorney who drafted the will or in some other location, such as secure storage that some states or their courts make available to testators. The will should not be kept in a safe deposit box because many financial institutions seal the box upon the death of the testator. If multiple people have keys to the safe deposit box, there is also a risk that someone will remove the will and destroy it.

And, as noted above, one way to revoke a will may be by writing on it. This is poor practice because writing on a will does not always revoke it. It may also be revoked by tearing it up or otherwise destroying it. Making a new will revokes all old wills. Old wills should also be physically destroyed to avoid confusion after the decedent's death. It may also be partially or entirely revoked by operation of law. Divorce causes a partial revocation by causing certain provisions regarding the divorced spouse to be invalid.

## Intestate succession

If someone dies without a will, the state law determines how her or his property is divided and to whom it is passed. As noted above, neither intestate succession nor testate succession applies to survivorship property, property transferred by a beneficiary designation, or property passed through a trust. Different states use different formulae for dividing the decedent's property. If there is a surviving spouse, the surviving spouse will usually get a share of the estate. If there are children or their descendants, they will usually take a share of the estate. If there is no surviving spouse and no children or grandchildren, the statute usually looks to ancestors (e.g., parents). If there are no parents, spouse, or children, the statute will distribute the property to more distant relatives. If no relatives can be found, the property will escheat to the state. Example 11.6 illustrates a partial intestacy.

---

**Example 11.6** Larry had a formal written will that gave his farm to his stepson. Before he died, Larry bought an office building. Larry's will contained no residuary clause. A residuary clause disposes of property not otherwise devised in the will. Residuary clauses are essential for distributing property acquired after the last will was executed. As Larry bought the office building after he executed his will, it was not mentioned in his will. As there was a partial intestacy, the office building went to Larry's next of kin under the state's laws of intestate succession. This was a third cousin whom Larry had never met.

---

## Trusts

A trust is a legal arrangement whereby a grantor transfers the legal interest in certain property to a trustee. The trustee holds and manages the property for the benefit of the named beneficiaries.

If a trust is created by a living person, as opposed to being created under a will, that person may reserve the right to revoke it. This type of trust is called a revocable trust. Revocable trusts are also called living trusts. Living trusts are will substitutes because property in the trust at the death of the grantor does not pass under the terms of the grantor's will. Living trusts are created for a variety of reasons. Living trusts allow for professional management of the funds during the grantor's life, avoid probate for the trust assets at the grantor's death, and may provide more privacy than probate. Living trusts are very useful in states with high probate taxes or lengthy probate proceedings. As the grantor has the right to revoke the trust, the trust assets are considered part of the grantor's estate for federal estate tax purposes. The trust assets remain subject to the claims of the grantor's creditors. In most states, use of the living trust will not protect the assets from the statutory rights of the surviving spouse and children to a share of the estate. Example 11.1 illustrates a failed effort to use a living trust to protect one's assets from a surviving spouse.

A living person may also create a trust without reserving the right to revoke it. This is called an irrevocable trust. An irrevocable trust may also be set up under the terms of the decedent's will. Trusts set up under the terms of a will are also called testamentary trust. A grantor who sets up an irrevocable trust gives up the right to revoke the trust. An irrevocable trust is a separate legal entity from the grantor. The trust, not the grantor, owns the trust assets. Except for simple trusts, trusts must file federal and sometimes state income tax returns and pay tax on their income. A simple trust is a trust that does not retain income. All income is paid out to the beneficiaries every year. It is the responsibility of the beneficiaries to report income received from the trust on their federal and state income tax returns. All other irrevocable trusts must file income tax returns and pay tax as a trust. Compared to individuals, trusts are heavily taxed. Assets in an irrevocable trust set up during the grantor's life are not part of the grantor's estate for federal estate tax purposes.

Creation of an *inter vivos* irrevocable trust may result in federal and state gift tax liability to the grantor. Irrevocable trusts are separate legal entities that are treated for gift tax purposes in the same manner as individuals. It is the responsibility of the grantor who created the trust to file gift tax returns and pay any gift tax due. Sound tax advice by an experienced tax professional is required prior to the use of an irrevocable trust as part of an estate plan. Most attorneys, unless their practices are tax practices, do not have the expertise to handle tax issues associated with complex trusts.

Selecting a trustee requires planning. The choice is usually between a professional trustee and a family member or friend. Professional trustees are paid a percentage of the value of the assets held in trust as their compensation. Trustees who are family members or friends may be paid a fee but often are not. Powers that are given to the trustee vary depending upon the grantor's objectives. A major issue is whether the trustee has the power to sell farmland. If the grantor wishes to keep a farm in the family, the trustee would usually be denied the power to sell a farm. Where agricultural assets are the major part of the assets held in a trust, it is critical that a trustee familiar with agriculture be accepted.

## Beneficiary designations

A substantial amount of wealth is transferred at death through contractual arrangements with beneficiary designations. These arrangements include life insurance, pensions, individual retirement accounts, and employee death benefits. Tax issues differ by type of contractual arrangement and require the services of the tax professional to avoid inadvertently triggering substantial tax liabilities. For example, life insurance death benefits are included in the federal taxable estate of the decedent if the decedent owned the policy at the time of his or her death. This problem may be avoided through ownership of the policy by the beneficiaries.

## Transfers under a power of appointment

Powers of appointment are found in deeds or wills. A power of appointment gives a person who does not own specific property the power to transfer ownership of that property to another person. Powers of appointment may be general or particular. The person upon whom the power of appointment is conferred is called the "donee." Powers of appointment are often used to allow the decision as to who receives property to be made long after the deed or will was executed. Under a general power of appointment, the donee may give the property to anyone, including himself. A particular power of appointment specifies to whom and under what conditions the property may be conferred.

---

**Example 11.7** Harold felt very strongly that his farm should belong to whichever of his children intended to continue farming it after his death. In his will, he created a testamentary trust for his wife, Helen. Under the terms of the trust, the trustee was required to release the farm to whichever of his children wanted to farm it. Under a particular power of appointment, he directed the trustee, at the death of Helen, to confer the farm upon whichever of his children demonstrated the greatest interest in continuing to farm the land.

## Probate

Probate begins with presentation of the will to the probate court, acceptance of the will by the probate court, and appointment of the executor or administrator. An executor is appointed if the estate was testate, and an administrator is appointed if the estate was intestate. The term personal representative is used to mean either an executor or an administrator. Every state has certain qualifications for personal representatives. Most states require that the personal representative be a resident of the state where the probate is conducted. Other rules for qualification of personal representatives vary significantly from one state to another.

Any person with an interest in the estate has standing to challenge the validity of the will. In most probate proceedings, the validity of the will is never challenged. Probate assets are all those assets under the jurisdiction of the probate court. After being appointed, one of the first things the personal representative does is inventory the assets of the estate and determine the debts of the estate. Other assets, such as those in trust, are not assets of the probate estate. In some states, real property passes by operation of law at the date of the decedent's death. In those states, the real property of the decedent is not a probate asset. In other states, real property is a probate asset. This makes a substantial difference in the amount of probate tax assessed. It also determines, in part, the advisability of using a living trust, discussed earlier, to pass some of the assets outside of probate. One of the important jobs of the executor is to notify creditors of the probate proceeding and to advertise to provide notice by publication to those creditors of the decedent that may be unknown to the executor. Probate assets of a decedent will be distributed pursuant to his or her will or to applicable intestate succession laws. The personal representative of the estate is responsible for gathering and valuing the assets, paying all debts and claims against the estate, filing all required inventories and accountings with the court, filing all necessary tax returns, and distributing the property to the beneficiaries. A major advantage of probate is that once creditors have been notified, either individually or by advertisement, no other creditor may make a claim against the assets of the estate.

# Chapter 12

# Family law, health, and end-of-life care

## Introduction

Family law encompasses marriage, the marital relationship, children, and divorce. One might well ask what families have to do with agricultural law. The short answer is everything. The 2007 Census of Agriculture, conducted by the National Agricultural Statistics Service, an agency of the U.S. Department of Agriculture, reported that almost 96 percent of the 2,204,792 farms in the United States are family-owned farms.[1] For most farms, family events such as marriages, the birth of children, and divorces are important events in the life of the farm business and the farm family. Some of these events may strengthen the farm business whereas others may very well destroy the farm business.

## Marriage

Most states set a minimum age for marriage and require that both parties to the marriage be mentally competent. If this seems similar to the requirements for a valid contract, it is. There is a contractual nature to marriage. Most states set the age of marriage at the age of eighteen, as is the case with the capacity to enter into a valid contract. Most states also allow marriage at younger ages if a child has the consent of his or her parent or guardian. If either party to the marriage is mentally incompetent, the marriage is void. Most states require a marriage license and that the marriage be solemnized. The person authorized to solemnize the marriage must be either authorized by a church or other religious body or an authorized civil authority. The parties must express their intentions in front of this person and each other, and there must be two or more witnesses to the ceremony. The person who solemnizes the marriage must return the completed license to the appropriate government office for recording in the public records. With the advent of same-sex marriages and the marriages of more people at advanced ages, the law of marriage in U.S. states is in flux.

Some states recognize common law marriage. Common law marriage is marriage without any of the formalities of a marriage license or solemnization. In those states that allow it, two elements must be proven. First, that the couple lived as husband and wife for the requisite time period and, second, that they represented themselves as husband and wife. The Full Faith and Credit Clause, Article IV, Section 1 of the Constitution, requires that states that do not recognize the doctrine of common law marriage recognize common law marriages that arose in other states.

---

**Example 12.1** John and Alice lived in South Carolina as husband and wife for a sufficient period in South Carolina that they were married under South Carolina law. Eventually, they moved to North Carolina, a state that does not recognize the doctrine of common law marriage. John and Alice had no children. Neither had wills. At John's death, his nephew, Ebenezer, contested Alice's right to an intestate share of John's estate. Ebenezer claimed that Alice was not married to John under North Carolina law and that, as John's closest living relative, he was entitled to John's entire estate. The North Carolina probate court held that both the Constitution and North Carolina precedent required it to recognize the validity of a South Carolina common law marriage.

---

Marriage brings with it certain rights and obligations for each party. There is a mutual right to spousal support. Each spouse has a right of consortium with the other spouse. The right of consortium includes the affection and comfort of the other spouse and conjugal relations. At common law, a woman, on the death of her husband, was entitled to claim a certain portion of her husband's real and personal property. This right is called dower. A similar right, curtesy, belonged to husband, on the death of his wife. However, these common law rights have been replaced in most states by a right to property of the deceased spouse that is defined by state statute. That right is no longer differentiated by gender.

At common law, the husband had the right to manage the property of the wife during coverture. Coverture was the condition of a married woman who as such had no right to manage the property that she brought into the marriage. The right of the husband to control his wife's property no longer exists in any U.S. state. There is a split among the states as to how property acquired during the marriage is handled. In most states, each spouse is presumed to be the sole owner of property acquired individually by a spouse with his or her own income. The issue of marital rights comes into play only in the event of divorce or death of a spouse. A minority of states are or were community property states. In community property states, the law presumes that all property acquired during marriage is owned on a fifty-fifty basis without regard to either the source of the money used to acquire the property or the name or names on the title to the property.

Under the doctrine of necessaries, each spouse is liable to third-party creditors for "necessary" items such as food, clothing, medical services, or shelter furnished to the other spouse even though the first spouse is not contractually bound on the debt. The existence of this doctrine and what are considered necessaries vary greatly from one state to another. Spouses are liable for their own torts against third parties but are not held liable for torts committed by the other spouse. Each spouse has a right to bring a tort action against the other spouse for injury to person or property. A spouse is not liable for the crimes of his or her spouse. Many states grant spouses a privilege that prevents one spouse from testifying against the other in a criminal action.

---

**Example 12.2** John and Jane were husband and wife. They owned a farm together as tenants by the entireties. They had no health insurance. John succumbed to a debilitating illness. They lived in a state that classifies medical care as a necessary. The hospital treated John in his final illness. His probate estate was inadequate to pay his hospital bill. The hospital sued Jane for John's unpaid medical expenses and obtained a judgment. The hospital docketed the judgment and forced the sale of the farm held by Jane. From the sale proceeds, the hospital recovered the money that John owed for his medical care.

---

## Marital contracts

Most states allow the parties to enter into an agreement prior to marriage. These agreements are called prenuptial agreements. These agreements address significant topics such as spousal support and the division of property upon divorce or death. An agreement will not be enforceable if either party is under duress, does not have an opportunity to consult with his or her own lawyer, or fails to fully disclose his or her property and financial obligations. Alimony or maintenance cannot be reduced to such a level that the ex-spouse would become a public charge. Provisions as to child custody and support are not binding on the court. Some states also recognize marital contracts made during the marriage. Rules governing validity of those contracts are similar to those governing the validity of premarital agreements.

Premarital agreements are very important to the well-being of multifamily farm businesses. Divorce and property distributions can be extremely disruptive to farm businesses. Divorce is a major source of farm business dissolution. Premarital agreements protect not only the married couple who makes the agreement but the interests of the other families in the farm business.

When the parties separate, but before they are divorced, their marital rights and obligations will continue during the separation period. To change the rights and obligations, the parties may enter into a separation agreement. This contract, if validly executed, may be binding against even third parties such as creditors.

These agreements are usually combined with a property settlement that divides the couple's property. If the parties decide to reconcile, they may also enter a contract to nullify the terms of their prior separation agreement and define their future relationship. Such an agreement is called a reconciliation agreement.

---

**Example 12.3** John and Jane separated and signed a separation agreement. Each agreed that neither would make any claim upon the estate of the other in the event that one died before the divorce became final. John died. Jane filed a claim with the probate court for payment of her statutory spousal share. John's children from a prior marriage successfully argued that they were third-party beneficiaries of the separation agreement and that Jane had waived her right to a spousal share.

---

### Children

Both parents of a child have an obligation to support the child until the child reaches the age of eighteen, or older under some circumstances. The obligation to support applies even if the child has his or her own resources. Children born of a marriage are presumed to be legitimate. In general, states will not allow the legitimacy of a child to be questioned even where evidence exists that the child was not the biological child of the father. The legal term for children born of a marriage is legitimate. The legal term for children born outside of marriage is illegitimate. If a child is legitimate, the father and the mother have all parental rights and obligations, and the child can inherit real and personal property from both parents. Children born to an unwed mother may automatically inherit only from the mother. Most states have procedures by which a child may be legitimized, allowing that child to inherit from the father.

A decree of adoption makes the child the legitimate child of the adoptive parents and may sever the parent-child relationship with the biological parents. States laws vary in the extent to which a child's relationship with his or her biological parents are severed. The biological parents generally no longer have parental rights and obligations. In many states, the child thus adopted may inherit only from his or her adoptive parents and not from the biological parents. Some states allow inheritance from biological parents. Stepparents have no obligation to support stepchildren. Stepchildren cannot inherit from stepparents; however, stepchildren can receive property from stepparents under the wills of the stepparents. Most adoptions are formal adoptions with the adoption approved by a court; however, some states recognize common law adoptions. Common law adoptions are usually recognized where there was an attempt at a formal adoption but for some reason the paperwork was improperly completed and the adoption never became effective. The states that recognize common law adoptions do so to avoid injustices.

A parent is liable to a third-party provider of necessaries supplied to a minor child, even if he or she does not have custody of that child. Under common law, a parent is not held liable for a child's tort merely because of the parent-child relationship. Some states impose vicarious liability on the parents under the relationship of principal and agent. Under the rules of agency, a parent is liable for any tortious acts of a child that the parent directs, consents to, or ratifies. A parent may be responsible for the criminal acts of his or her child if those acts were done at the direction of or with the consent of the parent. It is a criminal offense for a parent to abuse or willfully to neglect his or her child. In severe cases, courts may terminate parental rights and declare the child a ward of the state.

---

**Example 12.4** John drove his nine-year-old son, Johnny, and the family four wheeler to Larry's farm. Neither John nor Johnny had permission from Larry to be on his farm. John put Johnny on the four wheeler. John said to Johnny, "Have fun. I will be back to pick you up in a couple of hours." Johnny destroyed Larry's ripening wheat crop. Under these circumstances, most states would hold John civilly liable to Larry for the value of the wheat crop that was destroyed. Many states would also find John criminally liable for neglect because he left a child of such a young age alone with a potentially dangerous vehicle.

---

Custody is a term used to describe the rights of parents, grandparents and others regarding minor children who have been placed in their physical care. Custody may be determined in a divorce suit or by a separate civil action. Custody orders can be changed by the court at any time for the best interest of a child. The court will determine whether a parent or other person is fit to be the custodian.

### Divorce and related issues

The common law recognizes two types of divorce: absolute and divorce from bed and board. Absolute divorce dissolves the marriage ties and releases the parties from their marital obligations, leaving the parties free to remarry. Divorce from bed and board is a separation where the parties remain husband and wife with the legal right to refuse to live together. The parties are not free to remarry. A similar result can be reached with a separation agreement. Different states allow different grounds for divorce. Almost all states now allow some form of no-fault divorce where it is sufficient to allege the statutory period of separation and irreconcilable differences.

Unless there is a valid premarital agreement or property settlement agreement entered into before, during, or after marriage, the presumption followed by most courts is that the "marital" property of the couple will be divided equally. This is based on the concept that a marriage is a partnership to which each spouse makes valuable contributions, whether by earning an income outside the home or by being the full-time housekeeper. Marital property is any real or personal property acquired by either spouse during the marriage and before the date of separation unless it can be classified as "separate" property. In most but not all states, separate property is property acquired before the marriage or received by gift or inheritance during the marriage. There are substantial variations in the definition of marital property from state to state. When marital property and separate property are commingled, all the property becomes marital.

---

**Example 12.5** John and Betty were married. Prior to their marriage, Betty purchased 100 acres of farmland. After their marriage, John and Betty built a house on the land. They financed construction of the house and made the monthly payment from marital funds. The entire 100 acres and the house are marital assets due to commingling.

---

To be entitled to alimony or maintenance payments, a spouse, either husband or wife, must be actually dependent on the other spouse for maintenance and support or in need of that support. Alimony may be ordered by the court, or it can be the result of agreement in a properly drafted and executed agreement. It may be paid in a lump sum or in periodic payments. If payments extend beyond the death of either spouse, it is not alimony. The court has discretion to decide whether alimony is equitable under the circumstances and the amount, duration, and manner of payment. Marital fault, often adultery, is a factor in most states in determining whether alimony should be awarded. If alimony was established by agreement, the court may generally change it based upon changed circumstances, such as loss of employment. Remarriage by the dependent spouse generally ends the obligation to pay alimony.

### Torts against the marriage

A few states continue to recognize torts against the marriage. Alienation of affection is a common law tort that is typically, but not necessarily, brought by one spouse against the paramour of the other spouse. It may be either an intentional or a negligent tort. As a precondition, there must have been affection between the spouses before the tort-feasor began to tortiously interfere in the marital relationship. The tort consists of interfering in the marital relationship to such an extent that one spouse is persuaded to abandon his or her affection for the other spouse. Though most alienation of affection actions are brought against paramours, sexual relations are not an element of the tort. A meddling in-law may tortiously interfere with the marital relationship. Criminal conversation is a strict liability tort that consists of engaging in sexual relations with a person who is married to another. These common law torts have been abolished by statute in most states. The rationale for abolishing these torts is that they are anachronisms based upon an earlier view of women that regarded women as quasi-property, that the existence of these torts encourages revenge seeking by jilted spouses, and that the existence of these torts can interfere with post-divorce healing.

## Health and end-of-life care

### Introduction

Health care is a critical issue for farm families. Farm families often have difficulty in purchasing affordable health insurance in the market. Many farm families solve this problem through a spouse's off-farm job that provides health insurance coverage for the family. Health insurance is governed by a complex maze of federal and state laws. Although health insurance is of critical importance to farm families, its complexity dictates that it is beyond the scope of what can be covered in this book. A chapter of this length cannot capture health care law in all of its complexity. The purpose of this chapter is to provide a brief summary that will guide the reader to areas of interest that may be pursued in greater depth.

End-of-life issues include planning for disability and planning for long-term care. These are issues for all families; however, these issues are particularly important for farm families. Poor handling of these issues can jeopardize a farm business. Even where these issues are handled well, they can sometimes jeopardize a farm business.

### Advanced directives

Advanced directives are documents that are prepared in advance of need that determine how end-of-life decisions are to be made. These documents include the health care power of attorney, the living will, the physician orders for life-sustaining treatments (POLST), and do-not-resuscitate orders.

A living will is a document that expresses a desire to die a natural death. It directs medical care providers not to use "heroic measures" such as cardiopulmonary resuscitation to prolong life when there is no reasonable hope of recovery. A signed original of the living will must generally be provided to every health care provider that is likely to treat the person signing it.

A health care power of attorney is a specialized power of attorney that gives one person the power to make medical decisions for another, when that other person is no longer physically or mentally capable of making health care decisions. The person who holds the power is called the "health care agent" of the person who signed the health care power of attorney. The health care agent has the power to make decisions on behalf of the person who signed the power when that person is no longer physically or mentally capable of making decisions. In choosing a health care agent, one should select a person who is likely to make decisions in a manner that the person who signed the power would approve. This means that a discussion of what is desired in end-of-life care is necessary. It is also necessary that the person holding the power be willing to make those decisions.

POLSTs[2] are physician orders setting the parameters for end-of-life care. These programs are not available in every state. Some states use a name different from POLST. POLSTs are not substitutes for advanced directives, including a living will and a health care power of attorney. The health care power of attorney and the living will may be separate documents, or they may be combined into a single document. The form that these documents take will to some degree depend upon the governing state law.

There is no substitute for communication in handling end-of-life issues. Good communication with physicians, nurses, and hospital and hospice staff is essential. In addition, social workers and chaplains are invaluable resources. Chaplains who serve hospitals and hospices serve all patients. Though chaplains come from various faiths, they generally serve all patients including those with no religious affiliation. Family members who are caring for a dying family member should ask any question to which they do not know the answer or need an answer. End-of-life issues are complex.

## Managing the finances

Managing the finances of an elderly person is often challenging. One's ability to handle one's own finances declines as one ages. For most, this is a gradual decline. Even though individuals' ability to handle their own finances has declined, most will remain legally competent to handle their own financial affairs. This can present a serious problem because fraud on the elderly is very common. There are many criminals that prey on the elderly. Most state attorney general offices have a hotline that one may call if one suspects that an elderly relative, neighbor, or friend is a victim of fraud. Unfortunately, the money may already be gone by the time the fraud is uncovered. If children or other caregivers recognize the problem before the money is gone, there is much that can be done. Attorneys with practices focused on elder law can be extremely helpful. Often, such an attorney may need to be retained by children or other caregivers who recognize the need for help.

There are two ways that a lack of ability to handle finances can be addressed. The durable power of attorney is a document that gives another person the power to manage the financial affairs of the person who executed the power. The durable power of attorney is distinguished from an ordinary power of attorney in that it continues to be effective after the person who executed the power becomes legally incompetent. The person designated to act on behalf of the person who executed the durable power of attorney is called an "agent" or "attorney in fact."

The person who has the power to act under a durable power of attorney is usually not an attorney despite the terminology. The agent, or attorney in fact, is usually a family member, although there is nothing to prevent an attorney's being designated as an attorney in fact under a durable power of attorney. Durable powers of attorney generally end at the death of the persons who created them.

The powers granted to the agent under a durable power of attorney may be narrow or very broad. The grant of power under the durable power of attorney may be as narrow as the power to use the checking account to pay bills or as broad as the power to make gifts of property or money. If the durable power of attorney allows it, the agent may make gifts to him- or herself. Broad durable powers of attorney carry the risk that the agent will steal the money or squander it. Any person appointed as an agent under a durable power of attorney should have a reputation for handling money well and for honesty.

The second way that the finances of a person who is legally incompetent may be handled is through appointment of a guardian through a court proceeding. For a court to appoint a guardian, the court must first determine that the person, whose property the guardian is to manage, is legally incompetent. The appointed guardian is required to make periodic reports to the court. Guardian proceedings are costly, time-consuming, and emotionally wrenching. A durable power of attorney executed prior to incompetence may often allow a guardianship proceeding to be avoided.

### Paying for end-of-life care

The cost of health care and health insurance can be quite expensive. The Patient Protection and Affordable Care Act (ACA)[3] was signed into law on March 23, 2010. It is a complex piece of legislation that ensures that no person can be rejected for health insurance because they have a preexisting medical condition. It also establishes subsidies for individuals who fall below specified income thresholds. It applies penalties to individuals who failed to purchase coverage and who do not have a recognized exemption or excuse. It does not cover those who are qualified for Medicare. It also does not cover those who qualify for Medicaid due to low income. Both because the validity of parts of the ACA are currently before the Supreme Court and due to its complexity, detailed coverage is beyond the scope of this book. Farm families are well advised to obtain the assistance of insurance brokers and tax professionals who understand the nuances of the ACA. As of this writing the continued existence of the ACA and possible replacements are both uncertain. The current president includes replacing parts or all of the ACA as an important part of his agenda.[4]

Medicare is a federal program that pays for medical care for the elderly and disabled. It does not pay the full cost of all medical care, so many individuals covered by Medicare buy supplemental health insurance. A diminishing number of employer group plans continue coverage after retirement that may include supplemental coverage. Medicare does not cover long-term care.

There are two ways to pay for long-term care. The first is to purchase longterm care insurance. Long-term care insurance is expensive and may have certain limitations on coverage. The second way to pay for long-term care is through Medicaid.

Medicaid is the federal program that is operated under delegation to the states that pays for health care for those with incomes below certain thresholds. Qualifying for Medicaid is complex. Medicaid currently has a five-year look back that is designed to prevent people from transferring their assets to another family member prior to applying for Medicaid. One way that family businesses are lost is through the high cost of end-of-life care that may require the sale of farmland. Some of the elderly engage in what is known as a "Medicaid spend down." The purpose of this is to avoid capture of the farm assets to repay the money spent by Medicaid on a person's medical care. If one is going to engage in a Medicaid spend down, it is highly advisable to obtain the services of an elder law attorney. Elder law attorneys have the expertise to understand the Medicaid rules. The failure to conduct a Medicaid spend down well may result in being denied care. In some situations, criminal penalties may apply.

## Notes

1 National Institute of Food and Agriculture. *Family & Small Farms*, Retrieved June 22, 2018, nifa.usda.gov/family-farms.
2 Institute of Medicine of the National Academies. *POLST*. Retrieved June 22, 2018, www.polst.org/.
3 Pub. L. No. 111-148, 124 Stat. 119 (2010).
4 The White House. *Healthcare*. Retrieved June 22, 2018, www.whitehouse.gov/issues/healthcare/.

# Chapter 13

# Water law

## Introduction

In addressing legal questions about water, there are several questions that must be asked if one is to arrive at a satisfactory answer. First, what is the legal type or category of the water? The various types of water are discussed in this chapter. Second, how does one wish to use the water? Water may be used for many purposes. Some of these uses include consumption by humans or animals; domestic uses such as bathing, cooking, and washing dishes; irrigation of crops or lawns; cooling for power plants and other industrial processes; and providing power either directly or through the generation of electricity. Bodies of water are also used for recreation, transportation, and to provide the boundary for properties of different landowners or political entities. When there is an excess of water, either from precipitation or flooding, people wish to dispose of water. Water is also used as the vehicle for disposing of domestic, agricultural, and industrial waste. A chapter of this length cannot capture water law in all of its complexity. The purpose of this chapter is to provide a brief summary that will guide readers to areas of interest that may be pursued in greater depth.

Law governing the right to use water varies dramatically from one state to another. Laws governing pollution of water are much more unified because there is unifying federal law regulating water pollution. There are two primary systems governing the right to use water: the system of riparian rights and the system of prior appropriation. The system of riparian rights is based upon the English common law. At the risk of oversimplifying, the U.S. states bordering the Mississippi River on the west and all states east of the Mississippi River use some form of riparian water rights; three states—California, Nebraska, and Oklahoma—use a hybrid system; and Hawaii uses a unique system.[1] All these states have statutory water withdrawal systems that, to some extent, regulate water quantity used.[2] Some states apply the doctrine of riparian rights to groundwater but not to surface water.[3] The states of the Central Plains and the West, including Alaska, use some form of prior appropriation.[4]

## Types of water

There are six types of water: natural surface waters; runoff or diffuse surface waters that arise from precipitation (rainfall, snowmelt); underground streams; percolating groundwater; springs; and water in artificial channels, lakes, and ponds.

Natural surface waters are those that are found in creeks, rivers, streams, ponds, lakes, sloughs, swamps, estuaries, oceans, and any other body of water that humans had no hand in creating. Some very old artificial bodies of water, such as very old ponds or canals, may be regarded by the law as natural. These bodies of water generally contain water during periods of normal weather. A natural watercourse or stream has a well-defined channel with a bed and banks that are capable of retaining water. A natural watercourse has a flow. Natural surface waters also encompass some streams that are seasonal. For seasonal streams, the flow does not have to be continuous. In arid areas, some streams contain flowing water only at times of heavy rains. There is considerable disagreement at the margin about which seasonal streams are sufficiently defined to be included within the category of natural surface waters. The test is always fact-specific and may require the testimony of experts. There is also considerable disagreement about the point at which an artificial body of water will be considered natural for purposes of the law.

Runoff or diffuse surface waters arise from precipitation. The type of precipitation that produced runoff does not matter. It also does not matter that the runoff is separated in time from the precipitation event because the precipitation was held for a time as snow or ice. What does matter is whether the water is found in a defined watercourse with a bed and banks that are capable of retaining the water. Once the water is within a defined watercourse, it is natural surface water. Floodwaters are not natural surface waters but are instead runoff. What distinguishes floodwaters from high water in a natural watercourse is that floodwaters are not bounded by a bed and banks. Distinguishing runoff from natural surface waters is a question of fact. Relevant to that analysis is whether the water was within a defined channel or somewhere else. If somewhere other than a defined channel, it is floodwater that is classified as runoff.

Underground streams are like natural surface waters except that they flow through defined channels (i.e., caves that are below the land surface). Underground streams are typically found in areas of karst geology. Many of these underground streams have never been fully mapped.

Percolating groundwater is diffuse. It is found in either cracks in rock, between soil particles, or in spaces in other unconsolidated material. The water table is the level below which the soil or rock is saturated with water. An interconnected area that is saturated with groundwater is called an aquifer. An aquifer may range in size from an isolated pocket of water, such as might be found in the Appalachian Mountains and its associated Piedmont Plateau of North Carolina, to a huge multi-state aquifer, such as the Ogallala Aquifer found in eight states of the U.S. Great Plains.

Springs are formed by the emergence to the surface of water that was underground. The source of a spring may be either percolating groundwater or an underground channel. In most states, the source is not usually relevant to the legal treatment of the spring. Whether the spring gives rise to a natural watercourse determines the applicable law.

Artificial bodies of water are generally governed by the law under which the body of water was created. Artificial bodies of water include lakes created by damming a stream or river and canals. To understand the law governing any given artificial body of water, it is useful to know whether the body of water was created by a federal entity, a state entity, or a private entity. If a federal or state entity, it is also necessary to know which one. The anticipated uses of the water are also important to understanding the law under which the body of water is governed. The law governing bodies of water created primarily for power generation is quite different from the law governing bodies of water created primarily as municipal water supplies. USDA Natural Resources Conservation Service farm ponds are artificial bodies of water; the water usually belongs to the farmer.

## Law governing the right to use water

### The law of riparian rights

The rights that owners and occupants of land adjoining a watercourse have to use that water are called riparian rights. The humid Eastern states have traditionally followed the riparian doctrine of water rights. Riparian rights attach to both surface and subterranean watercourses and to other definite, natural sources of water supply on the surface of the earth. This law also applies to springs that give rise to a natural watercourse. The nature of these rights is determined using either the natural flow theory or the reasonable use theory. Under the natural flow theory, each riparian owner has a right to have the water of the stream remain substantially in its natural state, free from any unreasonable diminution in quantity and quality. Under the reasonable use theory, each riparian owner has the right to make the maximum reasonable use of the water so long as it does not interfere with use by others. Most states that use the system of riparian rights use the reasonable use theory. The reasonable use theory is more consistent with industrialized society with large commercial and agricultural needs for water than is the natural flow theory. The natural flow theory is very restrictive because downstream riparian owners are entitled to the water in essentially the same state that it was in when the upstream owner received it.

The system of riparian rights makes a distinction between domestic uses of water and other, commercial uses of water. This distinction is more important for the application of the natural flow theory than it is for the reasonable use theory. Domestic uses are those arising from the necessities of life, such as household use, drinking, bathing, irrigating small gardens, or watering domestic animals. The riparian owner may not take all of the water to the exclusion of the other downstream owners for artificial uses, which are those uses that are not for domestic use. Artificial uses would include commercial stock watering and irrigation of commercial agriculture. The riparian landowner who raises stock on a commercial scale cannot exhaust the stream flow unless other riparian owners' domestic needs have been met. The right to irrigate applies only to the excess water available after domestic purposes and watering domestic animals are supplied. Riparian owners have the right to hunt, fish, and swim in an adjoining watercourse. A landowner whose land does not abut the water has no right to use the water.

Riparian owners may not sell or give water to one who is not a riparian owner. Riparian rights are a right to use the water but not ownership of the water, even if the landowner owns the land under the water. Riparian rights may not be sold or transferred without also selling or otherwise transferring the land. Water users in riparian jurisdictions have typically secured their water supplies by purchasing easements from the downstream riparian owners. These easements act like a covenant not to sue and are binding on all future owners of the property.

---

**Example 13.1** Harry and Owen owned adjoining farms. There is a spring on Owen's farm that gives rise to a stream that flows onto and through Harry's farm. Owen decided to irrigate his farm, and his irrigation system used the entire output of the spring. A deed of easement, in favor of Harry's farm, gives the owner of Harry's farm the right to all of the water from the spring in perpetuity. The deed was executed in 1790 by the respective owners of the two parcels at that time to protect the water supply for a gristmill that was being built on the land that now belongs to Harry. Harry asked Owen to immediately cease irrigating from the spring. When Owen refused, Harry brought suit asking the court for permanent injunction to bar Owen from using water from the spring for irrigation. Finding no factual issues in the case, the court granted summary judgment in favor of Harry and issued a permanent injunction that barred Owen from using the spring's water for irrigation. The court ruled as it did because an easement runs with the land, potentially in perpetuity. The owner of the land that now belongs to Harry purchased the easement from the owner of the land that now belongs to Owen to secure his water source.

---

The right to riparian rights in a watercourse or lake are not lost by non-use alone. If someone without a right to use the water is using the water in a manner inconsistent with the riparian owner's rights, and the riparian owner fails to act within the statutory period, riparian rights may be lost by prescription.

### The law of prior appropriation

Most Western states use a system of prior appropriation applicable to both surface and groundwater. It is a system where first in time is first in right. Beneficial use is the basis, measure, and limit of the right appropriated. If water is, at any time, not put to a beneficial use, the right is lost.

To appropriate water, one must make a notice of intent to appropriate. In all states (except Colorado) that use a prior appropriation system, there is an administrative agency to which the intent to appropriate must be made. In all states, the intent to appropriate must specifically identify the location of the water supply. To avoid losing the appropriative right, a diversion of the water must be made within a reasonable time. Water is diverted by removing it from its source or, for in-stream diversions, by controlling its natural course by artificial means. No appropriation is perfected without putting the water claimed to a beneficial use. Some states allow junior users to use water claimed by a senior user who is not actually using it. Other states strictly limit the water that may be withdrawn.

Waters that may be appropriated include natural surface waters. When a water user reduces water used as the result of conservation practices, the water saved may be claimed as saved water. When water that was previously appropriated is captured and reused, that water may be appropriated. Springs whose water remains on the land where it originated are not subject to appropriation by others. Springs whose waters serve as the source of a watercourse are subject to appropriation by others. Developed waters are waters produced by mining or other activities. Developed waters are not subject to appropriation by others.

Appropriative rights may be transferred incidental to a transfer of the property. Appropriative rights may also be transferred separately from the land so long as the water so transferred is put to an actual beneficial use. Abandonment is an intentional surrender of one's appropriative rights. Nonuse does not cause an abandonment. A forfeiture of rights may occur through the failure to comply with statutory requirements.

Some states use a dual system of riparian and appropriative of rights. Many states, both Eastern and Western, have developed administrative permit systems. Administrative permit systems are adopted under the state's police powers. These systems will not be overturned so long as these systems are rationally related to protection of health, safety, and welfare. Some administrative permit systems have run afoul of the Fifth Amendment Takings Clause or the Due Process Clauses of the Fourteenth and Fifth Amendments. A person whose water rights will be affected by an administrative permit system must be given notice and an opportunity to be heard under the Due Process Clauses of the Fourteenth and Fifth Amendments. A person who has been deprived of substantially all the value of the water rights as a result of imposition of an administrative permit system may have a claim for compensation under the Fifth Amendment Takings Clause.

---

**Example 13.2** The Piedmont Triad Regional Water Authority had U.S. Army Corps of Engineers (Corps) and state permits to build a dam and impound a reservoir to provide water to the cities that it served.[5] Several downstream hydroelectric power producers that sold electricity brought an inverse condemnation action. Their action sought compensation for the reduction in water flow caused by the impoundment. The NC Court of Appeals held that having valid permits to build a dam and impound a reservoir did not relieve the Piedmont Triad Regional Water Authority of its obligation as a governmental entity to pay power producers for their riparian property rights in the flow of the river that had been taken by impounding the river.

Prior appropriation generally provides greater certainty in business transactions than the doctrine of riparian rights. In reasonable use variant states, the test of reasonableness is ultimately a question for a jury or a judge—not a fact that gives investors or lenders in projects that depend upon water use a great deal of comfort.

**Example 13.3** Jones Farms purchased and installed a state-of-the-art irrigation system for its produce operation. The source of water for the irrigation system was a modest creek that bordered Jones Farms' produce field. Barnes, who was downstream from Jones Farms, found that the creek dried up, leaving him without water for his pond. The pond was a critical component of his agritourism business. Barnes sued in nuisance for an injunction to prevent Jones Farms from pumping. The trial court found a nuisance and granted the injunctive relief requested. As there was no adequate groundwater source, the irrigation system that Jones Farms had installed was rendered useless, valuable only for resale at a substantial discount in the used-equipment market.

## Percolating groundwater

States use a variety of systems for allocating percolating groundwater. These alternatives include the absolute dominion or ownership rule; the reasonable use rule or the "American rule"; the correlative rights doctrine; the beneficial purpose doctrine; and the prior appropriation doctrine (discussed previously).

Under the absolute ownership rule, all percolating waters under the land may be withdrawn by the owner without regard to reasonableness or the effect on other neighboring landowners. Most states that follow this rule make ownership of the groundwater subject to a prohibition on withdrawals where the intent is malicious.

Under the rule of reasonable use, water use by the landowner is limited to the amount necessary for some reasonable beneficial purpose in connection with the overlying land. It is essentially an absolute ownership rule with limitations imposed for negligent, wasteful, malicious, and any off-site use. Under the application of the reasonable use rule, a use such as dewatering a mine is permitted without any liability so long as it is non-negligently conducted, even if that use ruins the ability of neighboring landowners to use their wells.

---

**Example 13.4** Harry Homeowner owned the house near Mega Quarry. Mega Quarry operates a limestone quarry that must pump constantly to dewater its quarry so that quarrying operations can continue. The dewatering operations caused saltwater intrusion into the aquifer. The saltwater came from the nearby ocean. As Harry's house was served by a private well and there is no municipal or county water service, the saltwater intrusion rendered Harry's house unusable and nearly valueless. Harry sued for the lost value in his property. In granting Mega Quarry's pretrial motion to dismiss, the court held that Mega Quarry had acted as a reasonably prudent quarry operator. In applying the state's standard of reasonable use of groundwater, the court noted that the applicable standard is what a reasonable quarry operator would do under similar circumstances.

---

The correlative rights doctrine may be thought of as "riparianism on its side." This rule gives landowners whose land is above the aquifer preference but provides limited rights to non-landowners and transporters if the needs of landowners are satisfied.

The beneficial purpose doctrine attempts to allocate groundwater based upon the landowner's reasonable share and recognizes that groundwater uses may diminish surface waters as a result of the hydrological connection that typically exists between surface and groundwater.

## Artificial bodies of water and treaty waters

Artificial lakes and other such bodies of water are not governed by common law rules. Artificial lakes are generally governed under the law that was used to create them. This may be federal law if the lake was created by the Corps, or it may be state law if the lake was created by an entity governed by state law. The Federal Energy Regulatory Commission (FERC) plays a major role in regulating artificial lakes used for the generation of electric power. The Tennessee Valley Authority regulates much of the surface water throughout the Appalachian region. There are other similar federal and state authorities throughout the country that control vast acreages of surface waters. A landowner whose land abuts one of these artificial waters is not a riparian owner and will have only those rights to use the water that are permitted by the authority that created the artificial body of water.

Some bodies of water, even if natural, are governed by international treaties or treaties with Indian Tribes. There are many such treaties with the United States that limit rights of private landowners to certain waters. As federal law, those treaties preempt state common law and statutory rights by operation of the Supremacy Clause of the Constitution.

### Runoff (diffuse surface waters)

In riparian jurisdictions, runoff is subject to one of three rules: the civil law rule, the common enemy rule, or reasonable use. The civil law rule requires that a landowner not change the natural flow of runoff. Under the common enemy rule, all diversions and all retentions are allowed without regard to reasonableness. In the context of retentions, this is sometimes called the absolute ownership rule. In jurisdictions that apply reasonable use, both diversions and retentions must be reasonable. There are jurisdictions such as Virginia and North Carolina that apply the reasonable use rule to diversions and apply the absolute ownership rule to retentions. In prior appropriation jurisdictions in the western United States, there is usually an owner of diffuse surface water. The person onto whose land precipitation falls may not have a right to use it.

In riparian jurisdictions, the most common water dispute is usually over drainage. If a drainage system is not maintained, water may back into tile systems in farmers' fields. In addition to killing the crop, unwanted backup may cause serious damage to a tile drain system if left uncorrected. As drainage systems typically involve multiple landowners, many riparian states have statutory authority to create drainage districts or water authorities. Drainage districts or water authorities are governmental authorities with the power to compel landowners in the district to maintain their respective portions of the drainage system. Some drainage districts and water authorities have the power to levy taxes. In areas of suburban development, the subdivision of land for residential and commerce uses has presented drainage districts and water authorities with many challenges. Development multiplies the number of landowners and introduces landowners who may fail to understand the need to maintain drainage systems.

## Bodies of water as property boundaries and ownership of submerged lands

Water is navigable if it has historically been used for commercial or recreational transportation. The riparian owner does not own the land under navigable water. The boundary of the riparian owner's property is the mean or average high water mark or, in some states, the vegetation line. Lands under navigable waters are owned by the state under the public trust doctrine. There are exceptions to this rule for existing grants of submerged lands and for those submerged lands that have been leased. For non-navigable waters, each riparian owner along a watercourse owns all of the land to the middle of the main channel, unless a deed states otherwise. For non-navigable lakes, the boundaries are generally pie-shaped, with the submerged land diminishing in width as it reaches the middle. For bodies of water that are subject to the tide, the boundary is the average high tide line. Example 13.5 illustrates the principle that the public may use navigable water for transport without trespassing on the property of the riparian owners.

---

**Example 13.5** Larry canoed the length of Red Creek. Red Creek is a tidal body of water that is historically navigable even though it is narrow. John owns the land on both sides of Red Creek. As Red Creek is navigable, John owns only to the mean high tide line. Larry may canoe on the creek and set foot on its bank below the mean high tide line without trespassing on John's property. Larry may also fish in Red Creek from his canoe.

---

A riparian owner's boundary may change gradually with time. Accretion is a gradual increase in the landowner's property. It may occur as alluvion from sediment that is added to the land or from reliction as water levels permanently fall. The reverse may happen. Erosion may result in the loss of soil that reduces the property, or rising water levels may result in submergence that reduces the acreage of the property. Sudden changes do not change property boundaries. A sudden change in a stream's banks as a result of a storm is called avulsion. Artificial causes also do not change boundaries.

## Water pollution

The federal Clean Water Act (CWA)[6] and other federal laws define the federal effort to regulate water pollution. Jurisdiction for most of these efforts is with the Environmental Protection Agency (EPA). Many EPA programs are delegated to the states. The Corps is responsible for issuing permits for activities in wetlands. The effort of the Corps is coordinated with the EPA and state agencies.

As a matter of legislative convenience, Congress divided sources of water pollution into point and nonpoint sources. Point sources are easily identified and concentrated. Nonpoint sources are hard to identify and diffuse. There is not a bright line that separates point sources from nonpoint sources. The result has been much litigation over this issue. Nonpoint sources receive a much lower level of scrutiny. Some sources are defined by statute to be nonpoint sources, importantly the agricultural exemption in the CWA that defines normal runoff from agricultural and silvicultural activities to be nonpoint. The most common sources of nonpoint pollution are farming, construction, and mining.

All individuals who wish to use surface water for waste disposal are regulated by the EPA and the state in which the water is found. A National Pollutant Discharge Elimination System (NPDES) permit is required of any person making a direct discharge to surface water. Large, total-confinement livestock operations are defined as animal feeding operations (AFOs). AFOs are exempt from the permit requirement under the agricultural exemption. The CWA requires that confined animal feeding operations (CAFOs) have an NPDES permit. There has been much litigation about the question of when an AFO becomes a CAFO. In general, an AFO loses the agricultural exemption and becomes a CAFO if it has a history of actual discharges. An AFO can avoid this outcome by ensuring that there are no actual discharges and that all applications of waste to crops and pasture are at agronomic rates.

---

**Example 13.6** Larry raises corn on hilly ground. Sheet erosion from his corn fields fouls the creek that borders his farm. As sheet erosion is normal runoff from agriculture, it is protected as nonpoint source pollution under the agricultural exemption in the CWA. Larry does not need to apply for an NPDES permit.

---

**Example 13.7** Jones makes apple cider from apples that he grows in his orchard. Waste from his cider press flows into a small stream next to his press. As this value-added processing is not a normal agricultural activity within the agricultural exemption to the CWA, he must either obtain an NPDES permit or cease discharging into the stream. His failure to do so may subject him to civil and even criminal penalties.

---

Most activities in wetlands require permits under sections 404 and 401 of the Clean Water Act.[7] The Corps administers the section 404 permitting program, and states administer section 401 programs. Violation of wetlands rules may also make a farmer ineligible to receive farm program benefits.

There are many names for wetlands such as swamps, bogs, marshlands, and sloughs. Likewise, there are many ways to define wetlands. The CWA defines wetlands on the basis of three factors. A wetland must have wetland hydrology. A wetland must have hydrophilic vegetation. This is vegetation that typically grows in wet areas. Finally, a wetland must have hydric soil.

The Corps' *Wetlands Delineation Manual* provides guidance to wetlands delineators. If an area has water present for at least 5 percent of the growing season, it meets the hydrology requirements for wetlands. There are other factors to consider when evaluating hydrology. These include soil saturation within a foot of the surface, water marks, drift lines, water-stained leaves, remains of aquatic vertebrates, and sediment deposits. Wetlands vegetation is quite variable; however, it must be of the type of vegetation that can tolerate very wet conditions or that requires wet conditions. Hydric soils are those that develop under anaerobic conditions. These soils have unique characteristics.

Not all wetlands are within the jurisdiction of the CWA. Only those waters that are waters of the United States are within the jurisdiction of the CWA. Arriving at a workable definition of a water of the United States that can be used to determine jurisdiction is an issue that has been litigated for years. The Supreme Court decision in *Rapanos v. U.S.*[8] established two inconsistent definitions for the water of the United States. The first was the definition of the plurality that held that there must be a continuous surface water connection between the water to be regulated and a water that is navigable in fact. The second definition is found in Justice Kennedy's concurring opinion. He held that a water of the United States is one with a significant nexus to a water that is navigable in fact. Unlike the opinion of the plurality, Justice Kennedy's definition does not exclude waters that have a significant nexus to a water that is navigable in fact through a groundwater connection. In 2015, the Corps and the EPA jointly published a final rule defining the scope of waters of the United States.[9] In 2018, the Corps and the EPA jointly extended the effective date of this rule to February 6, 2020, preserving the *status quo* prior to the 2015 final rule. This reflects both a change of policy accompanying a change of administration and litigation that had enjoined implementation of the 2015 final rule.[10]

Section 404 regulates the discharge of dredged or fill material into a water of the United States. It does not regulate removal of material from a water of the United States. The Corps lacks authority to regulate incidental fallback that results from excavation, land clearing, channelization, and trenching in wetlands. Some courts have held that draining a wetland entirely is regulated under section 404 because it eliminates a water of the United States entirely. Any activity that substantially changes the character of a wetland is in that gray area that is likely to be regulated under section 404. Section 404(f)(1)(A) provides an exemption from the NPDES permit requirement for "normal farming, silviculture, and ranching activities such as plowing, seeding, cultivating, minor drainage, harvesting for the production of food, fiber, and forest products, or upland soil and water conservation practices."[11]

## Notes

1 E-mail from Drew Kershen, Earl Sneed Professor of Law (Emeritus), University of Oklahoma, College of Law (February 17, 2015).
2 Joseph W. Dellapenna, The Law of Water Allocation in the Southeastern States at the Opening of the Twenty-First Century, 25 *University of Arkansas, Little Rock, Law Review* 9 (2002).
3 Dellapenna, at 32.
4 E-mail from Drew Kershen.
5 L&S Water Power, Inc. v. Piedmont Triad Regional Water Authority, 211 N.C. App. 148, 712 S.E.2d 146, 2011 N.C. App. LEXIS 734 (N.C. Ct. App. 2011); aff'd mem., 737 S.E.2d 379; 2013 N.C. LEXIS 177 (2013).
6 33 U.S.C. §§ 1251 to 1388 (2013).

7  33 U.S.C. §§ 1341 and 1344 (2013).
8  547 U.S. 715, 126 S. Ct. 2208; 165 L. Ed. 2d 159, 2006 U.S. LEXIS 4887 (2006).
9  Clean Water Rule: Definition of "Waters of the United States", 80 Fed. Reg. 37,054 (2015).
10 Definition of "Waters of the United States"—Addition of an Applicability Date to 2015 Clean Water Rule, 83 Fed. Reg. 5,200 (2018); Memorandum to the Record: Consideration of Potential Economic Impacts for the Final Rule: Definition of "Waters of the United States" – Addition of Applicability Date to 2015 Clean Water Rule. (2018). Retrieved June 22, 2018, from the EPA Website: https://www.epa.gov/sites/production/files/2018-02/documents/2018-02429_0.pdf.
11 33 U.S.C. § 1344(f)(1)(A)(2014).

# Chapter 14

# Business entities

## Introduction

There are multiple types of business organizations. The choice of a form of business organization depends upon many factors. Reducing tax obligations is one of the first objectives that comes to mind with most people when they choose a form of business organization. For most businesses, it is not the most important reason for choosing a form of business organization. One also has to be specific as to which tax one wishes to reduce. There are state and federal income taxes, franchise taxes, excise taxes, state inheritance or estate taxes, federal estate taxes, real estate taxes, personal property taxes, sales taxes, and others that are as diverse as the governmental entities in the United States that assess taxes. In choosing a form of business organization, it is essential to determine the types of taxes that the business will face and estimate the taxes due for each under each of the types of business organizations being considered.

Developing a workable management structure is one of the most important factors in choosing a form of business organization. Businesses that assign different management functions to different members of the business are usually more successful than those where all the members of the business are responsible for all management functions.

Liability avoidance is another important factor in choosing a form of business organization. For family businesses, the protective function of a business entity is often quite limited because the family members are also directly involved in the activities of the business. A person who is directly involved in an activity that generates liability is likely to have personal liability because that person's acts or omissions gave rise to liability.

Providing an adequate vehicle for attracting outside investment is another reason for choosing a particular type of business entity. Some types of business entities are particularly well suited to shielding outside investors from liability. If there is interest in growing the business, some types of business entities may facilitate that growth better than others.

The choice of business entities is also important to business owners as they develop their estate plans. Certain types of business entities allow management and ownership to be separated. When one child wants to farm and the child's siblings have no wish to farm, management responsibilities may be vested in the child who wishes to farm. As owners of the business the other siblings will have a right to share in the profits even though they do not have a management role. For closely held businesses, restrictions on sales or other transfers of interests in the business can accomplish multiple objectives. These restrictions can prevent ownership from being fragmented. For large farm businesses, restrictions on transfers of ownership interests may result in asset valuation reductions of 40 percent or more that can reduce estate taxes.

Costs and formalities are closely related considerations when picking a form of business organization. Costs are both those expenses expected to be incurred in setting up the business entity and those of operating it. Expenses of setting up the business entity include the fees for attorneys and tax experts and fees charged by states to register the business entity. Costs of maintaining the business entity will also include fees charged for preparation of tax returns and annual fees charged by states to maintain registration of the business. Other costs will include that of mandatory meetings of directors and shareholders and that of required records. There are also fees for separate bank accounts for the business entity. Formalities are the steps that one must go through to maintain the business as a viable entity. There may also be requirements for periodic audits that can add considerably to the cost of operating the business.

The failure to keep records and observe required formalities can be catastrophic to a business entity. Where records are not kept, business funds are comingled with personal funds, and formalities are not observed, it is unlikely that a judge will honor the business form and the protections that it provides. This is sometimes called "piercing the corporate veil." Failure to pay required fees to the state may result in the state's canceling the business registration. This terminates the separate legal existence of the business entity from that of its owners. Income tax consequences can be disastrous when this happens, as the tax obligations of the business entity are transferred to the owners of the business entity. Any liabilities of the entity become liabilities of the individual owners. Given the catastrophic consequences of the failure to observe formalities, a business owner contemplating the use of a particular type of business entity must assess his or her ability to observe formalities and pay the necessary costs of maintaining the business. In general, the simplest form of business organization that will meet the needs of the business owners is the appropriate form of business organization to select.

## Sole proprietorship

A sole proprietorship is the simplest form of business. One person sells a service or product under his or her own name or a fictitious name. One person owns all the assets and holds all leases of real and personal property. One person is responsible for all the debts and liabilities. The income, for federal income tax purposes, is usually reported on the individual's Schedule C or Schedule F of

Form 1040. Though there is not an absolute prohibition on co-mingling personal and business funds in a sole proprietorship, it is a bad idea. Co-mingling funds complicates income tax reporting and makes responding to an IRS audit much more difficult. It is also a red flag for lenders that makes it more difficult to obtain funding at a good price.

A sole proprietorship has one important advantage over other forms of business organization. The owner of a business operated as a sole proprietorship may represent the business in court without the necessity of hiring an attorney. All other forms of business organization must hire a licensed attorney to sue in the business's name. Even the sole owner of an LLC cannot represent the LLC in court because the owner and the LLC are legally separate persons. For the owner to represent the LLC in court represents the unauthorized practice of law. There is one exception to this rule. A representative of the business entity other than a sole proprietorship may represent the entity in court to seek a continuance to allow time to find a licensed attorney to represent the entity.

**Example 14.1** George Jones created and registered George LLC as his business entity. He conducted his vegetable farm and community-supported agriculture (CSA) operation through George LLC. George LLC had its own bank account, and CSA customers wrote checks out to George LLC. George Jones is not a licensed attorney. Jones sued Slippery Sidney in small claims court for the $3,029.11 that was owed George LLC. Sidney asked the judge to dismiss the case because Jones was not a licensed attorney. Jones did not know that he could ask for a continuance to give him time to find an attorney for George LLC. For that reason, Jones did not ask the judge for a continuance. The judge dismissed the case. As the statute of limitations on collecting a debt had run, George LLC was barred from refiling the case with proper legal representation.

## General partnership

A general partnership is an association of two or more persons to conduct a business for a profit. The relationship is consensual and contractual. A partnership is treated as an entity for litigation, holding title to property, and bankruptcy proceedings. It is a pass-through entity for federal income tax purposes. That means that all income taxes are paid at the individual level on individual partner income tax returns. Most states have adopted the Uniform Partnership Act (UPA).[1] The UPA provides default provisions for partnership agreements. When a partnership agreement is silent about a particular issue, UPA provisions apply. Those forming a partnership are free to change most of those provisions in their partnership agreement.

A partnership can arise through conduct. If two people do business together and hold themselves out as partners, the law will treat them as a partnership. The UPA provides the terms of these oral partnership agreements.

Under the UPA, the partners have equal management authority and share equally in profits and losses. They have an equal obligation to contribute their time, energy, and skill without compensation to the partnership business. All these default provisions can be changed by provisions in the partnership agreement.

Each partner has unlimited personal liability to the creditors of the partnership. If the partnership agreement included the limited liability partnership provisions of the UPA, partners may have limited liability for the negligence of a partner. This provision applies only to sums owed for a partner's negligence. A partnership may file a statement that limits the authority of a particular partner or partners. Once filed, this statement is binding on third parties and limits the liability of partners for the acts of a partner who exceeded his or her authority.

A partnership files a federal information tax return (Form 1065) annually. However, all income flows through and is taxed to the individual partners. A partnership interest is personal to the partner. The partnership is dissolved by the death of a partner or by the sale of a partnership share. Most provisions of the UPA can be modified in a written partnership agreement (e.g., capital contributions, management, sharing of profits and losses, rights and obligations, terms of property ownership, termination and dissolution, and buy/sell agreements).

There are provisions of UPA that may not be waived. The right of each partner to have access to books and records cannot be unreasonably restricted. Each partner has a fiduciary duty to the partnership. The fiduciary duty consists of a duty of loyalty and a duty of care. The duty of loyalty requires that each partner account to the partnership for any property, profit, or benefit derived by a partner in the conduct or winding up of the partnership business. It also precludes a partner from working for a competing business without permission of the partnership. This duty of loyalty of each partner to the partnership cannot be waived except that the partnership agreement may identify certain categories of activities that do not violate the duty of loyalty to the partnership. With full disclosure and a vote of a certain percentage of the owners, certain individual transactions may be authorized by individual partners. The duty of care requires each partner to avoid grossly negligent, reckless, or unlawful conduct. Other provisions that cannot be waived include obligation of good faith and fair dealing that may be defined in the partnership agreement, various provisions having to do with the disassociation or expulsion of a partner, and the winding up of the partnership business.

**Example 14.2** James was a general partner in a farming business that operated a CSA. John, the owner of their largest competitor, offered to sell his CSA to James because debilitating illness forced him to sell at a very attractive price.

Rather than offer the opportunity to the partnership, James bought the business in his own name and began operating it. The partnership demanded that he sell the CSA to the partnership at the price that he paid for it. James' attorney told him that his fiduciary duty requires him to comply. Should he fail to do so, the partnership could sue and force him to do so.

Partnerships do not have unlimited life. A partner's notice of disassociation or death may result in dissolution and winding up of the partnership business. Partners may voluntarily agree to dissolve and wind up the partnership's business. Some partnerships are created for a particular undertaking. When that undertaking is complete, the partnership will be dissolved. The occurrence of an event upon which the partners had previously agreed that the partnership would be dissolved is another way that partnerships end. Any time a partnership is dissolved, there may be important tax consequences that require the assistance of a tax expert.

## Limited partnerships

A limited partnership has the characteristics of both a partnership and a corporation. It is used when some partners want neither management responsibility nor unlimited liability for the business venture. Most states have adopted the Limited Partnership Act (LPA).[2] Under this statute, a limited partnership is formed with at least one general partner and one or more limited partners. A general partner manages the partnership and has full personal liability for the debts of the partnership. A limited partner contributes cash or other property. Her or his liability for partnership debts is limited to the amount of his or her investment in the partnership. Limited partners do not participate in the management of the partnership. A limited partnership is a pass through entity that files an information return, but income is taxed to the individual partners. Though limited partners share in the profits of the business, the losses of limited partners cannot exceed the amount of their investment. The formula for sharing the profits is defined in the partnership agreement.

A limited partnership can be a useful vehicle for farm business estate planning. As estate planning vehicles, limited partnerships are usually called family limited partnerships, reflecting that membership in the partnership is usually restricted to family members. The limited partnership can be used to remove the generation that wishes to retire from active management and thereby remove their assets from exposure to business liabilities. As a limited partner, only the retired member of the farm business's assets that remain invested in a limited partnership can be taken to satisfy a judgment. The caution that must be exercised is that the retired member of the family business must refrain from engaging in any of the business management activities. This is often difficult for retired farmers to do if they still reside on the farm. If the retired farmer is in fact actually involved with the management of the business, a court may use that as a basis for stripping away the protection for the retired farmer's personal assets that the limited partnership was intended to provide.

---

**Example 14.3** Gus decided it was time to retire from farming. He created a limited partnership with his son, Junior, as general partner and himself as limited partner. Every morning, Gus gave Junior a "to do" list. Gus maintained sole control over the partnership bank accounts. As Gus is acting as a general partner, a court would hold that he is a general partner that is fully liable for all partnership debts.

---

**Example 14.4** Gus decided it was time to retire from farming. He created a limited partnership with Junior as general partner and himself as limited partner. Gus moved to his beloved North Carolina mountains, where he spent most of his time fly fishing. Junior had sole control over the partnership bank accounts. Junior called Gus once a week to discuss the farm business and ask his father's advice. Gus never told Junior to make a particular decision. A court would most likely hold that Gus is a limited partner who is not liable for the partnership debts.

---

A second use for family limited partnerships is to reduce asset valuations used in the calculation of the federal taxable estate. Family limited partnerships usually contain restrictions on selling the partnership assets. Assets thus restricted have less value than assets that are not subject to any such restrictions. The two most common valuation discounts are alienation and minority interest discounts. An alienation discount is available for the valuation of assets that cannot be easily bought or sold. The minority interest discount is available for the valuation of assets whose owner controls less than 50 percent of the limited partnership. Combining these two discounts routinely produces asset valuation discounts in the 40 percent range. Given a 40 percent tax rate on the portion of an estate subject to the federal estate tax, valuation discounts can reduce estate taxes from any family farms sufficiently to avoid having to sell farm assets.

Although beyond the scope of this chapter, the structure of a family limited partnership may have important consequences for federal farm program payment eligibility and limitation rules. These rules are complex and require competent legal advice to interpret correctly.

## Limited liability company

The limited liability company (LLC) is a distinct entity that is a hybrid of a partnership and a corporation. The Limited Liability Company Act (LLC Act) provides model provisions for state laws governing LLCs.[3] Although some states follow the current version of the Act, the majority of states follow older versions. The LLC is a relatively new form of business organization that was created to avoid the unlimited personal liability associated with general partnerships while preserving the pass-through character of the income. Prior to the development of the LLC, only the corporation provided the same level of protection from liability.

The LLC form provides a great deal of flexibility because agreements can be developed between members and managers to accomplish specific business goals. The LLC does not have to be for profit. It is often used as a vehicle for nonprofit organizations. Where there is one owner, the tax issues raised by an LLC are much easier to address than the tax issues raised by a corporation.

An LLC is created by making a filing with the state secretary of state. Additional filings can be made to put creditors on notice as to whether the LLC is a manager-managed LLC or a member-managed LLC. The filing can also indicate, for a member-managed LLC, which member has the authority to act on behalf of the LLC. These filings provide the LLC with protection against third parties based upon the unauthorized actions of a member or manager. The manager of an LLC need not be a member or owner of the LLC. There is no requirement that an LLC operating agreement be in writing; however, if it is not in writing, it cannot be filed with the state's secretary of state to provide notice to third-party creditors. There is generally an initial filing fee charged by the secretary of state and annual renewal fees thereafter. Failure to pay renewal fees may result in involuntary dissolution of the LLC by the secretary of state. An LLC that is dissolved by the secretary of state is automatically converted to a general partnership. This may have serious implications for both tax and other sources of personal liability.

An LLC operating agreement may contain restrictions on the transfer of owners' interests in a manner similar to those applicable to family limited partnerships. Conversely, the operating agreement may specify that the ownership interests in the LLC are freely transferable. This allows the interest to be used as security for debt under Article 8 of the UCC. Nonetheless, the purchaser of an interest in the LLC at a foreclosure sale does not automatically become a member of the LLC. The requirements of a duty of care and loyalty may be reduced in the operating agreement to an extent not allowed in partnerships. An owner of an interest in the LLC does not have a fiduciary duty to the LLC or to the other owners of the LLC, unless the owner is a majority owner of the LLC. In that case, the majority owner has a duty not to oppress the minority owners.

Whether the LLC or its members have a duty to buy out the departing member is a question of state law. The issue is best resolved in the operating agreement. One important difference between a partnership and an LLC is the ability of a member to bring a derivative action. A derivative action is an action brought by a member on behalf of the LLC to recover funds that were wrongfully taken from the LLC by its managers or members. This aspect of an LLC is much more like a corporation. Some states also allow a member to sue the LLC directly. There is a great deal of variation in state law, and the best way to resolve these issues is generally in the operating agreement of the LLC.

For purposes of federal income tax, the default rule is that an LLC with two or more members will be treated as a partnership and required to file Form 1065. If there is only one member of the LLC, federal tax law will treat it as a disregarded entity, and the owner will report income on his or her individual tax return. For purposes of other taxes such as excise taxes and employment taxes, it may be treated as a separate legal entity. The members of an LLC may elect to be treated as an association taxed as a corporation or an S corporation.

As with family limited partnerships, LLCs can be excellent tools for estate planning. The operating agreement can be crafted to provide for the orderly transfer of management control between generations. Restrictions on the transfer of membership interests may be used to create alienation and minority interest discounts that are useful in reducing valuations of farm property for estate tax purposes. There has been much discussion about whether the LLC form is as useful for creating valuation discounts as the family limited partnership. As the family limited partnership is a much older entity type than the LLC, there is more case law involving family limited partnerships. Lawyers are often more comfortable with the large body of precedents involving family limited partnerships than with the smaller body of precedents involving LLCs. In choosing between the two forms, the choice is ultimately the client's based upon an assessment of the comparative risks and benefits of each form. For purposes of the limitation on federal farm program payments, a LLC is treated differently from a family limited partnership. A LLC is considered a single entity, in contrast to a family limited partnership that is treated as multiple entities for purposes of the limitation rule. Where application of the limitation on federal farm program payments is an issue, a family limited partnership may be a better choice than a LLC.

## Corporations

Corporations are formed under state law. A corporation is a legal entity that has rights and liabilities separate from its shareholders. A shareholder of a corporation is only liable for the debts of the corporation to the extent of his or her investment in the corporation. Shareholders elect a board of directors who set policy and appoint officers to manage the company on a daily basis. Shareholders do not participate directly in management decisions (unless they are also directors or officers). A corporation has a potentially unlimited life, and it is not dissolved by the death of a shareholder, director, or officer.

A corporation formed under Subchapter C of the Internal Revenue Code is an ordinary corporation subject to double taxation, which means that profits are taxed as they are earned by the corporation and then, when those profits are distributed to the shareholders as dividends, they are taxed again to the individual. A corporation formed under Subchapter S is a close corporation that has elected to be taxed like a partnership. Instead of being taxed at the corporation level, the income flows through to the shareholders and is taxed only once, at the individual level (whether the profits are or are not distributed). Additional IRC requirements, which include limitations on the classes of stock and the number of shareholders, make qualifying as a corporation under Subchapter S more difficult than qualifying as a corporation under Subchapter C.

Generally, shares of stock are freely transferable by the stockholder. However, state law permits the creation of restrictions on stock transfers by the articles of incorporation, bylaws, and an agreement among shareholders or an agreement between shareholders and the corporation. A restriction must be authorized by the statue and not unconscionable under the circumstances, and there must be a conspicuous notice of the restriction on the certificate or in the information statement required by the statute. One type of restriction would be a buy-sell agreement between a stockholder and the corporation or other stockholders requiring the selling stockholder to offer her or his stock first to the other party to the agreement. The agreement would set a price to be paid for the shares, which would be particularly useful if the shares were not publicly traded.

Shares in a corporation can be defined as common or preferred, based on the rights and privileges that belong to the owner. Common stock represents a fractional proprietary interest in the property and assets of a corporation. Therefore, the common shareholder participates on a pro rata basis in the distribution of corporate assets upon dissolution, participation in corporate profits (dividends), and management of corporate activities (right to vote). Traditionally, holders of preferred stock are not creditors of the corporation and, therefore, do not share in corporate assets upon dissolution. Instead, they have a right to a fixed dividend, due and payable before any dividends to common shareholders. However, the articles of incorporation can grant rights to preferred shareholders to receive preference over common shareholders with regard to distributions of dividends and corporate dissolution proceeds.

---

**Example 14.5** James is the sole preferred shareholder in the Acme Best Farming Corp. Under the articles of incorporation, he is entitled to the first $20,000 of profits to be paid as a dividend. Should the corporation be dissolved, he is entitled to the return of his $100,000 purchase of his shares. His preferred shares have no vote. In 2013, Acme generated $10.13 of profits, all of which was paid to James. The common shareholders voted to dissolve the corporation in 2014. After sale of all the assets of Acme and payment of creditors, $5,343.44 remained. This was distributed to James. The common shareholders received nothing.

---

The shareholders are the actual owners of the corporation, and ultimately they choose the people who will manage the company. Under state law, the shareholders must elect a board of directors to whom they delegate the power of management. The board is responsible for all the business affairs of the corporation, such as issuing shares of stock and the rights of the shares issued, the sale of corporate assets, mortgaging corporate assets, declaring dividends, and the election of corporate officers. The senior management of the company, represented by the chief executive officer and the senior management team, are responsible for the day-to-day operations of the corporation. Their authority and duties are prescribed by the bylaws and the directors.

The articles of incorporation must be filed with the secretary of state where the business is incorporated. The filing must contain the following information: a corporate name; the number of shares that may be issued; the street address and mailing address, including county, of the initial registered office and the name of the initial registered agent; and the name and address of each incorporator. This document may also provide the names and addresses of the initial board of directors, provisions regarding the business purpose and par value of shares, and limitations on the personal liability of directors. At the organizational meeting of the corporation, bylaws should be adopted. This document may contain any provisions for managing the company and regulating the affairs of the company that are legal and consistent with the articles of incorporation. The bylaws are the continuing set of governing rules under which the corporation and its officers, directors, and shareholders exercise management powers, transfer shares, and hold meetings and all other activities related to the corporate objective.

There are two ways to dissolve and terminate a corporation: voluntary dissolution and involuntary dissolution. The directors and shareholders may voluntarily dissolve a corporation by passage of a resolution of dissolution and filing of articles of dissolution with the secretary of state. In addition, a corporation may be dissolved without its consent by court action or administrative action of the secretary of state. If the directors are not acting in the best interest of the company, any shareholder may obtain judicial dissolution. If the corporation fails to file annual reports or pay franchise tax, for example, the secretary of state may administratively dissolve the corporation. As with an LLC, this may have serious implications both for tax and other sources of personal liability.

## Cooperatives

Cooperatives are a time-honored form of business organization for farmers. Cooperatives are organized under state law and vary considerably from one state to another. Cooperatives may be organized on a stock or non-stock basis. In either case, farmers pool their resources either for buying inputs, marketing products, or both. Cooperatives retain revenue in excess of expenses for a period of time to cover contingencies. After some period of time, excess revenue is returned to the members of the cooperative. Cooperatives are rarely used as the business entity of the farm business. Cooperatives are typically used by groups of farmers to improve their market power when buying inputs and selling farm products.

One of the important benefits of farmer cooperatives is an exemption from federal antitrust laws under the Capper-Volstead Act, enacted in 1922.[4] The

Capper-Volstead Act is not a blanket exemption from federal antitrust laws. To claim the benefit of the exemption, a cooperative must operate for the mutual benefit of producers of agricultural products and must not deal in the products of nonmembers in an amount that exceeds the value of the products that it handles for its members. Cooperatives cannot engage in restraint of trade.

## Conclusion

Farm clients seeking to set up a business entity often look for "the answer." There is no such answer. Determining the type of business entity best for a particular farm will depend upon individual circumstances. The business owners' tolerance for paperwork and willingness to contract for professional legal and tax services are major considerations. Though avoiding liability is an important consideration, no type of business entity provides complete protection. This is especially true for smaller, family-owned farms where the owner is also the operator and the primary or only employee. Larger, multigenerational farms with potential federal estate tax liability, or the need to qualify for federal farm program payments, will need a more complex array of entities.

Operating agreements for partnerships and LLCs, and bylaws and shareholder agreements for corporations, are seldom given sufficient consideration. Operating agreements govern a wide variety of issues that include management, assignment of tax attributes including income and losses, and arrangements for succession. Bylaws and shareholder agreements do the same for the shareholders in corporations. Bylaws provide detail that was not included in the articles of incorporation. Corporate bylaws are much easier to amend than the articles of incorporation as articles of incorporation must be filed with the secretary of state. Shareholder agreements are contracts outside of the corporation between shareholders. Such agreements may include some or all of the shareholders of the corporation. Of particular importance in these agreements are buy-sell arrangements that govern how the share of a deceased or departing owner are to be paid out. These agreements may also contain provisions to protect the owners of minority interests from oppression by those who own the majority of the entity.

## Notes

1 Uniform Law Commission. *Uniform Partnership Act.* Retrieved July 26, 2018, www.uniformlaws.org/Shared/Docs/Partnership/UPA%20_Final_2014_2015aug19.pdf.
2 Uniform Law Commission. *Limited Partnership Act.* Retrieved July 26, 2018, www.uniformlaws.org/Shared/Docs/Limited%20Partnership/ULPA_Final_2014_2015aug19.pdf.
3 Uniform Law Commission. *Limited Liability Company Act.* Retrieved July 26, 2018, www.uniformlaws.org/shared/docs/limited%20liability%20company/ULLCA_Final_2014_2015aug19.pdf.
4 USDA Rural Development. *Understanding Capper-Volstead.* Retrieved July 26, 2018, www.rd.usda.gov/files/cir35.pdf.

# Chapter 15

# Animal law

## Introduction

Animal law encompasses a disparate body of law governing the treatment of animals and poultry. Animals are tangible personal property, as were enslaved persons prior to the ratification of the Thirteenth Amendment on December 6, 1865. As the acknowledged humanness of enslaved persons, largely based upon sentience, created tension with their treatment as tangible personal property, the acknowledged sentience of animals creates a tension with their treatment as tangible personal property.[1] There is a great deal of debate about the extent to which animals are sentient. Yet, there is no doubt that animals feel pain and have some degree of awareness. It is a matter of history that the debate between those with property interests in enslaved persons and those who favored abolition was a contributing factor to the Civil War. Though the debate over the treatment of livestock is unlikely to lead to another civil war, that debate is leading to the creation of a great deal of agricultural law. There has been widespread support for laws to ensure the humane treatment of livestock and poultry. For readers interested in a science-based approach to the humane handling and slaughter of livestock, various books and research papers by Temple Grandin, a professor of animal science at Colorado State University, are an excellent starting point.[2] No one opposes the humane treatment of livestock and poultry; however, there is sharp disagreement about what constitutes humane treatment. Most livestock and poultry producers believe that they already treat their livestock and poultry humanely. They argue that many proposals are not science-based and would result in less humane treatment. There is a small, but vocal, minority that believe that livestock and poultry have intrinsic rights and should not be eaten, sheared, or otherwise used for human purposes. Some of these individuals have engaged in civil disobedience and acts that the law defines as terrorism (bioterrorism in non-legal terminology). The livestock and poultry industry has responded with a variety of legislative efforts to criminalize the surreptitious photography and videography of the inside of slaughter plants and large livestock and poultry operations. These statutes are based on the police power of the state to protect private property. The livestock and poultry industry has sought to shield information about livestock and poultry farms, including the locations of those farms, from inclusion in public records. Individual livestock and poultry farms and slaughter plants have been forced to take steps to protect their operations from threats of terrorism.

The first part of the law governing animals and poultry addresses the rights and obligations of owners. As animals are capable of moving from one place to another on their own, owners have obligations to control their movement and prevent damage to the property of others. Animals also contract diseases, some of which may be transferred to humans. Diseases capable of transfer from animals to humans are called zoonotic illnesses. The law imposes obligations upon owners to prevent the transmission of disease to other animals or humans. Owners also have rights as animals are tangible personal property. When animals are killed or injured by others, owners may have a right to recovery. In general, owners may recover the fair market value of an animal that was wrongfully killed by another. Many people have invested emotions in animals that they own as pets; however, the law of most states allows only recovery of the fair market value of the animal. In the case of a pet, the value is often zero.

The second part of animal law addresses the welfare of the animals themselves. Concern for animal welfare is ancient. The Bible, out of concern that working animals be allowed to eat, states, "Thou shalt not muzzle the ox when he treadeth out the corn."[3] Many religious traditions, including both Judaism and Islam, have rules for slaughter that reflect respect for the animals to be eaten. These rules were also undoubtedly conceived to protect human health. Modern rules reflect both of these concerns. Local governments usually focus on preventing neglect of animals, cruelty to animals, and protection of public health. Slaughter of animals and poultry that are sold in interstate commerce are under the jurisdiction of the federal government. States provide regulation for small-scale, intrastate slaughter in sales of livestock and poultry. States provide the statutory framework for local regulations.

The third and most controversial part of animal law addresses the question of the intrinsic rights of animals. Centuries of English law have never recognized that animals have any rights apart from the rights of their owners. Under English law, animals and poultry are chattels, defined as tangible personal property. This is in contrast to other religious and cultural traditions that revere certain animals, birds, trees, and other forms of life. Whether those traditions recognize intrinsic rights in those animals or birds may be debated. There is a vocal minority within the United States that would recognize intrinsic rights in animals and birds as well as fish. That viewpoint has gained no traction in its effort to seek recognition of intrinsic rights in other forms of life. Though not successful in changing the law governing livestock and poultry, the movement has probably contributed to public concern for the welfare of livestock and poultry. Often missed in this debate over animal welfare is that a cultural reverence for life, including a refusal to kill or eat animals, often does not imply a cultural obligation to intervene to improve animal welfare.

There is an important distinction between livestock and poultry used in agriculture as compared to animals and birds used for other purposes such as pets and medical research. Equine species have characteristics of both pets and livestock. Although equine species are classified as livestock under common law, there are enough distinctions from other livestock that equine species are probably best treated as a special category for legal purposes. Animals and birds that are not domesticated are wildlife and are treated under the wildlife laws of the states and federal government. Dogs have both agricultural uses and roles as companion animals or pets. Dogs are not classified as livestock under the law. For that reason, the breeding and selling of dogs is not treated as an agricultural activity under the laws of most states. Agricultural uses and roles as companion animals are not mutually exclusive. As the subject matter of this book is agricultural, this chapter will primarily address the law governing livestock, poultry, equine species, and dogs as used in agriculture. As hunting is an important component of agritourism, the complex law governing wildlife will be addressed briefly.

## Livestock and poultry

### Fencing laws

Whether an owner of livestock must confine his or her livestock is a question of state law. In what are known as fence-in states, it is the obligation of livestock owners to build and maintain an adequate fence to contain their livestock. In fence-out or open range states, livestock owners have no obligation to contain their livestock. Some states have only portions of the state that are open range. Some states allow certain species of livestock, for example cattle, to roam at large, but prohibit other species, such as swine, from roaming at large.

In fence-out states, the owner of livestock has no responsibility for the damage that the livestock do to another person's property. It is a responsibility of the property owner to construct an adequate fence to keep free-roaming livestock off his or her property. It is also the responsibility of other property owners and the public at large to avoid either negligent or intentional injury to free-roaming livestock. In fence-out states, identity of free-roaming livestock is maintained through a system of brands or other permanent markings. Each fence-out state has laws to ensure that livestock owners are protected from attempts to steal the livestock by altering the brand or other permanent identifier.

The laws of fence-in states are in sharp contrast to those of free range states. In fence-in states, the livestock owner has the obligation to construct and maintain an adequate fence to keep his livestock contained. An owner is liable for injuries or damages caused by her or his livestock when they are trespassing on the lands of another only if the animals are at large with her or his knowledge and consent, or if their escape is due to his or her negligence. The owner has a legal duty to exercise ordinary care and the foresight of a prudent person in restraining his or her animals onto his or her property. Even though there is no presumption of knowledge or negligence when an animal gets loose from its owner, these may be inferred if the animal is repeatedly found at large. Some such states apply a standard of strict liability for damages that straying livestock cause. A livestock owner who either intentionally allowed his or her livestock to stray or acted with reckless disregard for whether they strayed could be liable for punitive damages under either an intentional tort or gross negligence theory. Most fence-in states apply criminal penalties to those livestock owners who intentionally permit their livestock to stray.

---

**Example 15.1** Speedy was driving down a lonesome highway in an open range state when he hit a Black Angus cow standing in the middle of the road. The cow was rendered dead and useless to its owner. Speedy's car was a total loss, and he himself was not much better. From his hospital bed, he hired an attorney who told him the sad news. He was in the wrong, and the cow was in the right. He would have to pay the owner the fair market value of the cow, which was prize breeding stock. For his own injuries and his car, those were his losses to bear.

---

**Example 15.2** Wilbur owned a small farm on which he raised cattle. He did not like repairing fences and seldom did so. The state where Wilbur's farm is located is a fence-in state. One night as Maude was driving along the public highway that bordered Wilbur's farm, she hit one of his cows that had strayed into the road. Maude's car was a total loss, and she had serious injuries. She sued Wilbur under a negligence theory for the damage to her car and her personal injuries. At trial, Wilbur conceded that he seldom repaired his fences and his cattle often strayed on the road where Maude hit his cow. Maude recovered both for her personal injuries and for the damage to her car. Wilbur had to bear the loss of his cow.

---

Damages and injuries to third parties on the livestock owner's property are generally treated under negligence rules. There is an exception for livestock that have a history of causing injuries. In those situations, a strict liability standard may be applied. The owner is presumed to know the general propensities of certain animals, even if her or his particular animal has not performed dangerous or vicious acts. He must exercise due care to prevent injury from reasonably anticipated conduct. For example, the owner has a duty to restrain his or her animal if that breed of animal has a general propensity toward viciousness when he or she knows of visitors to his or her property. The courts of some, but not all, states have used the general propensities of certain breeds of dogs and cattle to impose a duty to restrain animals of those breeds. The act of fighting dogs and cocks is against the law in all states. Persons who fight dogs and cocks and, in most states, hold and train them are subject to criminal penalties and are open to civil liability.[4] In most states, a person possessing dogs raised for fighting will be strictly liable for the injuries that they cause whether the injury occurs on or off the property of the person who possesses such dogs. Under some circumstances, a person holding dogs raised for fighting may be held liable for injuries that they cause under a gross negligence standard. Under a gross negligence standard, both punitive and economic damages may be imposed. Gross negligence involves willful or wanton behavior done with reckless disregard for the well-being of others. The distinction between gross negligence and intentional tort is that there is no intent in gross negligence, unlike intentional tort, to commit the acts that constitute the tort. For that reason, gross negligence falls within the rubric of negligence.

In many states, it is a crime to allow one's domestic fowl to run at large on the lands of another that are under cultivation for grain or feedstuff or while used for gardens or ornamental purposes. Even in states where allowing one's domestic fowl to run at large upon lands of another is not a crime, the poultry owner would likely be liable in tort. Whether the theory is applied with the intentional tort, negligence, or strict liability depends upon the facts of the case and the statutes and precedents in the state where the acts occurred.

---

**Example 15.3** Tilden raised chickens that he allowed to run at large. John warned Tilden to keep his chickens out of the strawberry field that he was preparing to open to the public for pick-your-own harvest. Tilden agreed but accidentally left his gate open. The chickens ate a large quantity of John's strawberries, pecked many more, and contaminated the entire field with feces. John's strawberries were a total loss. Tilden is liable in negligence for the value of John's loss.

---

Most fence-in states allow citizens, designated public authorities, or both who find straying livestock to impound livestock found running at large. In those states where citizens are allowed to impound straying livestock, such citizens are entitled to be reimbursed by the livestock owner for reasonable costs incurred in impounding the animal, including the cost of a reasonable search for the owner. The impounder can retain the animal until the costs are recovered, but he must give food and water to the animal during such time. Where the owner of impounded livestock is known, the impounder must generally make a demand upon the owner as soon as is practical to do so. Where the owner is unknown, the impounder must give notice to a designated public authority who is required to publish a notice of impoundment. Livestock not claimed may be sold at public auction. These rules vary from one state to another. A person who finds straying livestock is not allowed to avoid the legal requirements and simply slaughter and eat the livestock. Such a provision in the law would encourage livestock theft. Livestock theft is a major problem in some regions.

### Livestock and poultry health

The USDA Animal and Plant Health Inspection Service plays a key role in responding to animal disease epidemics and health emergencies. It provides laboratory services and veterinary certifications. It approves veterinary biologics for import. It screens and quarantines imported animals to ensure that animal diseases are not introduced into the United States. It also provides certifications for animal exports. The Centers for Disease Control and Prevention (CDC) tracks zoonotic diseases. The CDC has an initiative to address antibiotic-resistant bacteria that includes stewardship of antibiotics fed to livestock and poultry. The Department of Homeland Security plays a role by addressing biosecurity issues and threats from bioterrorism.

States are active partners in all these programs and have laws in addition to federal law that address issues of animal and poultry diseases. State laws prohibit movement or sale of livestock and poultry with certain diseases. Certifications must be provided prior to movement of animals into most states. Veterinarians are required to report certain diseases that they find in livestock and poultry during the course of their practice.

The Food and Drug Administration (FDA) under the Federal Food, Drug, and Cosmetic Act[5] prohibits the sale of adulterated or misbranded feed products. States license the sale of feed products in their respective states. State authority includes establishing label requirements for animal and poultry feeds. The FDA regulates animal drugs except for those that it has determined to be exempt. States license veterinarians. All meat and poultry products, including eggs, whether regulated by the Food Safety Inspection Service (FSIS) or the states, must meet the Federal Food, Drug, and Cosmetic Act prohibition against adulteration and misbranding. There is no minimum amount of food or feed to which this requirement does not apply. This requirement is sometimes not understood by small-scale producers.

The USDA FSIS provides inspection to federally regulated livestock and poultry slaughter plants. Meat and poultry products that move in interstate and international trade are subject to federal inspection. FSIS regulates imports of meat and poultry products and certifies products for export. States license and regulate small slaughter plants that serve intrastate markets. States regulate on-farm poultry slaughter, where allowed, and set rules for small-scale egg producers.

There is a developing conflict between large-scale poultry and livestock production on the one hand and small-scale local agriculture on the other. The concern of the large-scale poultry and livestock producers is that small free range poultry and livestock operations may serve as a reservoir for diseases that threaten large-scale poultry and livestock operations. A common remedy used to stop epidemics in livestock and poultry consists of the destruction of all of the livestock or poultry that were exposed to the pathogen. This can be devastating for small free range poultry and livestock operations because it can destroy their breeding stock. It can lead to the extinction of some of the relatively rare breeds upon which they rely. The varieties of poultry and livestock used in large-scale poultry and livestock production operations are often proprietary, subject to various intellectual property protections. Even if the varieties of poultry and livestock used in large-scale poultry and livestock production were available to small-scale producers, these varieties are often unsuitable to their needs. Heritage varieties of poultry and livestock are sufficiently different from those used in large-scale poultry and livestock production operations that they appeal to different markets.

Feral hogs have become a serious issue in many parts of the United States. Feral hogs serve as a reservoir of disease that is a serious threat to the multi-billion dollar U.S. swine industry. Feral hogs destroy millions of dollars' worth of crops and ornamentals every year. They constitute a serious risk to food safety because their feces contaminate vegetable crops intended for raw consumption with deadly pathogens that can lead to outbreaks of food-borne illnesses. Hogs are non-native to North America and Hawaii. They were introduced by the earliest European settlers to North America and to the Hawaiian Islands by Polynesian settlers. Much of the spread of feral hogs has been through unintentional means and the escape of domestic hogs. The spread of feral hogs has been accelerated by hunters who moved them to establish populations for hunting. Many states have enacted laws that prohibit the movement of hogs without a license. The most seriously affected states have developed control programs. Most states do not consider feral hogs to be wildlife. This allows them to be killed at any time of year without limit.

### Livestock and poultry welfare

Livestock and poultry are excluded from the federal Animal Welfare Act.[6] Protection of livestock and poultry used in agriculture is left to state law. Though most states provide some protection to livestock and poultry used in agriculture, only a handful of states regulate the on-farm treatment of livestock and poultry. Those few states that have addressed on-farm treatment have addressed specific issues that include gestation crates for sows, veal stalls, and battery cages. The Humane Methods of Slaughter Act[7] requires slaughter methods in plants under federal inspection that have been determined to be humane. The Humane Slaughter Act does not apply to poultry. The Twenty-Eight Hour Law[8] requires that livestock in transport may be held for no more than twenty-eight hours without food and water. Livestock in transit must be given food, water, and rest for five hours between periods of no more than twenty-eight hours in transit.

The Horse Protection Act[9] prohibits exhibition or transport of any horse whose hooves have been injured (sored) to alter its gate. Horse slaughter has been effectively prohibited in the Unites States by a combination of state law and a federal prohibition on funding for inspection of horse slaughter. Federal law does not prohibit the slaughter of horses; however, there are no operating plants that slaughter horses in the United States. The U.S. Department of Transportation regulates the transport of horses for slaughter.[10] These regulations set minimum standards for humane transport of horses in transit to slaughter plants, all of which are in Canada or Mexico. The lack of demand for older horses as the result of the loss of domestic slaughter capacity has led to tragic unintended consequences—widespread abandonment and neglect of horses.[11]

Much large-scale poultry and livestock production in the United States is conducted in small enclosures or cages designed to prevent the livestock and poultry from injuring one another or their young. Some of these practices have become an important source of controversy. A few states have attempted to restrict such practices. The ability of such states to do so is a current source of litigation. Some consumers have shown a willingness to pay a premium for products not produced through certain confinement methods. The extent to which labeling accurately describes production methods is also a source of controversy and potential litigation.[12] Issues in livestock and poultry production are complex, and humane treatment does not always result from reforms. For example, layers used in cage-free egg production suffer double the rate of mortality of caged layers—primarily the result of cannibalism.[13] As the author knows from personal experience, free range poultry may suffer severely from predation.

## Dogs

Dogs are most likely the first domesticated species of animal. Neither dogs nor cats are livestock under common law. With a long relationship that dogs and humans have had and in the many uses to which humans have put dogs, the law governing dogs is complex. Dog law varies substantially from one state to another although the broad outlines of dog law that are described here are fairly universal. The CDC recorded that 368,245 non-fatal dog bites that required emergency room services occurred in the United States in 2001, the last year for which data are available.[14] That is an incident rate of 129.3 per 100,000 of population.[15] To put this in perspective, there were about 68 million dogs in the United States in 2001. Most of these dogs were pets that were not employed in agriculture; however, significant numbers of farms continue to use dogs. The large number of dogs in the United States alone makes them an important topic, as does the high level of dog-related injuries. The importance of dogs to agriculture makes a discussion of dog law an essential component of any study of agricultural law.

Dogs were most likely domesticated before the development of agriculture and have likely served a role in agriculture since it began. The most universal use of dogs in agriculture is to protect agricultural assets. Agriculture makes use of valuable, untitled personal property for which there is often limited security. Dogs give warning of intruders. The mere presence of dogs serves as a deterrent to theft. Dogs are very effective for protecting livestock from predators. Dogs continue to be used in some livestock operations to assist with herding.

Hunting dogs are employed in agritourism operations as an essential component of some types of hunting.

When dog bites occur, the legal system allocates responsibility based upon a number of factors. Whether the dog was on the dog owner's property is a critical factor in assigning liability. Whether the dog had a history of prior attacks is also a critically important factor. Some states allow testimony about the propensity of a breed for violence even where the particular dog had no history of violence. One often hears states described as one-bite states or no-bite states. In the latter type of state, the dog owner may be held liable for the injury caused by the dog's bite even where the dog had no history of violence. In the former type of state, it is often said that the first bite is free because it engenders no liability on the part of the dog owner. This description of how states handle injuries from dog bites is simplistic. Most states take a more nuanced approach to the question of liability that depends upon all the facts and circumstances of a particular case.

Many states apply a strict liability standard to all injuries caused by a dog that occur off the dog owner's property. These are easy cases for the plaintiff to win because all that is necessary for the plaintiff to prove is that the dog caused the bite. Unless the dog and its owner had some relationship to the owner of the property where the attack occurred, the status of the victim of the attack as an invitee or trespasser is usually irrelevant to the analysis. Some states also apply strict liability standard to injuries that occurred on the dog owner's own property if the dog had a history of violence. This can produce the anomalous situation where the dog owner is liable to a trespasser even though the trespasser may have liability for trespass.

> **Example 15.4** John kept Bowser, a dog famous in the dog fighting circuit. The state where John lives has passed laws that make dog fighting a crime and deem all dogs kept for fighting dangerous. Alvin trespassed on John's land to cut walnut trees in John's century-old grove. Unknown to Alvin, John let Bowser have the run of his walnut grove to protect his trees from people such as Alvin. Alvin managed to cut and remove a tractor-trailer load of walnut timber before Bowser attacked and severely mauled him. John and Alvin counter-sued each other. The court award John damages for his lost walnut trees under theories of timber theft and trespass. Under a theory of strict liability based upon John's keeping of a dangerous dog, the court awarded Alvin damages for his medical expenses, lost work time, and pain and suffering caused by the injuries inflicted by Bowser.

An intentional tort or gross negligence theory may be used in some cases. An intentional tort is appropriate if the owner of the dog intended the dog to cause injuries. A gross negligence theory may be used where the owner acted with reckless disregard as to whether the dog would cause injuries. In such cases, punitive damages in addition to economic damages may be available.

**Example 15.5** Jerry bought a dog of the Saint Bernard breed from John. John had previously been hospitalized because the dog mauled him. John did not disclose this to Jerry because he was afraid that Jerry would not buy the dog if he knew about this mauling. In doing so, John has acted with reckless disregard for Jerry's safety. Should Jerry be injured by the dog, John may be liable for punitive damages. In some states, the mere sale or other transfer of such a dog without disclosure of the injuries that it has caused may be a criminal offense.

As a general rule, dogs may not be killed, even if the dogs are trespassing. An exception exists in most states where the dog is attacking humans, livestock, or poultry. A person has a right to defend him- or herself or third parties against a dog attacking or threatening attack. Likewise, the owner or caretaker of livestock or poultry has a right to defend the livestock or poultry from an attack by a dog. Dogs may also be killed by designated public officials such as animal control officers or wildlife protection officers. A state may authorize individuals to kill dogs under certain circumstances. Many states have serious problems with feral dogs and have made provisions for killing them. Large numbers of unwanted dogs are killed in animal shelters. The number of dogs that animal shelters receive far exceeds those that are placed in homes. Licensed veterinarians are authorized to euthanize dogs under circumstances defined by state law.

Most states not only permit but require individuals to kill dogs that are reasonably believed to be rabid. Rabies is a serious disease that is usually incurable and fatal in both humans and dogs once an active case develops. For that reason, most states require that dogs (and cats) be vaccinated for rabies. Most states require that any dog or cat that has bitten a person be confined for a sufficient period to determine whether the dog or cat is rabid. When a dog or other animal has bitten a human and was killed, most states require that the carcass be submitted to authorities for laboratory tests to determine whether the animal was rabid. Extreme care should be used in handling any animal, alive or dead, that is believed to have been rabid because rabies can be transmitted not only by bites but by contact with any of the animal's bodily fluids.

There are acts involving dogs that are fairly universally prohibited. Criminal sanctions apply to many of these. Female dogs have certain periods of time in which they are fertile and will breed with a male dog. This period is called "heat." Most states prohibit allowing a female dog in heat to run at large. Male dogs can smell a female dog in heat from as far as several miles away. Male dogs will break through fences and other obstacles in their attempts to reach female dogs in heat. For that reason, allowing a female dog in heat to run at large is prohibited in most states.

Some states apply criminal sanctions to dog owners who fail to kill dogs that have killed domestic livestock or a human. There is usually some discretion based on the circumstances of the attack. Additional sanctions may be imposed for allowing such a dog to run at large. Selling or transferring possession or ownership of such a dangerous dog to another without providing written notice may also result in criminal sanctions.

## Wildlife

Though it may seem strange to address wildlife in a book on agricultural law, the lines between domestic species and wildlife is blurring. Some species of deer are now being intensively bred for the large antlers that many hunters desire. These deer are used in agritourism operations. Many farms have very active hunting operations that employ cage-raised birds such as quail. It is important to understand how the production and use of these species changes the legal environment.

The common law rule applied to wildlife is the rule of capture. The common law rule defined wildlife as the property of the government. Ownership changes only at the point where the wildlife was killed through legally permitted hunting. In the terms of common law, an animal or bird legally killed was reduced to possession. The rule of capture states that a person who legally takes wildlife acquires ownership at the point that the wildlife was taken.

All states regulate the taking of wildlife. These regulations include seasons during which particular species can be taken and bag limits on the total number of a particular species that can be taken during a defined period of time. There are also many other regulations including regulations that describe how wildlife can be taken. For example, semi-automatic shotguns may require plugging to restrict the number of cartridges that the shotgun can carry. Migratory species are regulated under federal law. Federal law includes international treaties that have been ratified by the Senate. State law may also regulate migratory species where not preempted by federal law. Agritourism operations based upon hunting cage-raised game is facilitated in some states by licensing provisions that allow hunting outside the normal season.

Not all species of wildlife are considered game. State laws prohibit the taking of some non-game species such as songbirds. The taking of certain non-game migratory species such as the common raven is prohibited under federal law through the Migratory Bird Treaty Act.[16] The federal Endangered Species Act prohibits the taking of certain listed species.[17] There are other species that states have classified as nuisance species that may be taken at any time.

An issue that arises with farm operations based primarily on wildlife is whether they meet the definition of agriculture. There is no single definition of agriculture. One must look to a specific part of the statute in question. So, for example, a farm that breeds and raises deer for fee hunting operations may not qualify for an exemption from county zoning because deer are not considered livestock in the definition of agriculture that applies to the zoning statute. The same farm may, however, qualify for reduced liability exposure under the agritourism statute because fee hunting is specifically included within the definition of agritourism. Farms whose operations are based upon what has traditionally been considered wildlife must answer the question, "Is my business a farm?" separately for each purpose. These purposes include coverage under right-to-farm laws. Benefits include real property tax reductions, sales tax exemptions on purchases of input, and many other benefits. Many states have recreational use statutes or agritourism statutes that limit liability of farms that allow hunting. Application of some of these statutes depend upon whether a fee is charged. Though these laws are important, they vary greatly from one state to another. A detailed discussion is beyond the scope of this chapter.

## Notes

1 Jeffrey S. Kerr et al. A Slave by Any Other Name Is Still a Slave: The Tilikum Case and Application of the Thirteenth Amendment to Nonhuman Animals. 19 *Animal Law* 221 (2013).
2 Dr. Temple Grandin. *Livestock Behaviour, Design of Facilities and Humane Slaughter*. Retrieved July 27, 2018, grandin.com/.
3 Deuteronomy 25:4 (King James).
4 As fighting cocks, unlike dogs, rarely injure humans, there is little law that addresses civil liability for injuries caused by fighting cocks.
5 21 USC §§ 301–399f (2013).
6 7 USC § 2132 (g) and (h) (2013).
7 7 USC §§ 1901–1907 (2013).
8 49 USC § 80502 (2013).
9 15 USC § 1821–1831 (2013).
10 9 CFR §§ 88.1–88.6 (2014).
11 Brenna (Robinson) Koehler. It Costs How Much to Get Rid of My Horse?!? Why the Economic Down Turn Has Illustrated the Need for Horse Slaughter Facilities. 18 Drake Journal of Agricultural Law 375 (Summer, 2013).
12 David Kesmodel. Bwaawk! A Consumer's Guide to Egg-Carton Terminology, *Wall Street Journal*, March 16, 2015, at B2.
13 David Kesmodel. Do Cage-Free Chickens Produce Better Eggs?, *Wall Street Journal*, March 19, 2015, at B3.
14 Center for Disease Control. Nonfatal Dog Bite—Related Injuries Treated in Hospital Emergency Departments—United States. Retrieved July 27, 2018, www.cdc.gov/mmwr/preview/mmwrhtml/mm5226a1.htm.
15 *Id.*
16 16 USC §§ 701–719c (2013).
17 16 USC §§ 1531–1544 (2013).

# Chapter 16

# Organic, sustainable, fair trade, local, and urban agriculture

## Introduction

The concepts discussed in this chapter are diverse. The thread that ties them together is a desire for naturally produced crops and livestock. What it means for something to be naturally produced is a topic of considerable debate. The general goal is to maintain soil health and genetic diversity and to reconnect people with food production. Also tied into this is a desire for an agricultural industry that provides producers and agricultural workers with a fair return for their labor.

## National organic program

The Organic Foods Production Act of 1990[1] (OFPA) created the National Organic Program (NOP) that provides certification for the marketing of products that are organically produced. Prior to creation of the NOP, all certifications of organically produced products were provided by private certifying organizations under private voluntary standards or under state law. Prior to the OFPA, there was no uniformity in certification. This hindered market development and exports of organically produced products. Though certified organic production remains a small part of U.S. agriculture, it is rapidly growing and can be highly profitable.

The OFPA contains certain key provisions. The practices of producers and handlers of organic products were brought under federal regulation. Those practices were required to include a written organic plan. A process for the accreditation of private persons or state officials as certifying agents was mandated. These accredited persons or state officials are then responsible for the agency's certification of producers and handlers. Each state is allowed to implement its own certification program for producers and handlers.[2] State programs may be stricter than the NOP.[3] State programs and subsequent amendments must be submitted to the USDA for approval. Establishment of labeling standards was mandated. Prohibited practices were defined. Establishment of a national list of approved and prohibited substances was mandated.[4] The OFPA mandated establishment of the National Organic Standards Board (NOSB). The purpose of the National

Organic Standards Board is to advise on establishment and modification of standards and implementation of the OFPA.[5] Section 6519 of the OFPA requires establishment of record-keeping requirements for producers, handlers, certifying agents, and others.[6] Section 6519 also requires establishment of procedures for investigations and enforcement. Section 6520 provides for establishment of an administrative appeal process.[7] The OFPA required the Secretary of Agriculture to issue regulations no more than 540 days after November 28, 1990. The final rule that established the NOP under the direction of the Agricultural Marketing Service (AMS) was not issued until December 21, 2000.[8]

Appeals of noncompliance decisions by the NOP program manager are made to the administrator of the AMS.[9] Appeals of noncompliance decisions by state organic program's governing state official must be appealed under the rules of applicable state organic programs. Adverse decisions of certifying agents are appealed either to the administrator of the AMS or through applicable state appeals processes depending upon whether the state has its own USDA-approved organic program. The period for filing an appeal is short—thirty days from the receipt of notice. It can be longer, if a longer period is provided in the letter of notification.

Establishment of the NOP was highly contentious. The proposed rule, published on March 13, 2000, received 40,774 comments.[10] One of the most contentious areas is the interaction between certified organic producers and neighboring conventional producers. The OFPA provides no authority to AMS to regulate the activities of conventional agricultural producers that neighbor certified organic farms. To the extent that there are any limitations upon the activities of neighboring conventional producers, these are provided under state law. This is usually through a tort action based on negligence theory. If the action of a neighbor using conventional methods resulted in a decertification decision, it is often necessary to appeal the decertification decision prior to filing suit against the neighbor. If the decertification decision was in error, that error, not the neighbor's actions, was the cause of the loss of certification. Without a determination that the decertification decision was made correctly, any suit against a neighbor brought under a negligence theory is likely to be dismissed for lack of the necessary elements of a suit in negligence. Most states set a statute of limitations of two to three years from the date of occurrence for filing negligence suits. As an appeal of a decertification decision may take longer than that, there are serious obstacles, in addition to proving causation, for a certified organic producer to recover for losses associated with the actions of a neighboring conventional farmer under a negligence theory. When state law and the facts of the case permit use of an intentional tort theory (e.g., trespass or strict liability), the organic producer has a better chance of recovering damages. Intentional tort and strict liability are not available in many, if not most, situations. Drift of pesticides from a conventional farm to a certified organic farm is often discussed as a common source of conflict. Though there are some judicial decisions addressing the issue, there are not so many that one can determine that it is a widespread problem.

### Regulation of organic production and product handling

The regulations governing organic production and product handling are complex. Logic or guesswork is no substitute for thorough understanding of the regulations. Many erroneously believe that no pesticides may be applied to certified organic crops. Such is not the case. Subpart C of the NOP establishes requirements for organic production and handling.[11] Products that are labeled "100 percent organic," "organic," or made with specific organic ingredients or food groups must comply with subpart C.

Subpart C requires an organic production or handling system plan. This plan must be in writing. It must include a description of practices and procedures and the frequency with which they will be performed. Each substance used in production must be described. Monitoring practices must be described. The producer's or handler's record system must be described. Management practices and physical barriers to prevent co-mingling of organic and nonorganic products must be described in the plan. Any other information necessary for the certifying agent to evaluate compliance must also be included in the plan.

Any parcel of land from which organic crops are to be harvested must have been properly managed. Proper management includes practices designed to maintain and improve soil health. These practices are varied but typically include crop rotation, use of cover crops, and the application of plant and animal materials. Plant and animal materials used as soil amendments must not contain prohibited substances that would contaminate the soil. Animal manure must be composted unless it is applied to land not intended for growing crops for human consumption, or it is incorporated in the soil at least 120 days prior to harvest of the edible portion of the crop, or 90 days prior to harvest for crops whose edible portion does not touch the soil. Composted plant and animal materials may be used as a soil amendment if properly composted. Plant materials alone may be incorporated without composting. Synthetic substances may be used as soil amendments only if on the National List. With some exceptions, ash from the burning of plant and animal material may be used as a soil amendment. The compost must not contain synthetic substances that are not listed on the National List as permitted. Sewage sludge or biosolids are not permissible soil amendments. Seeds and planting stock must generally be from organic sources. Crop rotation must be used on land for organic production. Organic standards for pest, weed, and disease management must be met.

For livestock and poultry production, certain standards for the origin of the livestock and poultry must be met. Feed must meet standards described in the NOP. Although medications may be used for treatment of specific diseases, subtherapeutic doses of pharmaceuticals must not be provided to livestock and poultry that are certified as organic. For animals on pasture, there must be a plan for management of the pasture consistent with organic standards.

Handlers of organically produced food must use permitted mechanical and biological methods. Section 205.605 lists nonagricultural substances that may be used by handlers.[12] Pest management is a major issue for all food handlers. The methods of pest management that may be used by certified organic handlers are restricted by section 205.271.[13] Care must be taken to avoid commingling with prohibited substances. Certain events such as natural disasters or drought may be grounds for granting variances from the regulations. Some synthetic substances may be used in certified organic production.[14]

### Labeling and market information

The term "organic" may be used to describe only products produced and handled in accord with the NOP.[15] For a label to state that a product is "100 percent organic," all the ingredients in the product must be organically produced.[16] If residue testing reveals a prohibited substance in the product at levels greater than 5 percent of the EPA tolerance, the product may not be labeled as organic.[17] A product may be labeled as "organic" if it contains not less than 95 percent organically produced product. The "made with organic ingredients" label may be used if at least 70 percent of the contents are organically produced. Products that contain less than 70 percent organically produced content may identify only specific ingredients as organic.[18] Livestock feeds are labeled in a similar manner. Qualifying products may display the USDA seal.[19]

Contracts with private buyers may set residue levels at less than 5 percent of the EPA tolerance. Those exporting products must meet the standards of the receiving country. The NOP rules provide minimum standards for organic production and handling. The NOP rules do not restrict states and private parties from setting more stringent rules.

## Steps to certification

Anyone seeking certification must comply with the OFPA and submit an organic production or handling plan to an accredited certifying agent. On-site inspection and complete access are required. All required records must be maintained for at least five years beyond the date of their creation. Applicable fees must be paid to the accredited certifying agent.

The certifying agent must be notified any time a prohibited substance is applied to a field. This requirement includes drift of prohibited substances such as synthetic pesticides. The certifying agent must also be notified of any changes in the operation.

Certification must be granted within a reasonable time. Should the application be denied, the certifying agent must provide the applicant with information supporting the denial. Denial of certification may be appealed. Appeals must be filed within thirty days from receipt of the notification or within the time period provided in the letter. Appeals are made to the administrator of AMS unless there is an approved state organic program. Appeals of adverse actions under a state program are made through the state program. As noted earlier, the short window for filing appeals can be problematic.

Appeals made to the administrator of AMS that are denied may be appealed to the U.S. District Court for the district where the person making the appeal is located. Appeals that are denied by the administrator of state programs are appealable to the appropriate state court for the state where the person making the appeal is located. Appeals from decisions by state program administrators may involve questions of state law, federal law, or both depending upon the grounds upon which the appeal was denied and the applicable state program.

### Steps to accreditation

Accreditation is available to both qualified domestic and foreign applicants in areas that include crops, livestock, wild crops, handling, or any combination of these. The USDA may accept an accredited foreign certifying agent under an equivalency agreement negotiated between the United States and foreign governments.

Certifying agents may be either private or governmental entities. To be certified, the agent must demonstrate sufficient expertise in organic production or handling techniques. The agent must demonstrate that it has an adequate number of trained personnel. The conduct of all persons involved in certification must be reviewed annually, as must the entire program. Required records must be maintained. Confidentiality of individual client information must be protected. A process must be in place to ensure that those involved in certification do not have a commercial interest in that which they are certifying. Where an application for accreditation is denied, the agency denied accreditation may appeal to the administrator of AMS.

## The National List of allowed and prohibited substances

The National List defines both substances allowed and substances prohibited.[20] The USDA has the responsibility to provide exemptions for certain synthetic substances in organic production and handling. Such substances are permitted if not harmful to human health or the environment, if necessary for production or handling of agricultural products, if no wholly natural substitute is available, and if uses of the substances are consistent with organic farming and handling.[21] The USDA must consult Health and Human Services and the EPA to make these decisions. In addition, the substance must either be in certain designated categories such as sulfur compounds and toxins from bacteria or synthetic inert ingredients that are not classified by the EPA as inerts of toxicological concern.[22] Conversely, the National List may prohibit the use of certain natural substances if those substances are harmful to human health or the environment and inconsistent with organic farming or handling.[23] Additions to the National List are developed by the National Organic Standards Board. The public may petition the National Organic Standards Board for inclusion of substances on the National List. Additions to the National List are subject to notice and public comment.

## Sustainable agriculture

The definition of sustainable agriculture set forth in this section entered the law through the 1990 Farm Bill.[24] Sustainable agriculture is not limited to certified organic or small-scale agriculture. It includes intensive agriculture that may occur on a large scale.

The term "sustainable agriculture" means an integrated system of plant and animal production practices having a site-specific application that will, over the long-term:

(A) satisfy human food and fiber needs;
(B) enhance environmental quality and the natural resource base upon which the agriculture economy depends;
(C) make the most efficient use of nonrenewable resources and on-farm resources and integrate, where appropriate, natural biological cycles and controls;
(D) sustain the economic viability of farm operations; and
(E) enhance the quality of life for farmers and society as a whole.[25]

There are several points that can be taken from the statutory definition of sustainable agriculture. First, the definition makes no distinction between conventional and certified organic production. Second, economic viability of the farm business is required for agriculture to meet the definition of sustainability. Third, sustainability must be determined on a farm by farm basis. Congress did not envision any bright line test for sustainability.

The definition of sustainable agriculture does not make a distinction between conventional and organic agriculture. Both conventional and organic agriculture rely upon natural biological cycles, and both use biological controls. Both conventional and organic agriculture attempt to use integrated systems for plant and animal production. Significantly, federal law requires that large livestock and poultry operations that are regulated as confined animal feeding operations apply livestock and poultry waste to the land at agronomic rates. An agronomic rate is an application rate of animal and poultry waste at a level that does not exceed the ability of the crop to which it is applied to utilize nutrients in the waste. Agronomic rates are set to limit runoff of nutrients and damage to water quality.

The definition of sustainable agriculture is applied in a number of contexts that are important to agriculture. The definition is used as a measure for evaluating grants to universities, producers, and others. It is also used to set priorities in programs that include biofuels and rural economic development, agricultural assistance to foreign nations, and investments in rural infrastructure. Though there is not a regulatory standard for sustainable agriculture, it is relevant to much of what the USDA does.[26]

## Fair trade

Fair trade is a social movement. It consists of several loosely associated organizations that are located primarily in Europe and the United States. In the United States, most activities involve products imported into the United States.

Fair Trade Certified products are certified under private standards. Compliance with the standards is enforced through private contractual arrangements. The primary purpose of the certification is to provide farmers in poor regions with sufficient income that they may make a living wage from their efforts. In the United States, certification for many products is made through Fair Trade USA. Fair Trade USA is organized under section 501(c)(3) of the Internal Revenue Code.[27] As such, Fair Trade USA is a private, nonprofit organization that may receive donations that are tax-deductible on the donor's federal income tax return.

## Local and urban agriculture

There is no single definition of local agriculture. The exemption in the Food Safety Modernization Act (FSMA) for direct farm marketing from the produce safety rule is one such definition.[28]

(1)  In general
A farm shall be exempt from the requirements under this section in a calendar year if—

(A) during the previous 3-year period, the average annual monetary value of the food sold by such farm directly to qualified end users during such period exceeded the average annual monetary value of the food sold by such farm to all other buyers during such period; and
(B) the average annual monetary value of all food sold during such period was less than $500,000, adjusted for inflation.

(4)  Definitions

(A) Qualified end user

In this subsection, the term "qualified end user," with respect to a food means—

(i)  the consumer of the food; or
(ii) a restaurant or retail food establishment (as those terms are defined by the Secretary for purposes of section 350d of this title) that is located—

(I)  in the same State as the farm that produced the food; or
(II) not more than 275 miles from such farm.[29]

This definition is limited to the direct farm marketing exemption from the produce safety rule under FSMA. Many farmers markets use a narrower geographic definition of local. Some retailers use a broader geographic definition. Few farmers markets or retailers apply any monetary limitations.

Local and urban agriculture are not the same. As the largest and most lucrative markets tend to be in large urban areas, much local agriculture tends to be near-urban. Urban agriculture in particular faces many regulatory hurdles that agriculture in more remote rural areas does not face. The remainder of this chapter is devoted to examining some of those regulations and laws.

## Zoning

Many states provide farms with full or partial exemptions from zoning. These exemptions are often very important for allowing agriculture to exist at all. Zoning works on a system of listed uses for any particular zone. If a use such as agriculture is not listed, it is not allowed. This topic is also discussed in Chapter 6.

Where agriculture is subject to zoning, it may be excluded entirely because it is not a listed use. Often, the failure to list agriculture may have been inadvertent. Historically, urban zoning authorities have not considered the prospect of urban agriculture. This can be problematic for efforts such as community gardening. Under a zoning classification, gardening may be allowed as an auxiliary use to the primary residential use. A vacant lot cannot be used for gardening because there is no residence. Without the primary use (the residence), the auxiliary use (the garden) is not permitted. There has been a trend to apply conservation easements to farm land with the goal of keeping the land in agriculture. This cannot occur if the zoning does not allow agriculture. Conservation easements are discussed in more detail in Chapter 20.

Some states allow relief from zoning only in agricultural districts or areas. Although it is not always the case, these agricultural districts and areas tend to be in predominantly rural areas. A recent trend has been for cities to modify their zoning to allow commercial agriculture. Detroit and Baltimore are two examples of many that now allow agriculture. Some states have facilitated this through changes in enabling statutes that encourage or require cities to provide zoning flexibility to agriculture.

## Tax relief

There are several types of tax relief available to farms. One of the most important is a reduction in the property tax. Because local and urban agriculture tends to be near cities, the fair market value of an acre of land tends to be much higher than that of farmland in rural areas. Without tax relief, farming is often not economically feasible in urban and near-urban areas. Many states make tax relief available only in agricultural districts or areas. As these are predominantly in rural areas, the tax relief may not be available to agriculture in urban and near-urban areas. Even where it is available in urban areas, minimum acreages necessary to qualify are often lacking as urban agriculture is usually practiced on very small parcels of land. Some states also have minimum income requirements to qualify for tax relief. As most urban agriculture is small-scale, and some is operated on a nonprofit basis with food products given away to those who are in need, property tax relief may not be available.

Many states provide relief to farms by exempting them from sales tax on the inputs they buy for agricultural production. Some states require minimum incomes to qualify. Urban farms attempting to use the sales tax exemption may not qualify because their income is too low or they are not operated with a profit motive.

---

**Example 16.1** Shepherds of Charity, a nonprofit, faith-based organization, operates a farm that employs recovering addicts as part of their treatment. All food produced is given to an associated homeless shelter. Because it is not a place of worship, Shepherds of Charity did not qualify for the property tax exemption for places of worship. As it is not operated with the intent to make a profit, it did not qualify for the state property tax relief program for farms. As it did not make at least $10,000 per year in gross income from the sale of agricultural products, it did not qualify for the sales tax exemption for the purchase of agriculture inputs. The farm supply store from which it bought fertilizer required it to pay sales tax on the purchase.

---

## Right to farm

Most states have right-to-farm laws that are designed to protect farming from nuisance and trespass actions that arise from normal farming activities. This protection may be available only to larger farms or those in agricultural districts or areas. Chapter 4 provides more information about torts based upon a nuisance theory and protections provided by right to farm laws.

## Access to water

Many urban areas restrict well drilling. This may limit the ability of urban farms to operate. With the interest in local agriculture, there is a trend toward greater tolerance of private wells. This is important, as using city water is often not economically feasible. Chapter 13 addresses water issues in greater detail.

## Insurance

The Federal Crop Insurance Program provides federally subsidized risk protection that is sold through private insurance agents.[30] The program is not well-suited to the needs of small-scale, part-time local and urban farmers. The program requires a minimum of 50 percent of gross income to be derived from agriculture. The program requires that there be a production history for a particular product from a particular farm. The Federal Crop Insurance Program provides coverage neither for all crops nor in all geographic areas.

Private insurance is more expensive than federally subsidized crop insurance. In addition, there may be no coverage available for farmers in local and urban agriculture. Private insurers want loss history for any activity that they choose to insure because they cannot properly price an activity without such a loss history. As many local and urban agricultural enterprises are novel, there may be little or no loss history. Local and urban agricultural enterprises also tend to be small in scale, which makes them of less interest to insurers than larger farms.

## Marketing

Farmers in local and urban agriculture face unique marketing challenges. Farm stands may be prohibited by zoning, traffic control, or other regulations. Farmers markets are moving toward requiring product liability insurance that covers the farmers market as a third-party insured. This can impose significant expenses on farmers that want to sell in those markets.

One approach that some farmers have used with success is community-supported agriculture (CSA).[31] CSA is a farm or group of farms that sells crop shares to consumers in advance of production. This is usually done on an annual basis. CSA is based upon contractual arrangements.

One question that arises with frequency is whether a product may be labeled "natural" for marketing purposes. Unlike the term "certified organic," the term natural does not have a precise legal definition. Most courts that have addressed the issue have concluded that food and feed products that contain genetically modified organisms (GMOs) cannot be labeled natural. GMOs are discussed in more detail in Chapter 17.

## Labor

Farmers engaged in local and urban agriculture often use nontraditional labor arrangements. These arrangements include volunteers and interns. If interns are unpaid and the farm is for profit, such an arrangement may violate federal and state labor laws. Such interns may be due at least the federal minimum wage and sometimes a state or local minimum wage if it is higher. Unless all the labor done by such interns is agricultural, interns who work more than forty hours in a calendar week may be due additional pay for their overtime. The use of volunteers who are not covered by workers' compensation may raise liability and liability insurance coverage issues for the host farm. Chapter 21 covers labor issues in more detail.

The Fair Labor Standards Act (FLSA) is the basic federal law that governs labor in the United States.[32] The FLSA provides for federal minimum wage and overtime for work above forty hours per calendar week and prohibits child labor. The FLSA requires record keeping and defines how hours worked are to be calculated. Agricultural workers are exempt from the requirement of additional pay for overtime. Farmers engaged in local and urban agriculture may have employees who do such things as produce value-added products that may not be considered agriculture under the FLSA. If there is any nonagricultural work during a calendar week, all the hours worked in that week are considered nonagricultural under the FLSA. Farmers also have a partial exemption from the use of child labor. Farmers are generally allowed to use family labor, even if those family members are children. The degree of relationship to the farmer is important to determining whether the child labor provisions of the FLSA have been violated.

## Notes

1   7 USC §§ 6501–6523 (2013).
2   7 USC § 6503(b) (2013).
3   7 USC § 6507(b)(1) (2013).
4   7 USC § 6517 (2013).
5   7 USC § 6518 (2013).
6   7 USC § 6519(a) (2013).
7   7 USC § 6520 (2013).
8   65 Fed. Reg. 80548 (2000)(codified at 7 C.F.R. pt. 205).
9   7 C.F.R. pt. 205.680 (2013).
10  65 Fed. Reg. 80548 (2000).
11  7 C.F.R. §§ 205.200–205.290 (2014).
12  7 C.F.R. § 205.605 (2014).
13  7 C.F.R. § 205.270 (2014).
14  7 C.F.R. § 205.206(e) (2014).
15  7 C.F.R. § 205.290 (2014).
16  7 C.F.R. § 205.301(a) (2014).
17  7 C.F.R. § 205.671 (2014).
18  7 C.F.R. § 205.305 (2014).
19  7 C.F.R. § 205.311 (2014).
20  7 C.F.R. subpart G (2014).
21  7 USC § 6517(c)(1)(A) (2013).
22  7 USC § 6517(c)(1)(B) (2013).
23  7 USC § 6517(c)(2)(A) (2013).
24  Drew L. Kershen. 46 *Creighton Law Review* 591 (2013).
25  7 USC § 3103(19) (2013).
26  USDA National Agricultural Library. *Alternative Farming Systems Information Center*, Retrieved July 28, 2018, www.nal.usda.gov/afsic.
27  Fair Trade USA. *About Fair Trade USA*, Retrieved July 28, 2018, www.fairtradeusa.org/about-fair-trade-usa.
28  21 USC § 350h (2013).
29  21 USC § 350h(f) (2013).
30  7 USC §§ 150–1524 (2013).
31  National Agricultural Library. *Community Supported Agriculture*, Retrieved July 28, 2018, www.nal.usda.gov/afsic/community-supported-agriculture
32  U.S. Department of Labor. *Compliance Assistance—Wages and the Fair Labor Standards Act (FLSA)*, Retrieved July 28, 2018, www.dol.gov/whd/flsa/.

# Chapter 17

# Genetically modified organisms and intellectual property law

## Introduction

This chapter expands upon the brief discussion of intellectual property contained in Chapter 8. The application of the fields of genetic engineering and genomics to important crop varieties produces what are known as genetically modified organisms (GMOs), or genetically engineered (GE) varieties. There is no standard terminology used to describe these varieties, and even the terminology itself may be controversial. Almost all the intellectual property embodied in GMOs (the term that shall be used throughout this chapter) is protected by utility patents. Other types of intellectual property protection discussed in Chapter 7 have not, to date, been used to protect GE crops. The landmark 1980 Supreme Court decision in *Diamond v. Chakrabarty*[1] required the U.S. Patent and Trademark Office to grant utility patents on inventions embodied in living organisms. This decision set the stage for today's multibillion-dollar agricultural industry of developing and marketing GMOs.

Most of these utility patents protect one of two broad categories of inventions. The first are those that provide crops with resistance to herbicides that the crops did not naturally possess. This allows use of herbicides to kill weeds without damaging the crops. The second type of invention incorporates a gene or genes that produce a compound or compounds with pesticidal properties that protect the crop from certain pests. The second type of GMO is regulated under federal pesticide law that is discussed in Chapter 20. The first type of GMO does not require regulation as a pesticide. Both types of GMOs are the subject of other types of regulation that are discussed in this chapter. There are two other types of genetic engineering that affect agriculture, but which are not used directly in agriculture. The first is the use of GE organisms to produce pharmaceuticals for livestock. The second are GE organisms used in fermentation and other processes to process agricultural products for food or feed.

The sophistication of genetic engineering techniques has been increasing while the cost of those tools has been falling. Scientists have begun to refer to this developing field as synthetic biology. The cost of these tools has dropped so precipitously that there is an annual student contest to develop synthetic organisms, usually bacteria.[2] The ubiquity of synthetic biological tools poses immense challenges to regulatory agencies. These challenges include both the inadvertent and intentional release of organisms dangerous or detrimental to crops or livestock. Much thought has focused on pathogens dangerous to humans. Herbicide resistance in weeds has become a significant economic problem.[3] Herbicide resistance in weeds is not confined to those herbicides used in conjunction with GMOs.

## Regulation of GMOs

Congress has never addressed genetic engineering in a comprehensive fashion. The term GMO is not defined in the statutes that agencies rely upon for authority to regulate agricultural biotechnology because these statutes predate development of these technologies. Lacking legislation, agencies have defined these and related terms through regulations that depend for their authority on existing statutes. Regulation of agricultural biotechnology under federal law ranges from almost nonexistent to very restrictive depending upon anticipated uses and the technologies employed. Plant and animal breeding even as practiced in large-scale industrial agriculture is largely unregulated at the federal level because these technologies are well understood and have been practiced for millennia. Likewise, processes that employ microorganisms, such as fermentation and bread making, are also largely unregulated. Exceptions exist for known pathogens, non-native invasive species, and other pest species. Opinion about whether regulation of GE crops is adequate is highly polarized.[4] The consensus of most scientists is that there is no scientific basis for regulating crop varieties produced by genetic engineering differently from crop varieties with the same traits that are produced by other means.[5] The adverse impacts on ecosystems of introducing species with novel traits are well known. One need look no farther than the kudzu that blankets acres of the Southeast.

Table 17.1 provides a summary of the agency roles and responsibilities in the regulation of agricultural biotechnology. These roles are discussed in more detail later in this chapter.

## A brief history of regulatory coordination between federal agencies

The Cabinet Council Working Group on Biotechnology through the Office of Science and Technology Policy coordinated efforts that led, on December 31, 1984, to the publication in the Federal Register of a document that was optimistically described as a concise index of U.S. laws related to biotechnology.[6] The original publication was a joint effort of the U.S. Food and Drug Administration (FDA), the U.S. Department of Agriculture (USDA), and the U.S. Environmental Protection Agency (EPA). This effort became the basis of the Coordinated Framework for Regulation of Biotechnology (Coordinated Framework)

*Table 17.1* Summary of federal agency roles and responsibilities

| Responsibility | Agency | | | | | | |
|---|---|---|---|---|---|---|---|
| | EPA | USDA | FDA | OSHA | PHS | DHS | NSF |
| Plant-pesticide registration | × | | | | | | |
| Pesticide tolerances in food/feed | × | × | × | | | | |
| New (non-pesticidal) microorganisms | × | | | | | | |
| Environmental policy (NEPA) | × | × | × | × | × | × | × |
| Workplace standards for biotechnology | | | | × | | | |
| Research standards for biotechnology | × | × | × | × | × | × | × |
| Biological agents and toxins control | | × | | | | × | |
| Quarantine functions | | × | | | × | | |
| Border controls/ import/export | × | × | | | × | × | |

that was published in the Federal Register on June 26, 1986.[7] In addition to the FDA, USDA, and EPA, it included the National Institutes of Health (NIH), the National Science Foundation (NSF), and the Occupational Safety and Health Administration (OSHA). With some changes, the Coordinated Framework has provided the basis for the regulation of biotechnology in the United States ever since. The biggest change was the establishment of, and transfer of functions to, the Department of Homeland Security (DHS) in the wake of the 9/11 terrorist attacks.

The purpose of the Coordinated Framework was to coordinate efforts of federal agencies to regulate biotechnology under the authority of various statutes. Coordination was through the Biotechnology Science Coordinating Committee (BSCC) of the Office of Science and Technology Policy. Seven areas of statutory authority that were identified are licensing and other pre-marketing requirements; post-marketing requirements; export controls; research and information gathering; patents; air and water emission standards; and various requirements for federal agencies. The BSCC no longer exists. Its functions related to agriculture are now in the Agricultural Biotechnology Working Group of the President's National Economic Council.

The Coordinated Framework for Regulation of Biotechnology is coordinated only in the sense that it is more "coordinated" than what came before it and that the BSCC was established to coordinate oversight of biotechnology research and products. Terminology governing the regulation of biotechnology is inconsistent and confusing. Terminology varies by the agency or agencies responsible for regulating an activity. Terminology is governed by the statutory authority or authorities upon which the agency or agencies rely. This cannot be changed without Congressional action. Neither the BSCC nor any successor entities have ever had authority to compel agency coordination. Research policies are regulatory in nature for those organizations whose biotechnological activities are funded directly or indirectly, in whole or in part, by federal funds. This encompasses virtually all university research in agricultural biotechnology. This is also true of some private agricultural research, especially where there is a university partner involved. Use of the products of biotechnology and the fortuity of which agency to which Congress assigned particular products, and not the nature of the process by which they were created, determines the agency that has jurisdiction. This is discussed in greater detail in the following sections.

## Jurisdiction of the Department of Health and Human Services

The FDA is primarily responsible for food and feed products, food additives, human and animal drugs, biologics, and medical devices. The FDA is responsible for enforcement of pesticide and other chemical residues that are established by the EPA.[8] Slaughter of domestic livestock[9] and poultry[10] and processing of meat and poultry products are under the jurisdiction of the Food Safety Inspection Service (FSIS), an agency of the USDA. Enforcement by FSIS is conducted in cooperation with the EPA and FDA. According to non-binding FDA guidance, it intends to regulate GE animals as new animal drugs, except releases of GE insects whose release for pest control is regulated by the Animal and Plant Health Inspection Service (APHIS).[11]

Definitions are critically important to how a product is regulated and to the level of scrutiny. For food products, any substance that the FDA has determined to be generally recognized as safe (GRAS) is not a food additive. Substances determined to be GRAS are generally unregulated. The EPA has determined that nucleic acids—contained in human food products—that code for plant-incorporated protectants (also called plant pesticides) are deregulated without regard to whether they were introduced by genetic engineering or conventional breeding.[12]

The U.S. Public Health Service (PHS) is an agency of HHS that has the responsibility for responding to public health emergencies, including those biological in nature, if other federal, state, and local resources are inadequate. Federal law provides limited immunity from federal and state lawsuits for those who develop and produce products to counter pandemics and epidemics. The Surgeon General who heads the PHS has broad authority to prevent the spread of communicable diseases by means that include "inspection, fumigation, disinfection, sanitation, pest extermination, destruction of animals or articles found to be so infected or contaminated as to be sources of dangerous infection to human beings, and other measures" that in extreme cases may include involuntary quarantine.[13]

## Jurisdiction of the EPA

Authority for EPA regulation of microbial products of biotechnology that are pesticides is the Federal Insecticide, Fungicide, and Rodenticide Act (FIFRA).[14] Under FIFRA, the EPA has the authority to regulate the development, testing, manufacture, sale, and use of all pesticides. The definition of pesticides encompasses all economic poisons designed to prevent, destroy, repel, or mitigate pests. Pests are defined to include animal, insect, arthropod, fungal, viral, or microbial pests. The term pesticide, in addition, includes plant regulators, defoliants, desiccants, and nitrogen stabilizers. The definition of pests under FIFRA excludes viruses, bacteria, or other microorganisms living on or in humans or other animals. The drugs and other medicinal products that address these organisms are regulated by the FDA under the Federal Food, Drug, and Cosmetic Act (FFDCA).[15] The EPA sets the tolerances for pesticide residues in food under authority in the FFDCA. Pesticide law is discussed in greater detail in Chapter 19.

Although FIFRA applies to all microbial products with pesticidal properties, the EPA has elected to focus its resources on regulating small-scale field trials of GE, nonindigenous, and pathogenic microbial pesticides.[16] The EPA has the authority to exempt small-scale experimentation where the organisms are contained.[17] The EPA has authority to issue experimental use permits (EUPs) where it does not grant an exemption.[18] No EUP is required where the organism or product used in the field trial is not intended to be used as a pesticide.

## Jurisdiction of the USDA

The Plant Protection Act assigns responsibility for regulating plant pests, including products of biotechnology that have the potential to be plant pests, to the USDA APHIS.[19] Under the authority of the Plant Protection Act, APHIS may regulate or prohibit the release of living organisms to the environment. It must choose to deregulate those organisms that it determines lack the potential to be plant pests or noxious weeds because the authority under the Plant Protection Act extends only to plant pests or noxious weeds. The Plant Protection Act defines plant pests to include protozoa, nonhuman animals, parasitic plants, bacteria, fungi, viruses or viroids, infectious agents or other pathogens, and any other organisms that injure plants or plant products. So long as something is a plant pest or noxious weed, authority under the Plant Protection Act is broad. APHIS may prohibit movement of organisms within the United States or between the United States and other countries, designate noxious weeds, and engage in eradication efforts. It may also determine that some organisms no longer require regulation. APHIS has emergency authority to quarantine, seize, and destroy organisms without first publishing notice in the Federal Register. Compensation may be paid where the Secretary of Agriculture determines it is appropriate or where articles are destroyed by mistake. APHIS is charged with administering the permit program for the import, transit, domestic movement, and environmental release of organisms that impact plants, and the importation of plants and plant products regulated under the Plant Protection Act and the Honeybee Act.[20] These permits are divided into organism and soil permits and plant and plant product permits. For a plant GMO to be released, APHIS must either grant a permit or determine that the GMO is not a plant pest.

The authority of APHIS under the Animal Health Protection Act[21] to protect animal and human health is similar in many respects to its authority under the Plant Protection Act. The Animal Health Protection Act defines animal pests to include protozoa, plants, bacteria, fungi, viruses or viroids, infectious agents or other pathogens, arthropods, parasites, prions, vectors, and any other organisms that injure livestock. The Animal Health Protection law provides APHIS with authority to restrict or bar both import and export to prevent importation of livestock disease and to prevent spread of disease by restricting export. Interstate shipments of livestock may also be regulated by APHIS to prevent the spread of disease (e.g., mad cow disease). APHIS may require post-import quarantine as needed to prevent the introduction of disease. Domestically, APHIS may quarantine or destroy livestock as required. Compensation may be paid at the discretion of the Secretary of Agriculture. Warrantless searches of livestock entering the United State are authorized and, if probable cause exists, of those moving in interstate commerce and those in a quarantine area. All other searches require warrants. APHIS is responsible for administering the permit program for the import of controlled materials, animal products, cell cultures, live animals, semen and embryos, and veterinary biologics. Although regulation of GE animals might fit in this permit system, APHIS has made no attempt to use it for that purpose, other than for GE insects referenced above.

## A brief discussion of current regulation of genetic engineered products

The working group established by the administration in the spring of 1984 determined that the laws regulating traditional genetic manipulation were adequate to govern genetic manipulation done by genetic engineering—no additional action by Congress was required.[22] The working group did determine that additional regulation of microbial products that were the result of genetic engineering was needed and that this additional regulation could be accomplished under existing statutory authority.

The definition of a plant pest is sufficiently broad to extend to protozoa, non-human animals, parasitic plants, bacteria, fungi, viruses or viroids, and any other infectious agents or other pathogens that may directly or indirectly injure, damage, or cause disease to a plant. The release of GE organisms triggers APHIS jurisdiction under the PPA because of a variety of harms that may result from the release of such organisms. An example of one such harm is gene flow to non-target species that may introduce genes with undesirable effects into those non-target species.[23] APHIS operates a program for permits, notifications, and petitions for the introduction (defined as importation, interstate movement, or release) of GE organisms under its biotechnology submissions program using a definition of biotechnology that is limited to GE organisms.

In general, either an environmental assessment (EA) or an environmental impact statement (EIS) will be required under the National Environmental Policy Act (NEPA)[24] for any field trials or commercial uses of GE organisms where living organisms are released to the environment. There are categorical exclusions to the requirement of an EA or EIS for activities where avoidance or limitation of the environmental risk is built into the action itself. These include activities that are isolated or contained, limiting potential human exposure; water bodies including wetlands that are unlikely to be contaminated; protected species and their habitat that are unlikely to be affected; and that the use does not cause bioaccumulation. Research is, in most cases, categorically excluded from NEPA requirements.

The question of whether to prepare an EA or an EIS can, in itself, be controversial. As preparation of an EA is much less expensive and time-consuming than preparing an EIS, applicants generally try to structure their activities to reduce the time and cost of permitting. In the context of an application for a permit to sell seed for genetically modified alfalfa, the U.S. Supreme Court was ultimately called upon to resolve the issue.[25] Roundup Ready Alfalfa (RRA) is a type of alfalfa that has been genetically engineered to tolerate the herbicide glyphosate marketed by the Monsanto Company under the trademark Roundup. APHIS originally classified RRA as a regulated product under the PPA; however, as the result of a request by the Monsanto Company and others, APHIS prepared an EA and issued a Finding of No Significant Impact. APHIS deregulated RRA without preparing an EIS. Two growers of conventional alfalfa seed and several environmental groups sued APHIS, alleging that it had violated the PPA, NEPA, and the Endangered Species Act.[26] As no preliminary injunctive relief was sought by the plaintiffs, RRA had unregulated status for about two years during which time it was grown in forty-eight states on about 220,000 acres. The judgment of the district court vacated the deregulation of RRA by APHIS; required that APHIS prepare an EIS prior to deregulating RRA, either fully or partially; barred planting of RRA on or after March 30, 2007; and imposed conditions on RRA planted prior to March 30, 2007.[27] Those conditions prohibited the addition of pollinators to RRA fields grown only for hay production; required cleaning procedures for equipment used in RRA production and education of farmers about requirements imposed on RRA production; and identification of all sites upon which RRA was grown. The U.S. Court of Appeals for the Ninth Circuit affirmed the decision of the district court.[28] The U.S. Supreme Court held that the district court abused its discretion by enjoining partial deregulation and by prohibiting future plantings.[29] A court that has abused its discretion has acted unreasonably. In December 2010, APHIS published its final environmental impact statement that supported its decision to deregulate RRA.

The FDA has authority to regulate food products produced from GE crops the same as it regulates any food product under the Federal Food, Drug, and Cosmetic Act. For GE livestock and poultry, the FDA requires pre-market approval and shares authority with the USDA and EPA. As food derived from genetic engineering is generally of the same composition as conventionally produced food, the chemicals in these foods are generally deemed to be GRAS and not subject to regulation. GE livestock and poultry, and products made from them, would, as with all livestock and poultry products for human or animal consumption, be regulated by FSIS in conjunction with the FDA and EPA as to various residues. As the Federal Meat Inspection Act[30] and the Poultry and Poultry Products Inspection Act[31] contain significant exceptions for livestock and poultry subject to state inspection that are not found in the Federal Food, Drug, and Cosmetic Act, it is likely, although as yet untested in litigation, that some genetic engineering of livestock and poultry may fall outside the scope of federal regulations where the research was conducted without federal money; however, rules as to residues would apply. The FDA has a voluntary consultation process available for premarket review of new food products.[32] As a practical matter, the voluntary consultation process is mandatory, even if that is not true as a matter of law. No food or feed product produced using genetic engineering technology can be sold if it has not been submitted for voluntary consultation and all FDA objections have been met. No buyer of food or feed products is willing to accept the exposure to product liability torts associated with a product that has not satisfied the FDA.

The National Oceanic and Atmospheric Administration (NOAA) operates the Seafood Inspection Program under authority provided in the Agricultural Marketing Act of 1946[33] that provides it with authority to regulate genetically modified seafood. The NOAA National Marine Fisheries Service is required to consult with the FDA to report on the environmental impact, including the impact on wild species, of GE seafood.

New gene editing technologies that result in deletion of genes rather than addition of genetic material pose additional challenges for the current regulatory structure. How, or if, products produced using these technologies will be regulated is unknown as of this writing.

## Regulation of research using genetic engineering techniques and field trials

In general, research of concern to the EPA falls into three categories: plant incorporated protectants, genetically modified microbial pesticides, and herbicide-tolerant crops. Products in the first two categories are regulated by the EPA as pesticides under the Federal Insecticide, Fungicide, and Rodenticide Act.[34] The EPA regulates only the herbicides used on herbicide-tolerant crops, not the crops themselves. The USDA APHIS is responsible for regulating herbicide-tolerant crops under the Plant Protection Act. Internationally, the Organisation for Economic Cooperation and Development has tracked developments in agricultural, industrial, and medical biotechnology research and development.[35] The NIH issued guidelines in 1994 for the conduct of genetic engineering. These guidelines apply only to research funded by NIH.[36]

The Plant Protection Act grants the USDA broad authority to conduct or sponsor research on plant pests. The DHS has authority to conduct or sponsor research both on threats from microbial pathogens and biotechnological solutions to various security issues, for example, rendering various toxins harmless.[37] Some animal disease research and certain facilities were transferred from the USDA to the DHS. HHS, FDA, CDC, and the USDA are authorized to coordinate the surveillance of zoonotic diseases under the Animal Health Protection Act. The PHS law provides the HHS with broad authority to conduct research on a wide variety of topics in biotechnology as these relate to human health. Congress created the NIH and its constituent agencies as agencies of HHS to conduct research on a broad variety of issues that affect human health.[38] Congress has also established ethics rules, rules for the use of animals, and other rules for those who receive funding from HHS.

## Labeling Bioengineered (BE) Foods

On July 29, 2016, the National Bioengineered Food Disclosure Standard (the Standard) was enacted when signed by the president.[39] It required the U.S. Department of Agriculture to publish final regulations within two years of enactment. The Standard uses a broad definition of "bioengineered" that is flexible enough to encompass not only existing GMOs, but also new products produced by quite different technologies. The applicability of the Standard is limited to those products for which labeling is already required under the Federal Food, Drug, and Cosmetic Act, the Federal Meat Inspection Act, the Poultry Products Inspection Act, or the Egg Products Inspection Act.[40] The Standard broadly preempts any existing or proposed state and local regulations that require labeling as GE, GMO, or similar designations for any food or seed covered under the Standard.[41] Proposed regulations were published in the Federal Register on May 4, 2018.[42]

## Scope for state and local regulation of GMOs

States of the United States are sovereign entities that function much as independent nations except to the extent that they have ceded power to the federal government through the Constitution. The Supremacy Clause of the Constitution of the United States governs the relationship between the federal government and the states. Authority may be exclusively federal, exclusively state, or concurrent. Where power is either exclusively federal or concurrent but in conflict, the federal authority preempts the state authority. The U.S. Supreme Court is reluctant to find federal preemption except where Congress has expressly stated that state law is preempted or there is a conflict between state and federal law that cannot be resolved.[43] As a result of this relationship between the federal government and the states, the scope for state and local regulation is broad. Without either a truly comprehensive federal approach to regulating GMOs or legislation expressly preempting state and local regulation, state and local regulation is likely to expand.[44] The debate over the power of state and local governments to require labeling of products grown using a GMO has been resolved in favor of federal preemption.

States currently have the authority to regulate drift of pollen from GMOs through their respective tort systems. With a 5 percent tolerance level in the National Organic Program for non-organically produced product, pollen drift is unlikely to produce damages sufficient to support a tort suit. Where foreign or domestic buyers have set a lower or zero-tolerance standard, it is possible that a tort suit for pollen drift could arise.[45] For such a suit to succeed, a court would have to find that such a standard was commercially reasonable.

Approval of specific varieties of GMO crops is done on a country-by-country basis. Where a commodity such as corn is widely traded, serious trade disruptions can result because it is almost impossible to keep the unlicensed GMO separate from those that are licensed. Current litigation involves varieties of corn deregulated in the United States and approved for production but lacking approval in China. Allegations in the litigation include shipments refused due to contamination, contractual losses due to insufficient uncontaminated corn needed to fulfill contracts with Chinese buyers, and an attendant drop in the market price of U.S. corn as the result of the loss of the Chinese market.[46] Claims are based upon negligence and various violations of state statutes. Alleged damages claimed in the various actions filed run into billions of dollars.

Labeling products as "natural" or "all natural" has been a contentious issue.[47] The FDA requested comments (which closed on May 10, 2016) on the use of "natural" in product labeling.[48] Without guidance from the FDA, the regulation of claims of "natural" and similar designations remains a matter of state law. Many states regulate product claims under labeling, unfair trade practice statutes, or other consumer protection law. Without statutory definitions of what the term natural means, continued litigation is likely. The key to whether the term natural can be used is usually a question of whether the claim is deceptive.[49]

## Notes

1  447 U.S. 303, 1980 U.S. LEXIS 112 (1980)
2  The Chronicle of Higher Education. *Undergraduate Synthetic-Biology Contest Mixes Fun with Serious Warnings*. Retrieved November 16, 2014, chronicle.com/article/Undergraduate/135692/.
3  Heap, I. *The International Survey of Herbicide Resistant Weeds*. Retrieved November 16, 2014, www.weedscience. org/.
4  OECD, *Emerging Policy Issues in Synthetic Biology*, 115 (2014).
5  *Id.*, at 116; Committee on Environmental Impacts Associated with Commercialization of Transgenic Plants, Board on Agriculture and Natural Resources, National Research Council, Environmental Effects of Transgenic Plants: The Scope and Adequacy of Regulation, 3-4 (2002).

6  Proposal for a Coordinated Framework for Regulation of Biotechnology. 1984. 49 Fed. Reg. 50856. (1984).
7  Coordinated Framework for Regulation of Biotechnology. 1986. 51 Fed. Reg. 23302. (1986).
8  Federal Food, Drug, and Cosmetic Act. 2013. 21 USC §§ 301 –399a. (2013).
9  Federal Meat Inspection Act. 2013. 21 USC §§ 601–695. (2013).
10  Poultry and Poultry Products Inspection Act. 2013. 21 USC §§ 451–472. (2013).
11  GFI # 187 – Regulation of Genetically Engineered Animals Containing Heritable Recombinant DNA Constructs, Final Guidance, FDA Center for Veterinary Medicine (January 15, 2009). Online. Retrieved March 28, 2015, from the EPA website: http://www.fda.gov/downloads/animalveterinary/guidancecomplianceenforcement/guidanceforindustry/ucm113903.pdf.
12  Exemption from the Requirement of a Tolerance under the Federal Food, Drug, and Cosmetic Act for Residues of Nucleic Acids That Are Part of Plant-Incorporated Protectants (Formerly Plant-Pesticides). 2001. 66 Fed. Reg. 37817. (2001); Exemption from the Requirement of a Tolerance under the Federal Food, Drug and Cosmetic Act for Residues Derived Through Conventional Breeding from Sexually Compatible Plants of Plant-Incorporated Protectants (Formerly Plant-Pesticides). 2001. 66 Fed. Reg. 37830. (2001); Regulations under the Federal Insecticide, Fungicide, and Rodenticide Act for Plant-Incorporated Protectants (Formerly Plant-Pesticides). 2001. 66 Fed. Reg. 37771. (2001).
13  Public Health Service. 2013. 42 USC §§ 201–300jj-38. (2013).
14  Federal Insecticide, Fungicide, and Rodenticide Act. 2013. 7 USC §§136–136y. (2013).
15  Federal Food, Drug, and Cosmetic Act. 2013. 21 USC §§ 301–399a. (2013).
16  Coordinated Framework for Regulation of Biotechnology. 1986. 51 Fed. Reg. 23302. (1986).
17  Coordinated Framework for Regulation of Biotechnology. 1986. 51 FR 23302. (1986); Pesticide Registration (PR) Notice 2007-2: Guidance on Small-Scale Field Testing and Low-level Presence in Food of Plant-Incorporated Protectants (PIPs). EPA. April 30, 2007. Online. Retrieved November 17, 2014, from the EPA website: http://www.epa.gov/PR_Notices/pr2007-2.htm.
18  Chapter 12, Applying for an Experimental Use Permit. *Pesticide Registration Manual.* EPA. Online. Retrieved November 20, 2014, from the EPA website: http://www2.epa.gov/pesticide-registration/pesticide-registration-manual-chapter-12-applying-experimental-use-permit.
19  7 USC §§ 7701–7786. (2013).
20  7 USC §§ 281–286. (2013).
21  7 USC §§ 8301–8322. (2013).
22  Coordinated Framework for Regulation of Biotechnology. 1986. 51 FR 23302. (1986).
23  Connor, Thomas. Genetically Modified Torts: Enlisting the Tort System to Regulate Agricultural Contamination by Biotech Crops, *University of Cincinnati Law Review*, 75 (2007).
24  42 USC §§ 4321–4370h. (2013).
25  *Monsanto Company v Geertson Seed Farms.* 561 U.S. 139, 130 S. Ct. 2743, 2010 Lexis 4980. (2010).
26  16 USC §§ 153–1544. (2013).
27  *Geertson Farms, Inc. v Johanns.* (2007) U.S. Dist. LEXIS 32701. (N.D. Cal. 2007).
28  *Geertson Farms, Inc. v Johanns.* (2008). 541 F.3d 938; 2008 U.S. App. LEXIS 18752. (9th Cir. 2008).
29  *Monsanto Company v Geertson Seed Farms.* 561 U.S. 139, 130 S. Ct. 2743, 2010 Lexis 4980. (2010).

30  21 USC §§ 601–695. (2013).
31  21 USC §§ 451–472. (2013).
32  FDA. *Regulatory Submissions—Part VII: Biotechnology Final Consultations*, Retrieved March 28, 2015, www.fda.gov/food/ guidanceregulation/guidancedocumentsregulato ryinformation/ingredientsadditivesgraspackaging/ucm199073.htm.
33  7 USC §§ 1621–1638d. (2013).
34  7 USC §§ 136–136y. (2013).
35  OECD. *Biotechnology Update. No. 22*, Retrieved September 4, 2015, www.oecd.org/ env/ehs/biotrack/48464394.pdf.
36  Guidelines for Research Involving Recombinant DNA Molecules (NIH Guidelines). 1994. 59 FR 34496. (1994).
37  6 USC §§ 101–1405. (2013).
38  42 USC §§ 201–300mm61. (2013).
39  Pub. L. No. 114-216, 130 Stat. 834 (2016).
40  Pub. L. No. 114-216, § 292, 130 Stat. 834 (2016).
41  Pub. L. No. 114-216, §§ 293, 295, 130 Stat. 834 (2016).
42  83 Fed. Reg. 19860 (2018).
43  *Bates v Dow AgroSciences LLC.* 2544 U.S. 431, 125 S. Ct. 1788, 2005 U.S. LEXIS 3706. (2005).
44  Connor, Thomas. Genetically Modified Torts: Enlisting the Tort System to Regulate Agricultural Contamination by Biotech Crops. *University of Cincinnati Law Review*, 75 (2007).
45  Non-GMO Project. Retrieved November 24, 2014, www.nongmoproject.org/.
46  Plaintiffs' Complaint. *Cargill, Inc. v. Syngenta Seeds, Inc.* (No. 67061). (40th Judicial Distr., La. Sept. 12, 2014); Plaintiffs' Complaint. *Archer Daniels Midland Co. v. Syngenta Corp.* (No. 79219). (29th Judicial Distr., La. Nov. 19, 2014).
47  Tracy, Tennille and Annie Gasparro. Settlement on Natural Food Claims, *The Wall Street Journal*, (November 19, 2014), at B4.
48  FDA. Use of the Term "Natural" in the Labeling of Human Food Products; Request for Information and Comments; Extension of Comment Period. Retrieved July 28, 2018, www.regulations.gov/document?D=FDA-2014-N-1207-1827.
49  FTC. Advertising FAQ's: A Guide for Small Business. Retrieved March 28, 2015, www. ftc.gov/tips-advice/business-center/guidance/advertising-faqs-guide-small-business.

# Chapter 18

# Food safety

## Introduction

Food safety has historically been addressed by both the tort system and federal and state regulation. The particular area of tort law that addresses food safety is called products liability. The trend has been for federal regulatory law to play a larger role in food safety; however, the roles of the tort system and state regulatory agencies remain a crucial part of these systems that work both together and in parallel. States operate both federally delegated programs and those solely under state law. The products liability system is exclusively state law, although applicable standards may be set by federal law. The FDA plays a crucial role in determining what constitutes an adulterated food product.

## Products liability and insurance

States have generally allowed recovery of damages under either a negligence theory or a strict liability theory. A majority of states use strict liability in tort as the applicable theory. Historically, the recovery of damages from farmers for food-borne illnesses was often impossible because the pathogen in the food consumed could not be connected to the farmer who produced the food. Changes in technology that take advantage of the unique genome of a particular pathogen now make it possible to trace the contaminated food through the chain of commerce to the original producer. All in the chain of commerce that handled the contaminated food product are jointly and severally liable to an injured plaintiff. Under the principle of joint and several liability, the plaintiff may recover the entire damage award from one defendant even though that defendant did not bear the entire fault for the injury. Liability among defendants may be allocated through a separate contribution action among the defendants. In a contribution action, the court will allocate fault and require the other defendants to reimburse the defendant that paid the entire award for that portion of the award that was not equitably attributed to him or her. Statutes of limitations and other procedural hurdles often bar contribution actions. In those relatively rare cases where a person introduced an adulterated food or feed product into the chain of commerce with reckless disregard for the health or safety of others, punitive damages and economic damages may be available to the plaintiff under a gross negligence theory. Punitive damages are generally not available in either strict liability or ordinary negligence cases.

As noted earlier, the two tort theories usually used in products liability cases are negligence and strict liability. The choice of theory is dependent upon the law of the state in which the products liability cases are brought. Because, unlike actions based on negligence, fault does not need to be proven in a case based upon strict liability in tort; these cases are much easier to win. Cases involving personal injuries from contaminated food products are generally high-stakes cases because they involve serious injuries or death. Plaintiffs' attorneys will usually attempt to file their cases in states that recognize strict liability torts in products liability cases. In the typical case involving an adulterated food product that was produced in one state and consumed in another state, there will almost always be a choice of states in which to bring the case.

Whether gross negligence is a third tort theory or a subset of negligence is a matter of semantics. Recall from Chapter 3 that gross negligence requires proof that the defendant acted with reckless disregard for the health and welfare of others. Gross negligence may also constitute a crime in the context of food production. Example 18.1 illustrates some of the consequences of acting with gross negligence.

---

**Example 18.1** John raises strawberries in a U-pick operation where most of his strawberries are picked directly by the consumer. John advertises that customers can pick and eat as many berries as they wish while they are picking berries. John irrigates the strawberry field from a pond that he allows his hogs to wallow in. The hogs are part of his pasture-fed pork operation that is adjacent to the strawberry field. Thirty children who picked strawberries on his farm developed E. coli infections. One child died, and several will require medical care for the remainder of their lives. Testing determined that all thirty children were infected with the same variety of E. coli. Testing further determined that John's strawberries were contaminated with the same variety of E. coli and that his hogs were carriers of the E. coli. The attorney who represented the children and their families brought an action based upon theories of strict liability and gross negligence. He argued successfully that irrigating strawberries from a pond that was used as a hog wallow was reckless disregard for the health and well-being of the strawberry customers. The jury awarded damages for wrongful death, pain and suffering, past and future medical expenses, and punitive damages. At the conclusion of his civil trial, a sheriff's deputy arrested John on manslaughter charges. John's criminal defense attorney reached a plea agreement that required him to serve eighteen months in prison.

Many general farm liability policies include limited products liability coverage. Typically, the amount of coverage is low, almost never more than $1 million. Such policies also typically limit coverage to raw agricultural products produced on the farm. Such policies do not cover value-added products that have been further processed or products produced on farms owned by others. Most farms that produce fruits and vegetables require additional products liability insurance. If the farm does sufficient processing to qualify as a registered facility under the Food Safety Modernization Act (FSMA), the farm is likely to require a commercial liability policy and additional products liability coverage.

Many contracts with large buyers of fruits and vegetables contain indemnity clauses that require the farmer to indemnify the buyer for costs associated with recalls. Many large buyers also require that the farmer selling to them maintain some minimum level of products liability coverage, provide proof of coverage, and name them as a third-party insured on the policy. Some farmers markets also require that farmers who wish to sell at the market provide proof of products liability coverage and name the market as a third-party insured. Some of these indemnification clauses used by large buyers apply even if the farmer's products are not ultimately determined to be the source of the outbreak of food-borne illness that triggered the recall. Most products liability policies to not cover this risk. Neither do product liability policies typically cover the farmer's own recall costs, losses from depressed product prices associated with a widely publicized recall, or lost profits. If insurance products are available to cover these risks at all, additional coverage beyond that provided in a standard products liability policy will be required. Although insurance usually covers the cost of legal defense including attorney fees, it does not usually cover actions based upon gross negligence and almost never covers the costs of criminal defense. Insurance is a matter of private contract. What is covered depends upon what state law allows and what the insured can negotiate with his insurance company.

## The structure of federal regulation of food and feed

The Federal Food, Drug, and Cosmetic Act (FFDCA) prohibits introducing an adulterated or misbranded food or feed product into the chain of commerce.[1] Selling a food or feed product that contains a prohibited pathogen can subject the seller to civil liability that includes penalties and costs associated with the investigation and recall of the contaminated product. The Food and Drug Administration (FDA) may, at its discretion, refer the matter to the U.S. Department of Justice for criminal prosecution. The U.S. Supreme Court has ruled that selling an adulterated food product is a strict liability crime.[2] It is sufficient to obtain a conviction of the head of a company for violation of the FFDCA if the head of the company knew of the condition that led to introducing an adulterated food or feed product into the chain of commerce. It is irrelevant that the head of the company had no role in introducing the adulterated food or feed product into commerce. For this reason, sophisticated buyers of higher-risk agricultural products such as fresh fruits and vegetables that are likely to be consumed raw impose substantial contractual obligations on agricultural producers. This helps protect buyers from both civil and criminal liability. The FSMA, passed by Congress in December 2010 and signed by the president on January 4, 2011, enhanced the regulatory authority of the FDA.[3] The FSMA adds to the authority of the FDA to regulate both farmers and facilities that handle and process food products after they leave the farm gate. Although the FDA has much of the responsibility for protection of food and feed from adulteration, authority is spread through several agencies and states and local governments. Table 18.1 summarizes federal

*Table 18.1* Federal statutes applicable to food and feed

| Agency | Authority | Responsibility |
|---|---|---|
| FDA | FFDCA | • Adulterated or misbranded food products<br>• Prior approval of food additives (note GRAS list)<br>• Sanitation program for milk, shell fish, food service, and interstate travel facilities<br>• Hazard Analysis and Critical Control Point (HACCP) System for seafood and fish processing establishments<br>• Hazard Analysis and Critical Control Point (HACCP) System for establishments processing juice<br>• Food allergy labeling |
| EPA | FIFRA | • Set maximum pesticide residue levels in food |
| USDA FSIS | Federal Meat Inspection Act Poultry Products Inspection Act | • Inspection of meat and poultry products; adulteration and misbranding prohibited<br>• Hazard Analysis and Critical Control Point (HACCP) System for meat and poultry establishments |
| USDA FSIS | Egg Products Inspection Act | • Inspection of eggs and egg products; adulteration and misbranding prohibited; detention and destruction of eggs and egg products not in compliance |
| Department of Health and Human Services (HHS) (assigned to FDA) | Egg Products Inspection Act | • Jointly with the USDA, detention and destruction of eggs and egg products not in compliance if those products are outside of an egg processing plant (USDA authority is exclusive within egg processing plants) |

agency authorities and responsibilities. Note that much of this authority applies to those who handle food after it leaves the farm gate.

Many buyers of agricultural products now require that producers comply with certain voluntary standards to help to ensure that food or feed products are not adulterated. Among the most important of these are good agricultural practices (GAPs) and Hazard Analysis and Critical Control Points (HACCP). The use of both GAPs and HACCP is discussed in this chapter. Though these programs may be voluntary in the sense that they are not required by statute or government regulation, these programs are contractually required by many large buyers of agricultural products.

### Federal Meat Inspection Act[4]

Enforcement of the Federal Meat Inspection Act (FMIA) is the responsibility of the USDA Food Safety Inspection Service (FSIS). The FMIA requires inspection of animals prior to slaughter. The FMIA also requires humane slaughter as defined in the FMIA and regulations. Postmortem examination of carcasses is required. Carcasses that do not meet standards must be destroyed. Cattle, sheep, swine, goats, horses, mules, and other equines are covered under the FMIA. The sale, transport, offer for sale or transport, or receipt for transport of any animal product that can be used for human food is prohibited if the product is adulterated or misbranded or has not passed inspection. Any establishment subject to inspection that received or originated an animal product that it believes to be adulterated must notify FSIS. Each such establishment under inspection must have recall procedures in place to recall any adulterated or misbranded product. Such establishments must maintain records necessary to support a recall. Establishments under inspection are required to pay the USDA for the cost of inspection.

An adulterated product is one that contains a harmful substance or pathogen at potentially harmful levels. It also includes a product with pharmaceutical or pesticide levels that are above tolerances. Any animal that died by means other than through normal slaughter house procedures is considered adulterated. Road kill cannot be legally sold despite humorous cook books dedicated to the topic.

The FMIA provides an exemption from inspections for personal and custom slaughtering. Exempt custom slaughtering operations slaughter animals for the owner who raised them and may also slaughter game. Packages of custom slaughter animal products must be marked "Not for Sale." The exemption applies only to inspection and provides no exemption to the prohibition on adulterated and misbranded meat products. Retail stores and restaurants are exempt from handling regulations under the FMIA.

The USDA is authorized to enter cooperative agreements with states to establish state inspection programs. The USDA is authorized to provide advisory, technical, and laboratory assistance to states with state inspection programs. The USDA may cost-share with states so long as it does not exceed 50 percent of program costs. The availability of cost-share is subject to annual appropriations.

There must be a single state agency designated to coordinate the cooperative agreement. The state must enforce the same standards as applied in federal inspection. Slaughter houses under state inspection are small operations.

## The Poultry Products Inspection Act[5]

Like the FMIA, the Poultry Products Inspection Act (PPIA) prohibits introducing adulterated and misbranded poultry products into interstate commerce. Also like the FMIA, the PPIA requires inspection of poultry slaughter under the FSIS. The PPIA has provisions for cooperation with the states for establishing state inspection in a manner similar to that for state inspection of meat. Poultry slaughter operations under state inspection are small. As with meat inspection, poultry inspection is both ante- and postmortem. There are certain exemptions from the PPIA. Retail stores that cut up poultry products for sale to the consumer on the premises are exempt. Certain individuals slaughtering poultry under certain religious dietary laws are exempt. Personal and custom slaughter is exempt. As with meat, the exemption from inspection is not an exemption from introducing adulterated or misbranded product into commerce. Establishments under inspection are required to pay the USDA for the cost of inspection.

## Egg Products Inspection Act[6]

The Egg Products Inspection Act grants the USDA FSIS authority to regulate eggs and egg products. The Egg Products Inspection Act defines "adulterated" in the context of eggs and egg products. The Egg Products Inspection Act grants the USDA the authority to regulate eggs and egg products from domestic chickens, turkeys, ducks, geese, and guinea fowl. The USDA has the authority to regulate any egg processing plant except those that are exempt. No product with false, misleading, or non-approved labels may be used. Cooperation with the states is authorized. Inspection is not provided to any plant that processes eggs that are not for human consumption (e.g., for animal feed). Eggs that are not for human consumption must be labeled to deter their use for human food. Violations of the Egg Products Inspection Act may be punished by civil penalties, criminal sanctions, or both. Sales by a producer from his own flock directly to the consumer are exempt from inspection. Sales by any producer from a flock of 3,000 or fewer hens are exempt. Eggs sold in violation of the Egg Products Inspection Act may be detained and destroyed. The FDA shares authority with FSIS to detain eggs or egg products that are in violation of the Egg Products Inspection Act. The FDA does not exercise this authority within an egg processing plant that is under FSIS inspection. States are prohibited from imposing standards on eggs and egg products that are either in addition to or different from the federal standards. Establishments under inspection are required to pay The USDA for the cost of inspection.

## The Federal Food, Drug, and Cosmetic Act[7] as amended by the Food Safety Modernization Act[8]

The FFDCA broadly defines food to include food or drink for humans or other animals, chewing gum, and any article used in food or drink for humans or animals. Adulteration or misbranding of any food is prohibited under the FFDCA. Though the FFDCA has long prohibited adulteration and misbranding, FSMA significantly enhanced the authority to address serious problems arising from food-borne illnesses. FSMA was enacted as an amendment to the FFDCA. FSMA contains four titles. Title I is designed to enhance the capacity of the FDA to prevent food safety problems. The intent of Title I was to give the FDA a role in preventing outbreaks of food-borne illnesses. Title II was intended to improve the ability of the FDA to detect and respond to food safety problems. Title III addresses improving the safety of imported food. Title IV contains miscellaneous provisions. It includes a whistleblower provision that applies to food facilities.

The goal of Congress when it enacted FSMA was to move the FDA from a food-borne illness detection role to a prevention role. FDA authority to trace food-borne illness outbreaks was expanded, and development of a traceability system was mandated. Record-keeping requirements for high-risk foods were expanded. FSMA requires the FDA, in cooperation with the Centers for Disease Control and Prevention, to enhance food-borne illness surveillance systems to improve the collection, analysis, reporting, and usefulness of data on food-borne illnesses. Section 206 gave the FDA broad mandatory recall authority.[9] Previously, the FDA relied upon voluntary recalls. FSMA also reduced the evidence required for administrative detention of food to "reason to believe."[10]

## Food facilities

A food facility is any facility that handles food but is not a farm or a restaurant. Farms and restaurants are not regulated as facilities. Differentiating between a facility and a farm, or a facility and a restaurant, is not always easy. As facilities, but not farms, are required to register with the FDA, this is a critical distinction. Some farms also process product from other farms, and some facilities may also sell to the public in a restaurant-like setting. Through regulation, the FDA has attempted to distinguish facilities from farms and restaurants. Farms that handle raw agricultural commodities for other farms will generally not be classified as facilities. Further processing on the farm may result in classification of the farm as a facility. One of the conditions required for registration is that the owner or operator of the facility consent to FDA inspection of the facility. Inspection is conducted as set forth in FSMA and regulations that the FDA has and will develop under the authority granted in FSMA. By consenting to inspection, the owner or operator of a facility has waived its right under the Fourth Amendment to require a warrant prior to inspection. Should a facility owner not consent to this waiver, the FDA will deny registration. As a practical matter, owners and operators of facilities do not have a Fourth Amendment right to require a warrant prior to inspection because facilities that are not registered may neither legally operate, nor sell their product.

FSMA requires each owner, operator, or agent in charge of a food facility to identify and implement preventive controls to significantly minimize or prevent hazards that could affect food manufactured, processed, packed, or held by such facility. FSMA provisions allow the FDA to develop regulations that exempt certain facilities from some requirements if those facilities are small and engaged in low-risk activities. FSMA directed the FDA to allocate resources to inspect facilities according to the known safety risks of the facilities or food.

FSMA moves the FDA regulation of food facilities closer to the USDA regulatory model. The USDA regulatory model, described above, requires on-site inspection of livestock and poultry slaughter. Though FSMA does not move to require ongoing on-site inspection, it does adopt aspects of the USDA model. The FDA has the authority to set performance standards for contaminants as the USDA has done for pathogens in meat and poultry. Food facilities registered with the FDA will have to perform hazard analyses and implement preventive control plans similar to the HACCP plans required of meat and poultry establishments. FSMA requires the FDA to coordinate enforcement standards with the USDA.

Section 103 of FSMA establishes new hazard analysis and preventive control requirements for facilities.[11] The owner, operator, or agent in charge of a facility is required to identify hazards that could lead to adulteration or misbranding of a food product. The language of FSMA extends liability and responsibility to anyone with management responsibility for the facility. Preventive controls must be put in place to eliminate or minimize risks. These controls must be monitored with records kept of the performance of those controls over time. FSMA requires that any reasonably foreseeable risk be identified, monitored, and controlled. Such risks that are listed in FSMA include biological, chemical, physical, and radiological hazards. Also included are natural toxins, pesticides, drug residues, decomposition, parasites, allergens, and unapproved food and color additives. The range of hazards includes both those naturally occurring and those intentionally introduced. Intentionally introduced hazards would include those caused by sabotage of disgruntled employees, criminal acts, and acts of terrorism. Prevention of adulteration and misbranding as the result of acts of third parties is the responsibility of the person in charge of the facility. Records that must be kept include a written plan. Documentation must be kept for at least two years and must be available for FDA inspection. This section of FSMA does not apply to seafood, juice, and low-acid canned foods facilities already under FDA HACCP programs. Section 103 of FSMA does not apply to facilities covered by the produce safety rule under section 105 of FSMA.[12]

The requirements for hazard identification and preventive controls are modified for qualified facilities. Qualified facilities are very small businesses or facilities that sell more than half of the food handled in the facility to qualified end users. The three-year, average annual value of all food sold by such a facility must not exceed $500,000. A qualified end user must be the consumer of the food or a restaurant or retail food establishment. The restaurant or retail food establishment must sell directly to consumers and must be in the same state as the qualified facility or within 275 miles of the qualified facility. The labeling requirements for qualified facilities require only the name and business address of the facility that processed the food. The FDA may withdraw the exemption for a qualified facility if there is an active investigation of a food-borne illness directly linked to the qualified facility. The exemption for a qualified facility neither exempts it from the prohibition on selling adulterated or misbranded products nor preempts the common law or any state, local, county, or other non-federal law that governs food safety.

FSMA gives the FDA the power to suspend a food facility's registration. As with the USDA's power to suspend inspection, this puts the facility out of business until it complies with the FDA's requirements. Suspension is authorized when there is "a reasonable probability of causing serious adverse health consequences or death to humans or animals."[13] Suspension of operations is immediate with the FDA order of suspension. The due process requirements of the Fifth and Fourteenth Amendments are satisfied by providing a hearing to the registrant as soon as possible, but not more than two days after the order of suspension. At the hearing, the hearing officer may determine that the FDA's order of suspension was improper and order the suspension of the facility's registration rescinded. At that point, the facility is free to reopen. This outcome is rare. More often, the registrant may reopen only after it has submitted a corrective action plan that is acceptable to the FDA. As the FDA is required to review the corrective action plan within fourteen days of submission, the FDA usually makes this decision quickly. FSMA required the FDA to develop a small entity compliance guide to assist small entities with compliance with registration requirements.

---

**Example 18.2** Betty hated to see food go to waste at the end of the day at the farmers market where she sold her produce. She would gather up the fruit that vendors would otherwise throw out before they went home. She took it to her home kitchen where she turned it into delicious jellies and preserves. She then sold these at the farmers market. She was so successful that the produce that she produced was only a small part of her sales. As she was a small producer, state law exempted her from health department inspection. A customer who became sick with a food-borne illness complained to both state authorities and the FDA that she had been sickened from contaminated jelly bought from Betty. The FDA determined that she was operating a facility and ordered her to suspend operations. The FDA also suggested that she conduct a voluntary recall.

## Produce safety

The produce safety rules under section 105 of FSMA are an important addition to federal food safety law.[14] FSMA requires that the FDA consult with the USDA and the Department of Homeland Security and state departments of agriculture to develop science-based minimum standards for the safe production and harvesting of fruits and vegetables. FSMA gave the FDA broad authority to develop the produce safety rule. FSMA gave the FDA discretion to exclude low-risk fruits and vegetables produced by small and very small businesses from the produce rule. The FDA has issued guidance that defines small and very small business for the produce safety rule.[15] FSMA directed the FDA to avoid conflicts with certified organic standards. Rules prioritize FDA efforts based upon known risks of products such as leafy greens, tomatoes, sprouts, and melons. Variances may be granted from the rules in individual cases where the variance is not likely to increase the risk of adulteration. FSMA provides an exemption from the produce safety rule for direct farm marketing. The three-year, average value of all food sold by the farm claiming the exemption must be less than $500,000, and that sold to qualified end users must exceed the amount sold to other buyers. The definition of a qualified end user is the same as for hazard identification and preventive controls rule. Nothing in this exemption permits a farm to sell an adulterated or misbranded product. The FDA may withdraw the exemption should such sales occur. The produce safety rule does not apply to any fruit or vegetable produced for personal consumption.

The produce safety rule establishes standards for production and harvesting of fruits and vegetables. One of the most problematic aspects of regulating fruit and vegetable production has been sourcing of water for irrigation. Irrigation water is sourced from either groundwater or surface water sources. Groundwater is generally less likely to be contaminated with pathogens than surface water. Testing irrigation water to determine whether it contains pathogens or other harmful substances is essential to food safety. Some groundwater sources of irrigation water are highly contaminated. Some fruit and vegetable operations that use irrigation for frost prevention require large volumes of water that can be provided only from surface sources. Providing adequate volumes of water while protecting fruits and vegetables from adulteration has been a challenge. A complicating factor is that the blooms of some fruit varieties can be contaminated with pathogens from irrigation water. These pathogens may remain viable and dangerous in the fruit that is harvested some months later. The need for additional research to develop adequate science-based regulations means that any regulations that The FDA develops will likely require modification as the scientific understanding of pathogen contamination of fruits and vegetables improves.

## Food imports

Title III of FSMA addresses the need to improve the safety of imported food.[16] FSMA requires U.S. importers to perform risk-based foreign supplier verification to ensure that imported food is produced in compliance with applicable requirements for hazard analysis and preventive controls. FSMA requires that a program be established to expedite review and importation of food offered for importation by U.S. importers who have voluntarily agreed to participate in such a program. Import certification and agreements with foreign governments to facilitate the inspection of registered foreign facilities are authorized. Food may be refused admission into the United States if permission to inspect the food facility is denied by the facility owner, operator, agent of the owner or operator, or the foreign country. FSMA establishes a system to recognize bodies that accredit third-party auditors and audit agents who certify that foreign entities meet applicable FFDCA requirements for importation of food into the United States.

## Whistle-blower provisions

Title IV of FSMA includes whistle-blower provisions designed to protect facility employees and former employees who report alleged food safety violations at the facility. The whistle-blower provision of FSMA applies only to facilities. It does not apply to farmers, restaurants, or retail establishments. No entity that operates a food facility may discriminate against an employee who reports what he or she reasonably believes to be a food safety violation to his or her employer, the federal government, or the attorney general of a state.[17] For employee protections to apply, there need not be an actual violation. It is sufficient that the employee reasonably believed that there was a violation. If the employee reported the violation to a regulatory authority in a state department of agriculture, the provision does not apply. The provision applies only if the report was made to his or her employer, the federal government, or a state attorney general. The employee protection provisions also apply if the employee has testified about the violation, is about to testify, or is participating in a proceeding involving the violation. It also applies if the employee objected to a practice that he or she reasonably believed was a violation of the FFDCA.

If the employee protection provisions apply, the employee may file a complaint of discrimination with the U.S. Occupational Safety and Health Administration (OSHA) as designee of the U.S. Secretary of Labor. Discrimination includes any retaliatory act such as firing the employee, demoting the employee, or giving the employee undesirable assignments. After investigation, OSHA may order either dismissal of the complaint or relief that may include abatement of the violation, reinstatement of the employee with back pay and full privileges of employment, and compensatory damages. The complainant may request a penalty that includes attorney and expert witness fees. Should OSHA dismiss the complaint and determine that it was made in bad faith, OSHA may assess a $1,000 penalty against the complainant. Either the U.S. Secretary of Labor or the complainant may seek enforcement of any order against an employer through a civil action in federal district court.

An employee dissatisfied with the determination of OSHA may file a new action (an action *de novo*) in federal district court within ninety days after receipt of OSHA's written determination or after 210 days if OSHA has failed to act. The employee may ask for restoration to the same employment status that she or he had before the discrimination occurred. The employee may also seek back pay, with interest, and special damages. Special damages include litigation costs, expert witness fees, and reasonable attorney's fees.

## GAPs and HACCP

With the enactment of FSMA, HACCP programs have become mandatory for most processors of agricultural products. HACCP programs apply to few farmers. This is not true for GAPs. GAPs are designed for farmers. GAPs continue to be voluntary in the sense that GAPs are not required by statute. Most large buyers of fruits and vegetables require GAPs; therefore, GAPs are not voluntary if a farmer wishes to sell to these buyers.

GAP certification is privately administered. Third-party certifiers determine whether production of a particular crop on a particular farm qualifies for GAP certification. Many state departments of agriculture have grant programs to help smaller farmers pay the cost of third-party GAP certification. Areas that are covered in GAP certification audits include water use, fertilization, animal hazards, worker hygiene, and harvest operations. FDA covers all these aspects of GAP certification in its guidance for producers.[18] Water used for irrigation can be a source of pathogen contamination in agricultural products that are consumed raw. Manure and biosolids must be properly treated to minimize the likelihood of pathogen contamination. Steps must be taken to reduce animal hazards. Animal hazards include contamination of product with feces. This contamination may arise when domestic or wild animals or birds are allowed to defecate on product to be consumed raw. Steps such as fencing must be taken to minimize the likelihood of contamination. Workers with poor hygiene or suffering from illness can contaminate fresh produce or fruits. Proper worker hygiene must be ensured to avoid product contamination with pathogens. Harvest is another important source of contamination. Water used in packing fruits and vegetables for harvest can be a source of pathogen contamination. Poor sanitary practices in packing sheds and reuse of containers are additional sources of contamination.

## Notes

1  21 USC § 331 (2013).
2  US v. Park, 421 U.S. 658, 95 S. Ct. 1903, 1975 U.S. LEXIS 69 (1975).
3  Pub. L. No. 111-353, 124 Stat. 3885 (2011).
4  21 USC §§ 601–695 (2013).
5  21 USC §§ 451–472 (2013).
6  21 USC §§ 1031–1056 (2013).
7  2121 USC §§ 301–399f (2013).
8  Pub. L. No. 111-353, 124 Stat. 3885 (2011).
9  Pub. L. No. 111-353, § 206, 124 Stat. 3885 (2011).

10  Pub. L. No. 111-353, § 207, 124 Stat. 3885 (2011).
11  Pub. L. No. 111-353, § 103, 124 Stat. 3885 (2011).
12  Pub. L. No. 111-353, §§ 103, 105, 124 Stat. 3885 (2011).
13  21 U.S.C. § 350d(b)(1)(2013).
14  Standards for the Growing, Harvesting, Packing, and Holding of Produce for Human Consumption. 2015. 80 Fed. Reg. 74354 (2015).
15  FDA. *Standards for the Growing, Harvesting, Packing, and Holding of Produce for Human Consumption: What You Need to Know About the FDA Regulation: Guidance for Industry Small Entity Compliance Guide*. Retrieved July 31, 2018, www.fda.gov/downloads/Food/GuidanceRegulation/GuidanceDocumentsRegulatoryInformation/UCM574456.pdf.
16  Pub. L. No. 111-353, §§ 301–309, 105, 124 Stat. 3885 (2011).
17  Pub. L. No. 111-353, § 402, 105, 124 Stat. 3885 (2011).
18  FDA. *Guidance for Industry: Guide to Minimize Microbial Food Safety Hazards for Fresh Fruits and Vegetables*. Retrieved July 31, 2018, www.fda.gov/Food/GuidanceRegulation/GuidanceDocumentsRegulatoryInformation/ProducePlantProducts/ucm064574.htm.

# Chapter 19

# Criminal law

## Introduction

Criminal prosecutions against farmers and agribusinesses are not common, but not rare. Since the law governing agriculture and food is complex, it is quite possible to violate the law without knowing that one has done so. In most such situations, the violation will be civil rather than criminal. Nonetheless, it is important for every person engaged in agribusiness to understand the nature of criminal law. It is also important to understand the relationship between criminal and civil law.

An obvious distinction between criminal and civil law is that in a criminal prosecution one may lose their freedom, whereas this is unlikely in a civil action. Criminal actions also begin differently than civil actions. In the federal system, all criminal actions must begin with an indictment by a grand jury. The Fifth Amendment to the Constitution requires an indictment by a grand jury to begin a federal criminal action. Some states and their constitutions authorize what is called an information rather than indictment by a grand jury. Unlike civil actions that may be brought by private parties, all criminal actions must be brought by the federal government or the government of a state.

A major difference between criminal and civil actions is the amount of proof that must be provided to obtain a criminal conviction as opposed to a judgment or injunction in a civil action. In civil actions, plaintiffs must prove their case by a preponderance of the evidence. A preponderance of the evidence is more than 50 percent. In a criminal case, the government must prove guilt beyond a reasonable doubt.

The reasonable doubt standard is a very high standard of proof. For the government to prove its case in a criminal action, it must demonstrate to the members of the jury that no reasonable doubt exists as to the defendant's guilt. This is sometimes called proof by more than 99 percent of the evidence. An acquittal in a criminal trial is not an exoneration. It means only that there was not enough evidence to obtain a conviction. It is entirely possible to be acquitted in a criminal trial and found civilly liable in a separate civil trial.

**Example 19.1** Larry Lax operated a federally licensed grain warehouse. As a result of a fire, 1.3 million bushels of corn were allegedly destroyed. The federal government suspected that Larry intentionally set the fire to cover a shortage of grain that resulted from his fraudulent transfer of the grain prior to the fire. The USDA referred the matter to the Justice Department for prosecution. The Justice Department determined that there was enough evidence to present the case to the grand jury, which subsequently indicted Larry on various federal charges. Larry vigorously denied wrongdoing. After a trial, the jury returned a verdict of not guilty. Simultaneously, the owners of the grain brought a civil action against Larry to recover the value of the grain. They sought recovery based upon the strict liability tort of conversion and in the alternative common-law negligence. The jury determined that Larry was civilly liable for the tort of conversion. They determined, based upon the market price of corn at the time of the loss, that Larry was liable for $5 million in economic damages. In addition, the jury assessed punitive damages of $10 million.

Although criminal actions brought against farmers and businesses are uncommon, the influence that the possibility of such actions has in the realm of federal civil enforcement should not be underestimated. When responding to an administrative notice of violation or penalty, the respondent should always respond in a manner that reduces the likelihood that the federal regulatory agency will make a referral to the Justice Department for criminal prosecution. As a practical matter, this means that the respondent may be more cooperative with the regulatory agency than they would in the absence of the possibility of a criminal referral. For example, it is seldom prudent to force a regulatory agency to seek a search warrant to inspect a site and review documents.

The possibility of a criminal prosecution makes it essential to respond carefully to a civil investigation since admissions made in the civil investigation may be used as evidence in a criminal prosecution. Simultaneous criminal prosecutions and civil trials are particularly problematic due to the treatment of refusals to answer questions based upon the Fifth Amendment right to avoid self-incrimination. The Fifth Amendment right to avoid self-incrimination applies only in criminal matters. There is no right to assert the Fifth Amendment in a civil matter. A refusal to answer a question in a civil matter entitles the other party to an inference of the most negative possible answer to the question. As a practical matter, an attorney representing a party in a civil action for which there is also a corresponding criminal action will almost always request a stay of the civil action until the criminal action is complete. While such a stay is often granted, it is within the discretion of the trial judge. A trial judge has discretion to refuse to stay the civil action.

As part of the planning process, farms and agribusinesses must anticipate that inspections may occur based upon the businesses in which they are engaged. All employees should be instructed in how to respond. There should be a list of people readily available that should be called in the event of a surprise inspection. It is generally reasonable to ask the inspector what he or she intends to inspect and to confine the inspection to the stated purpose of the inspector. The planning process requires both individuals with subject matter expertise and knowledge of the business and competent legal advice. In some situations, competent legal advice may include the advice of a criminal defense attorney.

## Strict liability criminal actions and *mens rea*

The U.S. Supreme Court held, in *United States v. Park*, that introducing an adulterated food product into the chain of commerce in violation of the Federal Food, Drug, and Cosmetic Act (FFDCA) is a strict liability federal crime.[1] The Supreme Court held that cases under the FFDCA have "reflected the view both that knowledge or intent were not required to be proved in prosecutions under its criminal provisions, and that responsible corporate agents could be subjected to the liability thereby imposed." The criminal action was brought against Acme Markets, Inc. and its president, John Park. Acme plead guilty but Park contested criminal liability. The action arose from the all too common situation in the food industry of a rat infestation in a warehouse in which Acme stored food. Penalties for violations of the FFDCA are:

> Violation of section 331 of this title; second violation; intent to defraud or mislead
>
> (1) Any person who violates a provision of section 331 shall be imprisoned for not more than one year or fined not more than $ 1,000, or both.
> (2) Notwithstanding the provisions of paragraph (1) of this section, if any person commits such a violation after a conviction of him under this section has become final, or commits such a violation with the intent to defraud or mislead, such person shall be imprisoned for not more than three years or fined not more than $ 10,000, or both.[2]

Mr. Park was convicted of five violations of 21 USCS § 331 without any intent to defraud or mislead. The jury fined him $50 per violation. Since this was his first offense, the misdemeanor penalties under 21 USCS § 333(a)(1) were applied. For second offenses and first offenses involving an intent to defraud or mislead, the felony penalties under 21 USCS § 333(a)(2) would apply.

Mr. Park admitted that he knew of the infestation and had received a letter from the FDA about it. A second inspection of Acme's Baltimore warehouse found that conditions had improved but the rodent infestation remained. To summarize Mr. Park's argument on appeal to the Court of Appeals for the Fourth Circuit, he noted that a large organization requires delegation of responsibilities. He agreed that he had ultimate responsibility for Acme's operations but that it was unfair to hold him criminally liable for every possible violation, given the impossibility of him personally visiting every operation in a large national company. The Fourth Circuit agreed with Mr. Park; however, the Supreme Court reversed. In reversing, the Supreme Court cited its opinion in *United States v. Dotterweich*.[3] Reversing the Fourth Circuit and reinstating the Mr. Park's conviction, the Supreme Court held that the FFDCA

> imposes not only a positive duty to seek out and remedy violations when they occur but also, and primarily, a duty to implement measures that will insure that violations will not occur. The requirements of foresight and vigilance imposed on responsible corporate agents are beyond question demanding, and perhaps onerous, but they are no more stringent than the public has a right to expect of those who voluntarily assume positions of authority in business enterprises whose services and products affect the health and well-being of the public that supports them.[4]

There are several lessons that can be drawn from *US v. Park*. The first is the need to respond vigorously to the first notice of violation and not wait for a second inspection and second notice. If the rodent infestation could not have been immediately remediated, the facility should have been shut down until it could be remediated. As long as the rodent infestation remained, Acme was violating the FFDCA by shipping adulterated product. A second lesson that can be inferred from *US v. Park* (although it was not specifically stated) is that exposure of food to a rodent infestation is sufficient to prove adulteration. No one in *US v. Park* argued that a likelihood of actual harm need be proved because a likelihood of actual harm is not an element of this crime. This is an important principle under the FFDCA. A third lesson is that everyone in the corporate chain of command has potential criminal liability for shipping an adulterated product. A fourth lesson, alluded to by the Supreme Court in its conclusion, is that juries have the power to mitigate the harshness of strict liability for corporate officers.

> We are satisfied that the Act imposes the highest standard of care and permits conviction of responsible corporate officials who, in light of this standard of care, have the power to prevent or correct violations of its provisions. Implicit in the Court's admonition that 'the ultimate judgment of juries must be trusted,' *United States v. Dotterweich* [citation omitted], however, is the realization that they may demand more than corporate bylaws to find culpability.[5]

**Example 19.2** Cynthia raised artisanal lettuce for restaurants. In violation of regulations adopted pursuant to the Food Safety Modernization Act (FSMA), she failed to instruct her workers to avoid picking lettuce in the prescribed area around wild bird feces. This violation came to light as the result of a whistle-blower complaint to the FDA by a former employee who had a wage dispute with Cynthia. The FDA referred Cynthia's case to the Justice Department for prosecution. A federal jury fined her $1,000 for each of seven counts of shipping an adulterated product. The government offered no proof that the lettuce was actually harmful.

*US v. DeCoster*[6] is a recent decision involving strict liability under the FFDCA. Jack DeCoster owned Quality Egg, LLC, and his son, Peter, served as his chief operating officer. Jack DeCoster also owned egg production operations in Maine. His son also worked in those. They both plead guilty to misdemeanors and were sentenced to three months' imprisonment each under 21 USC § 333(a). They appealed their sentences to the Eighth Circuit based upon procedural and substantive unreasonableness. Quality Egg plead guilty to bribing a federal official and to both misdemeanor and felony violations for introducing eggs adulterated with *salmonella enteritidis* into interstate commerce. Quality Egg was not a party to the appeal. The Eighth Circuit decision distinguished strict liability under the FFDCA from vicarious liability. Strict liability, unlike vicarious liability discussed in Chapter 3, arises from the failure of corporate officers to correct conditions that were within their power to correct.

The Eighth Circuit held that the absence of *mens rea* as an element of the crime did not violate due process. This is sometimes known as a scienter requirement, which means that the defendant has a guilty mind. This does not mean that a defendant must know which statute he violated. A general knowledge that one has done wrong is sufficient for scienter. Historically, one could not be convicted of a crime in the United States if one did not have scienter or a guilty mind. The federal criminal justice system, in particular, has long been moving away from the requirement of scienter toward strict criminal liability for a wide variety of violations. The Eighth Circuit's conclusion illustrates the importance of the climate that corporate leaders create within their company.

> Furthermore, the district court did not abuse its discretion by considering the Quality Egg employees' pattern of deceiving the FDA. A sentencing court may consider "any information concerning the background, character, and conduct of [a] defendant." See United States v. Rogers [citations omitted]. Here, the court considered such background information and found that the DeCosters had "created a work environment where employees not only felt comfortable disregarding regulations and bribing USDA officials, but may

have felt pressure to do so." In fact, one employee alleged that Jack DeCoster had once reprimanded him because he had not moved a pallet of eggs in time to avoid inspection by the USDA. Peter DeCoster was similarly personally implicated in the company's violations because of inaccurate statements he made to Walmart about Quality Egg's food safety and sanitation practices.[7]

Another much publicized outbreak involved cantaloupe shipped by Jensen Farms, owned by Eric and Ryan Jensen in 2011.[8] Cantaloupe shipped by Jensen Farms was contaminated with *Listeria monocytogenes* that caused 33 known deaths and 147 known illnesses. They plead guilty to misdemeanor charges under 21 USC § 333(a).[9,10]

A good contrast to those cases based upon strict liability is that of Peanut Corporation of America and its owner and president, Stewart Parnell. He received 28 years in prison for knowingly shipping peanuts contaminated with salmonella that caused a 2009 outbreak. There was ample evidence that Parnell knew of the salmonella contamination and chose to ignore it.

## Other sources of criminal liability

There are other sources of criminal liability. This chapter will identify activities most likely to give rise to criminal liability for farmers and agribusiness persons. Where there may be criminal liability, it is important to hire a competent criminal defense attorney to provide advice. Handling disasters well is one of the keys to avoiding criminal liability. One must always address the question of criminal liability when an employee or other person dies or is seriously injured as a result of some activity engaged in by one's business. If one's farm or agribusiness has a release of chemical waste that kills fish, there is likely to be criminal liability.

### Destroying or altering evidence and lying

Any time that litigation has begun or is likely to begin, the manager of a business must set in place procedures to ensure that potential evidence is preserved. In the age of electronic communications and personal computers, this became much more difficult because many devices automatically delete emails and other information on a scheduled basis. These deletions must stop when litigation begins. Even if there are no criminal repercussions, the impact on one civil case of allowing evidence to be destroyed can be devastating. It is often advisable to hire information technology professionals to ensure that evidence is properly preserved.

To avoid having a large volume of potentially damaging evidence, every organization should have policies that govern what employees create and how long that information is retained. A retention policy that ensures documentation is deleted once it is no longer needed helps to avoid discovery costs of sorting through old and obsolete information. Once litigation has begun or is likely to begin, it is too late to destroy that information.

Altering evidence is an indication of intent to deceive. Often altering evidence provides the scienter necessary to prove many crimes. This may include backdating documents.

One should always speak truthfully when speaking with government or court officials. Making a false statement to any federal official is a federal crime. Contrary to what many people believe, one does not have to be under oath when one makes a false statement to a federal official for that false statement to be a federal felony. There is a natural human tendency to try to be helpful. This is not a helpful tendency with legal matters. When one speaks to a federal official or testifies in court, one should speak only of that which is in one's personal knowledge. If it is not within one's personal knowledge, one should not speak about it or speculate on the matter. It is better to simply say that one "doesn't know" or one "doesn't recall."

### Financial crimes

Those engaged in agriculture often use federal programs including federal loan programs. It is important to be truthful on these applications. Overstating income or understating expenses when applying for federal loans may be a federal crime. Making such false statements when applying for financing from private sources may also be a federal or state crime.

When a farm must file for bankruptcy, the case will be heard in federal bankruptcy court. Fortunately, agricultural incomes have been generally good and few bankruptcies have been filed by farmers in recent decades. Nonetheless, agricultural incomes are cyclical and it could be expected that at some time there will be more bankruptcies. Debtors and creditors have a duty of candor to the court. Violation of this duty may result in severe civil penalties, including dismissal of the bankruptcy case. There are also criminal violations that apply to misstatements and false information provided to the bankruptcy court. It is important to work with one's bankruptcy attorney to ensure that information provided to the court is as accurate as possible.

Perhaps a surprising area for financial crimes in agriculture is in grain warehouses that handle the grain and soybeans produced by farmers. Grain warehouses are highly regulated under both federal law and state law because unfortunate events ranging from deterioration of the grain stored in the warehouse to outright theft occur frequently. Farmers should take steps to protect themselves from possible fraud or other loss. The most important thing a farmer depositing grain or soybeans in the warehouse can do is obtain a federal warehouse receipt. In the event of a failure of the grain warehouse, the holder of the federal warehouse receipt has rights superior to producers who have only a sales slip. The holder of a federal warehouse receipt is a secured creditor whereas the depositor of grain or soybeans with only a sales slip is an unsecured creditor. Unsecured creditors are the last to be paid in the event of a grain warehouse bankruptcy and typically receive only a tiny percentage of what was owed.

### Tax fraud

Tax fraud includes both underreporting income and over-reporting expenses. It also includes mischaracterizing personal expenses as business expenses. Farm businesses are one of the areas that the IRS gives additional scrutiny because some farms have relatively large cash businesses that make underreporting of income relatively easy. The IRS uses statistical models to identify returns that are problematic. While most of these situations will be resolved as a civil matter, some will be referred by the IRS to the Justice Department for criminal prosecution.

It is important to have one's federal and state tax returns completed by professional tax preparers. This will help ensure their accuracy and reduce the likelihood of a serious mistake. If one is audited, it is important to be represented by a tax professional. Any statement that the taxpayer makes to an official of the IRS can be used as an admission against interest in either a subsequent civil or criminal trial. A statement of a tax professional made to the IRS in error is regrettable but is much more correctable than a statement made to the IRS by a taxpayer.

Sources of criminal liability are not limited to state and federal income taxes. Sales taxes and various excise taxes are often problematic. Sales taxes are particularly complicated because there exist various agricultural exemptions. Often these exemptions are quite complicated in terms of what the exemption applies to and that to which it does not apply.

### Wetlands

Section 404 of the Clean Water Act regulates what can be done in a wetland. This is a problematic area of law because it is not always obvious what is a wetland. If one has any doubts about whether property contains jurisdictional wetlands, it is advisable to hire a professional wetlands delineator to determine whether the property contains wetlands and map any such wetlands. Use of a professional delineator is an indicator of good faith and tends to negate the government's allegations of scienter. The regulation of wetlands is discussed in greater detail in Chapter 21.

### Pesticides

Violations of pesticide laws are a source of criminal liability. Criminal liability usually arises from gross misuse of a chemical. Typically, these are uses for which the chemicals are not labeled. Such violations can be avoided by following chemical labels. Pesticide law is discussed in greater detail in Chapter 20.

Those engaged in aerial application using manned aircraft or drones need to exercise particular caution. The Federal Aviation Administration (FAA) regulates both types of aircraft.[11] Pesticide aerial applicators also must comply with laws governing aviation. Most states apply a stricter level of regulation to aerial application than ground application. Unfortunately, the law governing the use of drones is not well-settled in many states. The FAA has issued over 100,000

Remote Pilot Certificates since the inception of the licensing program on August 29, 2016.[12]

## Waste disposal

Improper disposal of waste is another source of criminal liability. Many rural areas have major problems with the improper dumping of solid waste. Many local governments have programs to identify those engaged in illegal dumping and to punish the perpetrators.

Hazardous waste is heavily regulated. The first step in avoiding liability is to determine whether one generates hazardous waste. If one generates hazardous waste, one will need to contract with licensed hazardous-waste disposal companies. Improper disposal of pesticide containers and unused portions of pesticides can be a source of criminal liability.

Improper disposal of livestock waste and other wastes to surface water is not an uncommon source of criminal liability. *Freedman v. United States*[13] provides an example of the consequences of discharging hog waste to surface waters. The corporate defendant's plea agreement provided for a $500,000 fine and $1 million in restitution. The petitioner was sentenced to six months in prison and six months of home confinement. The court also made him jointly and severally liable with the corporate defendant for the restitution amount.

## Occupational safety and health

Both the federal and state governments regulate employers to protect the health and safety of workers. Violations that result in death or serious injury are likely to be a source of criminal liability.

## Agroterrorism

Agroterrorism is a crime that is increasingly victimizing some farmers.[14] Many livestock and poultry producers have had to take steps to improve the security of their operations. This is necessary to protect not only their operations but their workers and customers. The failure to take reasonable steps to protect customers and employees from criminal acts of agroterrorism can be a source of civil liability for the farm or agribusiness.

The development of new, less costly, gene editing technologies increases the likelihood of either state sponsored or third-party acts of agroterrorism using deleterious organisms. Appropriate protective means as well as law governing such acts are only in the earliest stages of development.

## Notes

1   US v. Park, 421 U.S. 658, 95 S. Ct. 1903, 1975 U.S. LEXIS 69 (1975).
2   21 USC § 333(a) (2017).

3  United States v. Dotterweich, 320 U.S. 277; 64 S. Ct. 134; 88 L. Ed. 48; 1943 U.S. LEXIS 1100 (1943).
4  US v. Park at 672.
5  US v. Park at 678.
6  US v. DeCoster, 828 F.3d 626 (8th Cir. 2016).
7  US v. DeCoster at 636.
8  Clay D. Sapp. Food with Integrity? How Responsible Corporate Officer Prosecutions Under the Federal Food, Drug, and Cosmetic Act Deny Fair Warning to Corporate Officers. 70 *Arkansas Law Review* 449 (2017).
9  *Id.* at 468–471.
10  *Id.* at 474–476.
11  FAA, *Certification Process for Agricultural Aircraft Operators*, AC No. 137-1B. Retrieved August 5, 2018, www.faa.gov/documentlibrary/media/advisory_circular/ac_137-1b.pdf.
12  FAA. *Unmanned Aircraft Systems*. Retrieved August 5, 2018, www.faa.gov/uas/.
13  Freedman v. United States, 2013 U.S. Dist. LEXIS 110452 (E. Distr. N.C. 2013).
14  Nathalie N. Prescott. Agroterrorism, Resilience, and Indoor Farming. 23 *Animal Law* 103 (2016).

# Chapter 20

# Pesticide law

## Introduction

The Federal Insecticide, Fungicide, and Rodenticide Act (FIFRA)[1] is the basic federal law under which pesticides are regulated. Pesticides are sometimes called economic poisons. The term implies that pesticides are toxic substances with economic value as opposed to those toxic substances without economic value. For agriculture, pesticides are essential for a variety of purposes. As discussed in Chapter 16, pesticides, albeit those from natural sources, are used even in certified organic production.

The use of pesticides raises a variety of issues. At the top of the list is potential toxicity to humans. Acute toxicity of most pesticides is well understood. Longterm effects of pesticides are not as well understood. Interactions of pesticides with other chemicals and particularly with pharmaceuticals is generally poorly understood. Animal testing of pesticides does not always produce reliable predictions of the effects of these pesticides in humans.

Concern about the impact of pesticides on the environment is a second important concern. Many pesticides persist in the environment for long periods of time. Some of these pesticides are concentrated in the food chain and cause toxicity in predators. Some of these predators, particularly fish, are eaten by humans.

A pest includes an insect, a rodent, a nematode, a fungus, or a weed. It also includes any terrestrial or aquatic life form. That may include animals, plants, viruses, bacteria, and other microorganisms. It does not include viruses, bacteria, or other microorganisms that are on or inside a human or other animal. The reason for this exclusion is to distinguish pests upon which pesticides are used from diseases that pharmaceuticals are used to control. Pharmaceuticals are regulated under the FFDCA rather than the FIFRA.

Pesticide is a generic term that includes both compounds and mixtures. The definition of pesticide encompasses more than those substances whose value is in toxicity to kill pests. It also includes plant regulators, defoliants, desiccants, and nitrogen stabilizers. Among the broad classes of pesticides are insecticides, herbicides, fungicides, and rodenticides. Some genetically engineered plants may be regulated as pesticides. Plant growth regulators either retard or accelerate or otherwise change the growth of a plant from its normal pattern. Defoliants cause plants to lose their leaves. Defoliants are important for the mechanical harvesting of cotton so that the leaves are not in the way of the harvesting process. Desiccants cause plant material to die and dry faster than normal. Insecticides are designed to kill insects. Herbicides are designed to kill plants. Fungicides are designed to kill fungus. Rodenticides are designed to kill rodents such as rats and mice. Pesticides may unintentionally kill non-target organisms that include humans, pets, and wildlife. For that reason, their production and use are regulated.

## Registration of pesticides

Manufacturers must submit accurate and truthful information in support of registration and must keep records on all pesticides manufactured and sold. Every pesticide must be registered with the EPA before it can be transferred or sold. The registration process for new pesticides is an expensive, multiyear project. Applicants for registration of a new pesticide must provide a complete copy of the proposed labeling for the pesticide that includes all claims made for it and the directions for its use. The labeling must comply with FIFRA. The application must indicate how the pesticide is to be classified. In evaluating an application for registration, FIFRA requires that the EPA consider both the benefits and risks associated with use of the pesticide proposed for registration. The EPA may deny registration only for those products that pose an unreasonable risk to public health or the environment.

Pesticides may be classified for general use, restricted use, or both. There are a variety of factors that the EPA uses in making this determination; however, in general, general-use pesticides are safer for both humans and the environment. Reasons that pesticides might be classified as both general-use and restricted-use may depend on factors such as a particular formulation or concentration. Formulations with higher concentrations of active ingredients are more likely to be restricted-use.

A great deal of testing goes into the development and registration of the pesticide. The EPA may request a full description of all tests made and the results of those tests. The test results that contain active ingredients initially registered after September 30, 1978, may not be used in support of an application of a competitor for ten years after the initial registration of the pesticide. The EPA is required to keep confidential the data that manufacturers submit in support of registration. The purpose of this rule is to protect the investment that the manufacturer has in developing registration data. Each manufacturer is expected to develop its own data in support of registration even though those data may have already been developed for the same chemical by another manufacturer. EPA employees face severe penalties for unauthorized disclosures of these data. The policy behind this rule is to encourage manufacturers to invest in the development and registration of new pesticides. When the pesticide is registered for a minor use, the period of exclusivity may be extended. Minor-use pesticides are pesticides that are used on specialty crops and in other uses where the total volume of pesticide used is small. Given the small volume of pesticide used, development costs must be recovered from a smaller sales volume.

As the original purpose of FIFRA was to protect consumers of pesticides from fraudulent and misleading claims, a registrant must prove to the EPA that the pesticide's composition is such as to warrant the proposed claims for it. The second purpose of FIFRA, protection of the environment, was added to FIFRA by amendments only in 1972 when responsibility for FIFRA was transferred to the EPA from the USDA.

The registrant must prove to the EPA that the pesticide will perform its intended function without unreasonable risks to people and the environment. This is determined by taking into account economic, social, and environmental costs and benefits of the pesticide. When the pesticide is used in accordance with commonly used practice, the pesticide should not cause unreasonable risk to the environment.

Factors for evaluating risks that the EPA weighs when deciding whether to register a pesticide include carcinogenicity, reproductive effects, immunological effects, neurological effects, impacts on groundwater, impacts on wildlife and fish, toxicity, and the availability of effective alternatives. As the question of unreasonable risk is a matter of judgment, there is often controversy about the registration of particular pesticides.

Since 1996, new registrations last for a period of fifteen years. Prior to the 1996 amendments to FIFRA, registrations were for five years. The 1996 amendments require the EPA to re-register all previously registered pesticides. Under current law, the EPA is required to publish a notice of cancellation in the Federal Register if no request for renewal is received within thirty days prior to the end of the registration period. Manufacturers have thirty days to protest such proposed cancellations. The EPA has the authority to suspend registrations of any registered pesticide on an emergency basis and to cancel the registration for unreasonable risk to humans or the environment. The EPA may grant conditional registration where certain supporting data are not submitted. There must be substantial similarity and uses to existing products, and there must be no significant risk of harm or other adverse effects.

## Application of pesticides and related issues

States have primacy to regulate the use of pesticides. Primacy means that the states are the primary point of contact for pesticide use regulation and registration of applicators. The EPA requires certain minimum elements in every state pesticide program.[2] Every state with a cooperative agreement with the EPA must have a basic pesticide program. Required program areas are pesticide applicator certification; management of pesticide containers and proper containment of pesticides; management of soil fumigation and soil fumigants; and protection of water resources from pesticide contamination. Should a state fail to meet minimum federal requirements, the EPA may withdraw that state's primacy to regulate pesticide use.

## Regulation and enforcement

A basic pesticide program includes regulations and enforcement necessary to ensure that applicators act in a manner consistent with protection of human health and the environment. States are primarily responsible for monitoring the compliance of pesticide applicators with FIFRA and applicable state laws. These monitoring programs are conducted by the states and Indian tribes under cooperative agreements with the EPA. State actions against farmers and other pesticide users for violations of pesticide laws constitute the single largest category of environmental violation. Thousands of actions are brought every year. Most state programs are generally conducted through their departments of agriculture. States, under section 24(c) of FIFRA, may register additional uses for pesticides by promulgating supplemental labels. This 24(c) authority provides states with the opportunity to allow pesticides to be used for minor crops that the registrant did not include on the national label. Registrants often choose not to register minor uses because it is not profitable to do so. Section 24(c) labels are valid only within the states that issue the labels. The EPA may disapprove a state's 24(c) supplemental label. Such labels are valid for only ninety days from the date of issue if the EPA disapproves the supplemental label. The EPA may withdraw a state's 24(c) authority if it determines that the state is not exercising adequate controls. States may not add additional labeling requirements. States may not issue supplemental labels for pesticides for which the EPA has revoked the registration. States may regulate pesticide applicators more stringently than required by FIFRA so long as those requirements are not inconsistent with FIFRA. These additional applicator requirements are imposed by state regulation. As states are not permitted to add these requirements to the label, such requirements are usually imposed as a condition of maintaining one's applicator certification.

Every person who uses a pesticide must comply with the label. In pesticide education programs, one will often hear the statement, "The label is the law." This means that any deviation from label requirements is a violation of FIFRA and applicable state law. Label requirements are often very detailed and dictate the conditions under which the pesticide may be applied. Excessive wind usually means that the pesticide cannot be applied in an outdoor setting. For many crops, there is a pre-harvest period of time in which particular pesticides cannot be applied. The purpose of this is to reduce the likelihood of illegal residues in food products. Pesticide containers cannot be legally reused. Example 20.1 illustrates an unexpected result of this rule. They must be disposed of in a legally permitted manner. There are also very specific storage requirements for certain pesticides. As drift is a major problem, most labels address application techniques for drift avoidance. As the recent problems with dicamba drift have demonstrated, coverage under existing insurance products may be problematic.[3]

---

**Example 20.1** Farmer Jones had a farm next door to Farmer Smith. Farmer Smith discovered that he could reduce his costs by stealing insecticide from Farmer Jones. Farmer Jones was reasonably sure that Farmer Smith was stealing his insecticide. Farmer Jones decided to put a stop to Farmer Smith's theft. Farmer Jones had a number of empty pesticide containers. He poured a powerful herbicide into the containers and put them into his pesticide storage room. Sure enough, they disappeared. Soon thereafter, Farmer Smith's 200-acre field of cotton that he had planted a month-and-a-half ago was brown. Each time that Farmer Jones drove by Farmer Smith's field, he chuckled. He quit chuckling after he received a letter from Farmer Smith's attorney demanding payment for the value of the lost crop, reasonable attorney fees, and an amount equal to punitive damages that a jury could be expected to award. His chuckling turned to anger, and he went to his own attorney. At his attorney's direction, he wrote out a check to Farmer Smith's attorney for the value of lost cotton plus reasonable attorney fees. With check in hand, Farmer Jones' attorney negotiated a confidential settlement that required Farmer Jones to pay for the value of lost cotton plus reasonable attorney fees and refrain from discussing the matter with anyone or reporting Farmer Smith to any authorities for either trespass or theft. In return, Farmer Smith agreed not to report Farmer Jones to either state or federal authorities and to refrain from discussing the matter with anyone. For you see, Farmer Jones committed a federal felony when he mislabeled an herbicide by putting it in empty insecticide containers.

---

## Laboratories and testing

Laboratory support is one of the key elements of any basic pesticide program. Laboratory support must be adequate to support pesticide monitoring and enforcement. The basic pesticide program includes technical assistance to the regulated community. This includes developing outreach materials to improve compliance, conducting seminars and public meetings with members of regulated industries, providing remedial training for violators, and development of self-audit programs for members of regulated industries. Common inspections include targeted inspections of pesticide producer establishments; inspections of contract manufacturers; inspections of pesticide dealers, distributors, and retailers; and the monitoring of e-commerce in pesticides. A state program must monitor for pesticide misuse, monitor exempt activities such as emergency spraying for mosquitoes after hurricane disasters, and monitor additional uses of section 24(c) registrations. The EPA refers information about potential violations to the states for enforcement.

State laboratories are a very important link in the process by which those who have been adversely affected by drift and overspray can obtain compensation from those responsible. A laboratory test that confirms the off-target presence of a pesticide on property, livestock, or people is essential to the success of any plaintiff's tort case. State laboratories meet the chain of custody requirements and laboratory certification requirements necessary for the test results to be introduced into evidence in a tort case. The typical mistake that victims of pesticide drift make is to wait too long to call the state regulatory agency and get testing done. Many chemicals dissipate quickly, and time is of the essence.

## Worker protection standard

A major required element of any state program is implementing the worker protection standard (WPS) for the safety of workers handling pesticides. Worker training is a key element of the WPS. States have primary responsibility for enforcing the WPS and imposing sanctions for violations.

## Applicator certification

Pesticide applicator certification is another key component of a basic pesticide program. States have a great deal of freedom in setting up applicator certification programs. Some states have only a few certification categories while others have many more. Much of this will depend on the needs of the particular state. The usual distinction is between applicators who apply pesticides in agricultural and forestry uses and those who apply pesticides in buildings. The latter applicators are commonly called exterminators or pest-control contractors. The technical term usually used to describe these applicators is structural pesticide applicators.

Certification of all applicators of restricted-use pesticides is required. There are two basic categories of certification: private and commercial. These applicator certification requirements are managed by the states under delegation from the EPA. Most of these programs are operated by state departments of agriculture. States are free to add additional subcategories within the two basic categories of certification. Private applicators may not apply pesticides for hire and are generally restricted to property that they own or lease. Commercial applicators may apply pesticides for hire.

For purchasers of pesticides who plan to use the pesticides on their own property, no applicator certification is required if the pesticides to be applied are classified as general-use pesticides. General-use pesticides may be purchased by the public without restriction. No records of purchases are required for general-use pesticides.

There are two reasons that applicator certification may be required. The first reason to have certification is the ability to purchase restricted-use pesticides. Restricted-use pesticides may be purchased only by certified applicators. Restricted-use pesticides must be used under the supervision of a certified applicator. Supervision does not mean that the applicator holding the certification has to be physically present when the pesticide is being applied. It is sufficient that the applicator holding the certification be available to answer questions from the individuals who are actually applying the pesticide.

The second reason that an applicator may be required to have certification is that he or she is applying the pesticide to property that he or she neither owns nor rents. To apply a general-use pesticide on property that one owns or rents does not require certification.

Each applicant for applicator certification must take courses tailored to the specific certification category for which he or she is applying. After courses are completed, he or she must take and pass a test. Certified applicators are required to take additional periodic continuing education.

For those seeking certification as applicators for agricultural and forestry uses, training programs must promote integrated pest management (IPM).[4] IPM is an approach to pesticide management that seeks to use the latest scientific information about chemicals to promote environmentally sound pesticide use that is economically sustainable. One of the key components to IPM is the concept of economic thresholds. An economic threshold is a level of pest presence at which the cost of the damage done by the pest equals the cost of pesticide treatment. It is not economically rational to use a pesticide at a level below its economic threshold for a particular crop. Waiting until an economic threshold is reached protects the environment by reducing pesticide use. Reducing pesticide use reduces costs and improves profitability by reducing the quantity of pesticide used and by reducing trips across the field, which saves labor and fuel. Some insecticides and herbicides have negative effects on crop growth, so reducing the amount applied can promote better crop growth. There are many factors such as these that are taken into account in an IPM program. It is truly a situation where improving profitability can also reduce environmental damage.

### Record keeping

Everyone who handles a restricted-use pesticide, from the manufacturer to the end user, must keep and retain records. For the applicator, these records must include information about where and when the pesticide was applied and the weather conditions that existed at the time of application. The failure to keep adequate records is itself a violation of FIFRA.

### Enforcement

Enforcement responsibilities are divided between multiple federal agencies that include the EPA, FDA, USDA, DHS, and the states. The EPA is primarily responsible for registration and regulation of manufacturers. The EPA possesses a full range of civil and criminal penalties with which to enforce these regulations. States have primary responsibility for regulating the application of pesticides and certifying applicators. The FDA, EPA, and USDA have roles in regulating pesticide tolerances in foods. DHS has authority to stop transfers of pesticides that could be used in terrorism.

As stated above, states have primary responsibility for enforcement of pesticide use violations. Where states fail to adequately enforce use violations, the EPA may rescind the state's primary enforcement responsibility.[5]

## Pesticide tolerances

The EPA together with the FDA sets tolerances for pesticide residues found in foods. The USDA is responsible for pesticide tolerances in foods that are certified organic. A tolerance is the maximum acceptable level of a pesticide that may be found in food. Pesticide tolerances are regulated under the FFDCA. States may not set more stringent tolerances. In 1958, Congress added the Delaney Amendment to the FFDCA. The Delaney Amendment prohibited the use of any synthetic chemical with carcinogenic properties that left a residue in food products for human consumption. At that time, detection limits were in parts per thousand. The science has improved to the extent that parts per trillion or less can now be detected. Technological progress effectively banned the use of certain pesticides by allowing minute quantities of carcinogenic pesticides to be detected. In 1996, Congress repealed the Delaney Amendment in recognition of the fact that carcinogenic synthetic chemicals are not the only or even the greatest risk posed to the food supply. Congress directed the EPA and FDA to regulate risks to the food supply through the use of risk assessment. Thus, other risks beside the carcinogenicity of synthetic chemicals may be considered. Although risk assessment sounds good in theory, it is proving difficult to implement in practice. Much is not known about various risks to the food supply. There is also much disagreement about what constitutes an acceptable risk. For tolerances to have any meaning, there must be monitoring of the food supply. Monitoring is the joint responsibility of the FDA, EPA, and USDA. The FDA analyzes thousands of food samples annually to monitor compliance with pesticide tolerances.

### Price discrimination

FIFRA has the potential to be used as a price discrimination tool. There is nothing to prevent a manufacturer from registering the same chemical under two different labels for two different crops. The manufacturer can charge different prices for the different labels that are chemically identical based upon the differing ability of farmers of different crops to pay. Farmers cannot use the lower-priced, yet identical, chemical without facing civil and criminal liability. There is nothing in the EPA's authority under FIFRA to prevent this.

Prevention of monopolistic practices is the responsibility of the U.S. Department of Justice. Injured private parties have a theoretical right to bring a private antitrust action to protect their interests and recover damages. Antitrust actions are expensive, complicated, and time-consuming.

## Clean Water Act

A tension exists between FIFRA and the Clean Water Act (CWA). The CWA is discussed in greater detail in Chapters 13 and 21. The question is whether compliance with FIFRA negates the need for an NPDES permit under the CWA. The issue arises with widespread aerial application of pesticides on forestry and for mosquito control where pesticides inevitably enter bodies of water. The question also arises with irrigation return flows that contain pesticides. Although the issue is far from settled, some courts have ruled that compliance with the pesticide label negates the need for an NPDES permit.[6] Other courts disagree, having focused on the discrete means of conveyance rather than label requirements.[7] According to the EPA, "Point source discharges of biological pesticides and chemical pesticides that leave a residue into waters of the U.S. are required to comply with NPDES requirements."[8]

## Tort actions under state law

### Manufacturers

Both the common law and statutes of most states provide various causes of action against pesticide manufacturers. The Supreme Court decision in *Bates v. Dow Agrosciences*[9] addressed questions of federal preemption in a product liability case against the manufacturer. The case was brought by twenty-nine Texas peanut farmers whose peanuts were allegedly severely damaged by an herbicide manufactured by Dow Agrosciences. The gist of the complaint was that the herbicide was unsuitable for peanuts grown on high pH soils. The plaintiffs argued that the label should not have stated that the herbicide was suitable for all peanuts grown on any soils. The allegations made by the plaintiffs included violations of the Texas Deceptive Trade Practices-Consumer Protection Act,[10] tort claims based on theories of strict liability and negligence, and allegations of fraud and breach of warranty.

The Supreme Court held that section 136v(b) of FIFRA preempts state common law, statutes, and regulations that require labeling or packaging that are in addition to or different from those required by FIFRA. It held that state law may regulate the design of pesticide products. State laws that require manufacturers to design products that are reasonably safe, to be tested with due care, to be marketed free of manufacturing defects, and to honor warranties and other contractual commitments are not preempted by FIFRA. The Supreme Court did note that competing state labeling standards are preempted by FIFRA. It also held that statutory and common law rules that impose labeling requirements different from FIFRA are preempted. The Supreme Court's decision allowed the farmers' case against Dow Agrosciences to go forward.

### Applicators

Applicators are often sued when the chemical that they are applying is found off-site. Chemicals find their way off-site for a variety of reasons. The chemical may have been sprayed outside of the target area. This is called overspray. The chemical may have been sprayed on the target area but wind carried it off of the target area before it reached the target crop. The chemical may also have reached the target crop but volatilized to later be carried outside the target area. Volatilization is the process by which a chemical that was liquid turns into a vapor. This usually happens in the summer when the air temperature is high. The chemical may also be attached to soil particles and be carried off-site by the action of water. All these processes are referred to collectively as drift. Although not drift, a related issue arises when bees visit the target area and are adversely affected by the chemical. The trespassing bees may carry the chemical in either nectar or pollen or on their bodies back to the hive, where the entire hive is adversely affected.

The most difficult challenges that plaintiffs have is proving causation. Prompt testing for chemical residue in the affected area by a qualified laboratory is absolutely essential to any successful tort case against an applicator. These tests are best conducted by the official state laboratory. This allows the state to determine whether there has been a violation of FIFRA or state law. The state regulatory agency with primary responsibility for FIFRA enforcement can cite the applicator for a violation of FIFRA or state law. Most plaintiffs' attorneys will wait for the results of the regulatory investigation before filing suit against the applicator alleged to have caused the drift. If the state regulatory agency cites the applicator with a violation of FIFRA or state law, this makes it much easier for the plaintiff to win the case and makes a settlement without trial very likely. If the regulatory violation was the cause of the drift, negligence *per se* applies. Under the doctrine of negligence *per se*, proof of the violation establishes the first two of the elements in a tort based on negligence and duty and breach of duty. As the violation of a regulation is proven by the state, the plaintiff need only prove causation and actual damages. Without a violation, pesticide drift cases are difficult to win. Without test results that are admissible in evidence and which prove the identity of the chemical that caused the damage, pesticide drift cases are impossible to win.

The tort theory applied in pesticide drift cases in almost all states is one of negligence. There are a few states that apply strict liability in tort to aerial applicators of pesticides.[11] If the plaintiff can prove the applicator applied the pesticide with reckless disregard, a quasi-intentional tort theory might be used. As applicators are trained and require certification, the applicator's actions will rarely rise to this level of misconduct.

Often, pesticides are applied to farms by independent contractors. If the theory of the case is one of negligence, the farmer who hired the independent contractor has no liability. If neither the assets nor the insurance of the independent contractor cover the plaintiff's losses, the plaintiff is out of luck. Many states do not require that pesticide applicators carry liability insurance coverage. From the perspective of the farmer who hires the applicator, the farmer should require that the independent contractor provide proof of liability insurance coverage. The farmer should also require that the applicator's liability insurance cover the applicator's customers as third-party insureds. A certificate of insurance is usually sufficient to provide this evidence. In the event of serious damage done by drift, especially with personal injuries, the farmer is almost certain to be sued along with the independent contractor. If the independent contractor had previous regulatory violations, those violations may be used by the plaintiff's attorney to argue successfully that the farmer committed the tort of negligent selection of the pesticide applicator. The ability of the plaintiff to successfully make out a *prima facie* case of negligent selection will usually induce the farmer's liability insurance carrier to settle the case.

Honeybees provide some interesting issues. State law covering honeybees varies greatly. How responsibility is allocated between applicators and bee keepers is a major source of the difference in the laws. Some states require that beekeepers provide notice of the locations of their hives to neighboring farms if they wish to recover damages that pesticides used on neighboring farms cause their bees and hives. Other states keep lists of beekeepers and the locations of their hives and require that farmers applying pesticides notify the beekeepers before spraying. In states where beekeepers are required to provide notice, a farmer would have no liability for pesticide damage to the beekeeper if no notice was provided. In states where the farmer is required to provide notice, the farmer would have liability if notice was not provided and damage to bees was caused. Once the farmer gives notice, the beekeeper is responsible for protecting his or her bees from the spraying operation.

There are two problems with notification requirements. The first is that beekeepers often move their hives. This is particularly true for commercial beekeepers who often make the bulk of their money from using their bees as pollinators for farmers. The farmers pay the beekeeper a per hive pollination fee. The second problem exists when beekeepers are attempting to produce high-value specialty honeys. Those beekeepers often wish to keep the locations of their hives secret because they do not want their competitors to know where the most productive locations exist.

## Notes

1  7 U.S.C. §§ 136–136Y (2013).
2  EPA. *Fiscal Year 2018–2021 FIFRA Cooperative Agreement Guidance, EPA.* Retrieved July 31, 2018, www.epa.gov/pesticide-advisory-committees-and-regulatory-partners.
3  The Progressive Farmer. *Dicamba: Who's Liable? Insurance Claims Denied as Companies Grapple with Dicamba Injury.* www.dtnpf.com/agriculture/web/ag/news/article/2017/10/20/insurance-claims-denied-companies.
4  NC State University. *NSF Center for Integrated Pest Management.* Retrieved July 31, 2018, www.cipm.info/.
5  46 Fed. Reg. 26058 (1981).
6  *Peconic Baykeeper, Inc. v. Suffolk County,* 600 F.3d 180, 2010 U.S. App. LEXIS 6513 (2nd Cir. 2010).
7  *League of Wilderness Defenders/Blue Mountains Biodiversity Project v. Forsgren,* 309 F.3d 1181, 2002 U.S. App. LEXIS 22818 (9th Cir. 2002).

8  EPA. *Pesticide Permitting*. Retrieved July 31, 2018, www.epa.gov/npdes/pesticide-permitting.
9  544 U.S. 431, 125 S. Ct. 1788, 2005 U.S. LEXIS 3706 (2005).
10  Tex. Bus. & Com. Code Ann. § 17.01 et seq. (West 2002).
11  Theodore A. Feitshans. An Analysis of State Pesticide Drift Laws Revisited. 20 San Joaquin Agricultural Law Review 1, 23 (2010–2011).

# Chapter 21

# Conservation and environmental law

## Introduction

There is no sharp distinction between conservation and environmental law. Conservation efforts are considerably older than modern federal environmental law. Participation in conservation programs tends to be voluntary whereas compliance with environmental law is not. The conservation programs administered by The USDA are discussed in Chapter 25 and are not repeated here. There are numerous conservation programs under state law. The most important of these are discussed in this chapter. The remainder of the chapter is devoted to the major federal environmental laws that apply to agriculture and forestry.

## Conservation programs under state law

Most states with significant urban development pressure have programs to protect some land from development. One way to do this is through outright purchase by the state or local government for use as a park. There are divergent purposes for protecting land from development, and not all of these purposes are compatible with use of the land as a public park. Preservation of open space has as its purpose to maintain an esthetically attractive environment for humans. Preservation of land with unique geological or biological features preserves these resources for posterity. An example of a unique geological feature would be the point of highest elevation in a state or an unusual landform (e.g., Stone Mountain in Georgia. Somewhat smaller nearby mountains no longer exist as they were mined for crushed rock). Biological features would include habitat for rare or endangered species of plants and animals. Land preservation may also be motivated by a desire to preserve recreational opportunities (e.g., hiking trails and public beach access). Farm and forest land preservation is a priority for many communities. Reasons for doing so include promotion of agriculture and forestry, protecting local agriculture, preserving open space and recreational opportunities, and protecting the environment, particularly water quality. Depending upon the geology of the area, open space can be important for groundwater recharge. As the very purpose of protecting farm and forest land is to maintain the agricultural and forest industries, acquisition of the land by state or local government would be inappropriate.

One alternative is to use a conservation easement. The Uniform Conservation Easement Act (UCEA),[1] enacted by twenty-three states, is an important state tool for protecting agricultural and forest lands from development. Many states that have not adopted the UCEA have adopted similar legislation. The UCEA and similar legislation do several things. Through deed restrictions, these statutes allow conservation easements to be placed on private land. Conservation easements are one of the key state law tools used for land preservation. A conservation easement is an interest in real property that prevents the development of that property. A conservation easement may be either for a term of years or in perpetuity. In addition to the UCEA, provisions of the Farm Bill allow for creation of conservation easements under federal law. As the landowner is usually partially compensated for these easements, they usually do not qualify for favorable tax treatment.

Under the UCEA, a conservation easement may be held by either a unit of government or a land trust. A land trust is a private nonprofit organization set up under IRC §501(c)(3). As the creation of a conservation easement is a real property transaction, all the formalities in any real property transaction must be observed. The landowner must have good title to property that is free of security interests, hazardous waste, and abandoned underground storage tanks. If the landowner is married, the landowner must obtain the agreement of her or his spouse. The agency receiving the conservation easement must be satisfied that title is good and must conduct due diligence to set up the "innocent landowner" defense to Comprehensive Environmental Response, Compensation and Liability Act (CERCLA) liability (discussed later in this chapter).

To create a conservation easement, a deed must be prepared and recorded. The deed must include a legal description of the physical boundaries of the easement and the restrictions on the use of the property. The landowner and the receiving agency must agree to allocate closing costs between them. The landowner and agency should agree on a plan for transferring rights and educating subsequent owners of the property.

It is also wise to include a dispute resolution mechanism in the conservation easement. Arbitration and mediation are alternatives to litigation that can save parties much of the time and expense of traditional lawsuits. In mediation, a neutral third party attempts to help the parties reach a solution to their dispute. In arbitration, an arbitrator decides a dispute much as a judge would.

Application of a conservation easement to property will usually significantly reduce tax liability. The application of a conservation easement usually has the effect of substantially reducing the fair market value of the property. The property tax, based upon fair market value, will also be reduced. When the landowner is using some form of present use valuation program that reduces the value of the land to its value in agricultural or forestry uses, the reduction in property tax from applying a conservation easement may not be significant.

When a conservation easement is donated to either a government or a land trust, the fair market value of the conservation easement may be deducted on the federal income tax return as a charitable deduction. Donors are allowed to deduct the fair market value of their gift instead of the basis. The unrealized gain is never taxed. This is an added benefit. A charitable deduction or a credit on the donor's state income tax return may also available. The total amount of a federal charitable deduction in any given year is usually limited to 30 percent of adjusted gross income. The federal government allows the excess deduction to be taken over the subsequent five years' federal tax returns. For states that have an income tax, the treatment of donations of conservation easements as either charitable deductions or credits varies greatly.

The federal estate tax law allows the valuation of property subject to a donated conservation easement to be taxed at a value below the fair market value. The total amount of reduction in valuation that is allowed is limited to a maximum dollar amount. Conservation easements may be donated after a person dies. A charitable deduction is then taken on the estate tax return.

Many local governments and some state governments have purchase of development rights programs. These programs allow local and state governments to direct tax money and grants to preserving land that is deemed particularly worthy of protecting from development. Some local governments have taken this a step further and instituted transfer of development rights (TDR) programs that concentrate growth in designated receiving areas while reducing density in those areas where the land is to be preserved. The goal of TDR programs is to establish working markets so that those landowners in the sending area can sell their development rights to landowners in the receiving area. The sending area is the area that has been designated by the local government for development that is not so dense. The receiving area has been designated for dense development. Landowners in the receiving area that purchase development rights are then allowed even denser development. TDR programs have not been widely adopted.

Of more direct relevance to preserving farms are programs that allow agricultural, forest, and horticultural land to be taxed at its value in those uses. In areas with high urban and suburban land values, the use value for agriculture, forestry, and horticulture is likely to be much less than the fair market value of the property. States set various requirements for participation in these programs. Most states require an application. Some states allow participation only in areas designated as agricultural. Conversion to a non-qualifying use results in payment of additional tax in the year of conversion and all future years. It also results in repayment of the tax foregone in past years. This repayment of tax foregone, called the rollback tax, is usually limited to a set period of years. State laws vary as to the length of the rollback. The rollback can range from as few as three years to as many as fifteen years.

Agricultural areas or agricultural district programs are a major component of the efforts of many states to preserve agricultural land. Typically, each county or city establishes a program by enacting an ordinance. Ordinances establish minimum criteria for participating farms and boards to review applications from landowners. Conservation agreements are executed for a period of years. There are several benefits of participating in an area or district program. If a state or local entity proposes the condemnation of land in an area or district, many states provide procedural protections that include public hearings on the proposed condemnation. Certain assessments such as those for water and sewer may also be waived. Buyers of property within close proximity to land in an agricultural area or district are put on notice that they are buying near agricultural property. The existence of notice to buyers of land near farms can reduce the likelihood that the farms near the buyers' property will be found to be nuisances, should buyers object to the impact of practices on the farms that may devalue their property.

Zoning is another tool that has been used to preserve farmland and forest land. Typically, this is done with large-lot zoning. This type of zoning is very unpopular with landowners because it usually reduces property values. The same objective may often be accomplished by not building water and sewer lines to the areas where agriculture and forestry are to be maintained. This approach is less controversial than zoning. Lack of water and sewer lines limits development because any development will depend upon private wells and septic tanks. In many areas of the country, there is a limited supply of groundwater. Reliance upon septic tanks generally requires larger lots than a subdivision serviced by sewer lines. Some areas of the country will not support septic tanks at all. There are alternatives to private wells and septic tanks where water and sewer lines are absent; however, these alternatives are usually much more expensive than either of the options discussed.

## Federal environmental laws

The major federal environmental laws that regulate agriculture and forestry are discussed in this section. Agriculture is often exempt from the application of many aspects of these laws. These exemptions are usually not total.

### National Environmental Policy Act[2]

The National Environmental Policy Act (NEPA) was enacted on January 1, 1970. It was the first attempt to address the environmental impact of the actions of federal agencies. Unlike later federal environmental law, most of which is based upon the Commerce power, the constitutional basis of NEPA is the federal spending power. This is the power of the federal government to spend its money in any manner that it determines appropriate (subject to other constitutional limitations).

The primary vehicle through which NEPA operates is the environmental impact statement (EIS). The EIS is required for every action of an agency that

(1) is federal, (2) is major, and (3) has a significant impact on the human environment. Every action undertaken by a federal agency is a federal action; however, the definition of a federal action is much broader than this. It encompasses those actions undertaken by federal contractors and by recipients of federal grants, including states, universities, local governments, and private parties. Thus, the obligations of federal agencies under NEPA may not be avoided by having the action conducted by a third party. Whether an action is a major action has been the source of much contention. The courts, however, have helped to fill in the blanks in NEPA. The mere use of federal money does not make a project major; however, where the federal government retains significant discretion to control a project, the project is likely to be major.[3] Finally, the activity must have a significant impact on the human environment for an EIS to be required. This also has been the source of much litigation. Note that it is not sufficient for there to be a significant effect on the environment; the effect must have an impact on humans.

NEPA is implemented through the preparation of an environmental assessment (EA), an EIS, or a finding of no significant impact (FONSI). If an agency prepares a FONSI, no EIS is required as the agency has determined that its action is not subject to NEPA. As an interim step, an agency may prepare an EA. As a result of the EA, it may decide to prepare either a FONSI or an EIS depending upon the determination made in the EA. If it is determined that an EIS is required, the agency must prepare a draft and publish a notice of availability in the Federal Register. Comments from other agencies and the public are invited. After the comments are reviewed by the agency, a final draft of the EIS is prepared and a notice of availability is published in the Federal Register.

An EIS is required to have certain components. These include, of course, the expected environmental impacts of the project. Included in this part would be the scientific data upon which the expected impacts are predicated. Next, the agency must identify unavoidable adverse impacts that will occur if the action is taken. Alternatives to the action must be discussed. The economic impacts of the action are incorporated by including an analysis of the relationship between short-term uses of the environment and long-range impacts on the productivity of the economy. Finally the EIS must discuss any irreversible commitment of resources that will be made as a result of the action.

The federal courts have determined that NEPA is procedural. That means that after an agency has prepared a proper EIS, it can proceed with its proposed activity no matter how ill-conceived and environmentally damaging the activity may be. Nonetheless, NEPA has had a major impact on the way that federal agencies treat the environment. The preparation and publication of an EIS tends to focus public interest on an agency's proposed action. As a result, public pressure brought to bear through the political process may require an agency to change its plans even though NEPA does not require it to do so. NEPA applies to all federal programs that affect agriculture and forestry. Importantly, it also affects state programs that affect agriculture and forestry if those programs are funded with federal money.

### Comprehensive Environmental Response, Compensation and Liability Act[4]

Congress passed the Comprehensive Environmental Response, Compensation and Liability Act (CERCLA) in 1980 in response to several highly publicized hazardous waste incidents. Hazardous waste under CERCLA borrows definitions from the Solid Waste Disposal Act,[5] with modifications. The most important of these is that petroleum is not defined as a hazardous waste under CERCLA.

There are three components to CERCLA. The first is mandatory reporting of releases of CERCLA hazardous substances to EPA's National Response Center (which was established under the Clean Water Act[6]). Second, the EPA is authorized to respond to and remediate hazardous waste sites and spills. A fund, the Superfund, was established to provide money for this purpose. The EPA may seek reimbursement for its costs from the responsible parties. Third, the EPA is required to list the worst sites on the National Priorities List.

The most controversial part of CERCLA is the requirement that responsible parties pay for cleanup. There are three components to cleanup liability under CERCLA. First, liability is strict or without fault. If a person meets the definition of a responsible party, there is cleanup liability. It is not a defense to assert that the law permitted disposal of the waste at the time the disposal was made. Likewise, use of the best available technology is no defense. Second, borrowing from tort law, liability is joint and several. Joint and several liability means that when more than one person is a responsible party, the government can recover the entire cleanup cost from one, all, or some combination thereof. The person who pays the government may then sue the other parties for contribution. Contribution is defined as an action to compel codefendants to pay their equitable share of a damage award. Third, liability under CERCLA is retroactive. It does not matter when the waste was dumped. Liability can exist for waste that was created in the nineteenth century.

The CERCLA definition of potentially responsible party is very broad. It includes the owner or operator of a facility. This includes current owners who are unaware that the waste is on the property. Additionally, any person who owned the facility at the time of disposal and anyone in the chain of title between that person and the current owner is also a potentially responsible party. Any person who arranged for disposal, treatment, or transport of the waste is also a potentially responsible party. Any person who transported the waste is a potentially responsible party. The definition includes individuals, firms, corporations, associations, partnerships, consortiums, joint ventures, commercial entities, and local, state, and federal governments—indeed, almost anyone. The U.S. Department of Defense is one of the largest potentially responsible parties, with numerous sites scattered across current and former bases in U.S. territory.

There are a few defenses to CERCLA cleanup liability. If the waste was deposited on the property as the result of an act of war, an act of God, or the act of a third party to whom the property owner has no relationship, CERCLA cleanup liability may be avoided. A potential purchaser of real property may use the "innocent landowner defense" if the purchaser exercised due diligence prior to purchasing the property and found no waste. In the context of commercial property transactions, due diligence is usually fulfilled by conducting a preliminary environmental site assessment that reveals no waste problems with the property. As these defenses do nothing to restore the property, the buyer may be left with property that cannot be used. If the owner proceeds to move the waste around or otherwise disturb it, the owner may acquire liability. Thus, there may be very little value remaining in the property for the owner. It may be money well spent for a buyer to do more testing than that required for CERCLA due diligence to avoid buying a property that will later be found to be unusable.

There are also limited exemptions for lenders, heirs, fiduciaries, and governments that receive property by forced sale. The security interest exemption exempts lenders with indicia of ownership (e.g., a mortgage) who have done no more than engage in normal lending practices. Nonetheless, lenders who go beyond normal lending practices may find themselves on the hook for CERCLA cleanup costs.

As with many environmental laws, CERCLA contains a citizen suit provision that permits citizen enforcement of CERCLA if neither federal nor state governments have taken enforcement action. Attorney fees may be available to the prevailing party. The EPA has made a major effort to return hazardous waste sites to useful purpose through its brownfields initiative. A brownfield is a site where partial cleanup has been conducted. The use must be consistent with the partial cleanup of the site. Uses that could endanger public health are not allowed.

---

**Example 21.1** John was looking for a property to use for a child care facility. One of his requirements was that there be an outside area where the children would have the opportunity to play on real grass. John located a vacant property in an ideal location. Unfortunately, the soil was contaminated with heavy metals from a smelter operation that had been previously located at the site. Most state brownfield programs would place restrictions on such a property that would forever prevent it from be used as a child care facility.

---

CERCLA complicates agricultural real estate transactions. Though rural land may look pristine to the uninformed observer, it usually is not. Arsenic-based pesticides that were once widely used in agriculture are a major source of soil contamination. At one time, industries used rural land as unregulated dumps to dispose of hazardous waste. For this reason, it is often good practice for buyers of agricultural real estate to require a preliminary environmental site assessment prior to the purchase of the property.

## Solid Waste Disposal Act[7] as Amended by the Resource Conservation Recovery Act of 1976[8]

Most, if not all, productive processes produce more than one product, called "joint products." One or more of these products will be something desired, and the remainder is unwanted waste. There are few, if any, productive processes that do not produce any waste. Agriculture and forestry are no exceptions to this. For example, when timber is processed into lumber, a variety of sizes and shapes of boards are produced. In addition to these valuable products, bark and sawdust are left. It was once the practice to dispose of these waste products by burning them. This contributed particulates (smoke) and combustion gases to air pollution. Something that is waste now will not necessarily always be waste. Uses may be found for waste products and the mix of products may change. As an example of the latter, sawmill technology has improved so that less wood is converted into sawdust and more is converted into lumber. As an example of the former, bark is now sold to landscapers who use it as a groundcover, and sawdust may be pressed into useable boards. Thus, the percentage of timber converted to waste has been reduced.

Historically, solid waste produced by farms was pushed into ravines in open dumps or burned. Perhaps some still is, legally or otherwise. Greater concern for the environment, urban encroachment, and changes in the nature of the waste stream has reduced the viability of the traditional ways that people have disposed of waste. Open dumping has serious public health consequences that include creating a habitat for vermin that carry disease. Open burning contributes to air pollution and may be a fire hazard.

The Solid Waste Disposal Act (SWDA) encourages both recycling and source reduction. Recycling is a better way to dispose of waste because it turns waste into useful products. Unfortunately, not every waste product can be recycled, and there are many more that can be cannot be done so economically. Source reduction is another approach. Changes in technology can reduce the total waste produced. Unfortunately, it is often impossible to reduce waste production to zero, desirable though that result might be.

Under the SWDA, the two primary acceptable technologies widely used for waste disposal today are incineration and the modern lined and capped sanitary landfill. Incineration can produce air pollution and ash that may require disposal as a Resource Conservation Recovery Act (RCRA) regulated hazardous waste. Incineration does not require much land. Landfill technology is used as the primary means for disposing of solid waste in the United States because land costs make it relatively cheap compared with incineration. Agriculture and forestry have some additional options. In many rural areas, open burning of crop waste and timbering waste is allowed when the risk of wildfire is sufficiently low.

Certain livestock and poultry waste such as poultry litter may be spread on fields where crops or pasture use the nutrients in the waste. Disposal of empty pesticide containers is regulated under FIFRA as discussed in Chapter 20.

Amendments to the SWDA under RCRA require special handling for hazardous waste. RCRA governs the production, management, transport, and disposal of hazardous waste. By contrast, CERCLA governs abandoned hazardous waste sites. RCRA is designed to prevent the creation of any new abandoned hazardous waste sites. Hazardous wastes are either listed by the EPA as hazardous or determined to be hazardous based on their characteristics. These characteristics are ignitability, corrosivity, reactivity, and toxicity. Any one of these characteristics in a waste is sufficient for a determination that the waste is hazardous. Defining hazardous wastes based on their characteristics is necessary because the EPA has neither the budget nor staff to test and list all hazardous chemicals among the more than 70,000 chemicals in use in the United States today. Some infectious wastes such as certain hospital wastes are covered under RCRA as hazardous waste. The EPA also lists universal wastes: batteries, pesticides, mercury-containing equipment, such as thermostats, and mercury-containing light bulbs or lamps.

Wastes with concentrations of hazardous substances below threshold levels are not hazardous wastes regulated under RCRA. Even where concentrations of hazardous substances exceed threshold levels, some waste may be exempted from RCRA if the quantity produced by a generator is small. Such generators are called small-quantity generators. Excluded from the RCRA definition of hazardous wastes are "drilling fluids, produced waters, and other wastes associated with the exploration, development, or production of crude oil or natural gas or geothermal energy."[9] Intermediate products are not hazardous waste. An intermediate product is something that is the result of one process that is used in a second process to make something of value. To be waste, there must not be a further use for the material. Agricultural wastes are exempt from RCRA: "Solid wastes generated by any of the following and which are returned to the soils as fertilizers: (i) The growing and harvesting of agricultural crops. (ii) The raising of animals, including animal manures."[10] The exemptions for intermediate products and agricultural wastes can be problematic. If such a waste is used as fertilizer, it can introduce heavy metals and other toxins that may result in residues in crops. Most state fertilizer laws require testing only for beneficial plant nutrients, not for substances that might be harmful. When contamination occurs, bringing suit in the appropriate state tort system is usually the only available remedy.

RCRA requires "cradle-to-grave" accounting for hazardous waste. This includes every person who produced, handled, or disposed of the waste. Hazardous waste landfill standards are rigorous and require each hazardous waste landfill to be licensed. Groundwater monitoring in the area near the landfill is required. Those who handle or dispose of hazardous waste must demonstrate financial responsibility through adequate insurance or other means. State programs are authorized under RCRA. Citizen suits are authorized under RCRA. Any person who desires to bring a citizen suit must provide notice to the administrator of the EPA, the state, and the alleged violator. A citizen suit may not be brought if the administrator of the EPA or the state acts, or if an action is proceeding under CERCLA. Additionally, the violation must be continuous. Attorney fees are available to the prevailing party.

## Hazardous and Solid Waste Amendments of 1984[11]

Underground storage tanks, including those for agricultural use, are a major source of groundwater contamination. The Hazardous and Solid Waste Amendments (HSWA) were enacted as an amendment to SWDA. The philosophy of the underground tank program is prevention through replacement of tanks likely to leak with those that are not likely to do so. Contrast that with RCRA and CERCLA. The philosophy of RCRA is management designed to control hazardous waste from production, through transport, and disposal. The philosophy of CERCLA is one of remediation appropriate for abandoned hazardous waste sites. The regulations provide for several methods of protecting tanks and for a schedule to phase in the rules for existing tanks. Some tanks are excluded from the definition of an underground storage tank. Farm tanks of 1,100 gallons or less and those used to store motor fuel for noncommercial purposes are exempt. Tanks used for storing heating oil on-premises are also exempt. Even though these tanks are exempt from licensing, liability may still exist if there is contamination of groundwater or soil.

## Emergency Planning and Community Right-to-Know Act of 1986[12] [Title III of the Superfund Amendments and Reauthorization Acts of 1986]

Emergency Planning and Community Right-to-Know Act (EPCRA) provides a mechanism for public awareness and emergency planning to address chemicals stored, used, or released into a community. EPCRA has three primary components. The first is emergency planning and notification. Local emergency responders and their counterparts in local industrial facilities develop plans to handle emergencies. Also included is a mechanism for notification by the owners or operators of those facilities of any unplanned release of hazardous material from those facilities. The second part of the law requires all owners and operators of covered facilities to annually report all chemical releases from those facilities. The EPA publishes this information on an annual basis. The third part of the statute contains general provisions applicable to all information collected and reported. Not all chemicals are covered under EPCRA. Agricultural fertilizers are exempt from EPCRA.[13]

EPCRA required that states establish response commissions, planning districts, and local committees. It required the EPA to develop a list of covered chemicals and thresholds for each chemical on the list. Any facility with at least the threshold amount of a covered chemical was defined as a covered facility under

EPCRA, unless exempt. EPCRA explicitly authorized states to designate additional facilities as covered. The definition of covered facility goes well beyond what one ordinarily thinks of as industrial facilities. For example, community swimming pools typically store sufficient quantities of pool chemicals to make them covered facilities. Exempt facilities include vessels, motor vehicles, rolling stock, and aircraft, as these are covered under other law. Note, however, that releases from these must nonetheless be reported under EPCRA.

Much of the work under EPCRA is the responsibility of local planning districts that are required to develop local emergency response plans. Each plan must identify covered facilities and transportation routes for hazardous materials. Additionally, the plan must identify other facilities that are at risk as the result of their proximity to covered facilities or transportation routes. The plan must also contain detailed information about the methods to be used for handling specific releases. Community emergency coordinators facilitate the process for the community, whereas facility coordinators perform the same function for each covered facility. Notification in the event of a release is required, and the plan must list all parties that must receive notification for each anticipated type of release. The plan must also address the process for determining that a release has occurred and the affected population. The plan must describe emergency equipment, and list persons responsible for equipment and facilities. Evacuation plans, training programs, and constant practice are also essential parts of any good plan.

A key component of compliance under EPCRA is the safety data sheet (SDS; formerly called material safety data sheet) for each covered chemical. SDSs are usually provided by the manufacturer or supplier of the covered chemicals. All SDSs for a site should be kept in an accessible location at the site. First responders also need their own set of SDSs for all chemicals that are likely to be found within their jurisdiction. An SDS contains information about a chemical that is needed to respond to a release. This will include a description of the chemical and its properties including toxicity and appropriate handling and first aid procedures.

Absent an exception, all information provided under EPCRA is available to the public. This includes release data, emergency situations, and emergency response plans. An exception is made for trade secrets. A trade secret is any information not generally known to the public that tends to support the profitability of the owner's business. EPCRA provides procedures for the provision of confidential information to first responders and medical personnel without compromising the secrecy of the information. Those who receive trade secret information under this provision of EPCRA are subject to criminal prosecution if they disclose this information.

### The Clean Water Act[14]

The Clean Water Act (CWA) divided surface water pollution into point and nonpoint sources. Point sources are defined as easy to identify and concentrated.

Nonpoint sources are defined as hard to identify and diffuse. The classic example of a point source is a pipe from a factory that is dumping waste directly into a stream. The classic nonpoint source is runoff from a pasture. There is no bright line that separates point from nonpoint sources. Nonetheless, the distinction has enormous regulatory consequences. Section 319 of the CWA governs nonpoint source management programs.[15] Section 402 establishes the National Pollutant Discharge Elimination System (NPDES) of permits for point source discharges. Section 404 governs discharges to waters of the United States.[16] Section 401 preserves a role for state permitting programs by requiring state certification of compliance as a precondition to issuance of any federal discharge permit.[17] The CWA requires developing ambient water quality standards. This effort also was delegated to the states, with the EPA retaining ultimate responsibility for their development. Standards are based upon the uses that a body of water is expected to support. Thus, a stream in the coastal plain can accept more waste than a stream in the mountains that is expected to support a recreational trout fishery, as trout are more sensitive to most pollutants than are warm water fish. When a body of water is impaired (does not meet ambient water quality standards), the state where the water segment is located is expected to establish a total maximum daily load (TMDL) for each pollutant that impairs the body of water.[18] Although the TMDL program was part of the CWA of 1972, the states neglected it, and the EPA did not force the issue. Citizen suits against the EPA, beginning in the 1980s, have brought the issue of TMDLs to prominence. The EPA has ultimate responsibility for setting TMDLs where states have failed to do so. TMDLs must be set for impaired bodies of water without regard to whether the sources of pollution are point or nonpoint sources.

The major water pollutants regulated under the CWA are pathogens, organics, toxic organics, nutrients, heavy metals, and sediment. Pathogens are obviously a problem any time humans or animals can be expected to come in contact with the water. Organics are organic compounds of various sorts. In and of themselves they do not cause a problem; however, as they decompose, they reduce oxygen levels in water to such an extent that aquatic organisms may not survive. Toxic organics include substances such as some pesticides and other chemicals that have toxic characteristics. These include some of the worst industrial pollutants (e.g., PCBs and dioxin). Nutrients (phosphorus compounds [P] and nitrogen compounds [N]) lead to eutrophication of bodies of water. Rapid algae growth may result from excessive N and/or P in a body of water, if a lack of N and/or P had previously limited algal growth. When algae die, they decompose and reduce oxygen in the same way as do all organics. Excess N and/or P may change the ecological balance of a body of water leading to the growth of toxic organisms. Heavy metals (e.g., mercury, cadmium, and lead) are toxic and build in the food chain where they can harm people who eat aquatic organisms. In terms of volume, sediment is the single greatest pollutant. Sediment can alter stream channels and make the environment unsuitable for either recreation or aquatic organisms.

## Point source control

Point source dischargers must obtain an NPDES permit. The NPDES permit programs are delegated to the states. Each discharger's permit specifies in detail the pollutants that may be discharged. Permits must be renewed every five years. Both the initial permit and the renewal are subject to public comment. Large livestock and poultry operations that maintain livestock on non-vegetated surfaces may be defined as confined animal feeding operations if there is a history of actual discharges into waters of the United States. Without an actual discharge, an animal feeding operation cannot be regulated as a point source.

## Nonpoint source control

Nonpoint sources are scarcely regulated at the federal level. Most of the programs that exist are voluntary. The USDA's NRCS provides various cost-share, technical assistance, and conservation easement programs to farmers and other landowners. States are free to develop nonpoint source control programs under state law.

## Protection of wetlands

Section 404 of the CWA states that "[t]he Secretary may issue permits, after notice and opportunity for public hearings for the discharge of dredged or fill material into the navigable waters at specific disposal sites."[19] Nowhere in the text of the section does the word "wetland" appear. Widespread use of the word "wetland" is, itself, relatively new. These areas have more traditionally been called swamps or marshes. Correctly or incorrectly, these lands have often been viewed as sources of disease, or at best, wastelands. Until about fifty years ago, it was the policy of the U.S. government to promote the conversion of these lands by draining them or filling them. In areas of the United States where malaria was endemic, these marshes were often ditched to prevent standing water. The dramatic shift in U.S. policy that has occurred over the last fifty years has been in response to a belated recognition of the value of wetlands to ecosystems and to our economy. Coastal wetlands are home to most commercially valuable saltwater species, such as fish, oysters, and shrimp, during some part of their life cycle. Wetlands are also repositories of biodiversity, in part because most uplands have already been disturbed. Wetlands also serve an important filtering function. Plants and other organisms in wetlands use compounds of N and P, preventing those nutrients from reaching surface waters. Wetlands also trap sediment and toxic pollutants, thereby protecting surface waters. The result of this shift in understanding is that the federal government, which once paid people to drain wetlands, now holds these same acts to be the basis for imprisonment and lesser civil penalties. In part because these changes are so new and in part because the restrictions on the use of wetlands are so great, these regulations are very controversial.

Under section 404 of the CWA, the U.S. Army Corps of Engineers (Corps) has primary responsibility for wetlands permitting. The EPA has a subsidiary role in that it has the power to propose modification to or veto permits proposed by the Corps. Section 401 explicitly gives the states permission to operate wetland protection programs that are more stringent than the federal program so long as these programs are not inconsistent with the federal. Section 401 also gives the states explicit authority to veto or propose modifications to permits proposed by the Corps. Section 404 permits are of two types, general and individual. In most states, it is necessary to obtain a permit from the state in addition to the section 404 permit.

Where the activity proposed for a wetland is very minor, the Corps may issue a letter of permission rather than a permit. There are exceptions to section 404 for normal farming, silviculture, and ranching activities. The exception for normal farming activities continues to be heavily litigated. There are also exceptions for grandfathered activities and incidental movement and congressionally authorized dredging. However, if there is any doubt, the letter of permission should be requested. By requesting a letter of permission, the applicant protects him- or herself from an adverse regulatory action. Adverse actions may include civil fines and restoration orders and criminal actions.

General permits are issued to cover a specific category of activity. If an activity is covered under the general permit, the person conducting the activity need not apply for an individual permit. Preconstruction notification to the Corps and the public may be required before proceeding under a general permit. Mitigation may also be required. Mitigation involves restoring or creating a compensating wetland in the same watershed. A permittee is usually required to create or restore more wetland than was destroyed. If the state does not have an equivalent general permit, the permittee may have to apply for an individual state permit. General permits may be nationwide or regional. Nationwide permits are issued by Corps headquarters and cover the entire country. Those who intend to use nationwide permits should check with the regional Corps office before proceeding, because each Corps office has the authority to make regional modifications. There are also general permits issued by the regional offices that are applicable only to the region that issued the permit.

Individual permits are required where there is no general permit that covers the activity. Individual permits typically require two to three months of processing time unless an EIS is required. If an EIS is required, the average permit takes about three years to issue. Public comment is always required on an individual permit unless it is an emergency permit. Emergency exceptions are made for repairs and other activities that must occur after natural disasters such as hurricanes.

Typically, an applicant for an individual permit will hire an environmental consultant to manage the process. The initial action that the consultant typically takes is to delineate the wetland. This private delineation is not binding on the Corps but is nonetheless useful in negotiations over the size of the wetland. Wetland delineation is not an exact science. The next step is to ask the Corps for a pre-application evaluation. This step is not required but can save time and money. After the application is filed, there will be notice of the application to the public and opportunity for the public to comment on the application. There will also be public hearings. Next, the Corps will evaluate the application and prepare a statement of findings. At this point, the EPA evaluates the proposed permit and may veto it or suggest modifications. The state may do the same under its section 401 authority. If each step yields a positive result, the permit will be issued. Note that individual permits will typically be issued for water-based activities only. Permits will not be issued for activities that could just as easily have been conducted on an upland.

Jurisdiction of the Corps is based upon section 404 of the CWA. Federal courts have ruled that the Corps cannot use either migratory birds or incidental fallback to extend its jurisdiction. The latest attempt of the Supreme Court to establish the boundary of federal jurisdiction ended in a plurality decision.[20] The plurality held that a water of the United States must have a surface water connection to a water navigable-in-fact. In his concurring opinion, Justice Kennedy held that there must be significant nexus to a water navigable-in-fact for a water to be a water of the United States. As this was a plurality decision, lower federal courts are free to use either holding when establishing CWA jurisdiction. Recent regulatory efforts by the Corps and EPA to define federal jurisdiction under section 404 are discussed in Chapter 13.

Since 1986, each succeeding farmland bill has provided additional regulation of wetlands by prohibiting conversion to agricultural uses. This provision is more restrictive than section 404 and is discussed in Chapter 25.

## The Endangered Species Act of 1973[21]

The Endangered Species Act of 1973 (ESA) was enacted to protect species from extinction. It has had some notable successes. The American alligator was protected from illegal market hunting and is now no longer endangered throughout much of its range. The bald eagle has also made a remarkable comeback, in large part the result of banning the pesticide DDT. Despite these successes, the ESA remains controversial. The ESA is administered through the U.S. Fish and Wildlife Service, an agency of the Department of Interior.

The existence of endangered or threatened species on agricultural or forest land can result in significant restrictions on farming and forestry operations. In Western states where water is scarce, the ESA requirement to maintain minimum water levels in rivers can limit water available for agricultural irrigation. The ESA definition of "take" is very broad. It includes not only killing a listed species, but also includes modifying the habitat of the listed species such that the habitat is no longer suitable.[22]

This broad definition of "take" means that logging operations and agricultural irrigation from surface waters can constitute a "take". Restrictions arise from the identification of land as critical habitat for specific listed species. The efforts to protect the northern spotted owl have had a widely publicized impact upon communities dependent upon timbering operations on federal land under the management of the U.S. Forest Service. Equally publicized has been the impact of efforts to protect the red-cockaded woodpecker in privately owned long-leaf pine forests of the Southeast. In arid areas of the Southwest, the designation of certain rivers and streams as critical habitat has led the Fish and Wildlife Service to set minimum stream flows. Farmers who own the right to use the water under a state rule of prior appropriation discussed in Chapter 13 may be denied the right to use the water, as federal law preempts state law. Private timber land owners and owners of water rights have a Fifth Amendment right to compensation where the restrictions on their property use deprive them of its economic value. Those dependent upon timber on public lands have no such compensable property interest.

### State and local law

Most federal environmental law specifically preserves the state role. Unless the state law comes directly into the conflict with the federal law, states are generally free to enact environmental laws that are more stringent than federal laws. Many states have done this. Other states have limited their regulation to that required by federal law. There exists great diversity in the environmental law of the various states. Local governments are also a significant source of environmental regulation of agriculture and forestry in some states.

## Notes

1  Uniform Law Commissioners. *Conservation Easement Act*. Retrieved August 2, 2018, www.uniformlaws.org/Act.aspx?title=Conservation%20Easement%20Act.
2  42 U.S.C. §§ 4321–4370(h) (2013).
3  *Save Barton Creek Assoc. v. Fed'l Highway Admin.*, 950 F.2d 1129 (5th Cir. 1992).
4  42 U.S.C. §§ 9601–9675 (2013).
5  42 U.S.C. §§ 6901–6992k (2013).
6  42 U.S.C. §§ 1251–1387 (2013).
7  42 U.S.C. §§ 6901–6992k (2013).
8  Pub. L. 94-580, 90 Stat. 2795 (1976).
9  42 U.S.C. § 6921(b)(2)(A) (2013).
10  40 C.F.R. § 261.4(b)(2) (2014).
11  Pub. L. 98-616, 98 Stat. 3221 (1984).
12  Pub. L. 99-499, 100 Stat. 1728 (1986).
13  42 U.S.C. § 11021(e)(5) (2013).
14  33 U.S.C. §§ 1251–1387 (2013).
15  33 U.S.C. § 1329 (2013).
16  33 U.S.C. § 1344 (2013).
17  33 U.S.C. § 1341 (2013).
18  33 U.S.C. § 1313 (2013).
19  33 U.S.C. § 1344(a) (2013).
20  *Rapanos v. United States*, 547 U.S. 715, 126 S.Ct. 2208, 2006 U.S. LEXIS 4887 (2006).
21  16 U.S.C. §§ 1531–1544 (2013).
22  *Babbitt v. Sweet Home Chapter of Communities for a Great Oregon*, 515 U.S. 687 (1995).

# Chapter 22

# Labor

## Introduction

Federal labor law is complex. Agricultural employers are given preferential treatment in that they are not covered under many federal labor laws unless they employ a significant number of workers. The threshold number of workers varies from one statute to another. In addition to federal labor law, most states have their own labor laws. This chapter sets forth the basics.

## Wage and hour law

The Fair Labor Standards Act of 1938[1] (FLSA) is the primary federal law governing wages and hours. It covers most employees in the United States with some important exceptions. It does not cover elected officials and members of the armed services. The term *employee* "does not include any individual employed by an employer engaged in agriculture if that individual is the parent, spouse, child, or other member of the employer's immediate family."[2] Volunteers who perform services for agencies of states or their political subdivisions or interstate agencies are not employees for purposes of the FLSA. A volunteer is a person who receives either no compensation or is paid expenses, benefits, or a nominal fee. Volunteers cannot perform the same type of services for their employer that they perform as employees.

Many farms that use the community-supported agriculture (CSA) model use unpaid interns, apprentices, WWOOFers, or volunteers. Terminology varies from one farm to another. To the extent that these individuals are providing economic benefits to the farm, the FLSA generally requires that such individuals be paid minimum wage. State law may also require the payment of minimum wage. What differentiates farms from governments and charitable organizations, which may not be required to pay interns, is that farms are generally for-profit enterprises. This problem has apparently been avoided through the use of charitable organizations that accept volunteers who then participate in an education experience on farms. The World Wide Opportunities on Organic Farms, USA, hence WWOOFers, is the most widely known of these organizations.[3] There have been no test cases involving this model and almost no discussion in the legal literature.

Farm workers are generally exempt from the overtime requirement of the FSLA. If individuals are doing nonagricultural labor such as driving a truck to make deliveries to CSA customers, the farm may be required to pay overtime for any work in excess of forty hours per calendar week. If any labor during a calendar week was not qualifying agricultural work, all the hours worked in that week are treated as non-agricultural for the purposes of calculating the employer's obligation to pay overtime pay. There is a great deal of misunderstanding as to what the FLSA requires that should be resolved in an individual case by consulting an attorney concerning wage and hour laws.

Agriculture is broadly defined by the FLSA. Agriculture includes production of crops, livestock and poultry, and horticultural crops. It includes all those activities necessary to prepare and transport agricultural commodities to market, including storing them as an interim step. It includes forestry that is incidental to or performed in conjunction with agricultural operations. This can cause difficulties in interpretation. Growing, cutting, and trimming Christmas trees is not considered primary agriculture; however, some activities related to Christmas trees can be considered secondary agriculture. This means that such a person may be an employee but exempt from overtime provisions. The U.S. Court of Appeals for the Fourth Circuit disagreed with the U.S. Department of Labor position that labor employed in Christmas tree production cannot be primary.[4] The holding of the U.S. Court of Appeals for the Fourth Circuit applies only within the Fourth Circuit. The U.S. Department of Labor attempted to extend overtime pay rules to Christmas tree growers in the Fourth Circuit; however, the Fourth Circuit determined that the effort did not comply with the Administrative Procedure Act.[5] Examples 22.1 and 22.2 illustrate the effect of the split in the circuits.

---

**Example 22.1** Wilbur Nathan has a Christmas tree farm in Ashe County, North Carolina, near the border with Tennessee. He also owns another Christmas tree farm twenty miles away in Johnson County, Tennessee. Growing and selling Christmas trees is Wilbur's only business. His attorney has advised him that he must pay overtime pay in Tennessee but not in North Carolina. The reason for this is that Tennessee is in the Sixth Circuit whereas North Carolina is in the Fourth Circuit. His attorney explained that growing Christmas trees is a primary agricultural activity in the Fourth Circuit, as a result of Fourth Circuit precedent, but not in the Sixth Circuit. The Sixth Circuit has not ruled on this issue; however, he suggested to Wilbur that testing the issue in court was inadvisable. The attorney noted that such litigation would be expensive if Wilbur won and catastrophic if he lost. Wilbur's attorney also suggested to Wilbur that he avoid having any of his workers work in both states during a single calendar week. He advised that though there is no precedent, Wilbur ran the risk of being required to pay overtime pay for any worker who worked in both states during a calendar week. He also pointed out the obvious: that excellent records of time worked with the location of the work are essential to avoid liability under the FLSA.

---

**Example 22.2** Hiram Latham owns and runs a diversified farm in Johnson County, Tennessee. He raises vegetables, cattle, and a few free range chickens. He also has about ten acres of Christmas trees, a small portion of his 500 acre farm. He sells his trees at his roadside stand. His farm labor sometimes works pruning Christmas trees and selling Christmas trees, eggs, and vegetables at the farm stand. All products sold at his farm stand are produced on his farm. Both growing Christmas trees and working in the roadside stand are secondary agricultural activities under U.S. Department of Labor rules. Hiram is not required to pay time-and-a-half for overtime.

---

The FLSA currently requires a minimum hourly wage that is occasionally increased by Congress. Some states and some local governments have minimum wage laws that provide for a higher rate of pay than that required by federal law. Any nonexempt employee who works more than forty hours in a calendar week must be paid for overtime at a rate of one-and-a-half times the employee's regular rate of pay. The FLSA applies to any "[e]nterprise engaged in commerce or in the production of goods for commerce."[6] Any business that does not meet the definition of being engaged in commerce is not covered under the FLSA. Such a business is required to pay neither minimum wage nor overtime pay for hours over forty hours per calendar week. An important part of this definition is that the business must have gross income of $500,000 per year or more. Most states have enacted legislation that applies minimum wage and wage and hour provisions to businesses that gross less than $500,000 per year.

Hours worked are calculated based on when the employee is on the employer's premises, on duty, or at a prescribed place of work. If an employee voluntarily stays late to complete a task, that time counts as hours worked. Waiting time and on-call time are considered hours worked. Brief rest and meal periods are also considered part of hours worked. Bona fide meal periods of thirty minutes or more are generally not counted in hours worked. Travel for the benefit of the employer is generally considered hours worked, whereas commuting time is not. Commuting time is not part of hours worked only if the employee is doing no work during commuting time. If the employee is answering a cell phone for work-related activity, the commuting time counts as hours worked. Checking e-mail at home counts as hours worked. The ready availability of e-mail and other Internet-based connections to work has complicated the calculation of hours worked. Changing into clothes required for work is generally not part of hours worked. Specialty clothing such as that for protection from pesticides is another matter. Removing (doffing) such protective gear and putting on (donning) such protective gear is likely to be part of hours worked. Doffing and donning litigation is quite common.

Employers are required to display the official poster that explains FLSA requirements to employees. The FLSA requires that employers keep accurate time and pay records.

Exempt employees may be exempt from overtime provisions, and some are also exempt from minimum wage provisions. Executive, administrative, and professional employees are exempt from both minimum wage and overtime provisions. Certain employees in seasonal recreation businesses are also exempt from both. Farmers who use a very limited amount of labor per year (no more than 500 man-days of farm labor in a calendar quarter, defined as any day during which an employee works one hour or more of agricultural labor) are exempt from both the minimum wage and overtime pay requirements. As noted above, there are also exemptions from both the overtime and minimum wage provisions of the FLSA for agricultural workers who are immediate family members of their employer. Workers (cowboys) employed on the range are exempt from both. Local hand harvest laborers, who commute daily from their permanent residence and are paid a piece rate, are exempt from both so long as they were employed in agriculture for less than thirteen weeks in the previous calendar year. Nonlocal minors of age sixteen or younger, engaged in hand harvesting, and paid on a piece rate are exempt provided that they are working on the same farm that employs their parents and that the piece rate is the same as that paid to those older than age sixteen. It is worth reiterating what was said above: Good legal advice is essential to labor law compliance.

## Immigration

U.S. Citizenship and Immigration Services (USCIS) is responsible for administering the program for determining whether a person has the right to work in the United States. Form I-9, the Employment Eligibility Verification Form, is the form that all employers must use to verify employment eligibility.[7] To be eligible to work, every person must either be a U.S. citizen or have an immigration status that permits employment. Form I-9 is the form that employers use to determine employment eligibility.

The failure to determine employment eligibility can have serious consequences for an employer. Civil penalties may be assessed against employers who failed to adequately verify employment eligibility. Criminal penalties are also available. Violations may be assessed for the failure to correctly complete the Form I-9. The Form I-9 and supporting documentation must be retained during the period of employment and after the termination of employment. For noncitizen employees, documentation must be re-verified prior to the expiration of existing documentation. For agricultural employers, there is an additional risk to non-compliance. An employer may lose key employees at times that are critical to the farming operation.

Verifying employment eligibility is a double-edged sword. Certain practices are prohibited as unlawful discrimination. There are four basic types of discrimination. These include citizenship or immigration status discrimination, discrimination based upon national origin, document abuse, and retaliation. Document abuse consists of requiring information in preparing the Form I-9 that is not required by law or regulations. Retaliation consists of punishing an employee or terminating their employment status because that employee reported a discriminatory practice or testified in the proceeding concerning a discriminatory practice.

Employers, agricultural associations, and recruiters who refer agricultural employees for a fee must complete a Form I-9 for each of those employees when they are hired. Referring an employee without verifying employment status is prohibited.

The E-Verify system is a Form I-9-based system that allows employers to electronically verify whether a potential employee is eligible to work in the United States. The system has been heavily promoted by the government and is required for some federal contractors. To participate in the E-Verify system, an employer must enroll.[8] Rejection by the E-Verify system does not mean that a person is ineligible to work. It may simply mean that there is an error, such as an incorrect birthdate, in the government's database. Both the potential employer and employee are required to take steps to correct any discrepancy.

The H-2A program is a temporary agricultural worker program used by many farmers with seasonal labor needs. Though there are significant costs and paperwork requirements for participation in the program, many farmers have found it to be a valuable source of seasonal labor. The paperwork can be centralized by hiring through an agricultural association that does initial recruitment and provides record-keeping and compliance assistance to individual farmers.

## Employment at will

Many states apply the doctrine of employment at will to employer-employee relationships. Under the doctrine of employment at will, an employer may fire an employee at any time for any legal reason or for no reason at all. In most employment-at-will states, there is no requirement that any severance pay or other benefits be paid upon termination. The doctrine of employment at will does not prevent employers from offering employment for a specific term or from agreeing to provide severance benefits. The doctrine of employment at will serves to provide default contract provisions in the absence of other contract provisions mutually agreed upon by the employer and employee.

Although an employer may fire an employee without giving any reason for termination, many employers fire employees for fault to avoid successful unemployment insurance claims by those fired employees. Successful unemployment insurance claims can increase the unemployment insurance cost to an employer. For that reason, many employers try to have it both ways by avoiding an unemployment insurance claim while using the doctrine of employment at will. This can backfire. The doctrine of employment at will does not change an employer's obligation to terminate an employee for a legal reason. If the reason given for termination is not a legal reason, the employer may be subjected to substantial liability. This is particularly true where the reason given for termination was discriminatory. Many states that apply the doctrine of employment at will to employment contracts have exceptions to this rule in their law. Employers must know what those exceptions are. This varies greatly from one state to another. There are also many federal rules that prohibit a person in an employment-at-will state from being fired. Example 21.3, later in this chapter, provides an example of one such federal rule.

## Employment discrimination and harassment

Federal law prohibits discrimination based on race, color, religion, gender including pregnancy, national origin, age of forty years or older, disability, or genetic information. The Equal Employment Opportunity Commission (EEOC) has determined that it has authority to provide protection for lesbian, gay, bisexual, and transgender (LGBT) individuals based upon its authority to prevent gender discrimination.[9] The U.S. Attorney General takes a contrary view.[10] Most states also provide protection against discrimination. The greatest variation among states is in laws that protect those within the LGBT categories. State protection is particularly important for employees who fall into one of the federal exceptions, such as those for entities with fewer employees than the federal minimums.

### Age discrimination

Age discrimination violates federal law.[11] The prohibition against age discrimination applies only to employees or applicants age forty or older.[12] The prohibition against age discrimination applies to employers, employment agencies, and labor organizations. An employer is defined as a person in an industry affecting commerce with twenty or more employees employed each working day for twenty or more calendar weeks in the current or preceding calendar year.[13] The term *person* is broadly defined to include both flesh-and-blood humans and most forms of business organizations, labor unions, and state and local governments. Employers are required to post notices approved by the EEOC. These notices describe prohibited practices and provide contact information for the EEOC.

Employees or applicants who believe they have been discriminated against based on age may file a complaint with the EEOC.[14] The EEOC may order payment of back pay where the violation was willful. In addition to the option of filing charges to the EEOC, an employee or applicant may file a civil action in federal district court. Should the EEOC bring an action, the right to bring a private civil action terminates.

Many states have their own laws prohibiting age discrimination. Enforcement actions by state agencies may proceed unless an action has been brought under federal law.

### Disability discrimination

Employees are protected from discrimination based upon disabilities. This protection is provided by the Americans with Disabilities Act of 1990 (ADA)[15] or the Rehabilitation Act of 1973.[16] A covered employer is one with fifteen or more employees. Employment protection for those with disabilities includes protection from harassment. Harassment can include a disparaging remark about a person's disability. An employer may have liability for harassment perpetrated by the supervisor of the person with a disability. The employer may also be liable for the acts of other employees and third parties, such as even customers, where the employer does not take steps to prevent harassment.

Though all employers must avoid discrimination against employees and applicants with disabilities, additional requirements apply to those with federal contracts. Any person with a contract in excess of $10,000 with a federal agency for the purchase of personal property must take affirmative steps to employ those with disabilities.[17] Unlike other statutes that prohibit discrimination, this provision applies to businesses without regard to size. This provision can have significant impact on farms selling product to federal agencies.

The process of making a reasonable accommodation begins with a request from an employee for an accommodation. Making a reasonable accommodation for an employee with a disability is an interactive process. There must be direct communication with the employee about what sort of accommodation is requested. This need not be an onerous process. It is part of the ongoing communication with employees that is part of good management practice.

### Race, color, religion, gender, pregnancy, genetic information, and national origin discrimination

Title VII of the Civil Rights Act of 1964[18] prohibits discrimination based on race, color, religion, gender, or national origin. A covered employer is one with fifteen or more employees.

Religious practice must be reasonably accommodated. A reasonable accommodation includes allowance of dress and grooming practices that are based upon religious practice. An interactive process between the employer and employee may be required to determine what accommodation can be made without an undue hardship on the employer.

Racial discrimination occurs when somebody is treated unfavorably because he or she is a member of a particular race. It can also occur because he or she associated with a person of a particular race or even because that person has some characteristic associated with a particular race. Discrimination based on color is unfavorable treatment based upon skin color. It is an erroneous belief that discrimination cannot occur when the perpetrator and the victim are both of the same race or color. Federal law also prohibits harassment based on race or color. As with other forms of discrimination the perpetrator may be another employee or even a third party such as customer. Rules governing discrimination and harassment based upon national origin are similar to those for race and color.

Title VII prohibits all aspects of gender-based discrimination. This includes disparate treatment in hiring, firing, work assignments, promotions, layoffs, training, benefits, and anything else employment-related. As noted above, whether Title VII prohibits discrimination against transgendered, lesbian, gay, or bisexual persons is a matter of dispute between the EEOC and the U.S. Attorney General. Sexual harassment is also prohibited. The harasser may be another employee or even a third party such as a customer. Teasing and isolated incidents, if not serious, do not constitute sexual harassment. The test is whether a hostile work environment is created or an adverse employment action is taken against the victim. If the harassment is not sexual, it is generally not actionable under federal law unless it was based upon discrimination against one of the other protected classes discussed in this section. It is possible for the perpetrator of sexual harassment to be the same gender as the victim.

Retaliation is also prohibited by federal law. Retaliation is taking an adverse action against an employee who filed a complaint or brought a lawsuit alleging discrimination. In employment-at-will states, retaliation is a major exception to the rule that an employee at will can be dismissed at any time for any reason or no reason at all.

Paying unequal wages based on gender is prohibited by the Equal Pay Act of 1963.[19] The Equal Pay Act was enacted as an amendment to the FLSA. The Equal Pay Act applies to almost all employers without regard to how few employees are employed.

The Pregnancy Discrimination Act (PDA)[20] prohibits discrimination based on pregnancy. If the employer offers either paid or unpaid disability leave, that benefit must also be offered for disability due to pregnancy. Title II of the Genetic Information Nondiscrimination Act of 2008 (GINA)[21] prohibits discrimination against an applicant or an employee based upon genetic information. GINA was enacted as an amendment to FDCA.

### Disability

The requirements of the ADA go well beyond prohibiting discrimination in employment. Subchapter III applies to public accommodations and services operated by private entities.[22] The requirements of the ADA are triggered if a public accommodation is provided. Any farm that invites the public as part of its business must comply with the ADA. This means providing handicapped accessible bathrooms, wheelchair ramps, and other accommodations that are readily achievable. The ADA applies to many agritourism operations, farms that serve meals in a manner similar to a restaurant, farms that host corporate events and weddings, and farms with farm stores or similar facilities.

Any accommodation for disabled persons must be readily achievable. The ADA states that "[t]he term 'readily achievable' means easily accomplishable and able to be carried out without much difficulty or expense."[23] As with many statutory terms, the term *readily achievable* is in the eyes of the beholder or the court deciding a particular dispute. The analysis is very fact-specific. The ADA lists specific factors to be considered in determining whether an accommodation is readily achievable. Factors include the nature and cost of any requested accommodation, the financial resources of the facility, the number of persons employed at the facility, and the overall impact on the facility. The financial resources of the entity that owns or operates a facility is to be considered together with the total number of employees and the number, type, and location of its facilities. Other factors include the character of the workforce of the entity, the geographic distribution of its facilities, and the administrative and financial relationship of the facility or facilities in question to the entity.

Any farm that provides a public accommodation needs to have a plan for accommodating its customers with disabilities. Most family-owned farms are likely to be treated favorably under the ADA factors used to determine whether an accommodation is readily achievable. However, the lack of a plan makes a farm very difficult to defend in the face of a request for a reasonable accommodation. Many farms that provide public accommodations such as those engaged in agritourism have websites that promote their business. ADA requirements may apply to websites and to the farm's physical facilities. As it is not difficult to develop websites that can be read by a screen reader, that type of accommodation and others should be addressed when the website is developed. Though some accommodations both on the physical farm and on the farm's website may not be required as a matter of law, any accommodations that can be implemented easily and inexpensively should be. Even those lawsuits that are dismissed cost money, are unproductive distractions, and are bad for business. Noting available accommodations on the farm website and in other advertising can generate business. With an aging population in the United States, the number of families with a member who requires accommodation is increasing. Many of these families will not visit an agritourism or other farm facility unless they know that all of their family can be accommodated.

## The Family and Medical Leave Act of 1993[24]

The Family and Medical Leave Act (FMLA) covers employers of fifty or more employees. The FMLA provides for unpaid leave for employees who experience a serious illness or who have a family member who experiences serious illness and requires care. Unpaid leave may also be taken to as the result of the birth or adoption of a child. An employee who has paid leave may substitute paid leave for unpaid leave. Taking leave under the FMLA does not result in the loss of any benefits that were already accrued. An employee who takes leave under the FMLA is entitled to return to the same position as he or she left.

## Patient Protection and Affordable Care Act of 2010 (ObamaCare)[25]

The tax under ObamaCare for failure to provide health insurance for employees applies only to employers with fifty or more full-time equivalent employees. Full-time equivalent employees are calculated using a statutory formula in ObamaCare. The employer tax began in 2015 except for employers with at least fifty but fewer than one hundred full-time equivalent employees. For these latter employers, the tax began in 2016. Separate companies with common ownership are considered a single company for purposes of this calculation. Most farms in the United States have too few employees to be subject to the tax for not providing coverage; however, everyone is affected. Policy terms have changed as the result of mandated coverage in ObamaCare. Children of employees must be provided coverage until age twenty-six, with some exceptions. Lifetime benefits cannot be capped, and persons cannot be rejected for preexisting conditions. For farmers who are self-employed, the failure to obtain coverage may result in a substantial tax, depending upon income. The Tax Cuts and Jobs Act amended the ACA to set the penalty on individuals without health insurance at zero beginning after December 31, 2018.[26]

## Protected concerted activity

Under federal law, employees have the right to act in concert to complain about workplace conditions and to ask for other benefits or improvements.[27] Protected concerted activity includes union organizing activities and the right to form a union. However, protected concerted activities also include a wide range of concerted activities engaged in by either union or non-union employees. Example 22.3 provides an example of protected concerted activity.

---

**Example 22.3** Ebenezer Scrooge (no relation to the Dickens character) owns a large pecan grove and an associated cracking operation. The cracking operation is in an unheated metal shed. Cracking operations begin after the harvest is complete and sometimes continue into January. Several of his workers complained that he does not heat the cracking shed and that the temperature sometimes drops below freezing. Scrooge responded by saying, "You employees just want to waste my money. You are fired for getting together and bothering me. Now go!" The newly former employees of Ebenezer Scrooge filed a retaliation complaint against him with their regional National Labor Relations Board office. Scrooge eventually settled the complaint for $250,000.

Many states have right-to-work laws. Right-to-work laws do not prevent employees from organizing and joining or forming unions. Right-to-work law prohibit closed shops. A closed shop is created when an employer signs a contract with a union that requires that every employee be either a dues-paying union member or pay union dues, even if not a member. Right-to-work laws have nothing to do with protected concerted activities. Right-to-work laws and the doctrine of employment at will, although sometimes confused, are unrelated.

## Protection of migrant and seasonal agricultural workers

The Migrant and Seasonal Agricultural Worker Protection Act (MSPA)[28] governs employers that use migrant and seasonal labor. There is a small business exemption for very small employers that is the same as the exception to the FLSA.[29] All other agricultural employers must comply if they employ migrant or seasonal agricultural labor. Both agricultural associations and farm labor contractors who employ or broker labor and farms that employ labor are regulated under the MSPA. A migrant agricultural worker is a temporary seasonal worker who is required to be away from his or her permanent residence overnight. Seasonal agricultural workers are temporary workers who do not meet the definition of a migrant agricultural worker. Farm labor contractors are required to register with the U.S. Department of Labor (U.S. DOL).

The MSPA requires that every labor contractor, agricultural employer, or agricultural association that employs migrant agricultural workers pay them what they are due. No employer of migrant agricultural workers may require that the workers buy goods or services solely from him or her. The MSPA establishes housing standards for migrant agricultural workers and provides for inspection of those facilities. Recruiters, whether they be labor contractors, agricultural employers, or agricultural associations, must keep required records. Agricultural employers who do not serve as recruiters for others must nonetheless keep records on those migrant agricultural workers whom they employ. Agricultural employers must also post posters prescribed by the U.S. DOL that inform workers of their rights along with information on how to file a complaint. There are, in addition, standards for transportation provided to workers.

Enforcement is through a full range of tools. These include criminal and administrative sanctions and judicial enforcement. Workers are also given a statutory private right of action. Agreements to waive statutory rights are void. Non-payment of temporary agricultural labor remains a serious problem. Often, the farmer may not know that the broker who provided the labor was holding the workers in involuntary servitude. This problem is exacerbated by language barriers and the practices of some employers who hire undocumented foreign labor without asking questions. Federal law provides serious criminal sanctions for holding workers in involuntary servitude.[30] Federal law creates a private right of action against anyone who knowingly benefited from involuntary servitude.[31]

## Workers' compensation

States operate workers' compensation systems to provide compensation to workers who suffer work-related injuries and illnesses. Workers who are covered under workers' compensation cannot sue in a tort system. In return, the workers' compensation system is no-fault. No-fault means that even if the work-related injury or illness was the worker's own fault, the worker is nonetheless compensated for the injury or illness. Workers compensation systems vary substantially from one state to another.

Many farms have too few employees to be required to participate in the workers' compensation system of their state. Most states provide small employers, including farms, with the choice to opt into the system if they wish. The benefits to opting in are that an employee with the work-related injury or illness cannot sue in the tort system. Successful tort suits usually bring the injured worker a much higher payment than does the workers' compensation system. For that reason, it may be beneficial for a farm that is not required to participate to choose to participate. The downside of participating is that workers' compensation insurance for farms is generally expensive. The cost of insurance for any given industry is based upon its accident and illness record. Agriculture is a high-risk industry, and the cost of workers' compensation insurance is high.

In most state systems, an employer may object to payment to an injured or ill employee only upon the basis of its assertion that the injury or illness was not work-related. There is a great deal of workers' compensation litigation over this issue. There are also other issues that include whether the resulting disability is permanent or temporary and whether the worker will ultimately be able to return to work. An issue that is sometimes raised by workers is that the injury or illness was the result of the employer's gross negligence. In most states, a finding of gross negligence takes the claim out of the workers' compensation system and allows the worker to sue his or her employer in tort.

## Unemployment insurance

Unemployment insurance is a joint federal-state program that provides payments for a limited period of time to people who lose their jobs through no fault of their own. The Federal Unemployment Tax Act[32] defines the basic provisions that states must follow. All state unemployment laws are subject to federal approval. An agricultural employer is covered if he or she paid wages of $20,000 or employed at least ten individuals for some part of twenty days, with each day being in a different week for the current or the preceding year.

## Notes

1  29 U.S.C. §§ 201–219 (2017).
2  29 U.S.C. § 203(e) (2017).
3  WWOOF, USA. *About, World Wide Opportunities on Organic Farms, USA*. Retrieved August 10, 2018, wwoofusa.org/about/.

4 *U.S. Department of Labor v. NC Growers' Association*, 377 F.3d 345, 2004 U.S. App. LEXIS 15850 (4th Cir. 2004).

5 *NC Growers' Association v. United Farm Workers*, 702 F.3d 755, 2012 U.S. App. LEXIS 26136 (4th Cir. 2012).

6 29 U.S.C. § 203(s)(3) (2013).

7 U.S. Citizenship and Immigration Services. *Handbook for Employers M-274, Guidance for Completing Form I-9*. Retrieved August 10, 2018, www.uscis.gov/sites/default/files/files/form/m-274.pdf.

8 U.S. Citizenship and Immigration Services. *E-verify*. Retrieved August 10, 2018, www.e-verify.gov/employers.

9 EEOC. *What You Should Know about EEOC and the Enforcement Protections for LGBT Workers*. Retrieved August 10, 2018, www.eeoc.gov/eeoc/newsroom/wysk/enforcement_protections_lgbt_workers.cfm.

10 Office of the Attorney General. *Revised Treatment of Transgender Employment Discrimination Claims Under Title VII of the Civil Rights Act of 1964*. Retrieved August 10, 2018, www.justice.gov/ag/page/file/1006981/download.

11 29 U.S.C. §§ 621–634 (2017).

12 29 U.S.C. § 631(A) (2017).

13 29 U.S.C. § 630(B) (2017).

14 U.S. Equal Employment Opportunity Commission. *Disability Discrimination*. Retrieved August 10, 2018, www.eeoc.gov/laws/types/disability.cfm.

15 Pub. L. 101-336, 104 Stat. 327 (1990) (codified as amended at 42 U.S.C. §§ 12101–12213 (2017)).

16 Pub. L. 93-112, 87 Stat. 355 (1973) (codified as amended at 29 U.S.C. §§ 70–797b (2017)).

17 29 U.S.C. § 793(a) (2017).

18 Pub. L. 88-352, 78 Stat. 241 (1964) (codified as amended at 42 U.S.C. §§ 2000a, *et seq.* (2017)).

19 Pub. L. 88-38, 77 Stat. 56 (1963).

20 Pub. L. 95-555, 92 Stat. 2076 (1978).

21 Pub. L. 110-233, 122 Stat. 881 (2008).

22 42 U.S.C. §§ 12181–12189 (2017).

23 42 U.S.C. § 12181(9) (2017).

24 Pub. L. 103-3, 107 Stat. 6 (1993).

25 Pub. L. 111-148, 124 Stat. 119 (2010).

26 Pub. L. 115-97, 131 Stat. 2054 (2017) (codified as amended at 26 U.S.C. § 5000A (2017)).

27 National Labor Relations Board. *Rights We Protect*. Retrieved August 10, 2018, www.nlrb.gov/rights-we-protect.

28 Pub. L. 97-470, 96 Stat. 2583 (1983).

29 29 U.S.C. § 1803(a)(2) (2013).

30 18 U.S.C. §§ 1581–1597 (2013).

31 18 U.S.C. § 1595 (2013).

32 Aug. 16, 1954, ch. 736, Sec 1(d) [Internal Revenue Title, chapter 23], 68A Stat. 439 (1954) (codified as amended at 26 U.S.C. §§ 3301–3311 (2017)).

# Chapter 23

# Taxation

## Introduction

Farms pay taxes just as other businesses do. Among the most important of these taxes is the federal income tax. Federal income taxation is important for all farm businesses, even those that are not currently profitable. Also important are the federal estate and gift taxes and myriad state and local taxes. A chapter of this length cannot attempt to discuss these taxes in detail. The purpose of this chapter is to make the reader aware of the most important of these taxes and basic tax concepts.

## Federal taxes

The Internal Revenue Code (IRC) is Title 26 of the U.S. Code. The IRC is more than 4,000 pages long. The IRC includes the federal income tax, federal estate and gift taxes, federal employment taxes, federal excise taxes, and group health plan requirements as a result of the Patient Protection and Affordable Care Act. The passage of the Tax Cuts and Jobs Act (TCJA) (P.L. 115-97) in December of 2017 is an example of the continuing evolution of taxation in the United States.

Details of taxes change every year. Much of the IRC is temporary. Temporary means that there is a fixed expiration date for a particular provision, usually within the provision itself. Congress renews most of these provisions on an annual basis or as needed if the expiration date exceeded one year. When Congress renews these provisions, it often makes changes to them. These annual renewals of IRC provisions are called extenders.

The Internal Revenue Service (IRS) that administers the federal tax system makes changes to the application of these taxes. The IRS may do this by regulation. This is through the notice and comment provisions of the Administrative Procedure Act. The Notice of Proposed Rulemaking and the final rule are both published in the Federal Register.

Temporary regulations that apply until a final rule is published in the Federal Register are published as Treasury Decisions (TDs). TDs are also published in the Federal Register.

Revenue Rulings are official IRS interpretations of statutes, text treaties, and regulations. Revenue rulings are published in the Internal Revenue Bulletin (IRB). The IRB is a weekly publication of the IRS.[1]

Revenue Procedures provide specific information about filing returns and other information necessary to comply with an IRS position on a specific topic. Revenue procedures are also published in the IRB.

A Private Letter Ruling (PLR) is issued upon the written request of a taxpayer to resolve an issue that is unique to the taxpayer. If the taxpayer fully complies with the terms of the PLR, the IRS is bound by the PLR. PLRs cannot be used as precedents by other taxpayers or the same taxpayer in another matter. Nonetheless, PLRs are useful to tax practitioners as unofficial guidance as to the position that the IRS might take on a similar matter.

A Technical Advice Memorandum (TAM) is guidance provided by the IRS office of chief counsel in specific cases to help resolve issues in those cases. TAMs are issued only in closed cases with identifying information that can identify specific taxpayers removed.

The IRS uses the Notice to provide IRS interpretations of the IRC or other law. The Notice is used when regulations will not be issued soon. The IRS has a large backlog of regulations to issue, and it is not uncommon for some regulations to take years before being issued.

An Announcement makes no substantive interpretation. It may be used to do such things as remind taxpayers of an impending deadline.

A taxpayer may always file his or her own tax return without assistance of a professional tax preparer. For most farm businesses, such a course of action is ill advised due to the complexity of the IRC. Three types of tax return preparers have unlimited representation rights before the IRS. These are enrolled agents, certified public accountants, and attorneys. There is a fourth class of tax return preparers called unenrolled preparers who are classified as annual filing season program participants. Farm owners or operators should choose their tax return preparer based upon the level of complexity of their business and the sophistication of advice that they need.

Disputes with the IRS over the amount of tax due sometimes arise. There is an administrative process within the IRS to contest the initial determination of the IRS. Once administrative remedies in the IRS have been exhausted, there are two options that the taxpayer has to appeal. One is through federal district court and the others through the U.S. Tax Court. Both of these options are discussed in the following paragraphs.

The U.S. Tax Court was created by act of Congress under its authority in Article I of the Constitution. A taxpayer may file a petition in the Tax Court if he or she has received either a notice of deficiency or a notice of determination from the IRS. One may also file a petition for relief from joint and several liability under the innocent spouse relief provisions of the IRC if six months have passed and the IRS has not issued a determination letter. A taxpayer may represent him- or herself; however, that is usually not advisable given the complexity of the IRC. Representation may be by an attorney or other person admitted to practice before the Tax Court. Tax practitioners other than attorneys who are admitted to practice before the Tax Court may represent individuals in Tax Court matters. There are also some clinics that train law students who are authorized to provide representation at low or no charge for clients who cannot afford representation. A taxpayer who chooses to contest an IRS assessment in Tax Court need not pay the tax until the Tax Court makes its final determination. Interest on the tax and on some penalties may continue to accrue during the pendency of the case.

The other option that the taxpayer has is to pay the tax and file with the IRS for refund. Upon the IRS's refusal to refund the tax paid, the taxpayer may file an action for refund in the federal district court with jurisdiction. This has the advantage of stopping additional interest from accruing. A taxpayer may represent him- or herself in federal district court; however, doing so is quite difficult. Unlike Tax Court, only a licensed attorney who is admitted to practice before the district court where the action is filed may represent a taxpayer before a federal district court. If the taxpayer wins in federal district court, the court will order that the IRS pay a refund to the taxpayer.

## Calculating federal income tax liability

As a general rule, all income from whatever source is subject to the federal income tax unless subject to an exception. One common misconception is that only cash income is subject to tax. In-kind income, barter income, exchange of services, and any other exchange that was not a gift results in income subject to tax unless subject to an exception. Property or money received as a gift does not result in taxable income. When a gift is made, no values are exchanged, so no income results.

Adjusted gross income (AGI) is a starting point for calculating income tax liability. AGI is not one's total income for a given year. There are certain adjustments to income that are made on Schedule 1 of Form 1040 to calculate AGI.[2] These adjustments include deductions for qualified education expenses, certain business expenses, qualified moving expenses, various deductions related to health insurance and pensions, student loan interest deduction, qualified tuition and fees, alimony, and others. These deductions are sometimes called above-the-line deductions because they are subtracted from income on the tax form before reaching the line on which the AGI is calculated.

A taxpayer's personal itemized deductions are calculated on Schedule A of Form 1040. These are deductions for such things as home mortgage interest paid and property tax paid on one's residence now subject to limitations imposed the TCJA. One may elect either to take itemized deductions using Schedule A or take the standard deduction. The standard deduction is determined by one's filing status. The exemptions for the taxpayer, his or her spouse, and any dependents are suspended under the TCJA. At this point, taxable income and tax due on that income can be calculated. This is not the end of the calculation of the tax. Tax credits must be subtracted from the calculated tax to determine the tax. A tax credit is provided under the IRC for particular payment. For example, a credit for foreign taxes paid is deducted from the tax calculated on taxable income.

There are other taxes that are paid when taxpayers pay their income tax. The most important of these is the tax to support Social Security and Medicare. The Federal Insurance Contributions Act (FICA)[3] tax is paid as part of the employment tax paid by employers. The employees' share is deducted from their pay.[4] FICA supports both Social Security and Medicare. Those who are self-employed must calculate the self-employment tax and add it to the tax due. Self-employed persons are required to pay both the employee and employer's share of FICA.

FICA is paid only on earned income. Earned income is wages and similar payments for an employee and the equivalent of wages for the self-employed. For the self-employed, it is critically important to distinguish earned income from other income. Investment income, for example, is not subject to FICA. Income from the sale of timber is usually not earned income. Much of the income from timber sales by farmers is incorrectly reported as earned income. This results in the payment of self-employment taxes that are not required to be paid.

Many farmers are self-employed and pay the self-employment (Social Security) tax. The amount of tax paid determines, according to a complex formula, the retirement or disability payments that a person may receive from Social Security. Many farmers arrange their businesses to minimize the amount of self-employment and income taxes that they pay. This may be unwise as one approaches retirement age. It may be necessary to restructure one's income so as to pay more self-employment tax. This analysis requires the assistance of a competent tax professional.

Form 1040, Schedule F, is the form used to report income (and losses) from farming. Most farmers are allowed to report their income and expenses on the cash method. The cash method of accounting is a simple method of accounting that takes all the income received for the tax year and from it subtracting all the expenses paid during the tax year. For most farmers, the tax year is the calendar year; however, a corporate farmer may choose a fiscal year that is some year other than the calendar year. The choice of a fiscal tax year is a decision that cannot be easily reversed since it usually requires IRS permission to return to a calendar tax year. The cash method of accounting has significant advantages. First, it is simple and requires less effort than other accounting methods. Second, it allows for shifting expenses and/or income to two different tax years. Given the dramatic shifts in production and prices that can occur in farming from year to year, there are important tax advantages to being able to do this. The other method of accounting that could be elected is the accrual method. The accrual method generally produces a more accurate picture of income than the cash method because income and expenses are matched to each other.

## Basic tax concepts: rent

Rent is money received from a tenant that the tenant pays for the use of the land. Rent is not farm income (unless it is from a crop share lease, discussed in Chapter 7) and is not properly reported on Schedule F. Rent is not earned income and is, therefore, not subject to self-employment tax. Rent is generally investment income.

As with most investment income, rent may be subject to the net investment income tax (NIIT).[5] The 2017 Tax Cuts and Jobs Act[6] did not change this provision of the ACA. In most years, for most farmers, this will not be an issue because their AGI will be below the threshold for paying the NIIT. It does become an estate planning issue because renting farmland converts farmland from a business asset to an investment asset. Any gain on the sale of the farm real estate is investment income that is subject to the NIIT. Often, the sale price of the farmland together with any rents within the year in which the farmland was sold will be high enough to trigger the NIIT.

There is an important exception to this rule about rent. If the landowner materially participated in farming the land, the rent is farm income reportable on Schedule F and earned income subject to the self-employment tax. For a landowner to materially participate, the landowner must share in the risk of production. Rent from share lease arrangements is typically farm income to the landowner because a landowner in a share lease arrangement shares in the risk of production. If there is a crop failure, the landowner does not get paid.

## Basic tax concepts: farm program payments

Most of the farm program payments discussed in Chapter 25 are farm income reportable on Schedule F. Crop insurance and crop disaster payments are generally reportable on Schedule F. There is an election available to many farmers to report these payments in the year after the year in which the physical damage occurred. Feed assistance is reportable as income on Schedule F. This includes the market value of donated feed, the difference between market value and the price paid for feed provided at below market prices, and cost reimbursement.

## Basic tax concepts: conservation program payments

Payment received under the Conservation Reserve Program is income reportable on Schedule F. Conservation cost-share may generally be excluded from income. To be excluded from income, there are three tests that must be met. First, the expense must be a capital expense. That means if the farmer incurs the expense, it would not be an expense that can be deducted in the current year. Second, the cost-share payment must not substantially increase the income from the property. Third, The USDA must certify that "the payment was primarily made for conserving soil and water resources, protecting or restoring the environment, improving forests, or providing a habitat for wildlife."[7] The treatment of payments for USDA-held conservation easements depends upon the length of the easement. For those of less than thirty years, the payments are generally treated as rent. For those of thirty years or more in length, payments are treated as capital according to the rules for capital gains and losses.

### Basic tax concepts: cooperatives

Cooperatives are businesses owned by farmers for the purpose of selling farm products and buying farm supplies. The farm credit banks are also cooperatives organized for the purpose of providing credit to the farmer members. The key to understanding a cooperative is that it is owned by the persons with whom it does business.

As a cooperative is not organized to make a profit, it returns any excess funds to its members after it determines that those funds are no longer needed. These funds are called patronage dividends. The character of those funds in the hands of the farmer-owner of a cooperative depends on how those funds were generated. In most cases, funds that are returned to a farmer-owner in patronage dividends will be income reportable on Schedule F. Patronage refunds are typically paid in two parts: one part cash and a second part capital retained by the cooperative held in the farmer's account. The farmer will usually receive a Form 1099-PATR from the cooperative. A copy of the Form 1099-PATR is also provided to the IRS.

### Basic tax concepts: depreciation and the IRC section 179 deduction

The purchase price of a capital asset may not generally be deducted in its entirety in the year of purchase. An exception to this rule is the IRC section 179 deduction that allows the immediate deduction (expensing) of the purchase price of a depreciable asset up to certain dollar limits. A capital asset is any asset that is expected to have a multiyear life. Equipment, buildings, and pickup trucks are all capital assets with a multiyear life. Land lasts forever and is not subject to depreciation. For depreciating capital assets, deductions for those assets must be taken over a period of time. The amount of annual deduction allowed depends upon the asset class of the asset and the depreciation method elected. Congress changes depreciation rules from time to time so the choices of depreciation method available will vary from time to time. There are exceptions that allow expensing of the purchase price of some of these assets up to certain dollar amounts in the year of purchase. The total amount of the purchase price for a capital asset that can be expensed depends upon laws enacted by Congress and will vary from time to time. When a capital asset is sold, some of the depreciation taken must be recaptured as ordinary income. Amounts that were expensed in the year of purchase may also be recaptured.

Whether a sale is of an entire farm or a single depreciable asset, there will generally be depreciation or section 179 recapture. Even if the sale of a farm is done as an installment sale over a period of years, depreciation and section 179 recapture must generally be taken as ordinary income in the year that the agreement is signed, even if no income is received in that year.

Land can never be depreciated. Property not used in a trade or business cannot be depreciated. When property is no longer used in a trade or business, depreciation may no longer be taken, even though there is remaining basis to be depreciated.

> **Example 23.1** Bob bought a pickup truck. He deducted the entire purchase price under section 179. After three years, his business use of the vehicle dropped to 50 percent or less of the vehicle use because he no longer had another vehicle for personal use. This triggered section 179 recapture, calculated as the section 179 deduction taken, less the allowable depreciation for three years of use. Bob may increase his basis in the truck by the recapture amount. He will report the recapture amount as ordinary income in the year that his business use dropped to 50 percent or less of his total use.

### Basic tax concepts: basis

Basis is the purchase price of property less depreciation plus any improvements to the property. Basis in property must be reduced by any depreciation taken. It also must be reduced by depreciation that could be taken even if the depreciation was not taken.

The cost of repairs made to property is generally deductible as a business expense in the year that the repair was made. If the property was improved rather than merely repaired, the amount paid for the improvement is not deductible in the year that it was made. The cost of an improvement must be added to the basis and depreciated over time. An improvement to property makes it better or changes its use. A repair merely restores the property to its current useful condition.

When real property is purchased upon which there is standing timber, the purchase price of the property should be allocated between the land and the timber. Basis allocated to the timber may be deducted from the sale price of the timber when the timber is sold. Purchasers of real property often fail to make this allocation at the time of purchase. The problem can sometimes be corrected by doing a back cruise. A back cruise is done by a qualified forester to estimate what the timber was worth at the time the property was purchased. Such a back cruise must be completed before the timber is cut.

Basis is also adjusted at the time that property is received as an inheritance. In general, basis is increased or decreased to reflect its value at the date of the decedent's death, unless the alternative valuation date for purposes of the federal estate tax is used. It is very important that the new basis be established promptly. Attempting to establish the basis years after the property was inherited is much more expensive than doing it when the property was inherited. Basis can be established when the property was inherited through an appraisal of the property by a qualified appraiser. If a federal estate tax return must be filed, appraisals are required to support the wealth information on the estate tax return. Where the estate tax return is not required, some people will not obtain an appraisal to avoid the cost of hiring an appraiser. Basis in gifts is not handled in the same way as basis in inheritances. When a person receives property as a gift, that person receives either the basis of the property in the hands of the donor or the fair market value of the property at the time of the gift, whichever is lower.

When an owner of property sells it and acquires like property, the owner may elect to treat the exchange as a like kind exchange.[8] In that situation, the tax attributes of the old property are transferred to the new property. The new property has the basis of the old property plus any additional purchase amount for the new property. Paying taxes on any gain on the sale of the old property can generally be avoided by like kind exchange. Under the TCJA, like kind exchanges of personal property are no longer allowed. The exchange or trade value is deemed a sale and recognized on the tax return.

### Basic tax concepts: capital gains and losses

When a capital asset is sold, there is a gain if the sale price exceeded the basis. There is a loss to the extent that the sale price is less than the basis. If the asset was held for more than one year, gains are taxable at a lower rate than for ordinary income. Short-term gains (gains from the sale of a capital asset owned for less than one year) are taxed at the same rate as ordinary income. There is a limitation on the amount of the capital loss that can be deducted from ordinary income. Capital losses that cannot be deducted in the current tax year may be carried over to subsequent tax years.

Depreciable property used in a trade or business is not a capital asset. Inventory such as grain and storage is not a capital asset, except when wages are paid in commodities. Land used in farming is not a capital asset. Nonetheless, the gain on the sale of such land is taxed as a capital asset.[9] Note that depreciation may be recaptured as ordinary income, and amounts deducted for conservation expenses may also be recaptured as ordinary income if those expenditures were made within the last ten years preceding the sale.

### Basic tax concepts: forgiveness of debt

In general, the principal portion of a forgiven debt must be reported as income. This is based on the concept that the money received as a loan was not a gift so it is, therefore, income if it is not required to be repaid. There are several exceptions to this rule. Where the seller financed the purchase, a forgiveness of debt is treated as a reduction in the purchase price. The basis of the property must be reduced by the amount that the purchase price was reduced. To the extent that payments made on a debt are a deductible expense, any forgiveness of debt is not income. Debt discharged in bankruptcy is not income. Cancellation of debt that takes place while the debtor is insolvent is not income. Forgiveness of qualified farm debt does not create income. A qualified farm debt must be incurred in the farming operation, and at least 50 percent of the total gross receipts for the past three taxable years must be from farming. Qualified principal residence debt that is forgiven may also be excluded from income. In general, any forgiveness of debt that is not treated as taxable income reduces the debtor's basis in the property.

### Basic tax concepts: installment sales

A popular method for selling farm real estate is through an installment sale. Installment sales are particularly popular as an estate planning tool to transfer the farm to the current farmer's children. Often, a farmer's child or children who wish to take over the farming operation do not have either assets or the credit history to obtain a private loan. If the transfer is to occur, the parents must finance the transfer. Under the terms of an installment sale, payments are made over a period of years, sometimes as long as thirty years.

Most installment sales include the sale of many farm assets including real estate, equipment, and other assets. The sale of each of these assets must be treated separately for tax purposes. Even though a sale is structured as an installment sale, the seller can elect out of installment sale tax treatment. The election to do so may be revoked only with IRS approval. Income to the seller who does not elect out of installment treatment consists of interest, return of basis in the property, and gain on the sale of the property. Interest is reported as ordinary income. Even if the payment in the contract is not called interest, some interests must be imputed to the transaction. If the parties are related, which is often the case with farm transactions, certain minimum interest rates specified by the IRS must be used. After the amount of interest is determined, each payment is divided into a tax-free return of basis and a taxable gain. For most farm real property held for more than one year, the gain will be taxed at capital gain rates.

## Calculating federal estate and gift taxes

Recent changes in the federal estate tax mean that the estates of most farm owners will not be subject to the federal estate tax. The Tax Cuts and Jobs Act doubled, from $5 million to $10 million (before inflation adjustment), the basic exclusion amount for federal estate and gift taxes, and the exemption amount for the generation-skipping transfer tax. This change is applicable only to tax years after 2017, and prior to 2026.[10] The exclusion amount for estates of those who died in 2018 is now $11.18 million. The exclusion amount is the amount of a net taxable estate that is not subject to the federal estate and gift taxes. This is a lifetime exclusion amount that may be used to avoid either tax on lifetime gifts or tax on one's estate at death. It may be used only once. Using it to avoid tax on lifetime gifts reduces the amount available to offset the tax on one's estate. It is indexed for inflation. The taxable estate is calculated by deducting allowable expenses of the estate. A surviving spouse may now elect to pass any unused portion of the decedent's exclusion amount to her- or himself. This is known as "portability" and is done by filing IRS Form 706 (United States Estate [and Generation-Skipping Transfer] Tax Return) within nine months of the decedent's death, including extensions.[11] It should be emphasized that any of the lifetime exclusion amount used to offset gift tax on gifts made during the decedent's life is not available to offset the estate tax.

The fair market value of a qualifying family farm can be reduced by $1,140,000 for deaths that occur in 2018.[12] Any reduction taken under IRC § 2032A also reduces the basis in the property in the hands of the heirs or legatees. Property for which a reduction in value is taken must be held in continuing use for ten years to avoid recapture of any tax due. Estate tax payments are generally due with the estate tax return; however, installment payment of estate taxes may be elected under IRC § 6166.

The donor of a gift is generally responsible for filing a gift tax return and paying the gift tax. There is an annual exclusion amount that is $15,000 in 2018. This is the amount that any donor can give to an individual donee without an obligation to file a gift tax return. One donor can give up to $15,000 to as many donees as he or she wishes without filing a gift tax return. This annual exclusion amount is indexed for inflation. The annual exclusion amount is in addition to the life-time exclusion amount discussed above. A husband and wife may make a gift to an individual donee of up to $30,000 in 2018. The source of the money is irrelevant. It may all come from the husband or all come from the wife or come from a mix of the two. Payment of educational expenses and medical expenses directly to the provider is also excluded from the gift tax.

---

**Example 23.2** Bob's adult son, Ned, enrolled in Utopia College in 2018. Bob transferred $50,000 to cover tuition into Ned's account. Bob must file a federal gift tax return. He may apply his $15,000 annual exclusion amount to the first $15,000 of his gift to Ned. He must either pay gift tax or use $35,000 of his lifetime exclusion amount. Had he paid the $50,000 directly to Utopia College, the entire amount would have been a qualified educational expense excluded from the federal gift tax. He would have had neither a filing requirement nor a gift tax obligation.

Gifts of appreciated property such as farm real estate generally require an appraisal by a qualified appraiser to support the value claimed. For that reason, gifts of appreciated property can be expensive and complicated. There may also be other tax consequences such as depreciation recapture if business property is the subject of the gift.

## Federal excise taxes

Motor fuels are subject to federal excise tax. Farms that buy fuel for use in farming may be able to receive a refund of the excise tax. Fuel is dyed according to its use. Care must be taken not to use fuel in a non-qualifying use, as this can subject the user to penalties.

## Employment taxes

Farms that employ people must withhold employment taxes from their employees and issue W-2s to those employees just as any other employer. A farm employer is also responsible for paying the employer portion of FICA and for paying the Federal Unemployment Tax Act (FUTA) tax, if applicable.[13] The requirement to pay FUTA does not apply to farms that paid less than $20,000 in wages in any calendar quarter of the current or preceding calendar year and who have fewer than ten employees.

## Record keeping

Farmers must keep and retain records just as other taxpayers. Neither the IRS nor courts find the dashboard system of record keeping acceptable. (For those unfamiliar with it, the dashboard system is keeping all of one's farm records on the dashboard of one's pickup truck.) The failure to keep records will not prevent the IRS from assessing tax. The IRS will assess tax based upon the information that exists. Without records, a farmer will be unable to refute the IRS assessment.

## Hobby losses

Farmers who are not engaged in farming for profit cannot report their income and losses on Schedule F.[14] Income must be reported on Form 1040, and expenses may be deducted only to the extent of income. The farm business must be carried on in a business-like manner that indicates an intent to make a profit. The IRS has a list of factors that it applies to make this determination. An activity is presumed carried on for profit if it makes a profit in at least three of the last five years. For equestrian activities, the presumption is two of the last seven years.

## Pass-through, disregarded, and separate taxable entities

Farms organized as partnerships are pass-through entities. Farms organized as limited liability companies (LLCs) are also generally treated as pass-through entities.

This means that the partnership or LLC files an information return with the IRS, but each of the owners of the partnership or LLC reports gains and losses on his or her own individual tax returns. Subchapter S corporations are entities that have elected to file information returns with the IRS but, like LLCs, the owners report income and losses on their individual tax returns. Corporations (generally called Subchapter C corporations) and certain LLCs that have made an election to do so may file their own tax returns and pay their own tax. Payments to the individual owners are treated and taxed as dividends.

## State and local taxes

Many states levy income tax with which farm businesses must comply. States also generally have sales or use taxes that must be paid on some purchases. Both real and personal property used in the farm business is generally subject to property taxation. Laws governing taxation of real and personal farm property vary greatly from one state to another. Property taxes are discussed in Chapter 5. The state or local government where a farm is located may also have business taxes that apply to the farm. Vehicles are generally taxed in various ways. State taxes very greatly from one state to another. Even within a state, there can be considerable variation from one local government to another. Farm businesses often have full or partial exemptions from some of these taxes. Farm business owners or operators must be thoroughly familiar and well advised of state and local taxes.

## Notes

1  IRS. *IRS News and Published Guidance*. Retrieved August 11, 2018, www.irs.gov/government-entities/federal-state-local-governments/irs-news-and-published-guidance.
2  IRS. *Form 1040*. 2018. Retrieved August 11, 2018, www.irs.gov/pub/irs-pdf/f1040.pdf.
3  IRC Chapter 21 (2017).
4  IRS. *Form W-4*. 2018. Retrieved August 11, 2018, www.irs.gov/pub/irs-pdf/fw4.pdf.
5  IRC § 1411 (2017).
6  Pub. L. 115-97, 131 Stat. 2054 (2017).
7  IRS. *Farmer's Tax Guide*, Pub. 225 (2017).
8  IRS, *Farmer's Tax Guide*, Pub. 225 (2017).
9  IRC § 1231 (2017); IRS, *Farmer's Tax Guide*, Pub. 225 (2017).
10  Pub. L. 115-97, 131 Stat. 2054 (2017) (codified as amended at 26 U.S.C. §§ 2010, 2631 (2017)).
11  IRS. *Instructions for Form 706*. 2017. Retrieved August 11, 2018, www.irs.gov/pub/irs-pdf/i706.pdf.
12  IRC § 1232A (2013); IRS. *Frequently Asked Questions on Estate Taxes*. Retrieved August 11, 2018, www.irs.gov/businesses/small-businesses-self-employed/frequently-asked-questions-on-estate-taxes#513 IRS, Farmer's Tax Guide, Pub. 225, 81–84.
13  IRS, *Farmer's Tax Guide*, Pub. 225 (2017).
14  IRS, *Farmer's Tax Guide*, Pub. 225 (2017).

# Chapter 24

# International trade

## Introduction

International trade is critical to the profitability of some agricultural businesses. Trade in agricultural products was $140.5 billion in 2017.[1] Overall U.S. agricultural exports have been growing; total agricultural exports, for example, were only $96.3 billion in fiscal year 2009.[2] The composition of these exports has shifted toward consumer-oriented products. However, bulk commodities remain an important part of U.S. agricultural exports. China is currently the largest destination for agricultural exports from the United States; however, current trade disputes with China put this in jeopardy.[3] Table 24.1 lists selected U.S. agricultural exports by dollar value for calendar year 2017.

Though a small agricultural producer or processor may consider the laws governing international trade daunting, it is quite possible for even a family farm to export. Both the federal and state governments offer programs to agricultural producers and processors to help them export their products. There is now a significant number of consultants and attorneys who will help with the export process.

Trade over great distances between different groups of people has occurred for thousands of years. People learn fairly quickly that killing the stranger with cool stuff and keeping it is not the best way to get more. As a result, rules developed governing trade between peoples, although not necessarily countries, because countries or nation states, as we know them, did not yet exist. Initially, this body of law was not written. It was centuries or more after this body of international law developed that people wrote it down. This body of law is called customary international law. Customary international law is not as important as it once was because it has been replaced by bilateral treaties, multilateral treaties, customs unions, and conventions.

A bilateral treaty is an agreement between two countries that governs some aspects of the relationship between those two countries. There are many bilateral treaties that are important for trade between countries. The United States has tax treaties with many countries that are important for understanding the taxation of trade between countries. Working relationships exist with some countries, particularly Canada, that are not encompassed in treaties but are important for facilitating trade.

*Table 24.1* Selected export commodities in calendar year 2017[4]

| Commodity | Billion Dollars |
|---|---|
| Soybeans | 18.012 |
| Corn | 4.928 |
| Wheat, unmilled | 2.736 |
| Other feeds and fodder | 3.650 |
| Livestock, poultry, and dairy | 14.235 |
| Horticultural products | 17.365 |
| Soybean meal | 2.305 |
| Tobacco, unmanufactured | 0.622 |
| Cotton | 3.034 |
| Sugar and tropical products | 2.889 |

A multilateral treaty is a treaty between several countries. The North American Free Trade Agreement (NAFTA) is an agreement among the United States, Canada, and Mexico. There is no sharp distinction between a customs union and a multilateral treaty. NAFTA is also an example of a customs union. The European Union (EU) is another customs union; however, the EU agreements extend well beyond the facilitation of trade to shared governance and a common currency for some, but not all, of the EU members.

A convention is a multilateral treaty that may include anywhere from several dozen countries to most of the world's countries. A convention will typically establish an international organization to manage relationships between participating countries and resolve disputes. The World Trade Organization (WTO) that was established in 1994 by the WTO agreements is the most important example of a convention governing international trade. The WTO itself is headquartered in Geneva, Switzerland, and has 164 members as of July 29, 2016.[5]

## Selected international organizations, conventions, and multilateral and bilateral agreements governing U.S. trade

### *The World Trade Organization*

The WTO was preceded by earlier negotiations that established the General Agreement on Tariffs and Trade. The WTO agreements are not enforceable by individuals. The WTO agreements may be enforced only by countries. The Dispute Settlement Body has responsibility for settling disputes between countries.[6] Countries are encouraged and assisted with settling their disputes; however, if the countries with disputes are unable to settle, the Dispute Settlement Body will appoint panels. A panel engages in a quasi-judicial process to determine whether the accused country has violated the WTO agreements. If a violation is found, the complaining country is authorized to apply punitive tariffs to selected goods of the country found in violation.

In the United States, the Office of the United States Trade Representative (USTR) represents the president in trade negotiations and in negotiations with the WTO and other international organizations.[7] The U.S. International Trade Commission (ITC) provides the president and the USTR with independent analysis, information, and support for their negotiations in interactions with the WTO in member countries.[8]

Because agriculture is a critical sector for most countries, negotiating freer trade in agricultural products has been a difficult and time-consuming process. The Agriculture Agreement is one of the WTO agreements. It was negotiated as part of the 1986–1994 Uruguay Round. The continuing effort to promote freer agricultural trade is the responsibility of the WTO's Agriculture Committee. One of the major issues has been how to maintain food security. The WTO has devoted considerable effort to this issue and has developed resources to address the problem of food security.[9]

Trade in cotton has been a particularly difficult issue to address. The WTO's Cotton Sub-Committee has been assigned cotton trade issues by the WTO. As noted in Chapter 25, the 2014 Farm Bill removed upland cotton from the list of covered commodities to comply with an agreement with Brazil to settle Brazil's WTO complaint about U.S. upland cotton subsidies. Resolving trade complaints is a long and arduous process. Brazil's WTO complaint was originally filed on September 27, 2002.[10] For more detailed discussion of the Agriculture Agreement, the reader is referred to the book on the topic edited by Cardwell, Grossman, and Rodgers.[11]

## International Plant Protection Convention

The International Plant Protection Convention (IPPC) was established in 1952 to protect cultivated and wild plants by preventing the introduction and spread of pests.[12] There are currently 181 members of the IPPC. The governing body of the IPPC is the Commission on Phytosanitary Measures. The IPPC Secretariat is from the Food and Agriculture Organization of the United Nations (FAO). The IPPC receives regular support from the FAO.

The IPPC is currently working on a wide range of issues. One of these is sea container guidelines. Containers often provide a means for plant pests to move. The IPC is working on forestry guidelines to prevent the movement of forest pests. The entire standard-setting process is particularly important because harmonized standards among countries is a prerequisite to avoiding unfair trade practices. The IPPC does a great deal of work with developing training materials and with capacity building. Capacity building is particularly important for helping developing countries develop the capacity to both prevent the export of products that inadvertently carry plant pests and protect those countries from imports that carry plant pests. Developing countries need adequate phytosanitary institutions, pest surveillance, inspection systems, and export certification programs.

## The Food and Agriculture Organization of the United Nations

The FAO pursues three main goals of eliminating food insecurity, promoting economic and social progress, and advocating for the sustainable management and utilization of natural resources.[13] In particular, the FAO is focused on increasing the productivity and sustainability of agriculture, forestry, and fisheries. The FAO becomes involved in major animal and poultry disease outbreaks, supports work on mutation breeding techniques to produce better crop varieties, and conducts efforts to improve the safety of food.

## North American Free Trade Agreement

NAFTA became effective on January 1, 1994.[14] It regulates trade and investment between the United States, Mexico, and Canada. After a phase-out period, NAFTA eliminated tariffs on goods traded between the three countries if those goods originated in one of the three countries. Exporters that wish to obtain the benefits of NAFTA must have a certificate of origin that proves the goods originated in one of the three member countries. The U.S. International Trade Administration handles certificates of origin for U.S. exporters. Unlike the WTO agreements, NAFTA provides exporters with a direct route to address violations of NAFTA that affect their exports.

The United States, Mexico, and Canada have recently concluded a renegotiation of NAFTA. If ratified by the U.S. Senate, and approved by governments of Mexico and Canada, NAFTA will have a new name, the United States-Mexico-Canada Agreement (USMCA). The most important change for agriculture will be greater access to the Canadian milk market for U.S. producers. The negotiated draft also includes improved labor, environmental, and intellectual property protections.

## Organization for Economic Cooperation and Development

The Organization for Economic Cooperation and Development (OECD) provides a forum for thirty-four countries that account for 78 percent of the world's gross domestic product to discuss trade issues.[15] Though the OECD has given rise to some legally binding agreements, most of its work involves discussion and peer review. It collects data and performs analysis to support the efforts of member countries to understand and improve trade.

## Agreement on Trade-Related Aspects of Intellectual Property Rights

Agreement on Trade-Related Aspects of Intellectual Property Rights (TRIPS) governs intellectual property and is under the auspices of the WTO. It is

Annex-1C of the Agreement Establishing the WTO.[16] TRIPS required that member countries harmonize their intellectual property rules. TRIPS requires that member states provide some form of intellectual property protection of plant varieties. The agreement does not specify what that protection should be. Exemptions in TRIPS could be interpreted to allow countries to exclude patented seeds and plants from intellectual property protection.[17] This issue remains unresolved and will likely remain unresolved for some time because the WTO agreements do not provide any right of action to private parties. Resolution will require negotiation of the WTO agreements by member states, an arduous process.

## Bilateral trade agreements

There are numerous bilateral trade agreements between the United States and other countries. Each agreement is somewhat different. Exporters understand the terms of specific bilateral trade agreements that involve the countries that will be receiving their agricultural products.

## Federal agencies involved in agricultural trade

The U.S. International Trade Administration (ITA) provides a variety of services to agricultural exporters.[18] The Global Markets unit of the ITA provides individual exporters with expertise, trade promotion programs, and market access advocacy. The Enforcement and Compliance unit of the ITA helps to ensure compliance with international trade agreements. It handles individual complaints from exporters about unfair trade practices. It provides web-based assistance to potential exporters.[19]

The ITC protects U.S. intellectual property owners by handling complaints concerning foreign competitors that are attempting to ship goods to the United States in violation of intellectual property rights. The ITC has the power to exclude and seize goods that are in violation of U.S. intellectual property laws. The ITC works on a complaint basis. The services that the ITC provides are valuable to U.S. intellectual property owners. An ITC complaint is less costly, faster, and often more effective than filing an infringement action in federal court.

The USTR interfaces with the WTO on a variety of issues in agricultural trade including sanitary and phytosanitary (SPS) issues and regulatory issues. Regulatory issues include restrictions that other countries place on the import of agricultural products that were produced using genetic engineering technology and other technologies. The USTR has monitoring and enforcement responsibilities with regard to the WTO agreements and other free trade agreements.

The USDA Foreign Agricultural Service (FAS) provides many services to support U.S. exporters of agricultural products. The FAS maintains overseas offices that provide coverage in more than 150 countries.[20] The FAS partners with many U.S. agricultural organizations to help promote U.S. agricultural products abroad. Many of these organizations maintain supplier lists and databases that may be used by foreign buyers to locate suppliers of U.S. agricultural products. The FAS and its partner organizations participate in trade shows and other similar events around the world to showcase U.S. agricultural products.

The FAS operates the GSM-102 program. The GSM-102 program is an export credit guarantee program that reduces the risk of lenders who finance international transactions in U.S. agricultural products. It is available for consumer-oriented products, intermediate products, and bulk products. Consumer-oriented products include processed products. Examples of these products are frozen foods, wine, and fresh produce. Intermediate products are those that will be used as ingredients in other products. Examples of intermediate products include hides, paper products, and flour. Bulk agricultural commodities include grains such as corn, wheat, and rice.

Additional duties of the FAS include promoting food security abroad through food assistance and fellowships and exchanges. The FAS also has an important role in developing trade policy by advising the president and the USTR on trade negotiations and trade agreements. It addresses market access issues including those that arise from the use of new technologies such as genetic engineering and nanotechnology.

The USDA Animal and Plant Health Inspection Service (APHIS) is the primary point of contact with international trading partners for the discussion of phytosanitary issues management.[21] APHIS is the designated National Plant Protection Organization for the United States under the International Plant Protection Convention. Phytosanitary standards protect importing countries from the introduction of unwanted plants, animals, insects, diseases, and other pests. APHIS works with other countries to eliminate unfair phytosanitary standards that serve as trade barriers. Historically, phytosanitary standards have been distorted to serve as disguised trade barriers. APHIS works with other countries to harmonize standards. Harmonization helps to avoid trade distortions from phytosanitary standards.

U.S. products are sometimes excluded for legitimate phytosanitary issues such as disease and insect pests. Using science-based information, APHIS works with foreign governments to find solutions to these problems.

APHIS's Plant Protection and Quarantine program issues export certificates. Export certificates are required under phytosanitary standards to export most agricultural products. Many state departments of agriculture also issue export certificates.

### State programs

Most state departments of agriculture have an international trade office. These offices work with companies to help them to export their products. Most state-supported land-grant universities have international programs offices to facilitate work with counterparts overseas. Many of these international contacts directly or indirectly support export efforts for agricultural products. Many state departments of agriculture issue export certifications for agricultural products.

## Nongovernmental voluntary standards

Nongovernmental voluntary standards are voluntary only in the sense that they are not enforced by governments. Voluntary standards are usually required by buyers of agricultural products. Standards are established by a nonprofit, private organization. Inspections to ensure compliance with standards may be conducted by the organization that established the standards or may be conducted by a third-party certifier. The use of third-party certifiers is the more common approach. Nongovernmental voluntary standards are becoming increasingly popular in international agricultural trade. Voluntary standards typically offer more flexibility and specificity than conventions and other intergovernmental agreements. Voluntary standards are enforced through provisions in the multiple contracts between the various parties involved.

Examples of voluntary standards include Fair Trade, the ISO series of standards, and issue-specific standards. Fair Trade standards are designed to ensure that producers of agricultural and other products, primarily in developing countries, receive a fair return for their labor and capital.[22] Fair Trade standards also ensure that the environment is protected in the production process. The Rain Forest Alliance has developed issue-specific standards to promote preservation of rain forest ecosystems.[23] Some of its support comes from certification fees for products such as coffee that it certifies as being produced in an environmentally sound manner.

The ISO series of standards was developed by the International Organization for Standardization. The International Organization for Standardization is an independent, nongovernmental membership organization with its headquarters in Geneva, Switzerland. It is by far the largest developer of voluntary international standards. Standards developed include ISO 9000, quality management; ISO 50001, energy management; ISO 22000, food safety management; and ISO 14000, environmental management.

## Collections and dispute resolution

Collecting payment due for goods or services sold abroad is always a concern just as it is in domestic transactions. The typical way that payment is ensured is for a trusted third-party intermediary to hold the funds until the buyer certifies that the goods or services have been provided and meet contractual requirements. As the buyer is no longer in control of the funds, this removes the incentive for the buyer to pay slowly or not at all. An irrevocable letter of credit issued by a large international bank is one of the most common ways to ensure payment. The buyer of the goods or services purchases the letter of credit from the bank for a fee. The letter of credit is written in favor of the seller of the goods or services. After the goods or services have been provided, the buyer certifies to the bank that the goods or services have met contractual requirements. At that point, the bank pays the seller. The bank then collects the money that it paid the seller from the buyer. If the buyer does not pay, it is the responsibility of the bank to bring a collection action.

Using third-party intermediaries is costly. This is one of the major reasons why governments provide loan guarantees to subsidize international transactions by protecting banks from the risk of default. One interesting approach to reducing transaction costs has been the development of the Bitcoin.[24] Bitcoin is not the solution to this problem currently except for the bravest (or most foolhardy) of souls. Bitcoin currently suffers from huge price volatility, fraud, a lack of legal structure, and the hostility of governments. The IRS treats Bitcoin and other virtual currencies as property, not currency, for tax purposes.[25] Tax treatment of Bitcoin is unfavorable compared to transactions in recognized currencies. Despite the huge obstacles in structuring international transactions in virtual currencies, there is a need. Given the need, it is likely that it will become easier over the next decade to use virtual currencies to facilitate international transactions. Exporters of agricultural products would be among the major beneficiaries of such a development.

International dispute resolution is similar to domestic dispute resolution except that the costs and complexity are greater. The three basic ways of resolving disputes—mediation, arbitration, and litigation—are all employed in resolutions of disputes arising out of international transactions. There are a variety of organizations that provide mediation and arbitration services to help parties to resolve international trade disputes.[26] If litigation is required, determining the country that has jurisdiction over the defendant is a key threshold issue. Resolving disputes is often made easier through bilateral treaties between the United States and other countries. The terms of these treaties differ. What must be done to bring about a resolution of the dispute will also differ depending on the country to which product was being sold.

Sometimes it will be a third party that has liability when an international transaction does not work out as anticipated. Cargill, along with numerous other agribusinesses and individual farmers, recently sued Syngenta Seeds over corn shipped to China that was refused by Chinese authorities because the Chinese authorities found that the shipments were contaminated with genetically modified corn produced by Syngenta that was not approved for use in China.[27] The genetically modified Syngenta variety that contaminated the shipments was not licensed for sale in China. Because Cargill could not obtain sufficient uncontaminated corn, it was forced to delay or cancel contracts with Chinese buyers. In addition, Cargill experienced substantial disruptions at its export facilities due the inability to ship contaminated corn. Archer Daniels Midland Company has filed a similar suit against Syngenta.[28] A settlement was reached in the growers' class action in 2018.[29]

## Current Trade Disputes

The current Administration has imposed a wide variety of tariffs on many U.S. trading partners under section 232 of the Trade Expansion Act of 1962.[30] Section 232 allows the almost unlimited, punitive tariffs to be imposed to protect national security. While federal courts would be reluctant to second guess any president's determination of the nation's security, Congress may well curb the current Administration's appetite for tariffs.[31]

## Notes

1 USDA Economic Research Service (ERS). *Outlook for U.S. Agricultural Trade*. 2018. Retrieved August 13, 2018, usda.mannlib.cornell.edu/usda/current/AES/AES-05-31-2018.pdf.

2 USDA Economic Research Service (ERS). *Outlook for U.S. Agricultural Trade*. 2012. www.ers.usda.gov/webdocs/publications/35766/aes-73.pdf?v=0.

3 The Wall Street Journal. *Asian Nations Push Back at U.S. on Trade, Sanctions*. Retrieved August 13, 2018, www.wsj.com/articles/asian-nations-push-back-at-u-s-on-trade-sanctions-1533507560.

4 USDA Economic Research Service (ERS). *Outlook for U.S. Agricultural Trade*. 2018. Retrieved August 13, 2018, usda.mannlib.cornell.edu/usda/current/AES/AES-05-31-2018.pdfhttp://www.ers.usda.gov/topics/international-markets-trade/.

5 WTO. *Members and Observers*. Retrieved August 13, 2018, www.wto.org/english/thewto_e/whatis_e/tif_e/org6_e.htm.

6 WTO. *Dispute settlement*. Retrieved August 13, 2018, www.wto.org/english/tratop_e/dispu_e/dispu_e.htm.

7 USTR. *About Us*. Retrieved August 13, 2018, www.ustr.gov/about-us.

8 ITC. *About the USITC*. 2018. Retrieved August 13, 2018, www.usitc.gov/press_room/about_usitc.htm.

9 WTO. *Food security*. 2018. Retrieved August 13, 2018, www.wto.org/english/tratop_e/agric_e/food_security_e.htm.

10 WTO. *Dispute Settlement: Dispute DS267, United States—Subsidies on Upland Cotton*. 2014. Online. Retrieved August 13, 2018, www.wto.org/english/tratop_e/dispu_e/cases_e/ds267_e.htm.

11 Michael N. Cardwell, et al., Eds., *Agriculture and International Trade: Law, Policy and the WTO* (2003).

12 IPPC. *Who we are*. Retrieved August 13, 2018, www.ippc.int/en/who-we-are/.

13 FAO. *About FAO*. 2018. Retrieved August 13, 2018, http://www.fao.org/about/en/.

14 NAFTANOW.Org. *Frequently Asked Questions*. Retrieved August 2018, naftanow.org/.

15 USTR. OECD. Retrieved August 13, 2018, www.ustr.gov/trade-agreements/wto-multilateral-affairs/oecd.

16 Theodore A. Feitshans, TRIPS and the Protection of Intellectual Property in Biotechnology in the United States, in *Agriculture and International Trade: Law, Policy and the WTO*, 165, 165-192 (Michael N. Cardwell, et al., Eds., 2003).

17 John Linarelli, TRIPS, Biotechnology and the Public Domain: What Role will World Trade Law Play? in *Agriculture and International Trade: Law, Policy and the WTO* 196, 193-214 (Michael N. Cardwell, et al., Eds., 2003).

18 ITA. *About the International Trade Administration*. Retrieved August 13, 2018, trade.gov/about.asp

19 ITA. *Export Education*. Retrieved August 13, 2018, www.export.gov/export-education.

20 FAS. *Buying U.S. Products*. Retrieved August 13, 2018, www.fas.usda.gov/topics/buying-us-products.

21 APHIS. *Import Export*. Retrieved August 13, 2018, www.aphis.usda.gov/aphis/ourfocus/importexport.

22 Fair Trade USA. *Do the most good, every day*. Retrieved August 13, 2018, www.fairtradecertified.org/.

23 Rain Forest Alliance. *Working with you to rebalance the planet.* Retrieved August 13, 2018, www.rainforest-alliance.org/.

24 Wall Street Journal. *Why Bitcoin's Erratic Price Doesn't Matter.* Retrieved August 13, 2018, blogs.wsj.com/moneybeat/2014/12/21/why-bitcoins-erratic-price-doesnt-matter/.

25 I.R.S. Notice 2014-21, 2014-16 I.R.B.

26 National Agricultural Law Center. *International Treaties and Agreements.* Retrieved August 13, 2018, nationalaglawcenter.org/overview/international-trade/.

27 *Plaintiff's Petition for Damages, Cargill, Inc. v. Syngenta Seeds, Inc.* (No. 67061) 40th J. Dist. Ct., St. John the Baptist Parish, La. (Sept. 12, 2014).

28 *Plaintiff's Petition for Damages, Archer Daniels Midland Co. v. Syngenta Corp.* (No. 79219) 29th J. Dist. Ct., St. Charles Parish, La. (Nov. 19, 2014).

29 Syngenta Corn Settlement. Retrieved August 13, 2018, www.cacrecovery.com/case/syngenta-corn-settlement/.

30 Pub. L. 87-794, 76 Stat. 872 (1962) (codified as amended at 19 U.S.C. §§ 1801 et seq.).

31 Siohan Hughes and William Mauldin. Lawmakers May Curb Tariff Powers, *Wall Street Journal* (August 3, 2018), at A2.

# Chapter 25

# Federal farm program law

## Introduction

Federal farm program law is an exceedingly complex area of law. Much of federal farm program law is included in periodic farm bills. Farm bills are temporary enactments that amend permanent law. Permanent law is incompatible with many trade agreements to which the United States is party. Permanent law no longer reflects the current structure of agriculture and federal budgetary policy. A reversion to permanent law would result in much higher federal expenditures on federal farm programs than is currently the case. These periodic omnibus bills include much more than agriculture. Since the 1930s, there have been seventeen farm bills.[1]

There is much law in addition to that contained in the farm bills. This law includes statutes that cover specific topics that were enacted outside the farm bill process. Even though this law is part of what is often called permanent legislation, farm bills are often used to amend this law. Law outside of the farm bill process also includes treaties and conventions with other countries. Treaties themselves cannot be amended by a farm bill. Farm bills can amend legislation that implements a treaty. A farm bill can bring existing law into compliance with international agreements. An example of this in the 2014 Farm Bill is the removal of upland cotton from the list of covered commodities to comply with the WTO decision that upland cotton provisions under the 2008 Farm Bill did not comply with the WTO agreement.

## The farm bill

The current farm bill was enacted in February 2014.[2] There are twelve titles in the current farm bill. These are Title I, Commodities; Title II, Conservation; Title III, Trade; Title IV, Nutrition; Title V, Credit; Title VI, Rural Development; Title VII, Research, Extension, and Related Matters; Title VIII, Forestry; Title IX, Energy; Title X, Horticulture; Title XI, Crop Insurance; and Title XII, Miscellaneous. Title III, Trade, is omitted from the following discussion and is discussed in Chapter 24. Title IV, Nutrition, is not discussed because it does not relate directly to agriculture. Expenditures under Title IV are by far the greatest of any title in the 2014 Farm Bill because Title IV includes the programs to mitigate food insecurity. Title VI, Rural Development, is also not directly related to agriculture so was not included. The Value-Added Agricultural Market Development Program is part of Title VI. By encouraging producers and others to further process raw agricultural commodities, the program can increase farmers' incomes. The conservation programs of Title II, Conservation, are discussed in this chapter because many of these programs have a direct impact on agricultural production practices; however, the conservation compliance provisions of Title II are discussed in Chapter 21 along with environmental regulation of agriculture. Title XI, Crop Insurance, is discussed in a separate section that includes both a discussion of the crop insurance program and the amendments made by Title XI.

## Title I: Commodities

Commodity programs are designed to stabilize farm incomes by helping farmers manage risk. Commodity prices fluctuate widely. Drought, excessive rain, and other adverse conditions can cause crop failures. The result is often the financial failure of family farms. Congress recognized that a stable food supply is not only necessary to the well-being of the people of the United States as a whole but is a national security issue. Commodity programs are administered by the USDA Farm Service Agency (FSA). Farmers may enroll in these programs through their local FSA office.

The 2014 Farm Bill made some significant changes to the commodity programs as they existed in the 2008 Farm Bill. Direct payments to farmers were repealed. Persons or entities with an adjusted gross income (AGI) in excess of $900,000 were made ineligible for subsidies under the commodity programs. AGI is a measure of income before deductions as it appears on a person's or entity's federal tax return. The total subsidy that one person or entity can receive was capped at $125,000. The 2014 Farm Bill provided a choice of risk management tools to farmers to supplement federal crop insurance. Farmers who participate in these risk management programs must agree to maintain or implement conservation measures and protect wetlands.

There are a number of requirements for participation in commodity programs. To participate, a farmer must have base (base acres). Base is calculated upon the history of different crops planted on the farm. There are alternative means of calculating base in the 2014 Farm Bill. Farmers may elect between these alternatives. Only covered commodities participate in the commodity programs. Covered commodities include wheat, corn, grain sorghum, barley, oats, long and medium-grain rice, soybeans, other oilseeds, peanuts, dry peas, lentils, and small and large chickpeas. Farmers receiving benefits under Title I must comply with the highly erodible land and wetland conservation requirements. Upland cotton was removed from the list of covered commodities in response to Brazil's successful complaint to the World Trade Organization. Transition assistance was provided to upland cotton growers in the 2014 Farm Bill.

The 2014 Farm Bill created two new programs—Price Loss Coverage (PLC) and Agricultural Risk Coverage (ARC)—that replaced the repealed Direct and Counter-Cyclical Program and the Average Crop Revenue Election Program.[3] For the 2014–2018 crop years, farmers may elect to use the farm's 2013 bases for covered crops or reallocate base among covered crops. Once made, the election cannot be revoked. Yields used to calculate program payments may be updated to the farm's 2008–2012 average yield per planted acre. Years in which a covered commodity was not planted may be excluded from the yield calculation. As upland cotton is no longer a covered commodity, cotton base was converted to generic base. Generic base may be planted to covered commodities for which farm program payments may be received. These yields are used to calculate payments under the PLC. Payments are calculated by multiplying 85 percent of base times the difference between the reference price and the effective price times the program payment yield. ARC options include county ARC and individual ARC. County ARC is based upon actual county crop revenue for a covered commodity, rather than farm data, whereas individual ARC is based upon individual farm data. In 2014, all the owners of a farm were required to make a unanimous election between PLC/county ARC on a commodity-by-commodity basis (applicable only to covered commodities) or individual ARC for all covered commodities on the farm. If the first option was selected, an election to allocate base acres between PLC and county ARC was required. These elections cover the 2014–2018 crop years and are tied to the land, not the person farming the land. A change of lessee or owner does not alter the election. Those who did not make an election for 2014 were barred from PLC or ARC for the 2014 crop year and deemed to have elected PLC for subsequent crop years. Enrollment of the farm is still required to receive payments. Farms with ten acres or fewer of base acres in PLC or ARC are not eligible for payments unless the producer is a socially disadvantaged farmer or rancher[4] or is a limited resource farmer or rancher.[5] Producers that participate in the PLC and also participate in the federal crop insurance program may also participate in the Supplemental Coverage Option (SCO). SCO is a federally subsidized program that covers part of the crop insurance deductible. It is not available for those crops for which the producer has elected the ARC.

The marketing loan program was continued from the previous farm bill. The market loan program allows a farmer to borrow using a stored commodity that the farmer produced as collateral. These loans are non-recourse loans. If the price of the commodity falls below the loan rate, the farmer may default on the loan without penalty and forfeit the grain or other commodity to the federal government. The farmer is not liable for the government's loss on the commodity reflected in the difference between the loan amount and the market price of the commodity. Marketing loans are available for wheat, corn, grain sorghum, barley, oats, upland cotton, extra-long-staple cotton, long-grain rice, medium-grain rice, peanuts, soybeans, other oilseeds, graded wool, nongraded wool, mohair, honey, dry peas, lentils, small chickpeas, and large chickpeas.

The sugar program was continued without change from the 2008 Farm Bill. U.S. sugar prices are significantly higher than world market prices as a result of the sugar program.

The dairy provisions of the 2008 Farm Bill were repealed and replaced with two new programs. The first is the Margin Protection Program for Dairy Producers. This is a subsidized insurance program designed to protect the operating margins of dairy farmers. The second program is the dairy product purchasing program that allows the Commodity Credit Corporation to purchase dairy products to raise prices. Products purchased may be donated to schools and other approved outlets.

The Supplemental Agricultural Disaster Assistance Programs were enacted as part of the 2014 Farm Bill to provide assistance to producers whose livestock died from adverse weather or disease. The definition of livestock includes both beef and dairy cattle, bison, poultry, sheep, swine, horses, and other livestock. It also provides grazing assistance when grazing has been affected by drought. It continues the 2008 Farm Bill authority to provide relief from natural disasters that destroy grazing land, honeybees, farm fish, orchard trees, and nursery trees. The program also includes an indemnification program for farmers whose livestock was killed by reintroduced predator species, including both avian predators and wolves.

## Title II: Conservation

The conservation provisions of farm bills are designed to protect the productivity of agricultural and forest lands, improve wildlife habitat, and protect water quality. Setting aside land for conservation has historically been a way to reduce the amount of land in cultivation. This has the effect of reducing supply and increasing prices. Much of the funding under the conservation programs is provided on a competitive basis. Landowners seeking conservation funding must apply, and the applications are rated to determine which are funded. Farmers receiving benefits under Title II must comply with the highly erodible land and wetland conservation requirements.

The 2014 Farm Bill continued the Conservation Reserve Program (CRP). The CRP allows farmers to take land out of production and put it into conserving use such as trees or grass. Farmers receive an annual rental payment for land enrolled in the CRP. The term of CRP contracts is for ten to fifteen years. The FSA is responsible for the CRP.

The 2014 Farm Bill continued the Conservation Stewardship Program (CSP). The CSP is designed to help farmers to improve their conservation practices. There are two types of payments to farmers under the CSP. The first are for installing new conservation practices and maintaining existing practices. The second type of payments are for developing resource-conserving crop rotation systems. Contracts are for a five-year period. Total payment to any person or entity for the period of the 2014 Farm Bill (2014–2018) is limited to $200,000. Agricultural lands, cropland, grassland, pastureland, rangeland, and nonindustrial private forest land held by private owners or Indian tribes are eligible for the CSP. A wide variety of conserving practices are covered under the CSP. Enrollment in the CSP is through the USDA Natural Resources Conservation Service (NRCS).

The 2014 Farm Bill continued the Environmental Quality Incentives Program (EQIP). The EQIP provides farmers with cost-share assistance for conservation practices on working lands. Enrollment in the EQIP is through the NRCS.

The 2014 Farm Bill combined all easements into a single program that is called the Agricultural Conservation Easement Program (ACEP). ACEP has two parts: Agricultural Land Easements and Wetland Reserve Easements. Agricultural Land Easements are designed to protect working agricultural lands from development. Wetland Reserve Easements are designed to protect, restore, and enhance wetlands. Conservation easements such as those offered under the ACEP are deed restrictions on the use of land that are designed to protect conservation values. In the case of agricultural land, the primary conservation value would be keeping the land in agriculture. In the case of wetlands conservation, value is more complex and may include restoring integrated wetland and protecting wetlands from destruction. Under the ACEP, cost-share money is available for restoring wetlands. Money is also available to pay the landowner for a portion of the fair market value of the conservation easement. On private lands, both permanent and term easements are available. A permanent easement is one that lasts forever. A term easement is one that lasts for a period of years. Thirty-year contracts are available to enroll land owned by Indian tribes. Thirty-year contracts are available only to Indian tribes.

The 2014 Farm Bill combined several regional partnership programs into a single program, the Regional Conservation Partnership Program. Participation in the program is on a competitive basis. Other programs included in the 2014 Farm Bill include Conservation Innovation Grants (CIGs). CIGs are designed to encourage the adoption of practices that improve both environmental protection and agricultural production. CIGs are made on a competitive basis. The Voluntary Public Access and Habitat Incentive Program is designed to encourage landowners to create wildlife habitat and to open the land to hunting, fishing, and other outdoor recreation.

## Title V: Credit

American agriculture depends upon a readily available supply of credit. Credit is used for a variety of purposes. Long-term loans are used to buy land and build permanent agricultural structures. Equipment is generally purchased with intermediate-term loans. The costs of planting crops are covered through annual operating loans and trade credit. Annual operating loans are taken out at the beginning of the crop year and paid at the end of the crop year when the crops are sold. Trade credit is credit provided by suppliers. It is usually very-short-term credit.

There are three primary sources of credit for American agriculture. Private lenders that include banks, insurance companies, and other private sources provide a great deal of credit to American agriculture. The Farm Credit System is a second major source of credit to American agriculture. The Farm Credit System is composed of a network of independent cooperatives that provide credit to the farmers, ranchers, and rural residents who own these cooperatives. Farm Credit System institutions are regulated by the Farm Credit Administration, an independent federal agency. The Farm Credit Act of 1971[6] as amended[7] is the statutory authority for the Farm Credit Administration. The statutory authority for the Farm Credit System is permanent legislation and not part of the Farm Bill. The third major source of credit, which is part of the farm bill process, is direct loans made by the USDA. The USDA also guarantees some privately made loans.

The 2014 Farm Bill continued Farm Ownership Loans.[8] This program is administered by the FSA. The purpose of this program is to help beginning farmers and socially disadvantaged farmers obtain farm ownership. The eligibility requirements for both direct and insured loans are citizenship, status as a family farm, and an inability to obtain credit elsewhere. For direct loans, the applicant must have either training or farming experience sufficient to have a reasonable probability of success. Acceptable purposes for direct loans include acquiring or enlarging a farm or ranch, making capital improvements to a farm or ranch, paying loan closing costs for acquiring or enlarging a farm or ranch, paying for soil water conservation improvements, and replacing a temporary bridge loan made by a commercial or cooperative lender. Guaranteed loans may, in addition, be used to refinance indebtedness. Hazard insurance is required as a condition of both direct and guaranteed loans.

Subtitle B of the 2014 Farm Bill continued the farm operating loan program.[9] The rural residency requirement for operating loans was eliminated by the 2014 Farm Bill. Congress added authority for the USDA to make microloans. Authority to make emergency loans was retained by the 2014 Farm Bill.[10] Authority was included in the 2014 Farm Bill that allows the USDA to conduct pilot projects targeted to specific regions, sectors, and populations to determine the potential effectiveness of various loan programs.[11] The State Agricultural Mediation Program was extended by the 2014 Farm Bill.[12] The purpose of the program is to facilitate resolution of disputes with the USDA.

## Title VII: Research, extension, and related matters

Subtitle A of Title VII amended the National Agricultural Research, Extension, and Teaching Policy Act of 1977.[13] These amendments continue Congressional policy of supporting agricultural research, extension, and teaching at land grant universities. Subtitle A includes a competitive grant program to build capacity in non-land grant colleges of agriculture. Subtitle A also addressed the critical shortage of veterinarians in rural agricultural areas.

Subtitle B of Title VII amended the Food, Agriculture, Conservation, and Trade Act of 1990 (the 1990 Farm Bill).[14] Subtitle B includes continuation of programs to promote sustainable agriculture, protect genetic resources, conduct research on organic agriculture, provide weather information, improve farm business management, and conduct other relatively small but useful programs.

Subtitle C of Title VII amended the Agricultural Research, Extension, and Education Reform Act of 1998.[15] Congress used subchapter C to repeal some and to amend other programs in agricultural research, extension, and education. Subtitle D of Title VII amended several laws.[16] The Beginning Farmer and Rancher Development Program that provides education, training, outreach, and mentoring to the next generation of farmers was continued. Subtitle E of Title VII amended statutes to address bio-security.[17] Subtitle F of Title VII created the Foundation for Food and Agriculture Research.[18]

## Title VIII: Forestry

Title VIII amended acts that primarily address nonindustrial private forest land.[19] This is land that is privately owned rather than part of the national forest system that is managed by the U.S. Forest Service, a unit of the USDA. Nonindustrial private forest land does not include land that is owned by the large international paper companies. Most of these landowners own small acreages, and many do so as part of an agricultural operation.

## Title IX: Energy

Title IX, the energy title, addresses a number of opportunities for farmers to produce biomass, wood, and recovered waste that can be used to produce bioenergy.[20] Assistance is provided to both producers of biomass and to refineries that produce bioenergy.

## Title X: Horticulture

Title X includes provisions covering specialty crops and organic production.[21] This title includes provisions to support farmers markets and promote local foods.

## Title XI: Crop insurance

Title XI amends the Federal Crop Insurance Act.[22] Federal crop insurance has become a key component of the support network for American agriculture. This section discusses crop insurance generally and those changes made by the 2014 Farm Bill. Crop insurance is sold by private companies; however, policies are approved and subsidized by the federal government. The Federal Crop Insurance Corporation is the USDA agency that manages the Federal Crop Insurance Program.

Except tobacco, potatoes, and sweet potatoes, coverage applies only to the crop in the field. Certain acts of the producer may result in the denial of coverage. These acts include negligence or malfeasance by the producer, the failure to reseed the same crop where it would be customary to do so, and the failure of the farmer to follow good farming practices. Federal crop insurance covers crop losses due to natural causes.[23]

The Federal Crop Insurance Act preempts state insurance law except where cooperation with the states is encouraged. The Federal Crop Insurance Act creates a uniform, national statute of limitations for bringing suit when a claim is denied. No suit may be brought more than one year from the date of the final notice of denial of the claim.

---

**Example 25.1** Ralph grows wheat. He has two fields in which he grows wheat. He bought Federal Crop Insurance to cover losses for both of his fields. The crop in one field was a total loss due to a lightning strike that set the field on fire shortly before harvest. The second field was also a total loss because a motorist driving along the road next to Ralph's field threw a cigarette out of his car window that set the field on fire. The loss of wheat in the first field is covered by crop insurance because lightning is a natural cause of the loss. A cigarette tossed out the window of a passing car is not a natural cause, so there is no coverage for the second field.

---

Levels of coverage are based on historic yields. Transitional provisions cover farmers who have started producing a crop and have no or insufficient history. Rules governing the covered yield are complex.

In addition to coverage for catastrophic losses due to natural disasters, the Federal Crop Insurance Corporation may offer optional coverage to protect against prevented planting, wildlife depredation, tree damage and disease, and insect infestation. The Federal Crop Insurance Corporation may not offer coverage if coverage is available from private companies. For the 2015 crop year, Title XI of the 2014 Farm Bill makes available a Supplemental Coverage Option (SCO). To use the SCO, a producer must have underlying crop insurance coverage. Any producer who elects to participate in the ARC program under Title I of the 2014 Farm Bill is not eligible to participate in the SCO. The ARC is administered by the FSA.

The Stacked Income Protection Plan (STAX) is a new policy for cotton only that was created by the 2014 Farm Bill. It can be purchased either as a supplemental policy or as a stand-alone policy. It is based upon the county-wide revenue loss and can be purchased for up to 20 percent of expected county revenue. Payments are available when county revenue falls below 90 percent of the expected level. STAX was added as a crop insurance option because upland cotton was removed from the list of covered commodities by Title I of the 2014 Farm Bill.

There is now a whole-farm revenue protection policy that combines the previous adjusted gross revenue and adjusted gross revenue-lite policies. The whole-farm revenue protection policy is targeted at highly diversified farms and farms selling two to five commodities to wholesale markets.

The FSA is authorized to assist the Federal Crop Insurance Corporation with program monitoring. In addition to denial of coverage, a producer who files a fraudulent claim may be subject to criminal prosecution. In addition, the producer may be disqualified from receiving most farm program benefits for a period of five years.

Federal crop insurance is not available for all crops, nor is it available for some cover crops in some counties. The Federal Crop Insurance Act requires that the Federal Crop Insurance Corporation develop policies that are actuarially sound. When there are not sufficient data to do that, insurance cannot be offered.

Under the 2014 Farm Bill, beginning farmers are given certain preferences. The $300 administrative fee for catastrophic coverage is waived. The premium subsidy was increased by 10 percent for the first five years that a beginning farmer is farming. There are also provisions whereby the yield history can be adjusted if a beginning farmer experiences a poorly yielding crop. The 2014 Farm Bill also improves coverage for organic farmers by removing the 5 percent surcharge for organic price options and by allowing organic producers to choose either the organic or conventional policy coverage price.

A major change to the federal crop insurance program in the 2014 Farm Bill is the addition of conservation compliance. To qualify for crop insurance, producers must now comply with the highly erodible land and wetland conservation requirements. These requirements are already applied to FSA and NRCS programs.

## Marketing orders

Marketing orders are agreements initiated by producer groups. The purpose of marketing orders is to stabilize prices to control of supply. There are currently marketing orders for milk and for various fruits and vegetables.[24] Federal marketing orders are administered by the Agricultural Marketing Service (AMS). Requests for new marketing orders are initiated by producer groups. The AMS determines whether to establish a new marketing order through a quasi-judicial process supervised by an administrative law judge. Marketing agreements have a statutory exemption from antitrust laws.[25] The exemption from antitrust laws is not a complete exemption.[26]

Law governing marketing orders is complex and beyond the scope of this book. In recent years, provisions of marketing agreements and marketing orders have been a source of considerable litigation. A full discussion of that litigation is beyond the scope of this book.

*Cal-Almond, Inc. v. US Department of Agriculture*[27] involved a FOIA[28] request by the plaintiff for a list of almond growers entitled to vote in any referendum of almond growers on the continuation of the marketing order for almonds. The opinion sets forth an excellent discussion of how marketing orders work for readers who wish to know more. Marketing orders provide growers with sweeping powers to control the market in covered commodities.

## Expiration of the current Farm Bill

The 2014 Farm Bill expired at the end of September 2018. As of this writing, both the House and the Senate have passed bills; however, they diverge widely over work requirements for beneficiaries of the Supplemental Nutrition Assistance Program (SNAP),[29] formerly called food stamps.[30] The House work requirements are significantly stricter than those of the Senate. The President has threatened to veto any farm bill that fails to include the House work requirements. Farm bills often do not pass by the expiration date of the previous farm bill; however, Congress has always in the past passed one-year extensions of the current farm bill until it can pass a new farm bill. On December 20, 2018, President Trump signed the 2018 Farm Bill, entitled the "Agriculture Improvement Act of 2018".

## Notes

1 Congressional Research Service. *What Is the Farm Bill?* Retrieved November 30, 2014, nationalaglawcenter.org/wp-content/uploads/assets/crs/ RS22131.pdf.
2 Agricultural Act of 2014, Pub. L. 113-79, 128 Stat. 649 (2014).
3 FSA. *Program Fact Sheets: What's in the 2014 Farm Bill for Farm Service Agency Customers?* Retrieved March 23, 2015, www.fsa.usda.gov/FSA/newsReleases?area=newsroom& subject=landing&topic=pfs&newstype=prfactsheet&type=detail&item=pf_20140311_insup_en_fbil.html.
4 7 U.S.C. § 2279(e)(2) (2013).
5 NRCS. *Small & Limited and Beginning Farmers & Ranchers.* Retrieved March 24, 2015, http:// www.nrcs.usda.gov/wps/portal/nrcs/main/national/people/outreach/slbfr/.
6 Pub. L. 92–181, 85 Stat. 583 (1971).
7 12 U.S.C. §§ 2001–2279cc (2013).
8 Pub. L. 113–79, §§ 5001–5005, 128 Stat. 649 (2014).
9 Pub. L. 113–79, §§ 5101–5107, 128 Stat. 649 (2014).
10 Pub. L. 113–79, § 5201, 128 STAT. 649 (2014).
11 Pub. L. 113–79, §§ 5301–5306, 128 Stat. 649 (2014).
12 Pub. L. 113–79, § 5401, 128 STAT. 649 (2014).
13 Pub. L. 113–79, §§ 7101–7129, 128 Stat. 649 (2014).
14 Pub. L. 113–79, §§ 7201–7217, 128 Stat. 649 (2014).
15 Pub. L. 113–79, §§ 730–7311, 128 Stat. 649 (2014).
16 Pub. L. 113–79, §§ 7401–7410, 128 Stat. 649 (2014).
17 Pub. L. 113–79, §§ 750–7504, 128 Stat. 649 (2014).
18 Pub. L. 113–79, § 7601, 128 Stat. 649 (2014).
19 Pub. L. 113–79, § 8001–8306, 128 Stat. 649 (2014).
20 Pub. L. 113–79, § 9001–9015, 128 Stat. 649 (2014).
21 Pub. L. 113–79, § 10001–10017, 128 Stat. 649 (2014).
22 Pub. L. 113–79, § 1100–11028, 128 Stat. 649 (2014).
23 7 U.S.C. § 1802 (B) (2013).

24 AMS. *Marketing Orders and Agreements*. Retrieved September 4, 2015, preprod.ams. usda.gov/rules-regulations/moa.
25 7 U.S.C. § 608b (2013).
26 7 U.S.C. § 292 (2013).
27 960 F.2d 105, 1992 U.S. App. LEXIS 5425 (9th Cir. 1992).
28 5 U.S.C. §§ 551–559 (2013).
29 USDA Food and Nutrition Service. *Supplemental Nutrition Assistance Program (SNAP)*. Retrieved August 13, 2018, www.fns.usda.gov/snap/supplemental-nutrition-assistance-program-snap.
30 Wall Street Journal. *Trump Poses Wild Card in Farm Bill Negotiations*. Retrieved August 13, 2018, www.wsj.com/articles/trump-poses-wild-card-in-farm-bill-negotiations-1534078800.

# Index

CPSIA information can be obtained
at www.ICGtesting.com
Printed in the USA
LVHW051659130120
643457LV00005B/145/P

9 781138 606104